Panic, Prosperity, and Progress

Founded in 1807, John Wiley & Sons is the oldest independent publishing company in the United States. With offices in North America, Europe, Australia, and Asia, Wiley is globally committed to developing and marketing print and electronic products and services for our customers' professional and personal knowledge and understanding.

The Wiley Trading series features books by traders who have survived the market's ever changing temperament and have prospered—some by reinventing systems, others by getting back to basics. Whether a novice trader, professional, or somewhere in-between, these books will provide the advice and strategies needed to prosper today and well into the future.

For more on this series, visit our website at www.WileyTrading.com.

PANIC, PROSPERITY, AND PROGRESS

Five Centuries of History and
the Markets

Timothy Knight

WILEY

CHAPTER 1

Tulip Madness

In popular culture, there is probably no better-known event in the lexicon of unusual financial history than the tulipmania that seized Holland in the early seventeenth century. Whenever there is a financial bubble in modern times, the term *tulipmania* is bandied about, but few commentators who use the term have a grasp as to what actual events occurred.

It is a fascinating tale—perhaps somewhat apocryphal—and, if nothing else, entertaining. And it is surely the only chapter in this compendium of financial history that involves not one but two important biological maladies that shaped the story: a flower-distorting virus and a deadly human plague.

■ An Introduction to the Flower in Question

If you've ever grown tulips, you know all too well that, while beautiful, the tulip is a temperamental and relatively weak plant whose bloom is short-lived and whose likelihood of returning the next year is far from certain.

The flower itself was unknown to most of Europe in the sixteenth century, but around 1554, the Pope's ambassador to the Sultan of Turkey was charmed by the flower and collected seeds and bulbs for distribution. (The word *tulip* itself is said to be derived from the Turkish word for "turban," since the bloom somewhat resembles the same).

Cultivation spread throughout the region we today call the Netherlands as tulip bulbs found their way to Vienna, Antwerp, and Amsterdam. Planters took pleasure in the vibrant blooms and the fact that the plants were more tolerant of the harsher climate of the lower countries.

The bulbs themselves were classified into three groups: the single-colored, the multicolored, and the "bizarres." This last category is most germane to the tale of tulipmania, as *bizarres* were the rarest and most sought-after tulip. The reason these unusual flowers came about was a virus that interfered with the plant's ability to create a uniform color on the petal. It is today known as a "breaking" virus, since it breaks the plant's lock on a single petal color, although it does not kill the plant itself. The effect on the flower was striking, producing mosaic-like flames of color on each petal.

Even regular, single-colored tulips are difficult to grow from seeds. It took anywhere from 7 to 12 years to produce a flowering bulb from a seed, and once the bulb was at long last established, it would create only one or two clones (or "offsets") in a given year. The mother bulb itself would last only a few years before it died.

As challenging as it was to propagate *regular* tulips, it was even harder to do so for the exotic varieties, since the virus weakened the plant somewhat, and it usually failed to create offsets, meaning that any bizarre varieties required new plants be created from seeds. The length of time required for that growth meant that the most appealing varieties of tulips remained rare.

As knowledge of tulips spread, collectors of the bulbs began to give the exotic varieties inventive names such as "Admiral" and "General" to suggest the boldness of the plant's appearance. A sort of one-upmanship developed with the naming, leading to exalted titles like "Admiral of Admirals" and "General of Generals." For years, the cultivation and selling of tulip bulbs was little more than a curious hobby among horticulturists and the well-to-do.

■ Rise of the Tulip

As the sixteenth century turned over to the seventeenth, Holland was on the ascent. The area, formerly known as the Spanish Netherlands, had won its independence. Amsterdam, the capital of Holland, found itself as the driving force behind commerce, particularly as a trading partner with the East Indies. Newfound wealth and prosperity flooded the region, with single trading voyages yielding profits upwards of 400 percent to the financiers backing them.

A merchant class arose, and the new money in the area sought ways to show off its wealth. Grand estates begin springing up around Amsterdam, and nothing framed a handsome home better than a vibrant display of flowers in the surrounding gardens. And, naturally, there were precious few flowers more showy and eye-catching than the tulip.

This book is dedicated to Lee Barba, a fellow historian and student of the markets. Thank you for taking the risk that others lacked the courage to take.

CONTENTS

CONTENTS

As I suspect the case is with many others, my interest in history did not reveal itself until long after my formal education was complete. A school's offering of dates, places, and long-forgotten names captures the interest of very few children, and unfortunately it usually snuffs out any latent desire they might have to explore tales of the past that can offer up wisdom, insight, and previously unseen linkages.

For most of my adult life, I have had a deep and abiding interest in two related subject areas: history and financial markets. While the two might seem to be only obliquely related, they are actually engaged in a constant dance, with one informing the actions of the other. Historical events move currencies, stocks, debt, and all other flavors of fiscal instrument, and likewise movements—particularly exaggerated movements—in the financial markets can drive the decisions that shape history in real time.

When I first developed the outline of this book, I tried to gather up what I suspected were the most interesting and market-moving developments of the modern age. To my surprise, some of the events that I thought would have a major impact (such as the Kennedy assassination in 1963 or the London subway bombing of 2005) were, as far as financial markets were concerned, virtually immaterial; it was if they had never even happened. However, other topics I had initially left out, such as the Russian debt crisis of 1998, turned out to be monumentally important.

The completed book you are holding contains two dozen chapters of what I consider the most interesting and important episodes over five centuries that have had an impact on the thinking and behavior of financial markets. There are manias, panics, battles with inflation, the travails of war, and stories of riches both won and lost. The tales extend from early seventeenth-century Holland up to the twenty-first-century United States.

My hope is that, having read these accounts, the reader can gain perspective—specifically, perspective of how consistent human behavior has been over the centuries, and how in spite of extraordinary technological, political, and legal changes, the templates that govern humanity's relationship with both opportunity and fear are surprisingly steady.

There will undoubtedly be new "chapters" in your own lifetime of globally important events that move both markets and sentiment. In the end, I hope the reader can be better armed to comprehend the world's complexities and changes by way of the knowledge and insights this book endeavors to provide.

Tim Knight
Palo Alto, California
August 1, 2013

The tulip's reputation was on the rise, and by 1634, anyone with money but without tulips was judged simply to have bad taste. Whereas tulip bulbs used to be sold by the pound, their rising popularity and prices made them exponentially more precious, and soon much tinier weights were used as the basis of the tulip trade. A concurrent demand from French speculators for the bulbs only pushed the price higher.

The trading of the bulbs was framed by the growing season of the flowers themselves. Tulips bloom in the springtime for just a few weeks, and they enter a dormant phase from June through September. It is at this time they can be safely uprooted and moved about, so actual physical trades took place around this time of the year.

Because speculators did not want to confine their trading to just a few months, they put together what could be considered a futures market. Two traders could sign a contract in front of a notary, pledging to buy a certain quantity, type, and quality of bulb at the end of the season for a certain price. These contracts soon found an aftermarket of their own, so that people begin trading the paper instead of the physical bulbs.

■ Market Frenzy

In 1636, the tulip bulb was the fourth leading export of Holland (if you are curious, the leading three were gin, herring, and cheese). Because the margin requirements for tulip futures were minimal, the price of the contracts began to soar spectacularly. Some historians have noted that, due to the presence of the bubonic plague at the time, some individuals viewed life quite fatalistically, leading some speculators to trade with complete imprudence.

The Calvinists of Amsterdam viewed with dismay and concern the speculative frenzy that was springing up in their native land. The virtues of discretion, moderation, and hard work seemed to be shoved aside for the easy profits of trading in paper. The appeal of the profits at the time was understandable, however, as prices lurched forward. By 1637, a single bulb could fetch the equivalent of 10 years' salary of a skilled craftsman. Entire estates—one reported to be a full 12 acres—could be had for a single exotic "bizarre" bulb.

One of these bulbs, named the *Semper Augustus* (see Figure 1.1), was particularly coveted. In 1636, there were only two such bulbs in all of Holland. As trading spread throughout the country, it became impractical for

FIGURE 1.1 *Semper Augustus* **was one of the most-prized varieties of tulip.**

speculators to make the trip to Amsterdam, so smaller exchanges appeared in the taverns of small towns using similar trading rules as had been established in the capital city. To create an atmosphere of prosperity and opulence, these taverns were often adorned with large vases of tulips in full bloom and sumptuous dinners that traders could enjoy while doing their business.

The final spasm of buying was promulgated by a decision made in February 1637 by the self-regulating guild of Dutch florists. They agreed that, by their new rules, all the futures contracts that had been put in place since November 30, 1636, could henceforth be considered options contracts. This wasn't the exact language they used, of course, since such terms for financial instruments did not exist, but the effect was the same.

The difference between a futures contract and an options contract is subtle but crucial: with a futures contract, the buyer agreed to buy a certain quantity of a product at a certain price on a certain date; the obligation to buy was firm. With an options contract, the buyer had the right—but not the *obligation*—to execute a purchase based on the same terms.

To cite an example, if a person bought an option contract when the underlying asset had a value of 500, and the asset's value went to 800 by the expiration date of the contract, the buyer would presumably be glad to honor the terms of the agreement and purchase the product at 500 (since the market price was already up 60 percent). However, if the price had dropped to 250, the buyer could simply let the contract expire, losing only a small transaction fee equivalent to about 3.5 percent of the contract price.

With this new rule proposed, which the Dutch Parliament ratified, the risk of engaging in these contracts to the buyers decreased dramatically (indeed, by 96.5 percent). The reason is that those trading in tulip futures now bore very little risk, since they could simply walk away from the agreement if prices didn't behave favorably. If tulips ascended in price, the speculators made a lot of money. If the tulips fell in price, speculators lost only a small amount of risk capital.

It was at this time that trading reached its peak, in terms of both price and volume. Some bulb agreements changed hands 10 times in a single day.

The market finally broke down during a routine bulb auction held in Haarlem, Holland. A mass of sellers showed up to conduct business, but there wasn't a single buyer to be found. Some believe a severe outbreak of the bubonic plague kept the buyers away (although it seems to have done nothing to deter the *sellers*), but the simple fact is that the normal spot market for bulbs was suddenly one-sided and thus nonexistent. All sellers and no buyers does not a market make.

Within days, panic spread across the country, as people soon realized that their enormous trading profits were no more valuable than the paper on which the agreements were written (see Figure 1.2).

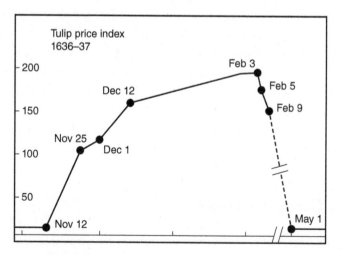

FIGURE 1.2 **After peaking in early February, tulip prices crashed hard, erasing the entirety of prior gains.**
Source: Used with permission from Jay Henry.

■ The Bloom Is off the Rose

The crash in tulip prices was even more rapid than the ascent. One bulb that had risen in price 26-fold by January 1637 lost 95 percent of its value in just one week. Speculators around the nation were facing losses that were in some cases ruinous.

Citizens demanded that their government do something about it, so the matter was referred to the Provincial Council of The Hague. After three months of discussion and debate, the Council made their announcement, which was this: they *had* no decision, and they would need more information. Not surprisingly, this provided cold comfort to the distressed populace.

The Council's follow-up suggestion wasn't much more helpful: they advised that every seller should meet with each corresponding buyer and, in front of witnesses, offer the tulips to the purchaser for the previously agreed price. If the buyer refused to complete the deal, the tulips could be put up for sale in a public auction, and the buyer would be held responsible for the difference in price.

In a market that had lost virtually its entire peak valuation, this was obviously a bad situation for buyers and sellers alike (but significantly worse for the sellers, who were stuck with bulbs that now weren't worth much more than onions).

There was no legal recourse to be had, either. The judges in Holland considered all the financial agreements pertaining to the tulip frenzy to be nothing more than gambling debts and, as such, were unrecognized by the legal system. Even if buyers were deemed responsible for the agreed-upon payments to sellers, those sums were unenforceable, and thus everyone who owed money simply ignored the entire matter.

As a final effort to shore up the badly rattled economy, the government offered to void any existing contracts for a fee equal to 10 percent of the contract price. Because prices had already plunged even more than 90 percent, this offer likewise provided no meaningful relief. In the end, most participants in the tulip madness suffered economic hardship, and the psychological scars would be with the nation for decades to come.

■ The Compost Heap

The events surrounding Holland's tulipmania have become the stuff of financial legend to this day, but modern historians speculate that perhaps the magnitude of the event was much smaller than some believe. Although there was indeed enthusiastic trading of tulip bulbs around 1636, it may have been confined to a very small number of merchants and craftsman, who for a time wanted to ape the exciting high-finance behavior of the nobility.

Some of the famous stories related to this time seem hard to believe. One oft-cited tale is of a sailor who, hungry while visiting a friend, plucked up a tulip bulb from his friend's table (thinking it was an onion), slipped it into his pocket, and boiled and ate it later. Once discovered, the poor sailor was pursued, captured, and thrown into jail for consuming a bulb whose value was equal to all the food the entire crew on the sailor's ship would require for a year.

Setting aside the fact that a tulip bulb bears little resemblance to an onion, eating a tulip bulb would be a wholly unappealing experience. The taste would be terrible, and even if the fellow managed to choke it down, the effects on his body would have been toxic. It seems a story such as this is more of an invention of propaganda than an account of an actual event.

The Dutch lunacy spread somewhat beyond its borders, creating miniature tulip frenzies in London and France, but attempts by brokers to push tulip prices to the levels seen in Amsterdam met with only moderate success. Even if the tale of flower-bulb speculation from long-ago Holland is more fiction than fact, it still is a fascinating anecdote into how the novelty of a new product (in this case, a flower, as opposed to an iPhone) can capture the public's imagination, if only for a few months (see Figure 1.3).

FIGURE 1.3 Jan Breughel's famed *The Folly of Tulip Mania*, painted in 1640 and displayed at the Frans Hals museum in Haarlem.

CHAPTER 2

The Mississippi Scheme

It seems hard to believe that an obscure Scotsman born over 350 years ago would have profound effects that persist in the financial world to this day, but it is true, and that man's name was John Law. The events surrounding Law's actions in the eighteenth century are the stuff of legend, and Law is considered by some economists to be the world's first Keynesian—that is, a person who supports the notion that flooding an economy with government spending is the best way to address a weak economy. Even the everyday English word *millionaire* was coined during the mania of Law and his so-called Mississippi Scheme. In this chapter, we will explore what led up to the scheme, its construction, and the devastation it wrought.

■ Law's Early Life

John Law was born in Edinburg, Scotland, in 1671. He was the oldest son of a banker, and as was the custom at the time, young Law apprenticed in his father's business beginning at the age of 14. For three years he worked in his father's counting house, learning the principles of banking.

In spite of being in a family of bankers and goldsmiths, Law did not have a passion for the business, and after his father died in 1688, the young Law took the opportunity to leave the family enterprise for an activity with far greater personal appeal: gambling. He set out for London and tried to apply his knowledge of statistics and probabilities to forge success as a professional gambler.

He did quite well for a while, managing to live a life of pleasure, pursuing his passion, but after nine years, Lady Luck began to neglect Law, and he lost more money than he could repay.

Law's plight was soon to exceed that of a mere gambling debt. He was quite taken with a lovely young woman named Elizabeth, and a suitor of hers, one Edward Wilson, didn't take kindly to the competition. Wilson challenged Law to a duel, which was unfortunate on his part, because Law shot him dead with a single shot.

Duels were a widespread custom in the eighteenth century, but they were not part of the actual rules of society, so Law was arrested and charged with murder. He soon stood trial at the Old Bailey before a judge who was known as a sadistic "hanging" judge who had no compunction about handing down stiff sentences to criminals. True to form, the judge sentenced Law to death after he was found guilty of murder.

Happily for Law, and for our story, his sentence was commuted to a fine, based on a decision that the killing was manslaughter and not murder. Wilson's brother was outraged and, while Law was still imprisoned, sought to have a harsher punishment foisted on his brother's killer. Law, however, managed to escape from prison and reached the continent of Europe, far away from London judges and grieving brothers.

On the European continent, Law resumed his gambling, spending three years both trying to earn a living and studying the monetary and banking affairs of the various countries he visited. The middle of the eighteenth century was an exciting, dynamic time for Europe, full of new ideas about science, the economy, and social experiments, and Law's penchant for numbers and knowledge of banking made him a quick study.

■ Franco Finances

The currency of old France was known as the *livre tournois*. The livre was originally established by Charlemagne as a unit of account equal to a pound of silver, and it was divided into 20 parts (called *sous*), which itself was further divided into 12 parts (*deniers*). (*Note:* To make reading and understanding the events in this chapter easier, I'll refer to the unit of currency as the *dollar*, although that is not the historically-accurate term.)

In the early 1700s, the French economy was a mess. King Louis XIV (see Figure 2.1) had waged a number of wars that left his country a financial basket case, and the country was at the brink of financial ruin. The national

FIGURE 2.1 Louis XIV, King of France, by the French engraver and artist Robert Nanteuil.
Source: Yale University Art Gallery.

debt was about $3 billion, and the wealth of the nation (largely in the form of precious metals) was mostly spent. Indeed, the shortage of precious metals meant that not enough money was in circulation.

Using the metaphorical image of the French economy as a body, the blood flowing within that body (in this case, gold and silver) had been largely drained away, so the body's health was in great danger. There simply wasn't enough blood to go around, since it had been spilled for unproductive wars.

It's important to know that during the course of Law's travels, he had become friends with the Duke of Orléans, who was the nephew of King Louis XIV. Although Law could not have foreseen the value of this friendship in years to come, being close to a royal family member usually isn't a bad connection to have.

Second, in spite of the shambles of the French economy, France did hold a vast expanse of territory in North America surrounding the Mississippi River known as Louisiana (of course, this territory was far greater in size than the state of Louisiana we know today, spanning from the Gulf of Mexico up into Canada). France was the first European country to settle this area, and the territory was larger than France itself.

As gigantic a piece of real estate as Louisiana was, virtually nothing was being done with it, and the vacuum of knowledge about the place was quickly filled with legend. Rumors began to circulate that Louisiana was rich in vast deposits of precious metals. It was heralded as a kind of paradise where beautiful but naïve natives would cheerfully exchange enormous chunks of gold and silver for whatever knives, magnifying glasses, or other near-worthless trinkets Europeans wanted to offer.

The notion of Louisiana being an utterly unexploited bed of wealth even conjured up a tale of an enormous mountain on the Arkansas River made of emeralds. And, in addition to all of the precious stones and metals said to be just beneath the surface of the landscape, it was also believed that a wide variety of furs were available from the fauna of the land, similar in value to the pelts actively traded with Canadian trappers. The truth is that any furry creature unfortunate enough to live in a climate like that of the Deep South would have perished long before.

In spite of all this folklore, the reality was that hardly any Europeans had colonized Louisiana, and those who *were* there found life to be extremely hard. Some attempts had been made to colonize the area with workers willing to till the land for its agricultural potential, but precious few French wanted to be involved in such a hard life in a strange and mysterious land. The government of France was so eager to prop up the image of its Louisiana territory that it hired artists who had never set foot outside of Paris to draw lush and inviting landscapes of the North American territory as if it were a differently situated French Riviera.

■ Paper Money

During the years that Law worked at his family's counting house, gambling his way through Europe and attending the salons of both royalty and common folk, he became somewhat of an economic philosopher. Quite aware of the stifling effect that the lack of precious metals was having on some European economies, he took the view that replacing metallic money with something more convenient and representative of a store of value would be superior.

In Law's mind, gold and silver coins were a crude and outdated method of exchange and that the currency that circulated through an economy didn't have to be wealth itself but merely serve as a means of exchange. National wealth, after all, depended on trade both within and without a country's borders, and the more currency that could flow within an economy, and the more effortlessly it could flow, the better it would be for the nation's collective fortune (see Figure 2.2).

FIGURE 2.2   John Law shown in a contemporary lithograph.

Back in his native Scotland, Law published a proposal for what he called a Land Bank. The idea was relatively simple: a given country (in this instance, Scotland, Law's native land) would "deposit," in a sense, the value of all its land holdings into a national bank. The bank, in turn, would issue notes whose collective value would never exceed the entire value of the land on deposit. These notes, each of which represents a tiny portion of the country's land-based wealth, would be the kind of paper money that Law envisioned as a more efficient means of exchange. It was a way of monetizing the value that the country already owned but had not yet unlocked—in this instance, the land—and pumping that value into the nation's economy.

Although the proposal garnered some scattered interest, it was not embraced by the Scottish government, and a disappointed Law abandoned his dreams of bringing his vision of paper money to his homeland and returned to his familiar role as a gambler. The idea did not leave him, however: in his own words, "When blood does not circulate through the body, the body languishes; the same way with money which does not circulate."

He spent the next 10 years moving between France and the Netherlands. During this time, he renewed his friendship with the Duke of Orléans. During their conversations, the duke was increasingly impressed with Law's apparent financial prowess, and he eagerly sought his advice on how to deal with his country's financial maladies. Louis XIV's reckless spending had put France in a bind, and there wasn't a clear way out of it.

As with Scotland, the notion of paper money was alien to the French, who perceived "money" as being either silver or gold.

■ A Golden Opportunity

As fate would have it, France's sovereign, Louis XIV, died in 1715, when the heir to the throne was still a young child, wholly incapable of leading a great European state (see Figure 2.3). That task therefore fell to none other than the Duke of Orléans, friend of John Law.

The duke was not himself made king, but he assumed the reins of government until such time as the young Louis XV reached majority age. Law shrewdly seized upon the opportunity and presented himself to the court, where he was warmly received.

Law proposed to the court that a great nation such as France should not be shackled by the inadequacies of a metal currency. France need not be a pioneer in this area, either, as both Great Britain and Holland had adopted paper money with success. Law proposed the establishment of a new bank that would manage the royal revenues and issue notes based on landed security, very similar to the scheme that had been rejected by Scotland.

FIGURE 2.3 Louis XV as a child in his coronation robe, as painted by Hyacinthe Rigaud, on display at the Metropolitan Museum of Art in New York City.

France was far more eager than Scotland to embrace Law's idea—and, given its dire straits, it perhaps felt there weren't any better choices to be had—so a royal edict was issued on May 5, 1716, granting Law the right to establish a bank.

The bank would be capitalized with one-fourth precious metal coinage and three-fourths French bonds. The capitalization was fixed at a sum of $6 million in the form of 12,000 shares at $500 each. The bank would also be responsible for the collection of taxes. The structure wasn't everything Law had proposed, but it was a good start, and the duke was willing to grant more privileges once Law and his bank proved themselves.

The public was all too willing to make use of the new, convenient banknotes as a form of payment. For one thing, the notes were assigned a specific value, backed by bonds and metal, which was permanently fixed. In prior years, the state had no misgivings about devaluing the metal coinage, which meant that a citizen could wake up poorer one morning not because of any fewer coins in his pocket but merely by those coins being deemed of lesser value by royal decree. These new paper notes, however, were not subject to that kind of depreciation, and the public appreciated the greater reliability of this new currency.

The name of Law's newfound institution was *Banque Générale*, and it was effectively the first central bank of the nation. The bank's notes were payable on sight, and the bank's issued paper was swiftly regarded as more valuable than the silver coinage that most citizens used, since the latter had a nominal value that was at the mercy of the state. Indeed, over the course of a year, the paper notes rose 15 percent in value based on their purchasing power. It seems that this modern view of money was swiftly accepted by the public with greater success than anticipated. Paper was evidently not just *as* valuable as metals— it was actually perceived as being safer and *more* valuable.

■ An Expansion of Power

So impressed was the French court by Law that it granted him a new title— *Comptroller General of Finance*—and greater powers to accompany his new title. Law set out to take down what he saw as encumbrances to the economy, such as canal tolls and overly large land holdings; he encouraged the building of new roads throughout France; and he put in place incentives, such as below-market low-interest loans, for new industries.

FIGURE 2.4 Philippe II, Duke of Orléans, was instrumental in putting Law in a position of great influence and power. He is shown here in a painting by Jean-Baptiste Santerre.

As France's de facto treasurer and finance secretary, Law also focused on the revival of overseas commerce. These pro-business measures aided the country with an increase in industrial output of 60 percent over two years. One simple metric that illustrates the power of Law's actions was that the number of French ships engaged in export jumped from merely 16 to a full 300 (see Figure 2.4).

Riding high on the success of *Banque Générale*, Law submitted a second major proposal to the regent: the creation of a new company that would have the exclusive privilege of trading with the province of Louisiana. This territory, stretching for 3,000 miles from the Mississippi Delta up to the frozen mountains of Canada, was rich with natural abundance, and Law saw it as a vast and untapped resource for France.

As with the national bank, the proposed capitalization and business of this new company was quite simple: Law proposed that the organization be capitalized with French bonds as well as the valuable exclusive trading rights with Louisiana. Shares in the company would be sold to the public, and that cash could be used to retire the aforementioned bonds (thus saving France the burden of continued interest payments on the bonds themselves).

The royal court agreed to Law's proposal, and in August 1717, *Compagnie d'Occident* (the Company of the West) was founded. The firm's capital was divided into 200,000 shares at a value of $500 each, and it was granted exclusive trading privileges with the Louisiana territory for 25 years, as Law had requested.

In spite of the attractive makeup of this new organization, the value of the shares languished. As mysterious as Louisiana was, it was generally recognized that very little was actually going on there, particularly since hardly any French citizens emigrated there to work the land, trap furs, or seek out fictional mountains made of emeralds. The shares in the Company of the West sank from $500 to $300, and Law's sterling reputation started to get tarnished.

Law then hit upon a simple but effective plan to reverse the poor showing of the company's shares. He announced that, in six months' time, the company would pay $500 for a certain number of shares in the company. This was the equivalent of a board of directors in a modern-day corporation issuing a stock-buyback program, and the effect was swift and exactly as Law had hoped. Individuals being told that a share that presently cost $300 could be sold for a 66 percent profit in a half-year's time pushed the price back up to its original offering value. The idea worked.

More important, the public surmised that the company's prospects must be far healthier than they had imagined, if the company itself was willing to pay such a premium on its own shares. It seemed to the investing public that the management was in the best position to know about its firm's prospects, so it was suspected that the Company of the West was being very discrete about just how bright its future looked.

■ Absorption and Ascent

The role of the *Banque Generale* took a dramatic turn in 1718 when it became the Royal Bank. Now the notes were not simply the paper produced by a private enterprise; they were now backed by the full faith and credit of the crown itself. The notes were guaranteed by King Louis XV. No guarantee had more strength or credibility.

Other important changes took place as well. The company acquired the right to mint new coins; it was made responsible for all of France's money minting and finances; and it had the right to collect most French taxes. Indeed, what had started out as an experiment quickly developed into France's first central bank and all its associated powers, with Law at the helm.

The Royal Bank was then made into a conglomerate. It absorbed the Company of the West as well as similar French companies, such as the China

Company, the India Company, and other rival trading outfits. Law had, in the span of just two years, created the most successful conglomerate in all of Europe, with vast powers to tax, coin money, enjoy worldwide trade monopolies, and retire the debt of the state. It was even granted a monopoly on the sale of tobacco.

The French national debt was about $1.5 billion, a vast sum at the time. The Royal Bank bought large amounts of this debt, which paid an interest rate of 4 percent, and extracted interest from France at a rate of 3 percent. From the crown's point of view, it was almost like free money: the state was able to eliminate a 4 percent debt burden in exchange for a 3 percent burden by means of an enterprise of its own creation. This was beneficial to the Royal Bank as well, since it was assured a healthy flow of dividends from the state to fund its future endeavors.

■ The Frenzy Begins

Law and his Royal Bank had magnificent prospects. He had exclusive privileges of trading in the East Indies, China, the South Seas, and, of course, Louisiana. His optimism manifested itself in a pledge of a yearly dividend of $200 per share, which, given the share price of $500, was an obscenely rich bounty for investors.

The investing public became increasingly enamored with shares of the Royal Bank, and a virtuous cycle was in place: paper notes, ostensibly backed by gold and bonds, were easy for the state to print; the public was all too eager to take these notes and give them to the Royal Bank in exchange for stock certificates in the Mississippi Company; and the trading public began trading the increasingly limited quantity of publicly traded shares among themselves, making its original offering price of $500 a distant memory.

Between May 1719 and August 1719, shares rose from $500 to $1,000, doubled again, and doubled yet again. Part of the reason for the near-vertical ascent in the share price was the very limited quantity of shares made available. Every couple of months or so, fresh shares would be made available to the public, and the men and women of Paris would stampede for the opportunity to get their hands on them.

The use of margin also poured fuel onto the proverbial fire, as it became a common practice for a buyer of shares to be given an entire year to actually pay for those shares. Thus, a person who wanted to acquire shares could do so on a 12-month installment plan. Given the near-vertical ascent of the company's stock, it seemed to be the closest thing to free money ever created. Law himself wrote at the time, *"The gates of wealth are now open to all the world. It is that which distinguishes the fortune of the old administration from those of the present"* (as quoted in Charles Mackay's *Extraordinary Popular Delusions and the Madness of Crowds,* published 1841).

Newfound wealth in sums formerly reserved for the highest ranks of the nobility found itself in the hands of the unwashed masses. Tales of vast fortunes being made by the lowest of society only exacerbated demand for the shares. There were tales of the chimney sweep who made $30 million in profits and the shopkeeper who amassed $127 million.

Even Law's own coachman appeared in front of his master one day to present two other coachmen as replacements. "But I only require one coachman!" said Law. His then-servant replied, "Yes, I know. The other one I shall engage myself."

There was no particular building in Paris dedicated to the exchange of common shares, but a narrow little street known as the *Rue de Quincampoix* took on the role (see Figure 2.5). This little lane became a daily frenzy of activity, with two gates set up on each end: one for the well-to-do, and the other for the common people. At a predetermined morning hour, both gates were opened, and people from both sides of the street rushed forward to begin the day's frenetic trading.

Of course, those lucky enough to own property on the heretofore unremarkable street enjoyed the dividends of this mania. Homes that in saner times had rented for $1,000 per year now yielded 16 times that amount. A cobbler rented out his tiny stall for $200 per day so that a trader could have

FIGURE 2.5 The *Rue de Quincampoix*. The street, near the Bourse, in which Law established his *Banque Generale* in 1716: after a contemporary engraving.

a reliable and comfortable location from which to trade. It is said that even a hunchbacked man seized upon the entrepreneurial idea of lending out his misshapen back as a writing desk to eager speculators.

In the autumn of 1719, as the share price vaulted to $7,000, $8,000, and $9,000, the financial orgy was in full swing, and *Rue de Quincampoix* was the epicenter.

■ A New Venue and a Plateau

Law recognized the need for a more civil place for traders of his wildly successful enterprise to convene each day—accidents among the swarming crowds were becoming commonplace—so he made an agreement with a French prince to rent out the *Hotel de Soissons*. It boasted a multi-acre garden, which would provide ample space for the swarms of traders, and the elegant statues and fountains in the garden certainly had greater appeal than the filthy road in which speculators were presently crowding.

As soon as Law had secured the property, an edict was passed stating that the only lawful place for the trading of securities was within the gardens of *Hotel de Soissons* (see Figure 2.6). Amidst the trees of the gardens, no fewer than 500 small tents were set up so that traders could conduct their business with some shade as well as a sense of place. The prince, already wealthy, enjoyed an avalanche of cash, as each of the tiny tents rented out for $500

FIGURE 2.6 Copperplate engraving of the *Hôtel de Soissons* drawn circa 1650 by an unknown artist.

each month, yielding a quarter-million dollars in pure profit merely for the use of the prince's enormous backyard.

As the share price lurched toward $10,000—a 20-fold increase in less than a year's time—the volatility of the share price became extreme. Prices could fluctuate 10 percent or 20 percent in the course of a few hours, and it was said that a man could rise poor in the morning and go to bed in affluence that very night.

Noblemen began to view the *nouveau riche* with scorn if not amusement, as the uneducated from the lower classes might have acquired some of the wealth of their betters but none of the refined mannerisms.

It should be remembered that all of this newfound wealth was not realized in the form of wheelbarrows of gold and silver being pushed throughout the streets of Paris. The nation's precious metal supply was safely tucked away in the vaults of the Royal Bank, and the people of France had wholly accepted the lightweight, convenient, foldable money stuffed into their pockets as being "good as gold." After all, any of the notes could be submitted to the bank at any time in exchange for the promised amount of "real" money.

Unknown to the common citizenry, however, was the fact that the value of the tidal wave of paper money flooding the citizens of Paris had long surpassed the value of the gold actually on hand. The royal court had become intoxicated with the sudden positive turn its financial situation had purportedly taken.

Sovereign debt was being retired, the economy was humming with the steady flow of this new paper currency, and the crown could dispatch with the fiscal woes that had plagued it only a few years earlier. Since wealth seemed as simple as cranking out fresh banknotes, the temptation was too great to resist.

Notes were not hoarded simply for the pleasure of having a large bank balance. New houses sprung up in every direction of the countryside, and a feeling of prosperity accompanied the "wealth effect" of rapidly escalating share prices. Luxury goods, formerly enjoyed only by the noble few, suddenly became commonplace.

Statues, paintings, linens, tapestries—all manner of high-quality manufactured goods began to grace the rooms of the middle class. It seemed that wealth was within the grasp of anyone willing to participate in the frenzy, and the pleasures of what can be acquired with wealth were likewise at hand for even the lowly born.

■ Cracks in the Mississippi

Unlike many modern legislative bodies, the French Parliament did not accept the financial machinations happening around them lightly. Parliament had, by and large, protested the introduction of paper money, and even as apparent prosperity pulsated through Paris, the Parliament viewed it with great skepticism.

A few of the more astute traders, however, sensed that the party would soon come to an end. Quietly, and in small quantities, savvy traders began making trips to the Royal Bank and exchanging handfuls of paper notes for gold coins. Some went even farther, not only exchanging notes for gold, but placing that gold within the safety of neighboring countries, just in case their country's disposition toward the metal and its confiscatory value might one day change. England and Holland became favorite storehouses for the coinage.

One astute trader is said to have exchanged a million dollars of bank notes for the equivalent amount of gold and, after dumping the metallic fortune into a cart, covered it with cow manure and escorted it far out of the city, unnoticed. He even went so far as to dress himself in the filthy clothes of a peasant so that his departure with such a vast fortune would attract no attention.

At the beginning of 1720, shares of the Mississippi Company started to succumb to gravity, which, given the highly leveraged ownership of many of the traders involved, caused alarm and concern.

Law proclaimed that the company would, in fact, *guarantee* the purchase of shares at a fixed price of $10,000, which pegged the price at that level for several months. The stock price wasn't falling, but the fact it wasn't rising anymore didn't go unnoticed. The only reason the share price was holding firm at $10,000 was that Law's company had pinned its pledge at that price.

All of the paper money circulating through France began to have the same effect that any overabundance of money has in any economy: it created inflation. Prices for houses, consumer goods, food, and everything else that could be bought with bank notes was on the ascent, and in early 1720, inflation was raging at a pace of 23 percent per *month*. As the paper notes could pay for less and less, confidence in the paper notes declined as well, while the perceived value of gold began a swift ascent.

Law began to view the situation with alarm, and wanting to suppress the public's newfound affection for gold, he had the crown issue an edict stating that payments in gold or silver for anything over $100 in value were prohibited, and that ownership of over $500 in gold was illegal. This is somewhat akin to all the financial institutions in the United States decreeing that credit cards could not be used for any charges greater than $20 and no card would be permitted a credit line greater than $250. The effect on the economy was stifling and immediate.

■ Economic Dictatorship

Because so much gold had already fled the country, spirited away by those prudent enough to ditch their paper money for something more tangible before the masses got wise to the situation, there was little coinage left in the country. The scarce quantity of gold and silver coins that were still around were hoarded, and the merchants in the economy, increasingly disinterested in accepting paper notes for transactions, brought business to a near standstill.

The crown began issuing edicts to take its economic dictatorship to a greater extreme. In February 1720, it was laid down that coins were banned as legal tender altogether, and only the notes from the Royal Bank could be used to transact business. The purchase of small and valuable hard assets, such as jewelry and precious stones, was likewise forbidden, and the citizenry was encouraged to police itself, offering handsome rewards to anyone who turned in a friend, neighbor, or family member for violating any of the economic decrees.

Thus, neighbor turned against neighbor. No evidence was required for a police investigation; mere suspicion was adequate to search a person's home and belongings for anything in excess of the tiny amounts of precious metals that were allowed.

The Royal Bank also took measures to try to slow down the extraction of real money from its vaults. For example, if a person came to withdraw gold in exchange for notes, the teller would count out the change at a comically slow pace, thus frustrating the others in line and reducing the amount that could be physically taken out in the business day before closing time.

Another trick was to put clerks in line who were instructed to withdraw some gold and then simply return the coinage to the vault immediately afterward, thus slowing down legitimate customers even further merely by making the lines longer.

As another desperate measure, Law ordered that a pile of banknotes be set ablaze in a bonfire, to try to convince the public of the growing scarcity of the notes. One can be excused for puzzling over why Law would think this a convincing display, since ink and paper are usually in abundant supply, bonfires be damned, but considering the pressures on the man, perhaps he wasn't thinking altogether clearly.

Shares of the Mississippi Company entered a free-fall, plunging from $10,000 to $4,000 in just a couple of weeks.

Another especially comic effort was made to try to convince the public that the Louisiana Territory was about to offer up untold bounty: Law arranged for 6,000 prisoners to be put into work clothes, equipped with shovels and pickaxes, and paraded around the streets of Paris before their purported departure to Louisiana.

Day after day, thousands of ostensibly Louisiana-bound workers made a show of it, but once their duties were done, they headed out to the countryside, sold the tools for whatever they could, and dispersed themselves, never to be heard from again.

So incensed was the president of the French parliament at these developments that he told the king to his face that he would rather have $100,000 in gold coin that $5 million in bank notes. Given that such an outburst to a crown would normally put one's life in jeopardy, it only goes to show how livid the French were becoming with the rapidly declining state of affairs.

■ A Rush and a Crush

The public became increasingly panicked about the dwindling value of their shares and the bumbling state of the economy. The rush to convert paper money into actual coinage became literally a life-or-death task, as the crush of humans at the bank's doors became fatal on a regular basis.

On one particular day, 15 individuals were crushed to death under the feet of desperate fellow countrymen. The enraged mob put three of the corpses onto stretchers, paraded *en masse* to the gardens of the royal palace, and screamed in fury for the king to see what misfortune his economic innovations had brought to the people of his land.

As runaway inflation continued to maul the economy, the increasingly haphazard Law urged the crown to devalue the currency in order to put a stop to inflation. Thus, yet another edict was issued, this one decreeing that, over the course of several months, step by step, the value of the currency would be trimmed by half.

Of course, when it is decreed that a given means of exchange is going to be cut 50 percent, it doesn't matter whether the trimming is instantaneous or scheduled to take place years ahead of time; the effect will be the same: an *immediate* drop of 50 percent in the value of a given currency. Shortly after this edict was issued, the Parliament overturned it, surely leading to maddening confusion among the increasingly frustrated citizenry, as well as the country's merchants

The share price of Law's firm continued to drop, first to $2,000 in September 1720 and, by December, to $1,000, a 90 percent plunge since the peak at the beginning of the year. Opposition to Law became so intense that the man began to fear for his own safety (see Figure 2.7).

A group of wealthy men decided to convert all their notes to coin *en masse* in order to exhaust the Royal Bank of its remaining supply of bullion. As a next step, they sought out all shareholders with questionable title to shares (mainly due to the fact they were purchased on credit) and confiscated the shares, thus reducing the public holdings of the stock by two-thirds. This greatly diminished ownership of the stock allowed Law's enemies to take control of the company altogether.

Clever corporate schemes were not the only tool used by the public to vent their fury against Law. As Charles Mackay tells it in his 1841 book *Extraordinary Popular Delusions and the Madness of Crowds:*

When John Law, by the utter failure of his best laid plans, rendered himself obnoxious, satire of course seized upon the French and the streets presented with songs in which neither he nor the king were

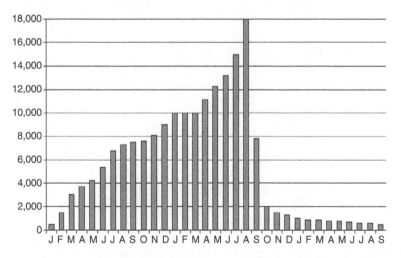

FIGURE 2.7 The stock price of Law's firm from 1719 to 1721, illustrating its steady rise and sudden, dramatic collapse.

spared. Many of these songs were far from decent, and one of them in particular counseled the application of all his [bank] notes to the most ignoble use to which paper can be applied.

The royal court itself began to strip the *Royal Bank* of its privileges: in November 1720 its right to manage tax revenue was removed, and before the year was out, it also lost all the privileges with respect to trade with other nations. Indeed, just about every privilege granted to the company was gutted, including its royal backing, leaving it an empty shell with no meaningful value.

Law was dismissed from his post as chief director of the bank at the end of 1720 and ultimately fled the country disguised as a woman for his own safety. (One can only imagine what Law was thinking as he fled across the French countryside in woman's clothing.) He moved back to Brussels as a pauper and spent the next few years gambling in Rome, Copenhagen, and Venice, never regaining his former prosperity.

When he learned of the death of the Duke of Orléans in 1723, Law realized he could never return to France, but, fortunately for him, he had been granted permission to return to London after receiving a pardon. He lived in London for four years and then, finally, moved to Venice, where he contracted pneumonia and died a poor man in 1729 (see Figure 2.8).

FIGURE 2.8   A political cartoon of Law published in 1720.
Source: Het Groote Tafereel der Dwaasheid, as published in *Harper's New Monthly Magazine*, No. 301, June 1875.

■ Aftereffects

The creation, inflation, and bursting of the bubble in the form of the Mississippi Company follows a template common to similar financial catastrophes throughout human history, running along these lines:

1. Some kind of shift happens (political, technological, or otherwise) that opens up extraordinary profit opportunities that did not exist before. Early participants thrive.
2. As word of the profits spreads, a larger and more diverse array of individuals participate, and as opportunities become more scarce, leverage, excessive trading, and outright fraud begin to creep in.
3. Once the original model can no longer support the participants, or once a fatal flaw is unveiled in the scheme, there is a rush to the exits, and after most participants are badly damaged financially, there is an outcry from the public for justice to be rendered against as many culpable parties as possible. Upon reflection, most of the participants recognize they really didn't know what they were doing in the first place.

Once fear replaces greed, the bubble bursts with great speed, and the speculative orgy comes to an abrupt halt. And, in spite of solemn pronouncements that no such foolishness will ever take place again, it always does: it might take a generation or two, but financial manias, like wars, are an unfortunate aspect of human nature that occur with disturbing frequency.

Markets tend to be efficient, and anything that appears to be "free money" is, at best, an extremely temporary displacement of market mechanics that will soon be rectified by those seeking to exploit the opportunity.

The French, feeling badly burned by their experiment with paper money, refused to touch the stuff again for the next eight decades. And although it held on to its massive Louisiana land holding for a while, France finally lost control of the area in 1763 after losing the Seven Years' War to England.

CHAPTER 3

The South Sea Bubble

A t roughly the same time John Law and the Duke of Orléans were turning France upside–down with the Mississippi Company, a largely identical situation was foisted on Great Britain with different actors. The parallels between what happened in France and Britain are remarkable, as we shall see.

29

■ Sovereign Debt and an Idea

The War of Spanish Succession was waged between 1701 and 1714, and in its prosecution of that war, Britain got itself deeply in debt. An internal audit of the various bonds yielded a sum of 9 million pounds owed without any specified means of paying it off. Indeed, prospects for the debt's being honored were so poor that the government bonds were priced in the public market at a near 50 percent discount to their face value.

In 1711, a scheme was conjured up to form a private organization to take over and manage the debt. The capitalization would be relatively simple: the company would be established with a government-sanctioned trading monopoly; specifically, it would be permitted to trade with the Spanish colonies in South America, a zone generally referred to as the South Seas. Thus, this new enterprise would be called The South Sea Company.

Holders of debt could exchange their certificates for shares in the newly formed company, and Britain would make interest payments on those bonds. Thus, the South Sea Company had two sources of income: (1) a reliable stream of cash from Great Britain for interest payments, and (2) lucrative trading profits that ostensibly would flow from South America.

One curious aspect of this arrangement is immediately apparent: a British company was conjured up whose principal business was trade relations with the colonies of a country presently at war with Britain itself. In spite of that, the company's shares did well, and the issue of national hostilities was put to rest with the Treaty of Utrecht in 1713, which ended the war.

As with France and its Louisiana territory, there was a profound sense of mystery (drawn wholly from ignorance) on Britain's part about the prospective riches of South America. It was widely believed that the ostensibly primitive souls residing in Mexico and South America would cheerfully trade their legendary mountains of gold and jewels for the relatively valueless wool and fleece clothing of Great Britain.

Of course, there were no natives waiting on the east coast of South America for the British to show up with wool to trade for gold. Indeed, it would be seven years after the formation of South Sea until a trading ship actually set sail to do *any* trading, and in that case, the trading was human cargo: slaves. So one aspect of the company's business plan—profits garnered from a monopoly over a single trade route—was illusory.

The other part of the business, collecting interest from bonds, was doing just as poorly. The government had failed to make any interest payments to the company, accruing back-interest of over a million pounds. In what would become a habit for the public/private enterprise, the issuance of more paper was offered as the solution to the problem, as the company issued more shares to stockholders equal to the value of the missed payments (since those shareholders were expecting dividends from those interest payments which would, in fact, never materialize) (see Figure 3.1).

FIGURE 3.1 Paper certificates such as this were offered in lieu of hard cash payments.

The South Sea episode exhibited far more corruption than what had taken place with John Law in France, both inside Parliament and on the streets of London. A form of "front-running" took place with the Lord High Treasurer who, being aware of subsequent purchases of government debt by the company, rushed out to the open market to acquire deeply discounted government debt before the word was out. Being able to purchase bonds at a 45 percent discount for certificates that would soon be retired at face value was a guaranteed moneymaker for those in the know.

■ A Useless Monopoly

The central appeal of the South Sea Company, of course, was the South Sea itself: that is, the valuable trade lanes sailed by Britain and graciously granted by Spain. It would seem the only task at hand was to fill some boats with wool and clothes, send them to South America, and return them to Britain filled with precious metals and gems.

The actual details of the agreement with Spain, however, would never allow such a financial bonanza. The treaty permitted Britain to supply the Spanish colonies with 4,800 slaves per year for a 30-year period, but for other cargo, the parameters were suffocatingly strict: the agreement stated that Britain would, in any given year, be permitted a *single* ship of no more than 500 tons.

In addition, if the trade produced by this aforementioned ship proved to be profitable, a full 25 percent of the profits (*plus* 5 percent of the balance) would be submitted directly to the King of Spain. Any trade monopoly, no matter how attractive, could hardly be lucrative to anyone under such terms except, of course, for the Spanish crown.

As unappealing as the terms were, they were soon rendered moot as war broke out between Britain and Spain yet again. What few assets the South Sea Company had established in South America were promptly seized, causing a loss to the organization of 300,000 pounds. The company at this point was little more than an office in England holding a bunch of government bonds whose interest income was being neglected.

In spite of this, rumors of John Law's success in France generated analogous excitement in Britain about some of the bold new frontiers of finance and enterprise, and tales of the soaring stock price of Law's bank conjured up hope of similar success in Britain. As 1720 began, enthusiasm for stock in publicly traded companies swiftly increased, not unlike the enthusiasm that swept the public for technology stocks in the United States 275 years later.

■ The Bubble Companies

What is most curious about what took place in 1720 is the excitement around publicly traded new enterprises. This excitement would be understandable if there were some recent example, but it was not preceded by the demonstrable success of South Sea or any other firm.

If, for example, the South Sea Company had enjoyed massive profits from a flotilla of ships returning from South America, groaning under the weight of gold bullion, the zeal for adventurous overseas businesses might be understandable. There were no such ships, however, and certainly no gold within them.

For whatever reason, the public was seized with a desire to invest in companies that possessed inventive and hard-to-measure business plans. Most of these new businesses made vague pledges about seeking gold in the New World, but some of the more outrageous new outfits were committed to such harebrained schemes as:

- Trading in hair.

- Horse insurance.

- Improving soap manufacturing.

- Creating a wheel of perpetual motion.

- Turning quicksilver into gold.

- And, history's favorite example of all, "carrying on an undertaking of great advantage but nobody to know what it is."

Comparisons to the Internet bubble of the late 1990s would be understandable, up to and including the "blank check" companies of that era, whose business plans were identical to that of the one mentioned in the preceding final bullet point (see Figure 3.2).

Naturally, plenty of unscrupulous stock-jobbers were happy to dream up a ridiculous business idea, exchange paper stock certificates for currency, and then disappear for parts unknown. This was an environment with no securities regulation of any kind, and the gullible fell prey by way of a combination of ignorance and greed.

The directors of the South Sea Company, however, were not happy with all of these new so-called "bubble" companies appearing. It was desirable that the public wanted to buy South Sea shares, of course, but these dozens of other unscrupulous outfits were mopping up the public's cash and diluting

FIGURE 3.2 One of the humorous "bubble cards" issued at the time.
Source: From reprint of 1841/1852 editions of *Extraordinary Popular Delusions and the Madness of Crowds* by Charles Mackay.

enthusiasm that the directors would rather have reserved for the South Sea enterprise exclusively.

Through the company's cash-based influence in Parliament (to put it politely), the directors saw to it that the Bubble Act was passed in June of 1720, requiring all publicly traded companies to receive a royal charter. Without such a charter, they were immediately disbanded; thus, dozens of swiftly created organizations were even more swiftly dismantled, and the investing public found itself much poorer. The South Sea Company, of course, received its royal charter promptly, and its already pricey shares shot up to 1,050 pounds, a 10-fold increase from six months prior.

■ Newton's Folly

The ascent of the South Sea Company stock was not unnoticed by one of the most brilliant men of the age, Sir Isaac Newton. Early in 1720, he purchased some shares in the company, and a couple of months later, concerned about the runaway stock price, he sold his position for a handsome profit of 7,000 pounds. He had ridden the stock from his purchase price of about 150 to his selling price at about 350.

FIGURE 3.3 Isaac Newton proved himself to be a better scientist than speculative investor.
Source: From a portrait by Sir Godfrey Kneller, 1689.

The stock continued to climb, however, and some friends of Newton's bought stock at higher prices, only to see them continue to 600, 700, and 800 pounds apiece. Newton could no longer stand missing out on padding his already-sizable profits from his earlier trade, so he tried to make up for lost time by purchasing as many shares as he could afford, even using borrowed funds to complete the purchase.

Although the great scientist got to enjoy the stock's final vault to above 1,000 pounds, he watched, dumbfounded, as South Sea succumbed to its own form of gravity. In the second half of 1720, Newton's holdings created a loss of 20,000 pounds for him before he dumped all his shares. His earlier profits were wiped out, and his misadventure with South Sea was a financial folly from which he would never recover. He said of the experience, "I can calculate the movement of heavily bodies, but not the madness of men" (see Figure 3.3).

■ Whirlpool in the South Sea

As the share price broke below its four-figure peak, people swiftly began to panic. For one thing, earlier in 1720, in a bid to accelerate the share price, people began to borrow money to buy the stock. The company itself allowed for purchases to be made on an installment plan. In August 1720, the first of these installment payments came due, and people became nervous about handing over actual cash in exchange for stock that already seemed to be slipping.

At the same time, news came from Amsterdam and Paris that asset values for speculative ventures were falling there, too. The "animal spirits" that had

FIGURE 3.4 The shares of the South Sea Company plunged far more quickly than they ascended.

compelled people to bid up South Sea disappeared with even more speed, and by the end of September, shares were down to 150 pounds. Banks and goldsmiths who had made loans based on South Seas shares as collateral found themselves holding the proverbial bag, as thousands of investors were ruined (see Figure 3.4).

Parliament was recalled for an emergency session in December 1720 to get to the bottom of the fiasco, and by the next year, fingers were pointed squarely at the directors of South Seas as the culprits. The political corruption, bribes, and widespread fraud among the company's management reached all levels of government, and heavy fines and prison terms were handed out to any miscreants who had not already fled the land.

The estates of the directors were confiscated in order to create a reparation fund for the victims of the company's collapse, and a resolution was

FIGURE 3.5 It was left to Sir Robert Walpole to clean up the South Sea mess.

Source: From a portrait by Sir Godfrey Kneller.

offered up in Parliament—only in half-jest—that the directors of the firm be tied up in snake-filled sacks, as in the days of ancient Rome, and thrown into the Thames to drown. A pamphlet of the day stated that:

> ... many poor families have been ruined, brought to poverty, and turned beggars. The trade of the City of London, one of the finest in the World, hath been very much shortened, few ships have been built, or fitted to Sea, during the Reign of the South-Sea Company.

The issue of shares was outlawed to prevent future bubbles, and the country's economy was left in shambles, taking nearly a century to recover. Robert Walpole, who had protested the South Sea Company from the start, took charge of the mess and later was appointed the first prime minister of England. The prohibition on public stock offerings was not repealed until 1825 (see Figure 3.5).

CHAPTER 4

American Revolution in the Colonies

When asked about the revolutionary war, most Americans probably conjure up images of a freedom-loving populace striving to unchain themselves from their distant British overlords. In popular folklore, the year 1776 is the kickoff point of a great political struggle that gave birth to our Constitution and a new land.

This is largely true, of course, but the American Revolution was as much about commerce and taxes as it was about political philosophy. The currency problems that the young nation grappled with during this period shaped the framework of our country, and the motivations behind the founding fathers' fight against Britain was not always as pure as has been taught to schoolchildren for centuries.

■ Prosperous Colonies

North America, as a thinly-populated landmass, offered its European settlers tremendous advantages that would be enjoyed for hundreds of years after its discovery in the late fifteenth century. It was a tremendously fertile land, replete with wildlife, vegetation, waterways, and natural resources that made it a vast, undiscovered treasure chest for its new inhabitants.

As the population tamed the wilderness in the late seventeenth and early eighteenth centuries, the 13 colonies enjoyed a long period of robust and steady economic growth. Between 1650 and 1770, the economy of the American colonies expanded 20-fold, and most historians agree that in spite of the abbreviated history of the colonial region, it already enjoyed the highest standard of living anywhere in the world in the 1770s.

The bounty of natural resources coupled with the industrial nature of the colonists made for economic abundance. The colonists exported rice, lumber, tobacco, and other valuable crops, and they did so in a business environment virtually free of taxes or tariffs. Besides a thriving export market to Europe, the colonists also enjoyed a prosperous trade relationship with each other (see Figure 4.1).

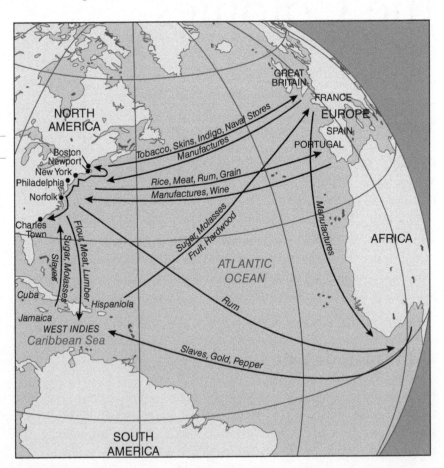

FIGURE 4.1 The "trade triangle" between North America, Africa, and Europe is illustrated here, showing principal exports and their destinations.

Some of this prosperity was fueled by credit offered by the British, who were willing to lend money to the wealthy landowners in the colonies in support of an increasingly lush lifestyle. Per capita debt in the Virginia colony, for example, doubled between the mid-seventeenth and mid-eighteenth centuries, and the desire to "keep up with the Joneses" (or, more accurately, the Washingtons or the Jeffersons) compelled the rich and almost rich to spend money on ostentatious luxury as visible evidence of their prosperity.

It was not necessarily the common man who would be agitating for revolution but the landed gentry as well. The rich landowners of the colonies not only had creeping debts to worry about, but many other economic motivations as well, from intrusive British laws to issues related to slaves.

Consider the skewed nature of slave ownership: In 1775, a full 40 percent of the population of Virginia was slaves. Half of the white Virginians owned at least one slave, but the richest 10 percent owned the majority. The upper one-*tenth* of white Virginians owned *half* of all the land, which meant the overwhelming majority of white Virginians had little in the way of property and were more vulnerable to boycotts and political turmoil than their wealthier compatriots.

Because of this vulnerability, the richest in Virginia did not consider the majority of freemen to be reliable political partners because their interests were so different. The risk of class warfare was very real, and as an actual fighting war approached, Britain made ample use of the potential divisions between slaves and their owners. After all, it would be hard for Britain to find a more dedicated soldier than a newly freed, newly armed slave to turn loose against his former master.

■ Intolerable Changes

Britain had, in the late seventeenth and early eighteenth centuries, engaged in a series of wars that had vastly increased its colonial holdings and worldwide wealth. There was the Nine Years War, the War of Spanish Succession, the War of Austrian Succession and, most germane to the forthcoming American Revolution, the Seven Years' War (1756–1763) between Britain and France.

After winning the Seven Years' War, Britain acquired from France all the land in North America east of the Mississippi River, in addition to Canada (from France) and Florida (from Spain). The North American colonies were no longer confined to the original 13 colonies but instead constituted the entire eastern half of North America (see Figure 4.2).

FIGURE 4.2 By 1775, Britain had control over the entire eastern half of the North American continent. This public domain map was obtained from an edition of the National Atlas of the United States.

Up until the conclusion of the war in 1763, the colonists were content to be under the power and protection of the British crown. After all, the colonists enjoyed a thriving trade with Britain, virtually no interference or taxes of any kind, and a guarantee of protection from foreign invasion thanks to being part of the British Empire. The colonies enjoyed all the benefits of being British with virtually none of the costs.

One of the few requirements laid down for the colonists was by way of the Navigation Acts, which required that the goods shipped to and from the colonies be on board ships that were constructed, owned, and staffed by the British. Given the importance of its thriving trade with Europe, and Britain in particular, this requirement was neither resented nor debated at its inception.

One important shift took place at the Seven Years' War's conclusion, however, pertaining to the land sandwiched between the Mississippi River and the Appalachian Mountains. This huge area of land, prior to 1763, was French territory, so the British crown had no misgivings about encouraging the colonists to explore, tame, and settle this land. It was the widespread usurpation of this land by the British colonists that aggravated the French into war in the first place.

At the war's end, however, France abandoned its claim to this territory, and Britain's attitude toward this land and its homesteaders reversed. Hungry to own the lucrative fur trade that was enjoyed in this region, Britain stated that the colonists were now foreclosed from owning or even setting foot on the land. Britain wanted all the settlers to return east to the colonies, making clear that the colonists would be excluded from this zone, which, until 1763, they had been encouraged to settle. The new rules forbidding the colonists were formalized in the Proclamation of 1763.

To add salt to the wound, the Proclamation also held that the territory would be patrolled by a standing army of 7,500 British soldiers, and that the funding of this occupation would be provided by none other than the colonists themselves. In short, the colonists who had been told to settle the land were notified, after they had accomplished this task, that they were now being *evicted* from their property and had to return far east to the colonies, where they would be required to *pay* for the soldiers that would, at gunpoint, make sure they did not trespass to the western side of the Appalachian range.

The colonists, naturally, deeply resented this sudden change of fortune. From the British standpoint, it was high time that the colonists started paying more taxes, since British citizens paid up to 50 times more in taxes than the colonists. Britain also was straining from the debts it had incurred by fighting the Seven Years' War, and it needed as much income as possible—be it from fur trade or from modest tax increases.

The desire to raise revenue via taxation did not end with the Proclamation of 1763 either. In 1764, the Sugar Act was passed, and the year after, the Stamp Act, both of which were crafted to extract revenue from the trading of goods. Also in 1765, the Quartering Act was passed, which required colonists to provide British soldiers with housing, food, and transportation as needed. So on top of paying for the soldiers that kept them from settling lands to the west, the colonists also had to serve as host to the infantry in their own homes.

■ Protests

The colonists did not accept all the new edicts from Parliament without protest. In 1765, 9 of the 13 colonies sent representatives to convene at the Stamp Act Congress in New York to discuss and implement a boycott of British goods. The boycott was effective (aided in large part by the relative self-sufficiency of the well-established colonies), and Britain's manufacturers pleaded with Parliament to eliminate the act, as it was harming commerce. Parliament complied, repealing the new taxes, and it likewise repealed the Sugar and Stamp Acts. The initiative of the colonists paid off quickly and handsomely.

In a peculiar move, however, Parliament passed a broader series of new taxes in 1767 known as the Townshend Acts. The colonists were emboldened by their prior success with a boycott, and undertaking a similar action in protest, they again met with success: in 1770, Parliament repealed the Townshend levies with one minor exception: the tax on tea. Parliament was, for the sake of its own commerce, willing to repeal the majority of the taxes, but it wanted to make clear that it was not forsaking its right to tax the inhabitants of its colonies. Modest as the one remaining tax was, it was important symbolically in the statement that it made.

Three years later, Britain extended its control of the tea trade by demanding, by way of the Tea Act of 1773, that the only company allowed to ship tea to America would be its own British East India Company. That December, a group of colonists dressed as Indians, boarded the ships, and tossed hundreds of tea chests overboard (known today, of course, as the Boston Tea Party) (see Figure 4.3).

Britain was furious at the misbehavior of its formerly compliant colonists. Parliament passed a series of acts intended to get the colonies back into line: the Boston Port Act, the Massachusetts Government Act, the Quartering Act, and the Justice Act were swiftly put in place to close Boston's port, alter Massachusetts's governing charter, and once again require colonists to house British soldiers without compensation.

The worsening relationship between Britain and America compelled the colonial congress to reconvene in Philadelphia for what was deemed the First

FIGURE 4.3 A rendering of the Boston Tea Party by Nathaniel Currier in his "The Destruction of Tea at Boston Harbor," painted in 1864.

Continental Congress on September 5, 1774. Encouraged by the success of the boycotts of the past, the colonists decided to enact a colony-wide boycott of *all* British goods and demand of Parliament that it repeal all 13 acts that were collectively described as the "Intolerable Acts" by the Americans. The Continental Congress stated to Britain that it was satisfied with the state of its relationship in 1763, and if the laws could be reverted so that the parties could return to the state of affairs enjoyed at that time, the discord could be eliminated.

Instead of agreeing to a peaceable settlement, Britain decided to crack down even harder on the colonies: it dispatched troops to occupy Boston, and the first shots of the American Revolution were fired in the spring of 1775 in Lexington and Concord, both in Massachusetts. A month later, the Second Continental Congress convened, and it was agreed that the time for peaceful compromise had passed. Instead, it was time to prepare for war, and in order to hold a war, they were going to need money.

■ Continental Paper

As prosperous as the colonies were, the government itself had very little in the way of assets. The public was not inclined to a strong government, particularly given the behavior of the British crown, and it was agreed by the colonial leaders that the issuance of paper money would be more palatable than the creation of a tax to fund the war. The colonists were, after all, already weary of taxes.

The new currency, the Continental dollar, was carefully designed to be difficult to counterfeit, and initially a prudent issuance of $6 million was distributed, with one Continental dollar being on par with one gold dollar. Over the course of time, however, the colonial government would succumb to the overwhelming temptation to print up more Continentals to pay the mounting expenses of the war.

General Washington intended to fight a war of attrition, counting on the British to eventually grow weary of the war, so it would be years before peace would finally be at hand. Thus, there were many years of substantial expenditures forthcoming, and the temptation to simply print up more Continentals to pay the soldiers and suppliers was hard to resist (see Figure 4.4).

As inflation started to slowly increase, colonial leaders became concerned that the diminishing value of the Continental would be an impediment to their chances of victory. Laws were passed declaring that anyone who refused to take Continental money, or refused to accept them at face value, was an enemy of the country. Early in the war, it was generally accepted that the unquestioning acceptance of the Continental was an act of patriotism, and anything else would be in aid of the enemy.

The same sentiment that promulgated a distrust of a strong central government likewise had a hearty respect for the independence of the individual states, so the states themselves elected to print their *own* currencies to address their specific financial obligations. With the increasing reams of paper flowing through the economy, the value of the currency inevitably declined. The amount of new Continental dollars issued was, over the course of five years:

1775: $6 million
1776: $19 million
1777: $13 million
1778: $63 million
1779: $140 million

And this was on top of $209 million of notes issued by the individual states. Thus, while it originally took $1 in Continental paper to buy $1 in gold, by April of 1781 it took $167.50. "Not worth a Continental" became a common phrase of denunciation for many decades after the currency's retirement.

FIGURE 4.4 A Continental Dollar, this one valued at one-third of a dollar, with the inscription "Mind Your Business."

As the paper money spiraled down in value, Congress resorted to "impressments," which was simply a polite term for theft. Soldiers were authorized to take whatever they needed, and they would leave what was basically an IOU. Had Britain won the war, these notes would have been worthless.

All of the colonists, of course, were taking a significant risk by confronting the British Empire. Britain had a large, world-class military, superbly trained and seasoned by years of fighting in Europe. The British war machine was well-funded with Britain's deep pockets and the country's ability to borrow whatever additional funds were required. The wealthiest colonists were taking an even more substantial risk, since they had the most to lose.

Those taking a particularly substantial risk were the 56 delegates who signed the Declaration of Independence. Most of these men were well-to-do, with a handful of famous exceptions, such as Samuel Adams. Nine of the men were large landowners, 11 were wealthy businessmen, and 24 were successful lawyers who, in the case of a British victory, would surely lose their license to practice their livelihood. Their willingness to sign their names to the document literally put their lives on the line (see Figure 4.5).

By 1780, with about half a *billion* dollars of federal and state currency floating around the colonies, Congress addressed the issue through the clever means of assessing a substantial tax, payable with fiat dollars (or, if one were so inclined, silver coins). This succeeded in mopping up a substantial portion of the supply of paper money, putting the young nation on a path to retiring the now-failed currency.

FIGURE 4.5 John Trumbull's painting, *Declaration of Independence,* created in 1816, shows the five-man drafting committee of the Declaration of Independence presenting their work to the Congress.

■ Peaceful Resolution

With all the advantages Britain had in its war against the colonies—skilled manpower, outstanding leadership, ample guns and ammunition, access to capital—they had one problem that could not be altered: the American colonies were very large. There was no practical way the British army could control such a vast population over such an expansive area, so they focused on securing the major naval ports.

After a couple years of fighting, the British were not making substantial progress, so they decided to seal off New England with the hope of trapping the Continental Army, thus securing it in a confined enough space to open up the prospect of defeat. At the Battle of Saratoga, however, General Burgoyne was defeated, and he surrendered to the colonial forces.

The British then adopted a form of financial warfare, counterfeiting Continental dollars and distributing them throughout the colonies with the goal of accelerating the plunge in the dollar's purchasing power.

The defeat at Saratoga greatly improved the public perception as to the colony's chance of actually defeating the British, and France decided to align itself with the colonial cause, signing a treaty with the Continental Congress. Britain took the news of the French alliance badly, still paying off the debts from its lengthy Anglo-French wars of the past.

In spite of some British victories in 1780, the war finally turned in 1781 as French and American forces defeated Cornwallis in Yorktown, Virginia. Britain at last abandoned its offensive posture in the war, and the Americans, after six long years of fighting, could claim their victory.

■ Economic Constitution

By the end of the Revolutionary War, the nations who had engaged in the conflict found themselves deeply in debt. The United States spent over $400 million (which was, not coincidentally, very close to the amount of paper money printed during the time); France spent 1.3 billion livres, and Britain had plunged itself 250 million pounds in debt. Having lost the war, the colonies, and the healthy trade relationship as well, the British saw their own taxes increase as they spent years paying off the indebtedness.

In spite of being the venue for years of warfare, the United States was by far the greatest victor, having won not only her independence but also a staggeringly large landscape. Now that the west was in its possession, the new country's territory extended all the way to the Mississippi River. The painful experience of America's experiment with paper money, however, played a large part in shaping the Constitution of the United States.

Most notably, the federal government learned that it was a severe mistake to allow individual states to create their own currency, so the Constitution expressly forbid states from creating any kind of legal tender. The job of gold and silver coinage was specifically reserved for the national government, and counterfeiting, which had been used as a weapon against the colonies during the war, was explicitly spelled out as a punishable crime by the framers.

The right to tax and tariff its citizens was also attached exclusively to the national government, since the colonies' inability to extract wealth directly from its citizens for the purposes of national interest (such as war) severely weakened early efforts against the British. Crucially, the Constitution also created what was effectively a common market between the individual states, reserving any laws with respect to interstate commerce to the national government. This "borderless" economy within the entire United States would obviously be a core reason behind the nation's future economic success.

From the point of view of an everyday colonist, he found himself paying and supporting one national government (that of the United States) in exchange for another (Britain); indeed, the fiscal burden on the citizens was much greater, now that the United States was on its own. The difference, of course, was that the individuals in North America were now citizens of their own country, no longer at the mercy of an overseas Parliament.

It was not long after that when 24 brokers met in 1792 underneath a buttonwood tree on a well-traveled dirt path in New York City called Wall Street to arrange for regular trading of company shares. Even though there were a mere five common stocks to trade (most of the financial trading of the day revolved instead around bonds, commodities, and various other tradable instruments), the so-called Buttonwood Agreement was the tiny seed that was planted in the fertile economic soil of the Constitution's framework that would eventually grow into the most important financial exchange in the world.

CHAPTER 5

The Panic of 1837

In the early history of the United States, there were two competing sets of thought with respect to banking. On one hand were those of Thomas Jefferson's mindset—the agrarians—who cherished individual production and self-reliance, and viewed banks and the legal entity known as the "corporation" with a tremendous amount of skepticism; on the other hand were the industrialists, who saw banks as a vital backbone of the economy and perceived the world as moving from a farm-based economy to a factory-based one.

One topic that was particularly divisive for these disparate groups was the notion of a central government bank. Europe's nations each had a government-sponsored bank that acted as the financial arm of the national entity; these banks would typically manage taxes, tariffs, the money supply, and other universal financial matters of the country relevant to the public interest. The government of the early United States decided to have one as well—named, not surprisingly, the Bank of the United States. The debate over that bank and the actions required to dismantle it were in large part responsible for one of the worst financial calamities the young nation had ever faced.

■ The Nation's Central Bank

The first Bank of the United States was established early in the nation's history, but the charter for the bank was, as with most banks, not permanent. It was chartered for 20 years, and in 1811, the end of the charter was drawing near. The House of Representatives rejected a motion to renew the bank's charter by just one vote, and in the Senate, the vote was evenly tied. As dictated by the Constitution, a tied vote in the Senate is settled by the vice president, and George Clinton, the VP at the time, voted against renewing the charter. Thus, the nation's first central bank was terminated.

The year that followed, 1812, had a war of the same name, and as is typical of wars, the nations involved spent much blood and treasure on its prosecution. If there was ever a time that the young nation needed a central bank, it was during a war, but the United States has done away with its own bank, so the nation's finances and ability to borrow suffered. As part of the recovery process, the *second* Bank of the United States was chartered in 1816 for a period of 20 years, just like its predecessor.

As the nation recovered and resumed its expansion, land speculation started heating up. The newfound economic prosperity was so widespread that the entire period was named by historians as the "Era of Good Feelings," and the second Bank of the United States began its business at the same time.

At this point in the country's history, there was no single paper currency. Instead, each bank was authorized to create its own bank notes. Thus, there were thousands of different kinds of paper money in the country, with a rainbow of colors and a wide variety of designs, each of them with varying amounts of reliability and safety.

Although the money was physically made of paper, it was, in most cases, backed by hard assets, most notably *specie,* a shorthand term for gold and silver coinage. Gold and silver were perceived as the very embodiment of "money," but paper was adopted as being much more convenient as a method of day-to-day business transactions. It was, after all, lightweight, foldable, and far more convenient than toting sacks of silver.

■ Jackson's Mistrust of Paper

One person who would get a painful lesson in the difference between paper and metal was Andrew Jackson, who, of course, would become the nation's seventh president (see Figure 5.1). Long before he did, in 1795, Jackson wanted to go into business with his own trading post, so he sold 68,000 acres of land in exchange for promissory notes from a man named David Allison. He in turn took these notes and used them as collateral to buy the supplies his trading post would require.

However, David Allison later declared bankruptcy, meaning that the promissory notes were literally worth the paper on which they were printed. Jackson therefore owed many vendors with money he didn't have, since the money he

THE PANIC OF 1837

FIGURE 5.1 The young Andrew Jackson had a series of very bad encounters with paper money, giving him a lifelong distaste for anything that wasn't hard currency.

thought he would be paid never materialized, and it took him the next 15 years to slowly settle up with the various parties to whom he owed money.

Understandably, this experience deeply scarred Jackson. He adopted a deep-seated aversion to any paper that held itself out to be an asset, whether in the form of promissory notes, bills of credit, bonds, or spending money. Jackson was a fairly active land speculator around this time, and he lost out on profits far too often because buyers would default on their notes and wind up not paying Jackson. The strain that these financial hits took on Jackson gave him a lifelong hatred of both bankers and paper money.

■ Biddle versus Jackson

The Bank of the United States had a rather clumsy start from the year 1817, when it opened for business, until 1822. Afterward, it was about to enjoy far superior leadership when it appointed its third president, Nicholas Biddle, in 1823 (see Figure 5.2).

Biddle was a highly intelligent, charismatic, and serious gentleman, who, at the young age of 37, was given the top post of what was effectively the nation's central bank. The years under Biddle's leadership are widely regarded as the best that the United Stated has ever enjoyed under any central bank, as it was a period of stable currency, steady growth, and prudent

FIGURE 5.2 Nicholas Biddle was a highly intelligent and effective banker who would lock horns with Jackson throughout his presidency.

expansion of credit. Biddle was terrifically well suited for the job, and the nation's prosperity was partly thanks to his consistently good guidance.

When Andrew Jackson became president in 1829, however, he took an instant dislike to Biddle without even knowing the man or appreciating his excellent management of the bank. Jackson was obsessed with eliminating the country's debt, which he viewed (as he did many things) as a nefarious plot by the bankers to line their own pockets.

He publicly called the debt a "national curse," and he pledged, "My vow shall be to pay the national debt, to prevent a moneyed aristocracy from growing up around our administration that must bend to its views and [will] ultimately destroy the liberty of our country."

It was unfortunate—and more than a little bewildering—that Jackson would take such a hostile view toward his government's own central bank. The second Bank of the United States had been a great asset to the nation, providing a currency that was healthy, stable, and well regarded.

Jackson not only denigrated the bank, but he also held that its very existence was unconstitutional (a view that had *already* been challenged and struck down by none other than the Supreme Court of the United States years earlier). Jackson even compelled Congress during his first year in office to investigate the bank and its constitutionality, and both houses returned with glowing reports of the bank's behavior, execution of its duties, and clearly documented constitutionality. Jackson's baseless vendetta against the bank's existence must have seemed preposterous to contemporary observers.

Andrew Jackson's own writing captures the intensity of his feelings against the bank; a small fragment of his long veto message to the U.S. Senate, dated July 10, 1832, reads as follows:

It is to be regretted that the rich and powerful too often bend the acts of government to their selfish purposes. Distinctions in society will always exist under every just government. Equality of talents, of education, or of wealth cannot be produced by human institutions ... every man is equally entitled to protection by law, but when the laws undertake to add to these natural and just advantages artificial distinctions, to grant titles, gratuities, and exclusive privileges, to make the rich richer and the potent more powerful, the humble members of society—the farms, mechanics, and laborers—who have neither the time nor the means of securing like favors to themselves, have a right to complain of the injustice of their Government.

An 1833 lithograph by Edward W. Clay, published by H. R. Robinson, N.Y.

FIGURE 5.3 An 1833 lithograph shows Jackson portrayed in a political cartoon heroically dispatching the wicked bankers, cheered on by an aide.

Jackson's worldview on such matters was simple: on one side were the common people: virtuous, industrious, hardworking, and honorable; and on the other side were the bankers: corrupt, inexcusably greedy, and eager to dole out patronage and favors to like-minded villains (see Figure 5.3).

Jackson saw himself as a crusader against such turpitude, and as the voice of the everyman, he would speak out loudly and frequently against the moneyed interests and their paper instruments of trade. Again, from the same veto message to the Senate, he continued:

> … we can at least take a stand against all new grants of monopolies and exclusive privileges, against any prostitution of our Government to the advancement of the few at the expense of the many, and in favor of compromise and gradual reform in our code of laws and system of political economy.

Such populist rhetoric appealed to many citizens of the country, and in Jackson's mind, he had captured the hearts and minds of every decent American. Besides attacking the debt, he held it as a sacred duty to attack the largest bank in the country: the nation's bank itself.

■ Death of the Second Bank

Jackson's contempt for banks was well known to Biddle, and the enmity between the two men grew over time. There is an account of a very rare personal meeting the two men had, and Biddle recalled the president stating, "I do not dislike your bank any more than all banks. But ever since I read the history of the South Sea bubble, I have been afraid of banks." It's interesting that Jackson's knowledge of financial history (the South Sea episode being chronicled earlier in Chapter 3 of this very book) would inform his political decision making.

Although it may seem almost unbelievable to the citizens of the United States today (who, as of this writing, are saddled with $16 trillion of debt, a number bound to be far higher by the time you are reading this), Jackson was able to bring the debt of the nation down to $0 in his second term of office, just as he had pledged. It was the first part of a two-pronged goal of his: eliminate the debt, and then eliminate the bank that made the debt feasible: that is, get rid of the nation's central bank. Andrew Jackson considered bankers to be, in his own words, the "moneyed aristocracy," and he perceived that any form of money other than gold or silver was little more than a fraud.

Besides Jackson's own negative experiences with commercial paper as a younger man, he was also inclined to misinterpret events and actions around him as conspiratorial in nature, even though they were far from it. He viewed the Bank of the United States not as an important quasi-government agency that was useful in the management of the nation's financial matters, but instead as a political rival whose assets could be used to mount attacks against him and his administration. In Jackson's overly active imagination, the leaders of the bank could grant generous loans, low interest rates, lucrative positions, and other favors to political enemies of the president.

Congress, however, had a more clear-eyed view of the bank, and when the issue of its recharter came up, the bill easily cleared both chambers, with a 28–20 affirming vote in the Senate and an even more lopsided 167–85 vote in the House. Although the veto power of the president had been used only a handful of times since the founding of the United States, Jackson took it upon himself to use this rarely used privilege to strike down the recharter bill.

The legislative branch of the government was flabbergasted, challenging whether what Jackson had done was even constitutional, but true to form, the president offered a very generous assessment as to the meaning of the Constitution, stating in a written response to the legislative body that "... the Congress, the Executive, and the Court must each for itself be guided by its own opinion of the Constitution It does not take a scholar to recognize what a breathtaking interpretation this was: allowing *each* of the three branches of governments its own "take" on what the Constitution really meant and how it should be applied in the course of the nation's behavior.

■ Waging a War with Words

Jackson penned an explanation as to his reasoning behind the veto. The bank's president, Mr. Biddle, thought the veto would be a political disaster for the president, and he egged on Jackson's political opponent, Henry Clay, who was putting together his own presidential campaign. Biddle wrote a letter to Clay on August 1, 1832, about a statement he had composed with respect to the veto:

> ... the President ... must pay the penalty of his own rashness. As to the veto message, I am delighted with it. It has all the fury of a chained panther biting the bars of his cage. It is really a manifesto of anarchy ... and my hope is that it will contribute to relieve the country from the dominion of these miserable people. You are destined to be the instrument of that deliverance, and at no period of your life has the country ever had a deeper stake in you. I wish you success most cordially.

Even though in retrospect it's plain to see that denying the United States a central bank was a horrendous error, it was, at the time, a politically astute decision. Jackson had done an excellent job convincing many of his countrymen that banks were the root of all evil. It was much evidently easier to convince the common folk of the early nineteenth century that rich men and their banks were a corrupt force that would do the nation harm than it would be for the President to actually read about and comprehend the benefits of a national central bank. Thus, with the masses behind him, Jackson took comfort in his actions.

This is shown in the newspapers of the time as well, which in those days had little compunction about coming down clearly on the side of one given political party or the other. One newspaper, the *Washington Globe,* rallied its readers with the antibank rhetoric: "Let the cry be heard across the land. Down with bribery—down with corruption—down with the Bank. ... Let committees be appointed in every township to prosecute every Bank agent who offers a bribe."

The Bank of the United States did not shutter its doors because of the veto, however. It had simply lost its charter as the financial instrument of the nation. It still had deposits, branches, and personnel. However, Jackson was going to strike another blow at it by seeking to withdraw all the deposits made by the United States from the bank and redeposit the funds into various state banks, which he considered less sinister and closer to the common man.

He told his secretary of the Treasury to execute the withdrawal, but the secretary refused to do so. The amazed Jackson immediately dismissed the secretary from his post and appointed the attorney general as the acting Treasury secretary, ordering him to carry out the same task.

The newly-appointed Treasury Secretary did as he was told, and now the bank found itself completely divorced from the affairs of the national government. This also meant it could no longer serve out its primary purpose, which was to provide the nation with a stable, well-managed currency. It was now simply the *United States Bank of Pennsylvania*, little different than any of the other hundreds of banks scattered throughout the young nation. (In a further expression of his peculiar worldview, Jackson stated that he had taken these actions since the bank had been "... attempting to influence the election of public officers," which surely had more basis in Jackson's active imagination than in reality).

■ A Flood of Paper for Land

Jackson's peculiar desire to disgorge the former Bank of the United States of its national deposits and distribute it to his so-called "pet banks" among the various states had quite the opposite effect from what was intended. His idea was to get capital into the hands of good, honest, everyday people from small capital institutions.

That may have been the case to some degree, but the broader result was that the state banks—which at the time didn't have stern (or even well-enforced) rules about how much specie they needed to have on hand in proportion to the bank notes they could print up (in other words, with relatively small amounts of gold and silver)—banks could flood the market with bank notes in the form of loans to customers.)

The special circumstance at the time was that the nation was growing, and the citizens of the nation were buying up land from what was then the world's largest real estate agent: the United States itself. The United States possessed countless millions of acres, and in the interest of taming the wilderness and turning it to productive purposes, it sold off parcels at very attractive prices to anyone willing to take the risk.

Thus, in the early part of the nineteenth century, investors of all types— from the common farmer to the well-heeled plutocrat—engaged in the increasingly fervent land speculation, made all the easier with access to generous credit from state-chartered banks.

There were many ambitious projects desired by the country to foment its growth, such as railroads, canals, and new roads. Business was growing and becoming more sophisticated in the country, and the industrialization of America would take the efforts of tens of thousands of investors, entrepreneurs, and industrialists. The national government was paving the way by selling huge tracts of very inexpensive land parcels.

In 1836, the land sales reached the highest point of the entire nineteenth century, when nearly 18 million acres were sold in the Northwest alone. A healthy agricultural market helped, with both wheat and cotton farmers increasing their holdings to help provide their goods to a receptive worldwide market. A historical article published in 1883 entitled *Oddities in Southern Life and Character*, captured the atmosphere succinctly:

> This country was just settling up. Marvelous accounts had gone forth of the fertility of its virgin lands; and the productions of the soil were commanding a price remunerating to slave labor as it had never been remunerated before. Emigrants came flocking in from all quarters of the Union, especially from the slaveholding States. The new country seemed to be a reservoir, and every road leading to it a vagrant stream of enterprise and adventure. Money, or what passed for money, was the only cheap thing to be had. Every cross-road and every avocation presented an opening, through which a fortune was seen by the adventurer in near perspective. Credit was a thing of course. The State banks were issuing their bills by the sheet … and no other showing was asked of the applicant for the loan than an authentication of his great distress for money.

The reader can be forgiven for recalling the real estate bubble from 2002 to 2007 when reading the above, since a wide array of banks eager to dole out easy credit to speculators, irrespective of creditworthiness, were realities in both past and present.

What greatly separates the two events, however, was the situation with the federal government's balance sheet. In the present day, the U.S. government is buried with debt and no clear way to ever pay it off; in the 1830s, the government had no debt, but instead had a growing *surplus* thanks to the vast land sales it was undertaking. After all, even though it was selling the land cheaply, it got it for free in the first place, so every sale was pure profit.

■ The Endangered Specie Act

Jackson witnessed with alarm the rapidly rising quantity of land sales—in 1835 there was three times as much land sold by the United States than just the year before—so he decided to turn once again to his reverence for "hard money" by means of what became known as the Specie Circular. It declared, in a stroke, that all future land purchases from the U.S. government would be done *only* by way of gold and silver.

This, of course, had an immediate and stifling effect on the "wildcatters" that were buying and selling land. Now that specie once again was king, those who actually had it in their possession (either the banks or individuals at home) hoarded it.

Banks that had leveraged their growth through the expansion of paper money teetered into bankruptcy, and farmers which had bought land at inflated prices on credit suffered a deadly one-two punch: (1) they had committed to purchasing property at high prices that were now rapidly falling due to the sudden restriction of credit; and (2) the crops that they did have, and upon which their livelihoods depended, were dropping in value, since the slowing economy reversed the trajectory of the prices of farm products, particularly cotton (see Figure 5.4).

In a case of terribly unfortunate timing for the next president, Andrew Jackson's philosophical twin, Martin Van Buren, won the presidency in 1836 and was inaugurated in March 1837, almost precisely when the economy of the country started falling to pieces. The new blow that struck the economy just two weeks before Van Buren's inauguration was that the banks of New York refused to redeem notes for specie, since their own gold and silver reserves had dropped to almost nothing.

Hundreds of banks across the country shut their doors permanently, and thousands of newly minted tycoons found their paper wealth worthless and their fortunes irretrievably laid waste. The economic data of the time all pointed to worsening conditions: a falling stock market, an increase in

FIGURE 5.4 A political cartoon of the time showed a pitiful family scene caused, according to the Whig party, by President Jackson. The father states, "I have no money and cannot get any work" as a child cries "I'm so hungry" and the mother chimes in, "My dear, cannot you contrive to get some food for the children? I don't care for myself."

bankruptcies, a growing unemployment rate, and a substantial drop in commodity prices. It was one of the worst recessions the nation would ever see, and it was laid at the doorstep of the White House right before Martin Van Buren took up residence there.

Former President Jackson very much had Van Buren's ear, and he encouraged him to stay true to the principles to which they both agreed: *not* to agree to charter a national bank, and *not* to overturn the Specie Circular. As usual, Jackson offered assurances based not on hard facts, but on what he and his paranoid personality supposed to be the case. From his residence, The Hermitage, former president Jackson penned a letter to Van Buren stating, in part: *"You may rest assured that nineteen-twentieths of the whole people approve of [these policies]—all except the speculators and their secret associates and partners."* Van Buren agreed, and in spite of the pleadings of businesspeople and bankers, the economy continued to worsen and would not fully recover for five years.

FIGURE 5.5 Pictured here is a thousand-dollar note, one of the last paper bills issued by the Second Bank before its closure.

Banks continued to fail for years, and even Nicholas Biddle's United States Bank of Pennsylvania—once the thriving bank of the country—lapsed into insolvency in 1841 (see Figure 5.5).

In the end, it is apparent that while the nation's expansion and growth would have occurred with or without Jackson's worldview and policies, the financial damage that took place by way of the land bubble and its subsequent deflation—exacerbated by the clumsy meddling in the nation's financial structure—deeply worsened a slowdown that would have been much shorter and much less severe had Jackson taken a different approach. The long-lasting and widespread economic downturn would be eclipsed in time only by the Great Depression nearly a century later, and most of the unfortunate episode was, we can see with hindsight, largely preventable.

CHAPTER 6

California Gold

The California Gold Rush is one of the most universally known eras of American history, but it is also one of the most widely misunderstood. It obviously altered the importance of California (which today reigns as one of the most important technological and business powerhouses on Earth), but it was just as important to the history of the entire nation in the decades that followed gold's initial discovery at Sutter's Mill.

There were not any meaningful financial markets for it to affect, but the gold rush laid the foundation for some important personal fortunes and fundamental Californian characteristics that lived far past the middle of the nineteenth century.

■ An Empty State

It seems hard to believe that a state that presently serves as the home to over 38 million people was, not that long ago, almost entirely uninhabited. In 1848, California was still a Mexican territory, and of the 34,000 or so people in the entire state, 12,000 were Mexicans, 20,000 were Native Americans, and a couple thousand were white soldiers and settlers.

One of these settlers was a young man named Sam Brannan who had started a newspaper called the *California Star* in the tiny settlement of San Francisco (see Figure 6.1). Brannan later had set up a store near a lumber mill owned by John Sutter, another newly established businessman in the area. Brannan had traveled out west with his fellow Mormons and at one point urged the church's leadership to establish its home in California (as opposed to Utah). Brannan was a hardworking, enterprising entrepreneur who enjoyed early success with both his newspaper and his store.

FIGURE 6.1 Sam Brannan was one of the first of a long line of California entrepreneurs. He would go on to become, for a while, the richest man in the state.

John Sutter, having befriended the Indians in the area, had established a large ranch of nearly 50,000 acres (which he called—of all things—New Switzerland) and, with the help of the Indians, had constructed a fort. He had great ambitions to become an agricultural powerhouse in the region, and he was building out the infrastructure of his holdings, including a lumber mill. So Brannan and Sutter, two businessmen in a state almost completely devoid of any inhabitants, nursed their business ambitions side by side.

On January 24, 1848, James Marshall, a trusted foreman working at Sutter's lumber mill, found several chunks of a bright, shiny, heavy metal in the water from the American River. Both Sutter and Marshall were intrigued and, referring to an encyclopedia on hand, learned how to perform some basic tests to determine whether it was gold or not. They confirmed that it was.

One might expect Sutter to be thrilled that precious metal was on his property, but he knew that if word got out, his land would be overrun with

FIGURE 6.2 In spite of finding gold on his property, John Sutter, pictured here in a painting by Frank Buchser, wanted to keep the metal's presence a secret so that his thousands of acres of land would be left undisturbed for farming.

strangers. He therefore sought to keep the discovery a secret. He asked Marshall to keep his mouth shut (see Figure 6.2).

After a few of Sutter's employees paid for their goods at Brannan's store with gold, though, it became much harder to keep the secret. Although Sutter didn't want word of the gold to leak, Brannan instantly realized that a flood of people in the vicinity of his store—the *only* store in the area—would be outstanding for his business, so he took it upon himself to return to San Francisco, vial of gold in hand, and shout out "Gold! Gold from the American River!" as he walked up and down the streets of the settlement. Naturally, word of the discovery spread like wildfire.

Brannan also would have liked to have printed a story in his newspaper about the discovery to dispatch the news further, but his staff had already rushed off, like most of San Francisco (which at the time was called Yerba Buena) to snatch up the promised gold from the American River. By amazing coincidence, right at this time Mexico signed over the California territory to the United States as a consequence of the Mexican-American War. Everything was in place for an astonishing transformation in the region.

■ A Challenging Trek

The earliest people to get word of the gold were those relatively close to California, such as Mexicans. By August 1848, word had finally reached the East Coast of the United States, and greatly exaggerated tales of the easy riches to be had in California swept the land.

There were, at the time, three ways to get from the eastern United States to California: (1) take a ship all the way around the coast of South America, and back up again, which took at least four months, and often much longer; (2) take a ship to Panama, then risk a malaria-infested journey to the other side of the isthmus to get on board another ship to complete the journey northward; (3) go overland, which had its own human-based peril. None of the three methods was safe or quick (see Figure 6.3).

FIGURE 6.3 This advertisement offered those on the East Coast a journey of a mere 100 days on the good ship *Spitfire,* so named for its supposedly rapid journey to California.

Even in faraway China, word spread about the *Gum San*, or Gold Mountain, that had been found, and enterprising agents distributed fliers in Canton and Hong Kong offering passage to California. Thousands of Chinese boarded ships to cross the Pacific Ocean, and within a few years, 20,000 Chinese would be in California (which constituted effectively the entire population of Chinese in the whole of the United States).

In the earliest days of the gold rush, there was a kind of excited camaraderie in the camps, since the feeling was that there was a vast treasure simply awaiting extraction for all brave enough to make the journey. A contemporary account held that "... the conviction was widespread that the mountains were a bank on which every man had a drawing account; if he came up short he need only seize his pick and pan and make a withdrawal."

The earliest miners were able to pan gold right out of the river with relatively little effort, and some of those who arrived in 1848 acquired staggering personal fortunes simply by the good luck of being there first (see Figure 6.4).

This was no panacea, however. California was truly "the Wild West"; there was no infrastructure, no enforced laws, no judges, no police, no plumbing,

FIGURE 6.4 The early arrivals to the gold rush used simple tools and methods to extract the gold, which was relatively easy to find. Their task would get exponentially more difficult as thousands more prospectors flooded the region.

and very little in the way of food or comfort. The territory had just passed into American hands, and whatever justice might be dispensed was often handled by "Judge Lynch" (that is, not an actual person, but instead a rope and an angry mob). Disease and discomfort were constant, and an alarming 30 percent of the original settlers died from sickness, violence, or accidents during the gold rush years.

The dangers to early miners were worth the profits, however, since a man armed with nothing but a pan could earn 10 to 15 times as much in a day as he could earn doing regular work. Making a lot of money suddenly didn't require education, a license, talent, or strength; it only took the will to show up and step into the river with a pan. Whatever you found was yours, free for the taking, and not even subject to taxation. It is not surprise, then, that the easy gold was found and removed within a year's time.

■ Disappointed Latecomers

Those from the East Coast who had traveled the 18,000 miles around the tip of South America expecting to find their fortune were soon disappointed. During the years of the gold rush, hundreds of thousands of people, all with the same dream, showed up, and while they made people like Sam Brannan rich, they usually found themselves completely devoid of the metal they came to acquire.

Brannan himself took a small place in California history by becoming the state's first millionaire, and he rapidly acquired land in San Francisco, Hawaii, and Southern California. (Incredibly, even though such land parcels were ultimately worth billions of dollars, Brannan died so broke that his estate couldn't even pay for his own funeral.)

Not surprisingly, the United States swiftly granted California statehood, skipping the traditional need to be a territory first, once its riches were known. As more and more people crowded into California to stake their claim, resentment and racism began to creep in. American miners looked down on the Mexicans, Native Americans, and especially the Chinese who had come to seek their fortune. The California state legislature cooperated in this racism, passing the Foreign Miners License Law, which required $20 per month (an exorbitant amount at the time) from anyone who was not a U.S. citizen.

One of the lasting legacies of this era was the influx of Chinese immigrants. Before the gold rush, the entire United States had essentially no

FIGURE 6.5 Having been chased away from the mining camps, many Chinese found reliable employment from the railroads, which needed them for expansion in the western United States.

Chinese at all. In 1852 alone, a full 20,000 Chinese came to California, and the large Chinese population on the West Coast of the United States today is a testament to the influx of immigrants who pursued the mountain of gold they had been told about (see Figure 6.5).

As the Chinese were chased away from gold mining, through both threats of physical violence and punitive legislation, they eventually found work in industries such as railway construction. Indeed, during the 1860s, the Chinese proved themselves to be reliable, brave, and hardworking, with over 10,000 Chinese employed by Central Pacific at one point. By 1870, there were nearly 70,000 Chinese in the United States, almost every single one of them living and working in California.

■ A Distorted Economy

The economic law of supply and demand became very apparent during the gold rush, since there was a surging demand (that is, the tremendous influx of humanity) and a relatively constant supply of goods. After all, only limited amounts of merchandise and foodstuffs could be had in a state that was almost entirely unpopulated before the gold rush commenced.

Some of the prices charged for everyday goods, adjusted for inflation, make clear how prohibitive living in the gold rush days must have been:

Beef: $280 per pound
Butter: $570 per pound
Cheese: $700 per pound
Eggs: $84 each
Rice: $230 per pound
Shovels: $1,000 each

Some stores would also offer services at very high prices, since time was precious to the miners. The miners were eager to hear from home, and their families would spend 40 cents to send a letter from the East to California. The store owner, in turn, would charge three times that much just to head into town where the post office was located and bring them back their letter. The store owners were just as happy to demand the same fee to take the miner's reply and bring it back down to the post office.

Services were so scarce that it was actually cheaper to ship laundry to Hawaii (then called the Sandwich Islands) for cleaning instead of having it laundered locally. Thus, shiploads of filthy shirts, pants, and undergarments sailed thousands of miles across the Pacific for washing. And San Francisco real estate—in a tradition that persists to this day—would yield handsome profits for those lucky enough to get in early. A parcel that might have sold for $16 before the gold rush would now yield 1,000 times that amount. It is not surprising that Henry David Thoreau, taking in the spectacle from the other side of the country, quipped in his journal, "Going to California ... is only three thousand miles nearer to Hell."

Another sign of how perverse the mindset of the time became was in the form of the ill-named Act for the Government and Protection of Indians, passed in April 1850 by California's new legislature. The law actually did nothing to "protect" the Native Americans; on the contrary, it expressly allowed for the white settlers to capture and enslave the Indians as workers.

In spite of California's piously disavowing the Southern practice of slavery, it permitted the buying and selling of Indians, particularly young women and children. During the gold rush years, about 4,500 Native Americans died at the hands of whites, and the overall population of Native Americans dropped from about 150,000 in 1845 to fewer than 30,000 in 1870.

■ On the Farm

During the gold rush years, the majority of people in California were miners. Even as early as 1850, about two-thirds of the state's entire population was engaged in gold mining, and since most workers left their regular jobs, those who were willing to remain in more pedestrian forms of employment saw their wages soar sixfold, since there was simply no one else around willing to do the work.

Those who were working the foothills of California for gold added greatly to the nation's available gold supply. As the easy-to-find gold disappeared, well-capitalized companies with large (and environmentally destructive) drilling tools took over and greatly increased the volume of gold extracted from the land. In 1848, not even a quarter-million dollars of gold was produced in California. By 1852, nearly $82 million was produced. (This year would be the peak of the gold production of the time, with subsequent years yielding substantial, but still slowly dwindling, figures) (see Figure 6.6).

Some additional perspective can be had from this fact: in 1849, well before gold production had reached its zenith, there was more gold extracted from California alone than had been extracted in the entire United States in the preceding 60 years. The U.S. monetary system was based on gold, so

FIGURE 6.6   As it became harder to extract gold with simpler methods, well-financed organizations expanded operations with equipment that individual miners could never afford.

the insertion of so much new metal into the economy also yielded inflation (somewhat like an equivalent amount of paper money's being printed), so wholesale prices increased about 30 percent between 1850 and 1855 across the United States.

California could not have found a more effective way to grow its population: the gold rush years pushed the population from its original 14,000 to nearly 20 times that amount, and although the vast majority of would-be miners abandoned their pans and pickaxes, some of them stayed in the state to find other gainful employment. Often, this would be in agriculture, as there was a growing demand for food, and California had ample arable land.

The commercial endeavor that would spring forth from California that would have a far longer-lasting impact on the nation was the railroad business. Four businessmen who had prospered, much as Sam Brannan had, with sales to the new California settlers, formed an alliance to create and manage the Central Pacific Railroad.

These "big four"—Mark Hopkins, Collis Huntington, Charles Crocker, and Leland Stanford (for whose son the famed university would later be named)—were in the proverbial right place at the right time. An intercontinental railway had long been the dream of the United States, but bickering between the North and South as to its pathway prevented the plan from ever going forward.

Once the Civil War was under way, and the South no longer had a voice in the U.S. government, the railroad was immediately approved (with, naturally, a relatively northerly placement of the tracks). The Pacific Railroad Act granted a $16,000 payment per mile for flat terrain, $32,000 for foothills, and $48,000 for the far-more-difficult mountain construction. Although it took most of the decade to complete, when the eastern-bound and western-bound construction finally met in Utah in May 1869, the nation was finally linked coast to coast (see Figure 6.7).

What this meant for California, of course, was that it suddenly had access to a worldwide (rather than statewide) market for its food. With access to the entire East Coast—and its ports for countries across the Atlantic—the points of destination for California agribusiness became global. By the late nineteenth century, while gold had been largely a thing of the past, agriculture had become California's most abundant and profitable business.

Thus, the exciting, get-rich-quick part of the gold rush lasted not even a year, as those early and eager enough were able to pluck their riches straight

FIGURE 6.7 The meeting of the railroads, one from the east and one from the west, was a historic symbolic moment in U.S. history, as the nation finally had a transportation system from coast to coast.

off the ground or from the streams of the Sierra foothills. The real impact of the mass migration into the state, however, was a vital intercontinental link, an amplified national money supply, and a large, ethnically diverse worker base in the new state of California that would have a profound and permanent effect on the character of the state and the nation.

CHAPTER 7

The American Civil War

For well over a century, schoolchildren in America have learned about the Civil War—the War between the States—and the narrative has usually focused on the slave-holding South versus the freeman North. The economic aspects of the American Civil War are hardly even considered, however, and the capital transformation that took place between 1861 and 1865 in the United States brought profound changes that are with us to this day.

■ Antebellum Nation

Eli Whitney's cotton gin was a deceptively simple device, but the change it brought to the world's economy was tremendous. At last, large volumes of cotton could be separated from the numerous, nettlesome seeds interspersed, and this new tool made the fiber a far more profitable and productive business (see Figure 7.1).

By 1815, the southern United States' most valuable export was cotton, and 25 years later, it was worth more than all the other exports of the entire country combined. The ideal soil and weather of the South put it in a position to produce two-thirds of the world's cotton, and a "triangle" economy was formed between the northern United States, the southern United States, and England. England bought the cotton from the South, ran it through its tremendous textile industry, and sold the finished goods to the growing northern U.S. population.

FIGURE 7.1 A deceptively simple but ingenious device, the cotton gin made the tedious, time-consuming task of separating cotton fiber from seeds easy, transforming the economy of the antebellum South.

The North and South of the United States were different in weather, temperament, and ambitions. The South modeled itself after the genteel, land-loving gentry of Europe, cherishing the abundance of the land and eschewing the smoke-belching ugliness of the factories and machines of the industrial age. The North endeavored to become an industrial powerhouse, making use of the growing immigrant population and seeking to be less dependent on the manufacturers across the ocean.

As the South contented itself with its agrarian growth, the North made impressive headway in building out its capital infrastructure. By 1860, a full 90 percent of the manufacturing output of the country was situated in the North. Although most of the farming continued in the South (where 84 percent of the population was engaged in agricultural pursuits, versus only 40 percent of the North), the North soon held a virtual monopoly on the nation's ability to actually create value-added products from the raw materials provided.

In spite of the nation's cotton emanating from the South, the North produced 17 times more textiles, 20 times more iron, 30 times more leather products, and—important for the war that was to come—32 times more weapons. It seems obvious in retrospect that in a contest between North and South, the North would handily win any battle, equipped as it was with

FIGURE 7.2 While lacking the charm of the agrarian South, the North had an enormous advantage in terms of industrial productivity, having almost complete control over the nation's ability to manufacture almost all its modern products.

firepower that would handily beat the cotton bolls and antiquated farm life of the South (see Figure 7.2).

A few years before the war began, in 1857, a financial panic swept the worldwide economy. It was, in fact, the world's first global economic panic, although it was not long lasting. The South was relatively unscathed, and the

North's ability to recover from the panic, thanks to the South's abundant supply of cash crops, deepened the South's already-strong belief that the northern states were highly dependent on the goodwill and agricultural output of what was to become the Confederacy.

After the 1857 panic, tensions between the North and South increased, driven largely by the growing nation's struggle with reconciling its profound differences with respect to slavery. When Abraham Lincoln won the 1860 election, New York's already-uncomfortable financial markets became far more nervous about the impact a divided nation would have on the country's commercial interests. *Harper's Weekly* reported in November 1860:

> Within the past fortnight a panic has prevailed in Wall Street, and stocks of all descriptions have declined from ten to fifteen per cent. Such an event, occurring simultaneously with the most bountiful crops and the most remarkable development of material wealth this country has ever known, has naturally puzzled the public, and given rise to much surprise and conjecture.

Movement toward a new, separate nation—the Confederate States of America—was taken, including the drafting of a constitution. The nation wasn't even 100 years old, and its survival as an intact republic was already in question.

The business problems of a Southern secession were obvious: raw materials would be reduced or withheld altogether; debt obligations might be ignored; the free flow of commerce would be suppressed by a hostile boundary. Indeed, the bankers of the North had $200 million of Southern debt on the books, and the likelihood of that debt's being honored and eventually repaid decreased dramatically in the event of a bellicose relationship. For these reasons, the moneyed interests of Wall Street had firmly opposed a Lincoln presidency, yet they had failed in their efforts to elect a different candidate.

In a way, the South was the one most responsible for the weaknesses it would face in the forthcoming war. First of all, it concentrated on lucrative cash crops such as cotton and tobacco, which, while very profitable during peacetime, would not provide the foodstuffs the population would need during war. Second, in constructing its constitution, the Confederacy sought to have a very weak central government, which itself was intentionally forbidden from raising taxes.

The political leaders of the South were convinced their strongest ally was one that could not even speak: cotton. The dominance of the Southern plantations in providing cotton to the world's textile mills, especially those in England and France, gave the South assurance that, in the case of secession, they would find powerful allies in those trading partners.

Britain and France needed cotton, and the southern United States was a prolific provider of it, thus, they would not only keep the South economically healthy, they would also prop her up by whatever means necessary to ensure her survival and protection. As we shall soon see, this was a grave miscalculation.

■ The Modern North

There were two fundamental strengths that would, over the course of the Civil War, lead the North to its victory: (1) its staggering superiority in terms of industrial infrastructure; (2) its access to capital, which, although almost nonexistent at first, would soon be borne out through the efforts of the federal government.

The South's dependence on slave labor made it slow to adapt to the changing world. The North, which didn't have the luxury of virtually free human labor, had to rely on the emerging field of modern agricultural tools and techniques. Even before the war started, the advantages of a mechanized approach to farming were evident: a threshing machine, for example, could process grain at 12 times the rate of six able-bodied men. As more and more men were taken away from the farms of the Union, in order to train as soldiers, those left behind had to become increasingly adaptive about their approach to farming which, in the end, would serve them well.

The North also had a substantial advantage with respect to transportation infrastructure. Not only was the North far better equipped with railroad lines than the South, but its manufacturing capability put it in a position to expand those lines at a far greater pace, even during the war years. In fact, the U.S. War Department created a special unit known as the United States Military Railroads, whose sole purpose was to design and build railways for the transportation of troops and supplies during the war, and by 1865, it was the largest railroad system on the planet.

Of course, wars in the middle of the nineteenth century were more about the quantity of soldiers than sophisticated weapons, and the North had a substantial advantage here as well. The North had 75 percent of the country's free population, and even though the passion about their cause and relative participation of the Southern population was greater than the North's, the absolute numbers were still greatly to the advantage of the Union army.

Before the Civil War began, there was no such thing as an income tax in the United States. People simply kept what they earned, and the (much, much smaller) federal government relied on import tariffs for the majority of its revenue.

This was yet another sore spot between the North and the South. The South favored low tariffs, because it made the finished goods (created with Southern-made cotton) more affordable and appealing to buyers across the country. The North, however, preferred higher tariffs, as it made American-made goods more affordable, and thus benefited American manufacturing versus that of England and France.

■ The Confederacy

After Lincoln's election to the presidency, the interest in seceding from the Union was rampant in the South. The presumed power of "cotton diplomacy" emboldened the political leaders of the Confederacy, and in spite of a two-to-one population advantage of the North over the South, the general belief was that any war would be short and decisively in favor of the Confederate states.

At the time of secession, the Confederacy had less than a million dollars of gold in its treasury, but it felt confident that its cotton crop would do a healthy job supporting the economy. The Union, however, was all too aware of the importance of cotton to Southern economic health, so among the earliest actions of the Union against its new opponent was to create a blockade of all the major ports. In doing so, it would cut off the lifeblood of the Southern economy.

At first, the South had a creative approach to this problem, selling bonds backed by the growing mountains of cotton in its storehouses. However, the blockades were persistent, effective, and very long lived, so the principal income source of the South was completely scuttled. Its economic starvation had begun. This was a major shock to the world's economy, given the magnitude of cotton on the world business scene. At the time, if the South had been considered an independent nation, it would have measured economically as the fourth largest in the world.

There was another serious problem in the Southern agrarian economy: lack of manpower. Because almost all able-bodied men were expected to leave their homes and fight the war, the productivity of farmland plummeted. The South didn't have the labor-saving devices of modern machines, and its slave labor was inadequate to grow and harvest the entire region's crops.

Although the modern perception is that all white farmers had slaves in the South, the reality was that most families had no slaves at all: only 384,000 out of 1.6 million families did, meaning over three-quarters of all family farms had virtually no one to tend them during the war. Thus, staggering amounts of land lay fallow, and untold quantities of crops went to waste.

During the course of the war, naturally, this led to widespread hunger and starvation, and in the latter stages of the war, grief-stricken letters from wives sent to soldiers would foment low morale and, in many cases, desertion from the armed forces. The South had optimized itself for the purpose of selling highly profitable crops during peacetime, but it was in no position to feed its own population during a time of war, with its ports blockaded and its manpower fighting and dying in battle.

■ The Greybacks

In the middle of the nineteenth century, there was no uniform currency in America. The general understanding of paper money was that it was a receipt for gold, payable on demand, at the bank of issuance.

Thus, hundreds of nationally and state-chartered banks across the nation had their own bank notes, and there were literally thousands of different kinds of currency in circulation (in much the same way that, in the modern world, there are thousands of different designs of checks and credit cards in circulation, but they are all recognized as being acceptable for the exchange of goods and services, due to the uniform value behind them—namely, a U.S. dollar).

In the earliest days of the Civil War, the South endeavored to create a currency for its newfound nation, but it didn't possess anywhere near the amount of hard assets to back up the bank notes. It thus created a series of bank notes of different denominations of a unit known as the Confederate States of America Dollar, which was backed by a promise to pay the bearer after the war was successfully concluded. In other words, the value of the note was based on a very uncertain future, and a completely unknown basis

FIGURE 7.3 A 20-dollar bill from the Confederate States of America.

for which hard assets, sometime in the same future, would be acquired (see Figure 7.3).

In spite of the shakiness of the value behind the bank note, it was initially widely accepted as being almost as good as gold. Due to the South's lack of widespread machinery, the printing of the bills themselves (known as *greybacks*) was a relatively shoddy operation: the printing quality wasn't especially good, and the sheets of money were often cut by hand with scissors and hastily signed by bank clerks in behalf of their superiors.

There was a legend at the top of the bill assuring that "Two Years After the Ratification of a Treaty of Peace Between the Confederate States and the United States of America the Confederate States of America will pay $1 to the Bearer" (or whatever the amount of the currency happened to be).

Given the relatively amateurish attempt to create the money, greybacks became very easy to counterfeit. As the war progressed, counterfeiting became more widespread, not only from Southerners desperate for cash to pay for goods, but by Northerners bent on diminishing the value of the paper money by flooding the market with more paper. The Confederate treasury secretary denounced the "Yankee scoundrels" in June 1862 by stating, "Organized plans seem to be in operation for introducing counterfeiting among us by means of prisoners and traitors."

With greybacks supported by nothing but a flimsy future pledge, and the abundance of bills flooding the South through both legitimate and counterfeit creators, the bills swiftly lost their value. When the bills were first introduced, one Confederate dollar was exchangeable for one gold dollar. Six months later, it would take $1.05 Confederate to buy a dollar of gold.

Six months after that, it was $1.25, and by February 1863, it would take $3 in Confederate money to buy a dollar of gold.

The greybacks acted as a good proxy for the general faith in the outcome of the war for the South, and as prospects for Southern victory dimmed, the value of the Confederate dollar began to plummet. This surging inflation made commodities increasingly expensive, and one measure of commodity prices between January 1861 and April 1865 increased from a value of 100 to over 9,000 (in other words, a basket of items costing $100 at the war's start would cost 90 times as much by war's end) (see Figure 7.4).

Although the South had counted on European financial support, very little was forthcoming. Both England and France had misgivings about lending money to a slave-based society. None other than Baron Rothschild wrote that "… all Germany condemned this act of lending money to establish a slaveholding government, and so great was public opinion against it that Erlanger and Company dare not offer it on the Frankfort bourse."

The importance of the South's economic weakness in the war's outcome was well understood by a contemporary, the famous General William

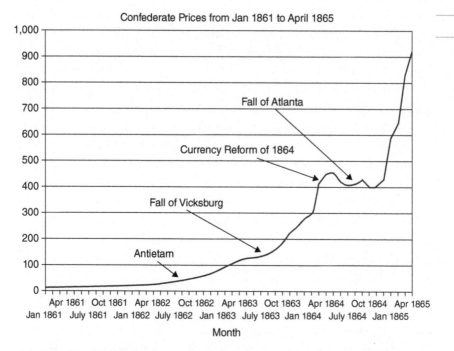

FIGURE 7.4 Inflation raged in the South through the entire Civil War, ultimately pushing prices up 90-fold.

Tecumseh Sherman, who wrote to a friend who lived in the South: "The North can make a steam-engine, locomotive or railway car, hardly a yard of cloth or a pair of shoes can you make. You are rushing into war with one of the most powerful, ingeniously mechanical and determined people on earth—right at your doors. You are bound to fail." He wrote this in 1863, but he was precisely correct about what was going to transpire over the remaining two years.

■ Bonds before Bombs

In 1860, the banking and finance industry was extremely primitive when compared to the present, and there has never been much incentive for the federal government to take a strong position in how the financial industry should conduct itself. The banking business was a hodgepodge of 1,600 state banks and 7,000 different kinds of currency ranging from good as gold to being worth less than the paper on which it was printed.

The money flowing in and out of the federal government did so in a very physical sense, because the government accepted only "hard money"— that is, physical gold—as its medium of exchange. Thus, tons of gold were hauled in and out of the Treasury's storehouses by horse-drawn carts to align the physical possession of money with the scribbles laid out in the ledger books of the federal government. It was a crude, unwieldy system, but it was a long-held tradition that the government would deal only in precious metal as its basis for its own currency holdings.

The trouble was, with a war looming, the United States didn't have enough physical gold to finance the weapons and manpower that would be needed. It may seem incredible to the modern reader, but the United States didn't even have a mechanism in place to *borrow* the money it needed. The small bond market that did exist didn't provide the size or liquidity the government needed, and the small placement of investors who might be interested in U.S. bonds in 1861 were demanding upwards of 12 percent interest. Simply stated, the government was effectively broke, and it had a war to pay for.

By March 4 1861, President Lincoln's inauguration day, not only was the government unable to pay the bills that had come due, but it had stopped paying members of Congress and was even unable to fund the stationery needed in its offices. The Civil War had not even begun, and the government's coffers were completely empty. On top of this, since the government depended on tariffs for 90 percent of its revenue, it could anticipate a large reduction in this income as blockades choked off any trade with the South, as the Southern states would be seceding from the country one by one.

The president had appointed as his Treasury secretary a stiff, pious, and pompous man by the name of Salmon P. Chase (who, four years later, would seek to run for president himself, even while in office). Chase had been a senator and Ohio's governor, but his training as a lawyer did not prepare him for a financial post. In spite of this, over the course of his tenure, he did an excellent job guiding and growing the Treasury into a crucial arm of the federal government (see Figure 7.5).

FIGURE 7.5 Salmon Chase had a long and storied career as a politician, serving as Lincoln's Treasury secretary and, in later years, as the chief justice of the U.S. Supreme Court.

Chase took a two-pronged approach to the government's desperate need for cash: first, he sought to appeal to the patriotism of the Union's citizens to fight the rebellion that was taking place. After all, those in the North did not perceive the pending war as between the United States of America and the Confederate States of America. As far as they were concerned, the CSA was a fictional daydream of their Southern brothers and sisters; it wasn't really a country, but instead was involved in a widespread uprising against the rightful government of the United States. Chase would use this patriotism as the basis for borrowing as much money as he could through bond sales.

Second, Chase endeavored to expand the nation's money supply by way of paper money. The gold needed to back hundreds of millions of dollars of currency was simply not there; the government would, in steps, need to move the public to a currency backed by the full faith and credit of the U.S. government, as opposed to the hard assets sitting in a vault—the system to which they had been long accustomed.

Chase first approached Congress with a request for $100 million in low-denomination Treasury notes that people could pay for over a five-month period in 10 equal installments. If this sounds like a modern-day pitch for a television or other large appliance, that's because the goal was the same: to compel everyday people to acquire something that they wanted (in this case, a victorious United States) with payment terms they could comfortably meet. The bond issue was approved, and it was a sweeping success.

Chase was well aware of the effect paper money might eventually have on prices, but he was resolute, informing a group of bankers, "Gentlemen, the war must go on until this rebellion is put down, if we have to out-paper [the South] until it takes $1,000 to buy breakfast."

In his discussions with bankers, he made a close acquaintance with Jay Cooke, a prominent and ambitious banker who, over time, became the principal marketer of U.S. bonds to the public. Cooke was as much a marketing wizard as a financial talent, since he took the innovative step of going directly to the people with modestly priced denominations paid for with attractive installment-payment terms.

Cooke advertised in newspapers and created handbills, and he is largely credited with revolutionizing the packaging and marketing of bonds. The teamwork of (1) Chase as the man who convinced Congress of the need to issue bonds and (2) Cooke as the man to get them sold to the everyday citizen was a potent combination that funded a large part of the war (see Figure 7.6).

FIGURE 7.6   Jay Cooke, the man who would single-handedly revolutionize the way bonds were marketed and sold to the public.

The text from one of the handbills nicely captures the sentiment and passion of the message and the broad audience it was addressing:

TO FARMERS, MECHANICS AND CAPITALISTS! You have a solemn duty to perform to your government and to posterity! Our gallant army and navy must be supported by every man and woman who has any means, large or small, at their control. The United States Government, to which we owe our prosperity as a nation, security of person and property of every sort, calls on each individual to rally to its support—not with donations or gifts—though who could withhold them—BUT WITH SUBSCRIPTIONS TO HER LOANS, based on the best security in the world, the untold and scarcely yet tried resources of this mighty Continent, which were developing rapidly when the rebellion broke out, and to maintain which, AS A PRICELESS HERITAGE TO POSTERITY, this defense against rebellion is made.

As the widespread buying and selling of securities became more commonplace, the financial industry matured and became more sophisticated. Wall Street had normally been considered a relative backwater in the global world of finance, but New York was soon second only to London in this domain.

The initial panic in the stock market, which pushed prices even lower than that of the Panic of 1857 was, with the help of Chase's and Cooke's guidance, replaced with a confidence and a prosperity, even in the shadow of the raging war. By 1864, Cooke was able to sell bonds faster than even the War Department could spend it. Bonds were, in the end, as critical an instrument of war as any gun or soldier on the battlefield.

■ Legal Tender

With literally thousands of different kinds of currency circulating around the United States, the public's perceived value of paper money was a liability to the nation's financial plans. Secretary Chase knew that a united nation needed a united currency, and it needed widespread public confidence in the currency, whether it was backed by the traditional hard asset of gold or not.

The opponents of paper money were numerous and vocal in their arguments against the adoption. Ever since Andrew Jackson dismantled the Second Bank of the United States in 1833, the country has contented itself with no central bank, no standardized currency, and minimal government meddling in the affairs of financial business. But the demands of the war made Chase's arguments for the issuance of a Federal Reserve note more compelling, and in early 1862, Congress finally agreed.

President Lincoln was grappling with the personal trauma of having lost his beloved young son Willie, so he left it to Chase to achieve the passage of the legal tender legislation, which Lincoln signed on February 25, 1862. Just as the greybacks acted as a proxy for the South's chances of an eventual military victory, so too did the newly printed Federal Reserve note act as a form of "stock" representing the United States.

By the spring of 1862, the North was beginning to muster enough victories on the battlefield to give hope that the Union would eventually prevail, so the citizens of the United States were willing to accept the Legal Tender Act as a necessity of the war.

The first issuance of the legal tender notes—popularly known as "greenbacks"—was in the amount of $150 million, and the money was immediately deployed to cover the mounting expenses of the nation's army

FIGURE 7.7 A greenback in the amount of one dollar, featuring none other than Salmon P. Chase.

and its suppliers. The importance of the congressional act that authorized the paper as legal tender was that all creditors, either public or private, would henceforth be *required* to accept the notes as payments for debt, in spite of the fact that they were not backed by gold or any other form of hard currency (see Figure 7.7).

Congress did not give unlimited printing authority to the Treasury, however, and soon there was a need for more cash. The Second Legal Tender Act, enacted in the summer of 1862, and the Third Legal Tender Act, enacted the following spring, expanded the limit of allowable currency from the original $150 million to $450 million.

Comprehending the growth of the money supply requires some perspective: in July 1861, the amount of federal paper notes in circulation was a mere $1 million, as it was backed by the same amount of gold in the Treasury's vault. By way of the Legal Tender acts, the amount of paper money in circulation was thus expanded 450-fold.

Another act of Congress that helped mop up some of this excess liquidity, and also helped provide for the nation's war efforts, was the enactment of the nation's first income tax. This tax legislation was put into effect roughly the same time as the First Legal Tender Act on July 1, 1862.

The tax was levied on a wide variety of manufacturers and employees. The principal reason the tax act was easily passed was that it was widely believed that the war would reach a successful conclusion in a few months, and the burden of the tax could be heaped on the backs of the Southerners as punishment for their insurrection. Thus, it was passed with the idea that those passing it would never actually have to bear its cost.

By today's standards, the tax was miniscule, levying a flat rate of 3 percent on anyone making over $800 per year (which, at the time, was a very good salary). The tax system became progressive in form and more substantial in percentage terms in the years to follow; by 1864, the system had three tiers: 10 percent for those earning more than $10,000, 7.5 percent for those earning between $5,000 and $10,000, and 5 percent for those earning between $600 and $5,000. For a nation that, before the American Revolution, was willing to riot over a few pennies in tax for English tea, it is remarkable that the same country so easily embraced an unprecedented garnishment on wages.

There was another goal to be achieved with the nation's new currency, and that was to replace the absurdly heterogeneous variety of other currency forms in the land. The president could not simply invalidate all the other forms of cash in circulation, but he could, over time, make it increasingly uncomfortable for state banks to issue and support their own currencies.

Lincoln started by issuing a 2 percent tax on all the notes in circulation from the state banks, and he increased this rate to 10 percent in 1865, thus making such notes a wholly inefficient and uneconomical means of exchange. By March 1865, Congress amplified the assault on paper currency not issued by the United States by doubling the taxation to 20 percent. This was the death knell of competing banknotes. All the banks, both state and federally chartered, adopted the federal reserve notes as the basis for exchange.

Inflation, naturally, did take place in the North, but to nowhere near the extent that it did in the South. The vastly expanded money supply created upward price pressures, sometimes as high as 80 percent in a year, but the management of the Union's finances was far more responsible than that of the Confederacy, which saw a 90-fold increase in its own price of goods.

■ Gold and a Hoax

Just as the value of the greyback behaved as a proxy for the South's war prospects, the value of gold reflected the military success (or setbacks) for the Union. Although financial markets were quite primitive at the time, necessity's being the mother of invention led to the creation of "gold rooms," where spirited bidding would take place. A contemporary account of one such room, excerpted from James K. Medbery's *Men and Mysteries of Wall Street* (published in 1870), evoked the intensity of the scene that isn't far removed from a modern-day account of a commodity exchange:

> The gloom or the gladness over success or defeat of the national flag mingled with individual passions. Men leaped upon chairs, waved their hands, or clenched their fists; shrieked, shouted; the bulls whistled "Dixie," and the bears sung "John Brown"; the crowd swayed feverishly from door to door, and, as the fury mounted to white heat, and the tide of gold fluctuated up and down in rapid sequence, brokers seemed animated with the impulses of demons, hand-to-hand combats took place, and bystanders, peering through the smoke and dust, could liken the wild turmoil only to the revels of maniacs.

The importance of gold to the Union's assets, and its value as a measurement of popular sentiment about the war's prospects, were not lost on President Lincoln. He followed gold's movement with a combination of tactical interest and feelings of resentment that any man would try to profit from the horror of the war happening around them.

One dinnertime anecdote holds that Lincoln asked, "What is the price of gold this morning? Is it going up or down?" The aide replied, "Up, Mr. Lincoln. The Street is wild." The president responded, "Well, now, they don't know everything. If I were a bear on Wall Street, and if I were short of gold, I'd keep short. It's a good time to sell." It seems incredible to imagine a near-deity like Abraham Lincoln speaking in the esoteric language of a financial speculator, but such was the account.

The gold rush that commenced in California over a decade earlier turned out to be a godsend for the United States, which relied heavily on whatever stores of gold it could attain. General Ulysses Grant himself remarked, "I do not know what we would do in this great national emergency were it not for the gold sent from California."

The opportunities to profit from gold's dynamic price movements were not missed by the unscrupulous, and one fascinating account from 1864 captures this neatly. In May of that year, after four years of war, the Union was growing hopeful that a successful conclusion might be in sight.

However, on May 18, two morning papers came out—the *New York World* and the *Journal of Commerce*—with shocking news: they stated that the president had ordered an additional 400,000 men to be conscripted into the

Union army on account of "the situation in Virginia, the disaster at Red River, the delay at Charleston, and the general state of the country."

The discouraging report and the demand for such a huge quantity of fresh soldiers sent a shock wave through the financial community, since it was obvious from the report that things were not going nearly so well in the war as once believed. Stocks tumbled, and hard assets such as gold soared in value. Some people became puzzled, however, because this important report was nowhere to be found in any of the city's many other newspapers.

Late that morning, crowds had gathered at the offices of both papers that had published the news, and the editors assured them that the story was true, producing the dispatch from the Associated Press with the matching information. The Associated Press, however, the ostensible source of the story, quickly issued a statement making clear that they had never sent out this account. This was soon followed by a statement from the State Department in Washington, in which Secretary of State William Seward declared the news dispatch to be "an absolute forgery."

It turns out that the forgery was a clever creation of Joseph Howard, the city editor of the *Brooklyn Eagle* newspaper. Howard, who was intimately acquainted with the workings of the city's newspapers, had come up with a scheme. He knew that bad news from the war would cause gold to rise in value. He also knew that the best way to get a dispatch into the morning papers would be to submit the information when the newspaper staff was most vulnerable—that is, in the wee hours of the morning, when there were hardly any personnel around to verify the facts (see Figure 7.8).

Thus, working with an accomplice, he crafted a realistic-looking Associated Press news release and, working with one Francis Mallison (a reporter for his journal), he distributed the news item at 3:30 in the morning to the city's newspapers. Most of them were reluctant to print such an important piece without verification, but two of them proceeded to run with the story.

Of course, before any of this took place, Mr. Howard had acquired as much gold as he could in his margin account, and once the grim news was raging throughout the financial community, he disposed of his position at a handsome profit, never suspecting the false item would be traced back to him.

It was, however, and President Lincoln himself ordered the closure of both of the papers that had printed the dispatch, which was an order later rescinded. Lincoln's furious demand for the paper's closures, however, became one of the few black marks on his presidency since, in spite of the

FIGURE 7.8   Joseph Howard, the mastermind behind the 1864 gold hoax.

ugly circumstances involved, the President's decision went right to the heart of freedom of the press enshrined in the Constitution.

Perhaps unsurprisingly, this was not the first instance Mr. Howard decided to try to fool the public. Years earlier, in 1861, he wrote a story claiming that President Lincoln had traveled throughout Baltimore disguised with— of all things— "a Scotch cap and long military cloak." Although Howard was thrown into Fort Lafayette for his crime, he was released a few months later.

The irony to the entire hoax was that only two months later, Lincoln did indeed order up the conscription of more men into the Union army. However, the figure demanded was not the 400,000 that Howard had dreamed up for his bogus news release. It was, in fact, a full *half million*. Howard's fanciful fraud was, in the end, both prescient and conservative.

■ A Nation Transformed

At the end of the war, the nation was reunited politically but had never been more different in other respects. The North had a solid financial base, a vastly-improved transportation infrastructure, and a modernized agricultural foundation. The South was a beaten, devastated land, with billions of dollars of business destroyed and a parched, burnt landscape where before there had been thriving, lush plantations.

The mechanical might of the North, powered by the financial wherewithal to support its cause, caused more American deaths than any other war before or since (in spite of vastly more efficient means of killing with modern warfare). The great capitals of the South—New Orleans, Mobile, Charleston, Atlanta—had been laid waste by fire and years of fighting, and the millions of slaves that had provided effectively free labor to the plantations for decades were now free citizens who would obviously no longer be making such services available to the desperate landowners of the former Confederacy.

John McMaster's 1927 publication *A History of the People of the United States During Lincoln's Administration* paints a picture of the devastation: "From Winchester to Harrisonburg scarce a crop, fence, chicken, horse, cow, or pig was in sight.... Extreme destitution prevailed throughout the entire valley. All able-bodied Negroes had left; only those unfit to work remained. The country between Washington and Richmond was ... like a desert

While both the North and the South had adopted a paper currency, the North's remained a valuable and universally accepted medium of exchange, whereas the South's was now worthless. The bonds, stocks, and currency of Southern business were worth no more than the paper on which they were printed, and countless families who had entered the war as wealthy patriarchs were in some cases reduced to begging.

The North's disposition to the South was a kindly one, however, as the nation sought to unify itself once more, and relief commissions were formed after the war to provide the food and shelter necessary to get citizens of the southern United States back on their feet. The prisoners of war held in the North were released and given rations.

One former soldier of the Confederate army was quoted in 1865's publication *Annual Cyclopedia of Important Events* that, "it must be a matter of gratitude as well as surprise, for our people to see a Government which was lately fighting us with fire, and sword, and shell, now generously feeding our poor and distressed.... There is much in this that takes away the bitter sting ... of the past."

From the modern vantage point, it is clear to see that in spite of the war's horrors, devastation, and loss of hundreds of thousands of human lives, the country was about to embark on one of the strongest and most bountiful periods in its history. The reunited states had five important legacies on which to build, brought about by the leadership of Lincoln, Chase, and the rest of his cabinet:

- *Federal taxes.* The first income tax imposed on the citizens of the United States was in 1861, and the Internal Revenue Act created a system for extracting revenue from the citizens, which became the principal source of revenue for the federal government, as opposed to the far more modest system of import tariffs that had supported Washington, D.C., before the war.

- *Legal tender.* After the war, the reunited nation had a unified currency as well, and the universal recognition of a single federal currency made commerce more efficient and the public's faith in paper money more stable. Alongside this new currency system was a stronger banking infrastructure, with the National Bank Act creating a national banking system.

- *Nationwide railroads.* As railroads began spreading across the nation, Congress sought establishment of a nationwide route. Before the war, Southern legislators sought a north-south route, whereas their Northern counterparts wanted an east-west route. Once the South had seceded, the northern half of the country got its way, and the Pacific Railway Act was established. In spite of the South's departure, the location of the intended railway was moved somewhat south, spanning from Omaha to Sacramento. The completion of this line, of course, would be a profoundly vital artery of commerce and people in the remaining decades of the 1860s, particularly given the vibrant growth of the American West.

- *Homestead Act.* This measure had been debated for decades, but it had been effectively blocked by the Southern members of Congress. During the war, with the South no longer participating in the legislative matters of the country, Congress was finally able to pass this law, which provided for free title of 160 acres of undeveloped land anywhere outside the original 13 colonies of the United States. Anyone willing to live on and cultivate the land could call it their own. In the second half of the nineteenth century, this alluring offer from the government compelled hundreds of thousands of people to settle the West and to cultivate and tame the vast wilderness on the continent.

- *Industrial colleges.* As the importance of mechanization became clear to those in the North who had to rely on fewer men to assist with farming, it was widely agreed that the nation's future would be aided by the promulgation of knowledge and development of such machines. The Morrill

Act granted each state land for the purpose of endowing agricultural and mechanical colleges (colloquially known as A&M, such as the famed school in Texas). The new schools were intended to teach "agriculture and the mechanic arts," which was a national investment that would pay enormous dividends as the country expanded and its farming opportunities became exponentially larger.

The president never lost sight of the importance of economics in his prosecution of the war, or the importance of providing for the men who fought it. On April 14, 1865, he told his new Treasury secretary, *"We must look to you, Mr. Secretary, for the money to pay off the soldiers."* It was literally one of the last expressions of his life, as the president was shot to death later on that very day.

CHAPTER 8

The Panic of 1893

The years following the conclusion of the American Civil War ushered in a vastly different America than the antebellum nation. In the first part of the nineteenth century, most citizens lived and worked on farms in small towns, lived a largely self-sufficient life, and at times struggled just to keep their families warm and fed. After the Civil War, however, the nation moved from an agrarian to an industrial economy, and as industry's growth became exponential, the Gilded Age would create characters of American business whose reputations persist to this day.

■ The Robber Barons

If there were ever a great time to be an ambitious American capitalist, it was just after the end of the Civil War. There was no income tax, no antitrust laws, no meaningful regulation, no unions, no minimum wage, vast plains of unexploited natural resources, frontier opportunities, and new industries. Some of the richest capitalists America would ever know would thrive during this period, including such storied names as:

- Jay Gould
- Mark Hopkins
- Andrew Mellon
- J. P. Morgan
- Cornelius Vanderbilt
- Leland Stanford

- Henry Clay Frick
- James Fish
- Charles Crocker
- John Jacob Astor
- Andrew Carnegie
- John D. Rockefeller

These men did not rise to prominence through gentle negotiations; it was a ruthless time for business, and these aristocrats had no reservations about bribing politicians, crushing competition through unscrupulous means, cheating investors, forming cartels, and both treating and paying workers as poorly as they could get away with.

While it is true that the leadership of these businessmen put America at the forefront of the worldwide economy, it did so at the expense of fair competition and the decent treatment of labor.

Business was growing so quickly, and its need for labor was so consistent, that the nation absorbed immigrants at a pace that at its peak approached a million per year. Although workers were by no means well paid, their standard of living did improve over time, and real wages doubled between 1870 and 1900. It was also an inventive age, with the number of patents granted between 1870 and 1900 being *10 times* the number in the 90 years beforehand, a 30-fold increase in the pace of inventions.

Although by 1890, for the first time in the nation's history, more people worked outside of agriculture than within it, the role of farming was still huge and vital. At the start of the nineteenth century, a full 74 percent of the population was in agriculture, but by 1880, that figure had shrunk to 40 percent, thanks to mechanization as well as the growth of other industries.

All of the progress and growth in farming, however, did come with a cost: falling prices. The amount of wheat, cotton, and corn increased twofold between 1870 and 1890, and since the population had not increased at the same rate, there was an excess of supply.

Because farming was increasingly efficient and large scale, and as other members of the global market such as India stepped up their own efforts to grow cash crops such as cotton and wheat, the price for these goods began to slump badly. By 1889, it cost farmers in Kansas twice as much to *grow* corn as the market price they could attain by selling it. And, as heavily mortgaged as farmers already were, they became severely distressed financially and sought a way out of their widespread troubles.

■ Silver and Gold

What was proposed was to deliberately create inflation by way of a change in how precious metals were treated in the United States. In 1890, the currency of the United States was officially backed by gold, and anyone in possession of gold (such as a prospector) merely had to pay a visit to any of the U.S. mints in the country, turn in their metal, and receive in return an equivalent amount in minted gold coins (minus a very small discount).

There were silver coins at the time as well, but not only could one not turn in silver metal for coins as the gold miners could, but the intrinsic value of the silver coins was less than the actual silver content, meaning that a portion of the silver coin's value was backed by nothing but government fiat (much like today's paper money, although these days the *entirety* of the currency is fiat based).

The widespread perception was that gold was the purview of the capitalists, the well-heeled, and the Northeastern (and British) moneyed interests, while silver—the "poor man's gold"—was the domain of the common man. The official exchange rate between the two metals—16 ounces of silver being equal to 1 ounce of gold—did not reflect market reality, which was more like 32 to 1, since silver's market value had plunged due to the large new supplies of the metal brought in from such places as the Comstock Lode in Nevada (see Figure 8.1).

The push for a greater role for silver was so strong that it prompted a massive political movement in the form of the "Silverites," who promoted bimetallism: that is, the use of both silver *and* gold as the basis for currency.

The political agitation was finally satisfied with the passage of the Sherman Silver Purchase Act in July of 1890, which required the Treasury of the United States buy 4.5 million ounces of silver every month, which would obviously drive up the metal's price. Western silver miners were delighted, since they could enjoy the inflated revenues from sales of their extractions, and farmers were likewise pleased that the increase in the money supply would reverse years of falling commodity prices.

There was a serious flaw in this plan, however. When the government purchased the silver, it exchanged special Treasury Notes for the metal, which themselves could be exchanged for either gold or silver (hence: bimetallism).

So if a person is able to sell silver at an *official* ratio of 16:1 when the *actual* market relationship is 32:1, the economically rational action is to redeem the notes for gold coins as swiftly as possible in an act of arbitrage. The U.S. government watched its gold supply—the foundation for its currency—rapidly dwindle, as investors sought to exchange their paper notes for gold coins acquired at unintentionally attractive values.

FIGURE 8.1 A group of miners from the Comstock Lode in Nevada in the 1880s.

These events worsened the gold/silver divide; in popular culture, silver symbolized regular Americans, unions, and the populist cause, whereas advocates of "sound money"—that is, gold—were the likes of J. P. Morgan. The U.S. government was forced to conduct a series of bond issues to shore up its shrinking supply of gold, since a lack of the metal would force it to abandon the gold standard, an event that would be calamitous for the nation's credit and currency.

On top of this, in the same year, the McKinley administration passed a tariff intended to protect the nation's beleaguered farms from the diminishment in cash crop prices. At a gruesome rate of 48 percent, the tariff acted as a hindrance to healthy global trade and would proceed to exacerbate the forthcoming slowdown.

■ Panic Sets in

The economic turmoil caused by the silver act was amplified greatly by two other financial events: the first was the declaration of bankruptcy by the Philadelphia and Reading Railroad in February 1893, just 10 days before the inauguration of Grover Cleveland. (It was to be his second term in office, although nonconsecutively, which is the only instance in American history of a two-term, nonconsecutive presidency.)

The other event, in May, was brought about by the largest-volume stock of the time: the National Cordage Company (a rope manufacturer). National Cordage attempted to corner the hemp market and failed to do so, resulting in a swift selloff of the company's stock. This selling pressure spread to other issues, and the stock market entered into a broad swoon.

The financial contagion spread rapidly: within a few months of the Reading Railroad's bankruptcy, bank failures occurred at a furious pace, with 600 shuttered initially and, by year's end, a full 4,000 closed. During the same period, about 14,000 different businesses closed shop, and the nation was entering what would be the worst depression in the country's history, with the exception of the Great Depression that would take place four decades later.

As businesses closed, unemployment began to climb, and the unemployment rate would persist in the double digits for years to come. Unemployment surged to 20 percent in 1894, and larger cities became flooded with jobless, homeless men looking for work. Policemen would be stationed at railroad stations to turn away newcomers trying to get into the city.

Those who were still fortunate enough to hold jobs saw their wages shrink, and discontentment began to spread, particularly as the contrast between the struggling masses and the breathtakingly rich robber barons was well known. Widespread strikes began taking place, numbering well over 1,000 in 1894, and 750,000 workers chose to be idle from their jobs in protest of either working conditions or wages. Management did not take a kindly disposition toward such work stoppages, and brutal crackdowns on strikes were rampant, resulting in injuries and even deaths in some cases.

One of the larger strikes of the time was by the Pullman workers in Illinois, and the statement they issued during the strike encapsulates their struggle and their harsh attitude toward the wealthy owner Mr. Pullman himself:

[Pullman's] Residences, compared with which ours are hovels ... no man or woman of us all has ever owned or can ever hope to own one inch of George M. Pullman's land. Why, even the very streets are his ... water which Pullman buys from the city at 8 cents a thousand gallons he retails to us at 500 percent advance and claims he is losing $400 a month on it. Gas which sells at 75 cents per thousand feet in Hyde Park, just north of us, he sells for $2.25. When we went to tell him our grievances, he said we were all his "children." Pullman, both the man and the town, is an ulcer on the body politic. He owns the houses, the schoolhouses, and churches of God in the town he gave his once-humble name.

One of the biggest protests from laborers was actually led and organized by a business owner named Jacob Coxey, who owned a steel mill in Ohio. He had to lay off 40 of his own workers, and he felt the federal government should do something large to address the worsening employment situation in the country (see Figure 8.2).

FIGURE 8.2 Businessman Jacob Coxey, who organized a small group of men into an "army" that would march to Washington, D.C., near the end of the nineteenth century

He proposed a national construction project of road building that would help employ tens of thousands of people and create infrastructure of lasting value, and in a suggestion that would make Keynesians of the next century proud, he suggested a half-billion dollars of new paper money be printed up, given to the unemployed in exchange for their work on such a project, and in turn get the country on the right path again.

He called his proposal the "Good Roads Bill," and he hoped 100,000 men would join him on a march from his native state to the nation's capital. He set out with 100 people on Easter Sunday in 1894 (including his son, whom he named, incredibly, Legal Tender Coxey), and even though only a few hundred others would join on the crusade, the so-called Coxey's army attracted a lot of attention and positive publicity (see Figure 8.3).

When Coxey reached Washington, D.C., with his followers on April 30, he did not find President Grover Cleveland awaiting his arrival with any kind of aid in hand. On the contrary, the president was ready to quell any sort of large march or protest, based on the prohibition of parades being held on the grounds of the Capitol, and the federal government arrested both Coxey and two of his men shortly thereafter. No half-billion dollar rescue package would be forthcoming.

■ Cleveland and Morgan

One man who had thrived as a rich, successful banker after the Civil War was J. P. Morgan, but as wealthy as he was, two circumstances were forthcoming in his career that, thanks to the events of 1893, would propel him to legendary status.

The first was the situation with the railroads, from which he had already garnered a large part of his fortune. The nation's railway infrastructure had become overbuilt, overleveraged, and fiscally unsound. Railroad after railroad toppled into receivership, and in this Morgan saw the opportunity of a lifetime.

A few years earlier, in 1887, Grover Cleveland had seen to the creation of the Interstate Commerce Commission (ICC). The ICC was crafted as a "fourth branch" of government, independent of the executive, judicial, and legislative branches, as a mechanism to ensure fair rates on the nation's transportation networks.

Ironically, Morgan made ample use of the ICC, which he populated judiciously with his own men in important ICC positions, as a mechanism for

FIGURE 8.3 On April 30, 1894, Coxey's army reached the capital and met with disappointing results.

acquiring bankrupt railroads on the cheap and assembling them into the nation's greatest railway cartel.

Since almost a third of the railroad companies in America were bankrupt, Morgan gained control over just about every railroad east of the Mississippi River at some point, ultimately settling on one-sixth of America's railroad track, or 30,000 miles total. Once the country got back on its economic feet, the entire revenue that the U.S. government received was only double the amount that Morgan himself enjoyed from his artfully constructed private railroad cartel. In other words, Morgan's railroad income was so substantial that in two years' time his revenue was equal to annual revenue of the entire U.S. government (see Figure 8.4).

Almost everyone else, of course, was suffering—not benefitting—from the nation's economic calamity, and shortly after President Cleveland began his second presidential term, he called together a special session of Congress and urged them to repeal the Sherman Silver Purchase Act, which had caused, and continued to cause, so much economic harm to the nation. A few excerpts of his message to Congress illustrate the gravity of the situation and the sense of urgency the president hoped to convey (emphasis on certain portions added by the author):

The existence of an alarming and extraordinary business situation, involving the welfare and prosperity of all our people, has constrained me to call together in extra session the people's representatives in Congress, to the end that through a wise and patriotic exercise of the legislative duty, with which they solely are charged, *present evils may be mitigated and dangers threatening the future may be averted.*

If, as many of its friends claim, silver ought to occupy a larger place in our currency and the currency of the world through general international cooperation and agreement, it is obvious that the United States will not be in a position to gain a hearing in favor of such an arrangement so long as we are willing to continue our attempt to accomplish the result single-handed.

The people of the United States are entitled to a sound and stable currency and to money recognized as such on every exchange and in every market of the world. Their Government has no right to injure them by financial experiments opposed to the policy and practice of other civilized states, nor is it justified in permitting an exaggerated and unreasonable reliance on our national strength and ability to jeopardize the soundness of the people's money.

FIGURE 8.4 In this contemporary cartoon from *Puck* magazine, J. P. Morgan is shown grasping his cornucopia of valuable assets, most prominently the clutch of railroads he had acquired.

This matter rises above the plane of party politics. It vitally concerns every business and calling and enters every household in the land. There is one important aspect of the subject which especially should never be overlooked. At times like the present, when the evils of unsound finance threaten us, *the speculator may anticipate a harvest gathered from the misfortune of others, the capitalist may protect himself by hoarding or may even find profit in the fluctuations of values; but the wage earner—the first to be injured by a depreciated currency and the last to receive the benefit of its correction*—is practically defenseless. He relies for work upon the ventures of confident and contented capital. This failing him, his condition is without alleviation, for he can neither prey on the misfortunes of others nor hoard his labor.

The president's desire for a "hands-off" government was persistent in his political philosophy. Even when it came to the modest requisition of $10,000 in seed for Texas farmers who had just suffered a drought, Cleveland voted the bill, and part of his explanation to Congress was:

> I can find no warrant for such an appropriation in the Constitution, and I do not believe that the power and duty of the general government ought to be extended to the relief of individual suffering which is in no manner properly related to the public service or benefit.... The lesson should be constantly enforced that, though the people support the government, the government should not support the people.... Federal aid in such cases encourages the expectation of paternal care on the part of the government and weakens the sturdiness of our national character.

It is indeed astonishing to know that the president of the United States was able to make such a statement only a little more than a century ago.

In spite of the president's success at getting Congress to repeal the Sherman Silver Purchase Act, the damage to the nation's gold reserves had been severe. By February 1895, the nation's gold was down to $68 million. The president asked Congress to float yet another bond issue, but they refused to do so. Cleveland then turned to the richest family in the world, the Rothschilds of England, but they insisted that if they were going to do business with them, he would have to go through J. P. Morgan himself (see Figure 8.5).

Cleveland, like most of the country, had a strong distaste for mega-wealthy, opportunistic tycoons like J. P. Morgan, so he did not approach the man. Morgan, however, recognized a golden opportunity (both literally and figuratively), so he went, uninvited, to the White House. Cleveland would not see him, but Morgan wasn't budging, proclaiming instead: "I have come down to see the president, and I am going to stay here until I see him!"

Finally, the president relented and agreed to meet with him along with the Treasury secretary and attorney general. During the meeting, in which Morgan largely sat in silence and listened, it was stated that the United States

FIGURE 8.5 Grover Cleveland's populist rhetoric was a strong balance to the surging power to the plutocracy around him.

was down to its last $9 million in gold reserves. At last, Morgan spoke, notifying the president that he was aware of a $10 million draft, payable on demand in gold, that was awaiting redemption. He told President Cleveland, "It will all be over by 3 o'clock." Cleveland finally buckled to the thinly veiled threat and sheepishly asked, "What suggestions have you to make, Mr. Morgan?"

Thus, Morgan's trap had sprung brilliantly. He just happened to have a proposal at hand that called for Morgan and the Rothschilds to loan the U.S. Treasury 3.5 million ounces of gold in exchange for 30-year government bonds. The deal allowed for Morgan and Rothschild to purchase the entire issuance of bonds at $104.50 and, in turn, sell them to the public at $112.50.

As good a deal as that was, it got even better for Morgan, because the investment world was already positioned for a fiscal failure from the U.S.

government. Morgan's shocking plan astonished (and ruined) thousands of speculators who were betting the opposite direction, and the demand for the bonds was so strong that the price garnered was not $112.50, but $119, and the entire pile of bonds was sold out in 22 minutes flat. Morgan had made a killing while simultaneously saving the United States from its own financial blunders.

■ The Man behind the Curtain

Those who were already contemptuous and suspicious of Morgan were incensed, and the leader of the Silverites, William Jennings Bryan, based virtually his entire presidential campaign on a populist pro-silver/anti-gold message. His famed "Cross of Gold" speech stated:

> Having behind us the producing masses of this nation and the world, supported by the commercial interests, the laboring interests and the toilers everywhere, we will answer their demand for a gold standard by saying to them: You shall not press down upon the brow of labor this crown of thorns, you shall not crucify mankind upon a cross of gold!

Bryan then stretched out his arms and stood there as a Christ-like martyr before the stunned, silent audience. A few moments later, the wild cheers began and the excited mob rushed up to their cherished candidate. The speech would remain one of the most famous ever made in U.S. political history (see Figure 8.6).

In the present, Bryan is largely unknown to the public, but a cultural artifact from the same era is known to nearly everyone to this day: *The Wizard of Oz*, familiar to most modern people from the movie, a fanciful and imaginative tale bearing the lesson that there's "no place like home."

The Wizard of Oz, however, was originally written as a novel and conceived as a political allegory. The book was written in the late 1890s, during the throes of the gold/silver political dichotomy, and the major elements of the book were represented by the circumstances and characters of Baum's surroundings:

- The yellow brick road was the gold standard.

- The silver slippers represented the silver standard (it should be noted that the slippers were silver in the book; the "ruby" slippers of the movie were untrue to the novel and were chosen for aesthetic effect, since color in movies was very unusual in those days and the ruby slippers were very showy on-screen).

FIGURE 8.6 William Jennings Bryan, speaking to a spellbound audience in his typical dramatic style about the oppressive gold standard.

- Dorothy Gale represented everyday American people who had been, metaphorically speaking, swept away to an unfamiliar circumstance by gale-like forces beyond their control.

- Emerald City represented the "greenbacks," which was the political contingent—that is, the citizens themselves—that supported unbacked paper money.

- The wizard, who runs Emerald City, was the disingenuous politician who appears to be powerful and wise but is, in fact, a foolish man behind a curtain who is trying to frighten and control regular people.

- The Scarecrow, stuffed with straw, was the American farmer.

- The Cowardly Lion was William Jennings Bryan himself (who, at the time, was widely characterized by critics as indecisive).

- The Tin Man represented American's industrial interests.

- The Wicked Witch of the West was a stand-in for the American West.

- The flying monkeys were the displaced Native Americans of the West (in the novel, the leader of the monkeys tells Dorothy, *"Once we were a free*

people, living happily...this was many years ago, long before Oz came out of the
clouds to rule over this land.")

In the end, of course, Dorothy simply has to make use of the silver slippers—which she could have done at any time—to return her to the simple, safe, and secure life she yearned for.

With the nation's finances stabilized through J. P. Morgan's aid and the artificial inflation of silver prices set aside with the repeal of the Sherman act, the nation was finally able to mend itself. By 1897, the economy was returning to health, and unemployment dipped into the single digits once more. It was prepared to enter the twentieth century chastened by the experience, but it would enjoy 10 years of relatively uninterrupted prosperity before the next financial surprise was be foisted upon the country.

CHAPTER 9

The Rich Man's Panic of 1907

O n a chart of the financial history of the United States, the downturn that took place in stocks in 1907 is a barely recognizable blip. What took place during that year, however, completely altered the financial structure of the world. It is an astonishing story of what the financial universe of the United States was like before the nation had its own permanent central bank.

In the early twentieth century, it was not as if the United States had never had a central bank to call its own. Indeed, there was one in place long before, but President Andrew Jackson let the charter of the Second Bank of the United States expire in 1836, and the banks of the United States relied on one another to navigate the roiling waves of the nineteenth century. Unfortunately, this system produced periodic panics and bank closures on a surprisingly frequent basis, and a depositor could not be assured of the safety of his money once it was deposited within an institution.

■ A Simpler Time

In sharp contrast to the modern financial world, understanding the mechanics of finance of the early twentieth century is relatively simple. As long as one has a basic understanding of the importance of supply and demand and how the interaction of those two elements affects price, it is relatively easy to comprehend the dynamics of what happened during those years.

113

In spite of its place as a relatively sophisticated urban center, New York City in the early 1900s was strongly subject to the cycles of agribusiness. The annual agricultural cycle had a profound effect on interest rates, money supply, and credit. Every autumn of every year, money would depart the city in order to pay for and ship the harvests taking place closer to the center of the nation.

At the same time, due to the scarcity of money, interest rates paid for deposits would rise, in an effort to attract deposits to replenish the depleted supplies of cash. Foreign investors could usually be relied upon to make those deposits. Thus, the financial rhythms of New York City were closely tied to the ancient cycles of the seasons.

Between October 1903 and January 1906, the Dow Jones Industrial Average had risen from 42.3 to 103, an increase of 143 percent in the span of just over two years. The start-of-year exuberance of 1906 would not last long, however, as a number of bearish events emerged:

- In April, San Francisco was badly damaged by one of the worst earthquakes in history, prompting a large outflow of money from the nation's money centers to the devastated region.

- In June, an offering of New York City bonds failed.

- In July, the Interstate Commerce Commission was granted power by the Hepburn Act to set railroad rates, thus depressing transportation stocks.

- In the same month, the copper market collapsed.

- In August, the Standard Oil Company was fined $29 million for antitrust violations, and a widespread anti-big-business sentiment was sweeping the land, personified by President Theodore Roosevelt.

By August, the Dow had lost about a third of its value. In retrospect, we can see that the vast majority of the approximately 50 percent drop that would eventually take place in the stock market actually transpired before the "panic" had even started.

It is also important to understand the role that trust companies had around this time. Trusts were formed in the nineteenth century as relatively conservative enterprises. They focused their business on managing estates, taking deposits (largely from the well-to-do), and holding securities. They essentially began as banks for the rich, but they were privileged not to have been subjected to the same regulations as state or national banks.

Because they were relatively lightly regulated, trusts were more at liberty to make investments from which other banks were foreclosed. For example, trusts were able to make collateral loans at high interest rates, whereas banks could not. This added to the profitability of the trusts, and both the profitability and the light regulation made them attractive enterprises to start. Thus, trust assets grew 244 percent between 1890 and 1910, compared to national bank assets' growing 97 percent and state-chartered banks' growing only 82 percent. In short, trust assets were growing at triple the rate of the assets at state-chartered financial institutions.

The state of New York did institute somewhat firmer regulations in 1906, requiring that a trust maintain reserves of 15 percent of its deposits, but it required only 5 percent of the deposits to actually be available in the form of currency at the bank itself. This relatively thin cushion made trusts susceptible to "runs," which were events in which panicked depositors would demand their cash back, thus threatening to exhaust the bank's supply of cash on hand (and, more important, the confidence in the institution).

Another political piece of the puzzle was that, in spite of Roosevelt's firm antitrust stance, the federal government was far less intrusive with respect to business and financial affairs than it is in the modern day. Indeed, for the entire summer of 1906, the President's cabinet didn't meet even once, and once the crisis was in full swing, Roosevelt was busying himself trying to hunt down a bear to kill in the forests of Louisiana (see Figure 9.1).

■ The Copper Magnate

Augustus Heinze was born in Brooklyn and was trained as a mining engineer. In Montana, he made a huge fortune as a mining promoter, and he earned a reputation as a combative businessman who was unafraid of taking large copper trusts to court.

His greatest success in court was due to a copper mine he owned, which happened to be located near Amalgamated Mines. Heinze claimed that veins of copper emanating from his mine extended beneath the land owned by Amalgamated, and even though it was their land, he claimed the rights to the mineral deposits. A lengthy court fight ensued, and in the end, an out-of-court settlement of $25 million was made (in 1906 dollars), half of it in cash and half in Amalgamated stock.

Heinze took his massive newfound fortune to New York and aspired to become a banking tycoon. Early in 1907 he had established firm relationships

DRAWING
THE LINE
IN MISSISSIPPI

FIGURE 9.1 A contemporary political cartoon, showing President Roosevelt engaged in one of his favorite recreational activities: hunting for bears.

with two of the city's more powerful—and rather unscrupulous—bankers: E. R. Thomas and C. F. Morse. In those days, it was common practice to expand one's banking empire through "chain banking," which involved buying stock in a given bank, using that stock as collateral to borrow money, and then using that cash to buy stock in yet another bank or trust (see Figure 9.2).

Thus, in short order, Heinze was soon in control of several banks and was on the board of directors of eight banks and two trust companies. With the right money and connections, it was not difficult to become a force to be reckoned with in New York's financial district. Morse himself was a director of seven New York City banks, three of which he utterly controlled. In those days, the personalities of individual businessmen (and

FIGURE 9.2 Augustus Heinze, a famed copper baron of Montana as well as an aspiring New York banking tycoon.

their reputation, whether good or bad) was closely linked to financial institutions, particularly given that there was no government insurance for everyday depositors.

■ Cornering United

Heinze and his cohorts hit upon a scheme they thought could substantially add to their fortunes: cornering the stock of United Copper. Morse himself was no stranger to cornering markets, as he had successfully cornered New York's ice market (when there was such a thing). Because Heinze already owned a substantial block of United Copper stock, a successful attempt on their part to push the price higher would prove very profitable.

The key to this plan was to create a "short squeeze." For those unacquainted with short-selling, it works like this: in regular stock investing, a person buys a stock at a given price with the hope that the price will rise and, in doing so, generate a profit. Thus the old adage, "Buy low, sell high."

Conversely, a short-seller seeks to turn this goal on its head: "Sell high, buy low." The pursuit of profit is the same, but the timing is reversed: a person *sells* a stock at a price he believes is high and, in the future, he hopes to *buy* the stock back at a lower price.

There are certain risks to shorting stocks, though, in contrast to standard long positions. If a person buys a stock, that stock is his forever. There is nothing that can be done to take it away, unless the company itself is purchased (which typically involves a premium and is an agreeable outcome to the shareholder in such a case).

When a person sells a stock short, however, he cannot synthetically sell the stock out of thin air (a practice sometimes referred to as "naked shorting"). The investor instead has to actually find a broker that *has* the stock in the first place and is also willing to sell it on his behalf. Once this is accomplished, the short-seller is at risk of the stock's being "called away" or demanded.

The reason for this possibility is easy enough to understand: suppose a given person ("Client A") uses a broker that had 100 shares of stock X in his possession (owned, obviously, by another client—in this example, "Client B"). The broker agrees to sell the stock from Client B's account based on the pledge that Client A will buy those 100 shares back at a later date. All of this happens without Client B's knowledge.

Further suppose that, a month later, Client B wants to sell his 100 shares of stock X. Given the circumstances, the shares are simply not present in the account to be sold. So the broker forces Client A to "cover" the short (buy the shares back at the market price), thus restoring the holding to Client B's account and allowing the regular market sale to take place. This situation puts the short-seller in a vulnerable position.

This takes on an added twist in 1907, long before the age of electronic transfers and records. The notion of owning a stock was still very much tied to the *physical* possession of a stock certificate, and in the relatively modest stock market of the day, there simply was a much smaller universe of traders and stocks around.

Augustus Heinze's brother, Otto, was the main brain behind the idea of cornering United Copper, and as the Heinze family was already in possession of a large quantity of United Copper stock, it was in their interest to see the price rise. It was Otto's belief that they were in a superb position to put the short-sellers in a very uncomfortable spot: by buying stock in the open market, Heinze could push the stock higher.

As the stock rose, more and more of the shorts, eyeing their growing losses, would want to get out of their positions. It was Otto's belief that, in many cases, most of the stock that the short-sellers had borrowed was, in fact, already in Heinze's possession, and that the short-sellers would have to purchase shares directly from Heinze in order to close their positions.

The other aspect to this idea was that Otto believed there were very few shares locally available on the market, because the stock had already been so heavily shorted. The Heinze family would have, in a way, a short-term monopoly over all the available inventory of United Copper stock and thus could demand an exorbitant price from the short-sellers that were desperate to cover their position and cap their losses.

As rich as Augustus Heinze was, cornering a public company was an expensive undertaking, and they needed financial backing to improve their chances of success. Otto and August Heinze, accompanied by the notorious banker Charles Morse, met with Charles Barney, the president of the Knickerbocker Trust Company, the third-largest trust in New York. Barney had successfully backed prior Morse schemes, but he was reluctant to provide funding, as their scheme was going to involve more money than Barney was comfortable lending (see Figure 9.3).

Thus, on their own, they decided to try to corner the stock anyway. On Monday, October 14, 1907, they started buying United Copper in the open market, pushing the price from $39 to $52 in a single day, an increase of one-third. The next day, Otto issued a demand from his brokerage, Gross & Kleeberg, that all borrowed shares be returned.

The hope at this point was that short-sellers would scamper around the city, find absolutely no stock to buy, and helplessly show up at Gross & Kleeberg to be told what exorbitant price they would have to pay.

Instead, it turns out there was, in fact, ample available stock in the open market, and the short-sellers who wanted to get out were able to cover their positions at regular market prices. The demand for the stock pushed it somewhat higher to $60, but once the market began to realize that the strong demand from Heinze was not going to push them collectively against a wall, the share price started slipping.

CHARLES W. MORSE
PRESIDENT CONSOLIDATED ICE COMPANY

FIGURE 9.3 Charles Morse, a New York banker of the early twentieth century with a notorious reputation for aggressive financial schemes.

By the end of the Tuesday, it had fallen to $30, even lower than when the squeeze began the prior day. The Heinze brothers and their affiliated interests were in sudden and unexpected trouble. In a word, the market had called their bluff, and the selling of the stock was spectacular.

By Wednesday shares were fetching a mere $10, and Otto Heinze was financially ruined. His brokerage house, Gross & Kleeberg, was itself forced to close based on a single client's horrifically bad trade.

Much of the trading going on during this pandemonium was taking place on the Curb market, which was, quite literally, the curb of the street outside the New York Stock Exchange (the "curb" would eventually become the

American Stock Exchange, which itself was referred to as "the curb market" for decades to come). The *Wall Street Journal* reported of the day, "Never has there been such wild scenes on the Curb, so say the oldest veterans of the outside market."

There was another Heinze casualty of the disastrous United Copper scheme: the State Savings Bank of Butte, Montana, which was owned by none other than F. Augustus Heinze. The bank held a large amount of United Copper stock as collateral for some of its lending, and with the collateral dramatically devalued, the bank declared its insolvency.

■ The Bank Runs Begin

At this point, any financial institution associated with Morse or Heinze became immediately suspect in the public's eye. One of the banks, Mercantile National, insisted that Heinze resign, which he did. In spite of this, fearful depositors rushed to the Mercantile to withdraw money as fast as they could. Other banks, including New Amsterdam National and National Bank of North America, were crowded with people demanding their money back, mainly because of their association with Morse.

To tamp down the embers of the panic, the New York Clearing House (which was a consortium of the city's banks) demanded that both Morse and Heinze resign *all* of their banking interests, which the men did. This was to little avail, because by the end of the week, a sweeping tide of anxiety was making its way across the city.

Famed tycoon J. P. Morgan was far away from all this tumult. A devout Episcopalian, he was attending a church retreat in Richmond, Virginia. He was hosting a number of bishops in the Rutherford mansion, which he had rented for the occasion. Morgan was 70 years old and had largely retired from the world of finance, but he was kept abreast of the reports from New York about the gathering clouds on the horizon of Wall Street.

By the end of Saturday, Morgan could no longer ignore the news, so he summoned his private rail car to take him back north (making sure the bishops were provided a comfortable journey in a second rail car). He arrived in New York City and went directly to the sumptuous new marble library he had built for himself on the corner of 36th Street and Madison. The library was already replete with bankers from the city who were eagerly awaiting his guidance, since Morgan had successfully guided the U.S. Treasury during the Panic of 1893.

As the discussion lasted until late Sunday evening, Morgan and his men examined the books of the trust most widely believed to be at risk, which was Knickerbocker. After examining the company's books, they decided it was already insolvent and could not be saved if the bank run continued the next day (see Figure 9.4).

On Monday, October 21, nothing seemed particularly out of the ordinary at Knickerbocker Trust Company. In spite of having 18,000 depositors and $67 million in deposits, the bank was not confronted with a line of clients when it opened for business. However, a steady and unending stream of customers pressed against the teller windows for the entire day, withdrawing all the money in their account one by one. By the end of the day, the management of Knickerbocker knew they needed help, so they called on J. P. Morgan.

Discussions with the management lasted until the early hours of the next morning. Morgan recognized that having the city's third-largest trust fail would be unhealthy for the fragile psychological environment in his financial world, so he sought to help with conditions. Primarily, lacking faith

FIGURE 9.4 The Knickerbocker Trust, whose building is shown here from the early nineteenth century, was initially declared beyond salvation by Morgan.

in the present management, he insisted on the resignation of Knickerbocker's president, C. T. Barney. Morgan pledged $12 million in support to short up the bank's diminishing cash reserves.

The next morning, Tuesday, October 22, was much worse for Knickerbocker. Unaware of Morgan's financial backing, persons with cash in the bank were eager to get it out, and a line of them stretched long down Fifth Avenue. By the afternoon, all of the cash in the bank was completely exhausted, and Knickerbocker declared itself insolvent with $52 million in liabilities.

At this point, fears of financial contagion began to spread. The *New York Times* reported of Knickerbocker, "... as fast as a depositor went out of the place, ten people and more came asking for their money and the police were asked to send men to keep order."

An immediate effect of the growing fear was that interest rates for very short-term loans (typically used for stock purchases, known as a call rate) skyrocketed from 6 percent to 60 percent. Very few banks were willing to lend in such an environment, and those that were willing wanted fantastically high compensation for it.

■ The Stock Exchange Teeters

As the call rate lurched from 60 percent to 70 percent and, later, 100 percent, the metaphorical air supply of cash that normally enlivened the stock market was choked off. Equity prices started to sink badly, and by the afternoon of Thursday, October 24, Ransom Thomas, the president of the New York Stock Exchange, went to Morgan's office to advise him that they were going to close the stock exchange early. Morgan correctly asserted that such an act would only add to the panic and tumult, and he implored Thomas to give him time to help (see Figure 9.5).

Morgan told the presidents of the city's banks to come to his office at once, which they did within minutes. Morgan informed them bluntly that unless they gathered $25 million among themselves to provide the exchange, 50 brokerage houses would fail that very day. Within minutes, the presidents pledged nearly the full amount to the exchange, and the money reached the market half an hour before the closing bell. Morgan also tried to shore up confidence by making a rare statement to the press: "If people will keep their money in the banks, everything will be all right."

The next day on the New York Stock Exchange was just as bad, and Morgan again had to lean on bank presidents to loan the exchange money—this

FIGURE 9.5 The stock market's ascent prior to the 1907 panic, and its subsequent collapse, is represented in this price chart of the Dow Jones Industrial Average.

time, in the amount of nearly $10 million—and the bankers were beginning to worry they were throwing good money after bad. Morgan knew he could not sustain this kind of cash infusion indefinitely, and that Friday he organized his team to form two committees, both bent on public relations: one of them was specifically for the nation's clergy, to calm their congregations on Sunday, and the other for the newspapers, to help explain the financial backing Morgan and his men were providing and why it would stabilize the situation.

The weekend proved to be just as restless and anxious as the prior had for J. P. Morgan. On Sunday, George Perkins, an associate of Morgan's, was told by the City of New York that if it did not receive $20 million in emergency funding within the week, it would also go bankrupt. The mayor himself, George McClellan, appealed to Morgan directly on both of the following two days, and Morgan quietly agreed to purchase $30 million in city bonds. He did not publicize this additional financial backing, since he felt revealing the precarious situation of the city itself would only exacerbate an already very bad situation.

■ Roosevelt's Reluctant Aid

During all of this, the president of the United States was enjoying himself in the wilds of Louisiana, hunting bear. He finished up his adventure and was slowly making his way back to Washington, D.C. On the way, he took time to give a speech lambasting the men of Wall Street and praising his administration's tough stance against financial manipulation and railroad conglomerates. These sentiments, of course, did nothing to shore up confidence back in New York.

Roosevelt and Morgan were at opposite sides of the political spectrum of the day, and they had a deep distaste for one another. In spite of this, with the magnitude of the problems at hand, Morgan contacted George Cortelyou, the nation's secretary of the Treasury (see Figure 9.6).

FIGURE 9.6 George Cortelyou, a lifelong bureaucrat who held the important post of Treasury secretary in the Roosevelt administration during the 1907 panic.

Cortelyou did not achieve his lofty post by being a luminary in the world of international finance. Instead, he had ascended, administration by administration, to successively more senior posts almost by happenstance. He started as a stenographer, and President Grover Cleveland brought him into his service based on Cortelyou's stellar shorthand skills.

He was later the private secretary to McKinley and, later, when the Department of Commerce was formed in 1903, he was given the secretary position of that department. Subsequent President Teddy Roosevelt made him postmaster general of the country, and then, curiously, he was given the position of secretary of the Treasury. This is where he found himself in the midst of the crisis.

So, at Morgan's urging, Cortelyou boarded the 4 P.M. train from Washington to New York. Awaiting him in uptown Manhattan was a suite Morgan had prepared as a meeting place for Cortelyou and a retinue of the city's bankers. The basis for the meeting was to retain the federal government's aid in yet another looming crisis in the form of the Tennessee Coal, Iron, and Railroad Company (TC&I).

One of the largest brokerage firms in the country, Moore & Schley, had borrowed excessively during the crisis, and the collateral used for the loans was their substantial holdings of TC&I stock. The stock itself had been weakening through the crisis, and the weaker it got, the more at risk Moore & Schley became of their loans' being called away based on the deteriorating conditions of their collateral.

Such a move would bring the brokerage to ruin and make a severe situation even worse. If the loans were called, Moore & Schley would have to liquidate their TC&I position swiftly, which would not only crush the stock but cause extensive collateral damage to other issues in the market as well.

J. P. Morgan concocted a plan that would not only stave off such a situation but benefit his financial empire as well. His plan was that the U.S. Steel Corporation (which itself was formed by Morgan via a merger of Andrew Carnegie's and Elbert Gary's steel empires) would acquire TC&I at a price of $90 per share. This would be, in itself, a positive acquisition for U.S. Steel, and it would eliminate the risk of Moore & Schley's prospective collapse worsening the financial contagion.

The problem, of course, was that in the current antitrust environment, a firm with a 60 percent market share (namely, U.S. Steel) was not in a position to legally acquire a smaller outfit. Thus, Morgan needed the blessing of the president of the United States for the deal to be permitted. He needed an exception, and given the crisis, his chances were good.

At the same time, the situation with runs on banks and trust companies had not abated, and one firm in particular—the Trust Company of America—seemed to be the next domino likely to fall. Morgan gathered 120 of the city's bankers and business leaders into his well-used library to get an update on the status of the trust companies in the city.

Morgan told the men that they needed to come up with a solution to the problem, and he left the library to attend to other matters. Only later did the bankers realize that Morgan had literally locked them inside the library, and he intended to keep the key inside his pocket until the men came up with a solution to the mess. They were trapped there and, at Morgan's behest, had to figure out a solution.

When Morgan entered the room some time later, no consensus had been reached, so he told the men that they needed to come up with $25 million to shore up the trust companies through the crisis or else the city would face unmanageable panic. After considerable prodding, Morgan was able to persuade the de facto leader of the group to sign an agreement to advance the funds, and the rest of the men followed suit. The agreement having been reached, Morgan produced the key and allowed the bankers to return to their homes at 4:45 that Sunday morning.

Cortelyou had finally arrived in New York, and the suite at the Manhattan Hotel uptown was crowded with some of the top finance men of the city, representing such esteemed family names as Rockefeller and Frick.

There was not much in the way of financial aid the Treasury could offer directly—its own coffers had a mere $5 million at hand—but the city's financiers needed the stated support of the Roosevelt administration with respect to stemming the crisis as well as permitting the TC&I sale to proceed.

Two of the bankers, Frick and Gary, got on an overnight train Sunday evening to have an emergency meeting with Roosevelt. Roosevelt's secretary denied them access to the president, but, by way of the secretary of the interior, they were finally granted an audience.

Frick and Gary told the president that, in spite of the prohibitions of the Sherman Antitrust Act, if he did not permit the acquisition of TC&I by U.S. Steel, the financial markets would enter a free-fall. With only an hour left until the market opened, they beseeched the president to make an exception for the good of the country's financial stability. Roosevelt assented to the exception, and the news received in New York was greeted with great relief.

■ Jekyll Island

Through the entire crisis, the one man in the middle was clearly J. P. Morgan. Without a central bank to turn to, the financial industry relied on Morgan's financial resources, connections, public pronouncements, and force of will to steer the collective ship through the storm.

Although the bankers of the city, and the populace in general, were grateful for Morgan's support and leadership, it had become apparent afterward that relying on a single wealthy individual to shore up the collective financial health of the nation put the country in a vulnerable position. After all, Morgan could have used the situation to his advantage even more than he had.

The next year, in May 1908, Congress passed the Aldrich-Vreeland Act to establish the National Monetary Commission. Its purpose was to investigate the causes of the panic from the prior year and explore ways to prevent such a panic's happening in the future. The chairman of the committee (and one of its namesakes), Senator Nelson Aldrich, went to Europe—a continent replete with central banks in each nation—to study their system for nearly two years.

It became clear to him there were significant benefits to having a central bank. The series of problems that took place during the crisis of the prior year could largely be attributed to a lack of credit. Without a central bank to turn to, the city's banks had to rely on the deep pockets of Morgan and his associates. Time and again, Morgan had to either come up with the cash or compel others to do the same, and having an industry rely on its own internal resources—particularly when its health affected the health of the economy as a whole—seemed shortsighted.

On his return in November 1910, Aldrich assembled a meeting under the most secret circumstances at the Jekyll Island Club, located off the Georgia coast. In attendance were senior administrators from the Treasury Department and representatives from the National City Bank of New York, J. P. Morgan, the First National Bank of New York, and Kuhn, Loeb & Company. Edward Griffin wrote in his 1994 book *The Creature from Jekyll Island*:

> Picture a party of the nation's greatest bankers stealing out of New York on a private railroad car under cover of darkness, stealthily riding hundreds of miles South, embarking on a mysterious launch, sneaking onto a island deserted by all but a few servants, living there a full

week under such rigid security that the names of not one of them was once mentioned, lest the servants learn the identity and disclose to the world this strangest, most secret expedition in the history of American finance.

The men decided the best course of action was for the United States to form its own central bank, with the banks themselves holding key spots on its committees. The National Monetary Commission submitted and published its final report in January 1911, and its recommendations were debated for a full two years. Finally, on December 23, 1913, Congress passed the Federal Reserve Act, which President Woodrow Wilson signed on the very same day, and the Federal Reserve System was thus formed (see Figure 9.7).

Ironically, or perhaps appropriately, J. P. Morgan himself died the same year, on March 31, 1913. It marked the end of one era—that of outsized personalities dominating the relatively shaky, clubby world of banking—and the beginning of a new one, embodied in the form of the Federal Reserve Bank.

FIGURE 9.7 The Federal Reserve, created in 1914, was the most significant result of the 1907 financial panic.

The United States had finally joined most of the rest of the industrialized world in the age of modern finance, and even a century later the value and objectivity of the nation's central bank would be called into question. The tight connections between the banking industry itself and Washington, D.C., in the form of the federal reserve system would not always sit well with the public, but there is no doubt that the presence of the central bank tamped down the prospects of more financial crises springing up on a regular basis, as they had so many times during the prior century.

CHAPTER 10

Billion-Dollar Bread— The Weimar Hyperinflation

There are many aspects to the hyperinflation that gripped Germany in the early 1920s that are remarkable, but two in particular stand out: (1) this was a crisis that didn't just affect an elite cache of speculators but had a sweeping effect on virtually the entire population of common citizens; (2) it laid the groundwork for one of the largest, devastating, and world-altering wars in history.

Many people, even though unacquainted with important financial events, have heard something about the hyperinflation of this era, but very few people understand its root causes, its effects on the common citizenry, and its subsequent implications. In this chapter we will explore this amazing era of world financial history and why it leaves scars on the German psyche to this day.

■ Funding a War

When Germany went to war in 1914, it made a very bad assumption, similar to the one made by both sides of the United States Civil War: that the fighting would be concluded in a short span of time. Based on this, Germany decided to borrow money in order to fund the war effort, as opposed to having the population pay for it by way of higher taxes.

On July 31, 1914, the *Reichsbank* (the German central bank) issued an order suspending the right of anyone to redeem German currency notes into gold. On August 4, three days after the Reich had declared war on Russia, parliament passed additional currency acts that allowed it to create an "exceptional" quantity of "unbacked paper notes" (that is, notes that were unable to be redeemed for gold until further notice by parliament).

The then-named Great War did not, as it turned out, conclude swiftly. Instead, four years of horrific warfare lay ahead, and Germany spent on the order of $160 billion marks on men and machinery, only to lose the war in the end. The only good news for Germany was that the physical plant of the nation was still largely intact, as most of the fighting had taken in other parts of Europe.

During this time, the quantity of marks in circulation increased dramatically, from 13 billion in 1913 to 60 billion by 1918. At the same time, the national debt increased from 5 billion marks to 156 billion marks, as Germany had printed and sold a staggering quantity of bonds to its own people.

■ An Expensive Peace

The victorious Allies of the First World War wanted to punish Germany severely once the war was complete, and it did so by demanding gigantic financial reparations for the damage caused. In 1919, at the Paris Peace Conference, the German delegates warned that such reparations would "crush all creative urges, the will to work, and all entrepreneurial spirit in Germany forever." This was not empty posturing on the part of the Germans; their prophecy would turn out to be quite prescient.

The exchange rate between the mark and the U.S. dollar was 4.2 at the start of the war. By the end of the war, due to the expansion of German currency, the rate had eroded to 8.91 marks to the dollar. Once the peace treaty was finalized, and the world realized how punishing the reparations would be to Germany (and what actions the country might take), the exchange rate plunged further to 47 marks to the dollar.

The printing presses kept running, albeit at a nonhysterical rate, and by the time the mark reached about 60 marks to the dollar in early 1921, things seemed to stabilize. Indeed, the German economy seemed to be relatively strong. The quantity and velocity of marks in the German economy actually helped invigorate reindustrialization, and unemployment throughout the nation was quite low.

The low value of the mark made German exports extremely attractive to consumers from other nations, and in the span of 1921 industrial output increased 20 percent, unemployment dropped below 1 percent, and German workers saw their wages rise handsomely. As burdensome as the forthcoming payments to the victors were, the German economy at least seemed to be recovering from its dismal circumstances.

The reparation payments began in June 1921, and the total amount due, 132 billion goldmarks, was more than the entirety of Germany's gold and foreign currency holdings. Germany was obliged to spend years making crushing payments in hard currency as well as industrial production and commodity products—indeed, a full 26 percent of the value of Germany's exports. The nation was, in a sense, being subjected to a profoundly heavy tax paid out to its neighbors, and such a burden would choke off any real growth in the economy.

■ The Printing Presses

Because Germany was required to make its payments with stable foreign currencies, it bought those currencies in the open market with freshly-printed German marks. Of course, the more marks that were printed and handed over, the less valuable they became. By November 1921 the mark-to-U.S.-dollar ratio was 330 to 1, meaning a mark—which used to equal about 25 cents—was now worth one third of one penny.

Financial disaster was augmented with political disaster the next year with an assassination. Germany's foreign minister—the equivalent of a U.S. secretary of state—was a moderate, intelligent, and well-liked man named Walter Rathenau. He was very popular with the public, perceived as rich, worldly, and good for the German state, particularly in the delicate postwar period, but he was murdered by right-wing fanatics on June 24, 1922.

This assassination dealt a hard blow to the German psyche, as the perception of a generally law-abiding society on the mend was damaged by such a shock. Germans were already very nervous about their rapidly declining currency, and this latest event made them even more anxious about their country's prospects. They were thus compelled to accelerate their acquisition of hard goods in exchange for marks, whose reputation as a legitimate currency was rapidly collapsing.

Money, after all, is intended to represent a store of value, but in the case of fiat money, the only thing that gives it value is its credibility as being valuable and stable. Broadly speaking, fiat currency is valued based on the state's perceived ability to tax its people and businesses, as well as manage its own internal affairs. The only thing that seemed universally recognized about the German mark was that there were a lot more of them than before.

By December 1922, the mark-to-dollar ratio was 2,000 to 1. Four months later, the ratio was 20,000 to 1, and by August 1923, the ratio was greater than a million to 1. All through this time, the printing presses were churning out bills at a furious rate. More than 130 companies were hired by the government to print the notes, and 1,783 presses were running, day and night, as long as there was paper to feed into them. Things were beginning to spiral out of control, thanks to the government's ceaseless creation of new paper money.

The impatience of the populace was shared by those abroad as well, who were becoming concerned at Germany's shaky situation. Germany was obliged to "pay" huge quantities of coal to France as part of the reparation, but a slight delay in delivery compelled France to march 100,000 troops into the Ruhr valley to seize the mines and confiscate all the coal therein.

This was not only an infuriating and humiliating event for the Germans, but it also meant that the other industries that relied on coal for energy ground to a halt. After all, with France firmly in control of the nation's principal energy supply, industrial production could not continue.

The next domino to topple was tax revenue, as industrial revenue collapsed. Worse still, since the Germans needed power to light its streets and houses, it shelled out precious foreign currency reserves to purchase energy from outside the country.

Each of these steps made a very bad situation even worse, and the growing ranks of impoverished, starving Germans made the circumstances explosive. Even young children suffered as deficiency diseases reached epidemic levels. Germans bitterly blamed France as the source of all their troubles, and this hatred would fester in the years to come, helping lay a solid foundation for a future dictatorship and another European war.

■ Widespread Suffering

As the severity of the mark's collapse widened, hardly any Germans were spared horrific financial trauma, irrespective of their place in society or the savings they had accrued over the years. The German government decided to issue relief payments to the workers who were rendered idle by the French takeover of the coal mines, and 300 paper mills were running at top speed to create the paper necessary to feed the nation's printing presses. By that point, over 2,000 presses were spinning both night and day, adding massively to the country's inventory of marks (see Figure 10.1).

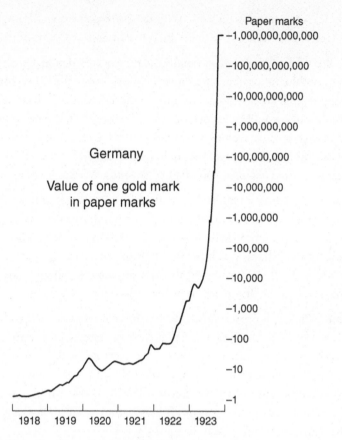

Paper marks

- −1,000,000,000,000

- −100,000,000,000

- −10,000,000,000

- −1,000,000,000

Germany   - −100,000,000

Value of one gold mark   - −10,000,000
in paper marks
                           - −1,000,000

                           - −100,000

                           - −10,000

                           - −1,000

                           - −100

                           - −10

                           - −1

1918 1919 1920 1921 1922 1923

FIGURE 10.1   Even on this logarithmic scale, the change in value of a paper German mark to a fixed amount of gold is breathtaking.

The best way to understand how the collapsing currency affected the common man is through a series of anecdotes from various citizens of the time (unless otherwise noted, anecdotes are drawn from Adam Smith's 1981 *Paper Money* and Alexander Jung's "Millions, Billions, Trillions: Germany in the Era of Hyperinflation," published in *Der Spiegel*, August 14, 2009):

- A lawyer had taken out an insurance policy in 1903 and, month after month, faithfully made payments into the policy. When the 20-year policy paid out, in 1923, the lawyer cashed out the proceeds and was able to buy himself a loaf of bread with it.

- An American visitor, at the end of a meal while in Germany, paid the cook a one-dollar tip. The excited family had a meeting afterward, trying to decide what to do with their newfound wealth. They decided a trust fund would be set up at a Berlin bank, with the cook as the beneficiary, and the bank would be entrusted with the investment and oversight of the dollar.

- Since the value of cash fell so rapidly, many workers demanded to be paid not bimonthly, or weekly, but multiple times every day. Therefore, each working day, all work would stop on several different occasions, and giant sacks of money would be handed out to each worker. They would rush these bundles over to their waiting wives who would, in turn, leave for shops to purchase just about anything that could be exchanged for cash. (Cited in *The Nightmare German Inflation*, published by Scientific Market Analysis in 1970.)

- A man walked into a coffee shop and ordered a cup of coffee, priced at 5,000 marks. After finishing the cup, he ordered a second. When he was done, he was presented with a bill for 14,000 marks. When he disputed the size of the bill, he was informed that the price had gone from 5,000 to 9,000 while he was enjoying the first cup, and he should have simply ordered two in the first place in order to save money.

- At one factory, there was just one payment made per day, and it took place at 11:00 each morning. At that time, a siren would sound, and all the workers would gather together in a courtyard. A bus would pull up, loaded with cash, and the cashier would call out names, one by one, and throw them bundles of the banknotes. The workers would immediately rush out to shops to purchase goods before they went up in price, as they always did several times each day of the week.

- Citizens across the land knew that virtually anything was better to hold than cash, so they took to buying anything they could get their hands on, no matter how irrelevant to their own lives. Pianos became treasured purchases, whether or not the buyer knew a single note of music. Hard assets such as gold, silver, and diamonds were purchased, as well as less commonly recognized stores of value, such as antiques, soaps, and hairpins.

- At the Junkers plant in Dessau, the company calculated each morning what the value of three and a half loaves of bread would be and paid its workers this amount. The wives of the workers would dash off to the nearby stores to beat the midday posting of new prices.

- Even doctors started refusing currency for their services, preferring to be paid in eggs, coal, sausages, and other things they could actually use. Stranger still, burying the dead took a turn for the worse, since cremations became impractical due to the cost of very scarce coal. Germans resorted to burying their dead in the cheapest coffins they could find, including a 50-centimeter tall box colloquially known as the "nose-squasher."

- Disgusted with the state of their country, a German family sold its house, intent on sailing to a new life in America. They took the cash from the sale of their home and, upon arriving in Hamburg to get on the boat, they were informed that the cash they had in hand wasn't enough to get on the boat to make the crossing. Indeed, the proceeds from the sale of the house were no longer even sufficient to get back on the train and return to the town from which they came.

- Eugeni Xammar wrote in the Spanish newspaper *La Veu de Catalunya*, "The price of tram rides and beef, theatre tickets and school, newspapers and haircuts, sugar and bacon, is going up every week. As a result, no one knows how long their money will last, and people are living in constant fear, thinking of nothing but eating and drinking, buying and selling."

As both the high and the low of society found themselves in an increasingly bizarre world, they became paranoid that some unknown, malicious force was at work behind the scenes. Their world didn't make sense anymore, so that started to point to unseen scapegoats—more often than not, the Jews—as the cause for their hardship. The seeds of hatred were being sown, fed, and watered in this alien environment. Even the mark itself was referred to sometimes as "Jew confetti" (see Figure 10.2).

FIGURE 10.2 The quantity of cash required to purchase even everyday items became so substantial that wheelbarrows were required to pay for goods being sold.

At the same time, many adults began to lose their moral grounding as they became more desperate. Thievery became commonplace, as citizens would steal whatever they needed to survive. Farmers were particularly vulnerable, as fellow Germans would raid their farms at night, digging up crops and spiriting them back to their homes. Copper pipes and brass fittings were ripped away from houses; fuel was siphoned out of parked cars; neighbors began to steal goods from one another.

The sweeping degradation took on more nefarious forms as well, as the populace adopted an attitude of nihilism. Drug use became widespread, with cocaine as the drug of choice, and prostitutes—both men and women— roamed the streets, ready to barter their bodies for food and goods. The most fortunate humans walking German soil were those who visited from abroad, since their pocket change could afford them a lifestyle of decadence and bohemianism that they could never know in their native land.

Famed economist Joseph Schumpeter wrote of "the disorganizing effects of the collapsing currency on the national character, on morals, and all branches of cultural life." Some states and cities within Germany even began printing their *own* money. One currency-printing outfit in southern Germany printed on its notes the tongue-in-cheek suggestion that "If coal is even more expensive, feel free to use me as fuel."

■ A Nation of Speculators

In this environment, everyone was unwittingly forced into the lifestyle of a speculator. Goods were bought and sold, bartered and exchanged, at a frantic pace, and in order to survive, common citizens had to adopt the mindset of a cunning trader.

Banks expanded dramatically in girth, as the economy increasingly relied on the management of comically large quantities of cash, and the quantity of bank workers ballooned from 100,000 in 1913 to 375,000 in 1923. At the same time, productive labor began to shrivel in efficacy, as regular laborers were obsessed with fighting for higher wages, trading cash for goods, and trying everything they could to not let hyper-inflation consume them.

Just about the *only* beneficiaries from this insanity were debtors. It didn't take long for people to realize that debts could be paid easily by simply sitting back and waiting a few days. Formerly difficult debts could, with a collapsing currency, soon be paid off by simply forgoing a loaf of bread and paying off the debt in full.

Indeed, businesses thrived in this environment, since the credit on which they had earlier relied to build their businesses became effortless to service and pay off. Before the war, bankruptcies occurred at a pace of 813 per month; by late 1923, there were barely even 10 bankruptcies recorded.

The most profitable way to run a business, therefore, was to borrow as much as possible. Companies would borrow to their maximum allowed credit and buy up machinery, raw materials, and any other assets. It was the closest thing to free goods one could imagine, since the assets being bought were tangible, useful, and valuable, whereas the debt undertaken was, in short order, meaningless. The most adroit businessmen borrowed marks, purchased foreign currency, and then soon repaid their debt, reaping an enormous profit by the vastly mutated exchange rate (see Figure 10.3).

It was noted that on October 25, 1923, the Reichsbank printed 120,000 trillion marks. The bank actually felt that announcing its valiant efforts to create more currency illustrated its dedication to assisting the nation, and it expressed chagrin that the target amount for that day, a *million* trillion marks, could not physically be achieved. They pledged, however, that currency production was being vastly expanded and that they would not let the nation down in this manner again.

■ The Retenmark Miracle

Finally, enough was enough. The introduction of the 1,000 billion mark note was the final, ludicrous conclusion of the endless money-printing. The Reichsbank finally took radical, appropriate action to stop the hyperinflation. In November 1923, they announced that:

1. A new currency was to be introduced, the *rentenmark*.
2. 2.4 billion of them would be created, and this figure would not increase except in small, measured steps.
3. The money was backed by land and industrial infrastructure.
4. Each rentenmark would be worth one trillion of the old marks.

The inflation stopped virtually instantly. The astonishing thing is that the *pledge* that the notes were backed by real estate and industrial plants was wholly impractical and meaningless. Being able to exchange notes for gold was one thing; being able to exchange notes for a miniscule fraction of a factory was quite another.

FIGURE 10.3 German marks, given their virtual worthlessness, were adopted by some citizens as interesting and inexpensive wallpaper.

FIGURE 10.4 A billion-mark note, which was a relic of the greatest excesses of the German printing press.

All the same, the citizenry of Germany was so desperate to adopt a currency in which they could actually believe, they embraced the rentenmark almost without question.

Although inflation was brought to a halt, the financial and psychological damage already done was deep and permanent. Anyone who had savings before now had nothing. Those who had exchanged their cash for goods were oftentimes neck-deep in possessions they didn't need or want. Businesses that acquired durable goods on credit now had far more equipment than they could ever put to practical use (see Figure 10.4).

At the same time, the nation had become prone to propaganda, hatred, and thoughts of revenge. Without the psychological and financial damage wrought by hyperinflation, it is doubtful that someone with Adolf Hitler's message and methods could have taken root in the German soil. Given the situation after 1923, however, Hitler found a receptive audience to his rantings.

■ Lingering Aftereffects

The effect on the psyche of the common person was expressed by Thomas Mann, who wrote, "The market woman who without batting an eyelash demanded 100 million marks for an egg lost the capacity for surprise. And nothing that has happened since has been insane or cruel enough to surprise her."

The nation, as a whole, had gone through a bout of collective insanity, and their worldview was permanently altered, with cynicism deeply ingrained into the character of a country that had until recently prided itself as a law-abiding and industrious nation.

The aftereffects of hyperinflation were felt most strongly by the middle class, who found themselves stripped of their savings, holding worthless insurance policies and meaningless bank books. In 1924, it was as if everyone was starting from scratch.

The principles that mothers and fathers taught their children—to save, be thrifty, avoid debt—were turned upside-down. The biggest losers in this era were the prudent and the sensible; the biggest winners were reckless debt hogs. The economy had donned a perverse and distorted mask, and the world simply stopped making sense anymore to everyday Germans in 1923.

The paper-printing madness, in the end, tallied up to 1.2 sextillion marks by July 1924 (that is, 1,200,000,000,000,000,000,000 marks). With hyperinflation behind them, Germans faced new, different challenges: the government took it upon itself to drastically increase tax rates, and with the economy on the mend, the German state actually announced a surplus in the 1924–1925 tax year.

But the spendthrift ways of hyperinflation created a substantial lull in the economy since so much cash had already been wasted on unnecessary and excessive equipment and inventory that would take years for regular industrial demands to absorb.

The holiday from bankruptcies that business had enjoyed in 1923 was also at an end, as declarations of bankruptcy exploded from only 263 in 1923 to 6,033 the next year. The day of reckoning had finally come for the enterprises that had relied on meaningless credit beforehand.

Hitler emerged on the national scene during this vulnerable time, with the failed *Beer Hall Putsch* taking place in Munich during November 1923. In spite of Hitler's failure there, Germany had found itself transformed into a nation with millions of latent radicals, hungry to make sense of what had just happened to them.

Everything understood by them before had been hurled out the window, and where there had once been faith was now distrust and cynicism. In the next election, the Nazi party won 32 seats in Parliament, and the right-wing Nationalist party also secured 106 seats, pledging to voters they would exact revenge on those who had put the German people through this nightmare.

The famed Pulitzer-prize winning writer Pearl Buck reflected on her 1923 visit to Germany and wrote:

> The cities were still there, the houses not yet bombed and in ruins, but the victims were millions of people. They had lost their fortunes, their

savings; they were dazed and inflation-shocked and did not understand how it had happened to them and who the foe was who had defeated them. Yet they had lost their self-assurance, their feeling that they themselves could be the masters of their own lives if only they worked hard enough; and lost, too, were the old values of morals, of ethics, of decency.

CHAPTER 11

The Roaring Twenties

The popular view of the 1920s in America was that it was a decade of excess, wealth, and decadence. While this was true in some cases, in a nation growing as rapidly as the United States—its population had doubled between 1890 and 1920—the truth was far more complex and nuanced.

The twenties were indeed "roaring" for the richest in the country, and for most of the population it was a time of growing wages, greater buying power, and technological marvels. In retrospect, it was also a time that set the stage for the most calamitous economic downturn in the nation's history.

■ The Great War's End

What we now call World War I—at the time, the *Great War*—ended in late 1918, having claimed the lives of 10 million men and expending nearly a third of a trillion dollars.

The war was, of course, devastating to Europe, but one of the unintended beneficiaries was the American farmer, who enjoyed selling his ever-growing basket of goods for continuously rising prices. The agricultural industry in Europe was devastated from the years of fighting, and America, safely on the other side of an ocean, was able to provide the world's food at price that had been pushed higher by the reduced supplies.

Once the war was over, however, the golden age of American farming came to a quick close. Cotton dropped from 35 cents a pound to 16 cents; corn plummeted from $1.50 a bushel to a mere one-third that price; many other foodstuffs and staples suffered similar plunges of 50 to 66 percent, causing financial trauma for the heavily mortgaged farms of America.

In a way, the Great Depression got a 10-year head-start for rural America, and commodity prices would not return to their Great War levels until the start of the next "great" war nearly 20 years later.

As the 1920s started, labor turmoil began spreading, and in the shadow of the recent Communist revolution in Russia, fear spread throughout the leadership of American business that "reds" were infiltrating capitalism by way of trade unions. In 1919, a general strike held by all workers in Seattle and a strike of the nation's steel industry ceased the output of hundreds of thousands of workers across the country.

These work stoppages, coupled with the rapidly rising interest rates of the Federal Reserve, created a recession in late 1920 and early 1921. The attitude of business toward labor unions was profoundly hostile in the early 1920s, and orchestrated violence against union members was commonplace. The threat of violent attacks was largely responsible for workers' being compelled to return to their jobs.

As the 1920s unfolded, there were essentially three distinct Americas that experienced the decade in different ways. The first, agricultural, suffered the most and enjoyed the fewest benefits of the period; lower commodity prices, suffocating mortgages, and both physical and cultural isolation from the rest of the country meant there was nothing "roaring" about the 1920s for the farmbelt. Even the most basic infrastructure was lacking in rural America, with only 10 percent of farmers having access to electricity as late as 1930.

The middle class enjoyed two beneficial economic changes: the first, steadily growing wages as demand for labor increased (about 20 percent over the course of the decade), and second, increasingly affordable goods—particularly new consumer goods—which increased their standard of living. The 1920s was the first decade in the country's history where anything that could be considered a "leisure" lifestyle became accessible to those who were not wealthy.

The highest echelon of the country thrived, benefiting from the increasingly *laissez-faire* disposition of government toward business and a plunging tax bite. For the rich, the Roaring Twenties were the party for which the decade has its reputation.

■ Lower Taxes, Higher Growth

The politics of the 1920s, most notably with Calvin "Silent Cal" Coolidge, took an almost completely hands-off attitude to business, in contrast to the trust-busting Theodore Roosevelt approach from early in the century. It may seem amazing to those reading in the modern age, but the U.S. government actually generated a *surplus* for every year of the 1920s, most of which was used to lower the modest debt of the country (see Figure 11.1).

When the federal income tax system was enacted in 1913, the rates started at 1 percent for those making $4,000 and ascending to the maximum of 7 percent for those making a million dollars a year or more (a fantastic sum at the time). As the fiscal demands of the Great War took their toll on the nation's budget, tax rates dramatically increased, and by 1918, the highest rate was 77 percent, a more than 10-fold increase on the highest income levels.

Luckily for the very rich, even though the rates never returned to the puny Woodrow Wilson–era levels, tax rates were severely cut by about two-thirds, and those earning income in America—particularly those at the very highest levels—were permitted to keep far more of their earnings.

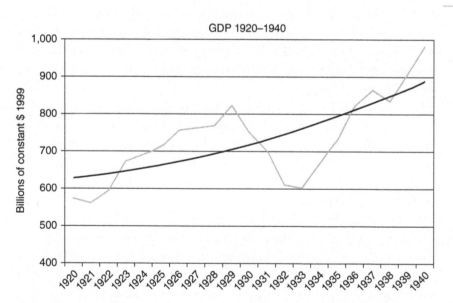

FIGURE 11.1   This figure of gross domestic product for the United States from 1920 to 1940 illustrates how, during the 1920s, there was a virtually uninterrupted trend of growth.

The records of the nation's treasury reflects the growing ranks of the super-rich in the country, with 21 taxpayers reporting annual income of over a million dollars in 1921, 75 in 1924, and 207 in 1926. Interestingly, even though the tax rates plunged from 77 percent to 24 percent for the highest paid, the total revenue the U.S. government enjoyed from taxpayers *increased* steadily with the nation's general prosperity of the decade.

■ Consumerism Blossoms

Two broad trends in the 1920s led to the rapidly growing importance of the middle class to the American economy: the widespread use of credit and the introduction of many new, relatively affordable technologies.

Many of these products are commonplace today, but at the time, such innovations as canned food, telephones, movies, refrigerators, washing machines, radios, and cars were life-changing innovations at the time. The car was particularly important, since the auto industry grew from almost nothing in 1900 to a full 10 percent of the GDP (and the employer of 4 million workers) by 1920.

Purchasing products on credit became convenient and socially acceptable after the war's conclusion, and the majority of relatively "big ticket" items were bought on credit—about 90 percent of furniture, 75 percent of cars and washing machines, 65 percent of vacuum cleaners, and over 50 percent of refrigerators, pianos, and radios. Credit put these purchases within reach for Americans that normally would have associated such items as being only for the wealthy (see Figure 11.2).

It wasn't just the *products* that people bought or the *means* by which they bought them that changed; the *manner* in which they bought products changed as well. Before the Great War, for instance, if you went grocery shopping, you would walk in, hand the clerk a list, and wait while the clerk went to the various shelves where the products were stored and assembled the basket of goods for you.

In the 1920s, the concept of "self-service" grocery shopping took hold, allowing people to push their own carts around, grabbing goods themselves off of shelves. Naturally, consumers who were free to wander about and grab products off shelves were apt to buy more than those who had written up a list in advance, so grocers enjoyed two benefits: greater sales and well as the reduced labor costs of not having clerks plucking out items from lists.

FIGURE 11.2 Among the many new consumer goods offered, one of the most popular was the electric refrigerator, promoted here by this ad from General Electric.

Other retail stores also enjoyed positive changes. For one thing, it was not a common practice before the 1920s to actually post prices for products. The goods would be displayed, and the customer would haggle with the clerk over the price for each and every product. This was obviously inefficient and created a lot of friction between buyers and sellers. The establishment of a "one-price" policy, while seemingly obvious in retrospect, was a revelation to consumers of the day.

In addition, mail-order firms that had thrived by shipping products across America's railways in the late nineteenth century recognized that the automobile was going to change where people lived and how they would buy products.

Instead of farmers placing orders with Chicago-based Sears Roebuck & Company and awaiting for delivery via rail, more and more consumers would be located in suburbs – made feasible by cars and roads – and would prefer to shop in-person at a local retail store stocked with similar products. Thus, in 1925, Sears opened up eight retail stores, and four years later that number had grown to 324 (see Figure 11.3).

The proliferation of automobiles and radios started to tie the country together culturally as profoundly as the coast-to-coast railways completed in 1869 had. The migration from the country to the city—as well as from the city to the suburbs—gained momentum, and the infrastructure demanded by the proliferation of automobiles generated employment and revenue for those involved in road construction, home construction, electricity infrastructure, or any of the other industries required by the building-out of modernity.

■ The Florida Land Rush

The growth of the middle class and the availability of the car also created a land boom peculiar to American history—that of Florida. Between 1920 and 1925, the population of the state grew from 968,470 to 1,263,540, and most of this was prompted by an urgent desire to acquire property that was believed to be an almost surefire profitable investment.

In the end, it would be discovered that Florida was not perfect, and that between the heat, mosquitoes, and hurricanes, Florida had problems just like anywhere else in the country. But to a nation relatively naïve about the potential paradise in the panhandle, the allure of a tropical splendor in the continental U.S. was too much to resist.

FIGURE 11.3 In the 1920s, Sears Roebuck was the most formidable and forward-thinking force in American retail.

In 1921, the frenzy for land acquisition began to gather steam, and by 1922, the *Miami Herald* was the heaviest newspaper in the country, since it was bulging with advertisements for land that was being sold. Countless stories began dotting newspapers in the rest of the country, recounting tales of quick, easy profits being enjoyed by regular folks who were willing to take the risk.

The towns and cities in Florida sought to grow their own populations (and tax bases) by attracting the newcomers, so bonds were floated at lofty interest rates to raise the money needed to build out the facilities and infrastructure of Florida's communities. The state, too, understood the benefits of a rapidly growing population, and in 1924 it eliminated state income tax, inheritance taxes, and took on a pro-construction, pro-business attitude, all of which fit nicely within the spirit of the decade.

The growing army of realtors in Florida offloaded the task of seeking and signing up sales prospects to "binder boys," who were typically young men and women who would stand post at any given real estate development, ready to take a deposit on a parcel of land.

This deposit—or "binder"—would let a speculator secure a parcel for which he would be required to fully finance 30 days later. In a way, these "binders" acted somewhat like options contracts, since aggressive speculators could secure a property at a given price with a relatively small down payment and, hopefully, sell their rights to purchase the property before the month was over at a handsome profit (see Figure 11.4).

After a few years of steadily advancing prices, the value of properties began to reach absurd levels. One old man had spent his life savings of $1,700 early in the boom on a piece of property in Pinellas County, and his sons, fearing for his mental state, had him committed to a sanitarium. Once the property reached $300,000 in value (over 175 times the purchase price), the man's lawyer got him released so he could sue his own children.

■ A Nation of Speculators

By early 1925, some members of the press began to question the sanity of their fellow countrymen in bidding up the prices of what was in some cases little better than swampland. *Forbes* magazine published a deeply skeptical article about the frenzy, and speculators who had been enjoying a brisk business flipping properties (similar to what their descendants would do from 2004–2006 in certain parts of the United States) suddenly found a dearth of buyers.

FIGURE 11.4   A contemporary advertisement praising Florida's consistently warm weather "where winter exists in memory only."

On top of this, the railroads that had been hauling down mountains of construction materials to the rapidly growing state had grown weary of the bottlenecks and headaches from the ceaseless press of rail traffic into Florida, so they formed an embargo. Starting in October 1925, the Seaboard Air Line Railroad, Florida East Coast Railway, and Atlantic Coast Railroad would ship only food, fuel, and perishables to the state. The flow of building materials was choked off at once.

The next disaster to befall Florida land speculation was the *Prinz Valdemar*, a 241-foot boat that sank in the mouth of the Miami harbor, thus blocking access to the one alternative route vendors had to get their wares to the state.

Later the same year, in September, a hurricane hit South Florida with winds of over 125 miles per hour. As news reports spread throughout the country of the kinds of natural disasters that could befall residents of the state, the magical allure of Florida fell away, and land prices continued their descent, causing damage to prices that would take decades to repair.

In spite of the boom-and-bust of the Florida real estate frenzy, the urge for quick profits was not gone for the rest of the nation, and a growing interest in the stock market was not hampered by the relatively confined catastrophe of the panhandle state. Much like the Internet boom of 1995, stocks of new technology companies like Radio Corporation of America caught the imagination of the public, and prices were bid up with increasing volume and accelerating prices.

The amount of leverage available to the small speculator was much larger in the 1920s than it is today, with some issues requiring as little as 10 percent of the purchase price fronted in cash.

A more insidious reason for the appreciation in stock prices was the widespread use of the stock "pool." The way a stock pool would work was similar to how "shills" function at an auction: a body of individuals agrees in advance to target a particular stock. They then buy the stock in the open market, purchasing larger and larger blocks.

As the ownership of the stock in a pool reaches a predetermined size, the members within the pool began buying and selling the stock with each other at higher and higher prices, drawing attention from those outside the pool at the unusual activity of the stock.

Members of the public would notice the surging volume and steadily rising price of the stock and assume something important and positive was happening beneath the surface, and they would at last join the bidding. The rising price would feed on itself, and once the price seemed to be reaching a

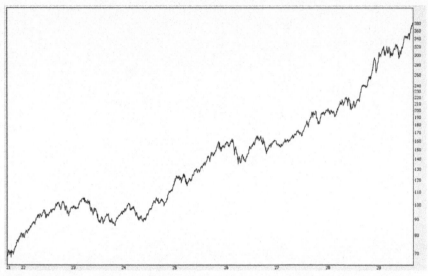

FIGURE 11.5 From September 1921 to September 1929, a period of eight years, the stock market rose continuously, almost without interruption. The Dow Jones Industrial Average gained nearly 500 percent during this time span.

speculative spike, the pool operators would dump their shares on an unsuspecting public at prices that were, in reality, far out of alignment with intrinsic value (see Figure 11.5).

As constructive as business fundamentals were for most of the 1920s, cracks were beginning to appear in the facade as early as 1928, but those fissures would not be recognized until it was much too late. As we shall see in the next chapter, the country was about to experience a hurricane far worse than those suffered in Florida across its financial landscape. And this disaster would commence when the nation seemed the least vulnerable to any kind of financial worries.

CHAPTER 12

The Great Depression

There is probably no financial era in world history more famous than America's Great Depression of the 1930s. It lasted longer, ran deeper, and had more long-lasting effects than any other financial calamity in the nation's history, and the economic thinking shaped during that time dominates the world's financial structure to this day.

The beginning of the Depression was flanked by two American presidents with vastly different turns of luck, based on their proximity to the event. On the one hand was Calvin Coolidge, who enjoyed a restful, crisis-free stay in the White House as the nation rollicked in the Roaring Twenties. The thriving economy was tagged as the "Coolidge prosperity," even though the man for whom it was named had little or nothing to do with the happy circumstances at the time. He was fortunate to depart the White House in early 1929, untouched by the maelstrom that was soon to come (see Figure 12.1).

On the other hand was Herbert Hoover, who, in spite of his best efforts, was widely regarded—particularly by his contemporaries—as hapless and ineffectual as the economic nightmare consumed much of the nation. Even today, the commonplace belief among those with a passing knowledge of the Great Depression is that Hoover had a hands-off, passive disposition toward the events swirling around him, when in fact he worked tirelessly to try to turn around the calamity to no avail. As with so many examples of other national leaders throughout history, one man was given credit where very little was due, and another was saddled with blame that was, on the whole, undeserved.

FIGURE 12.1 The taciturn Coolidge had the fortune of good timing, which permitted "Silent Cal" a relatively peaceful, stress-free tenure during his White House years.

■ The Orgy of Speculation

For the first two decades of the twentieth century, the stock market, as measured by the Dow Jones Industrial Average, was basically unchanged. Even though it went through five distinct boom-and-bust cycles, if one were to invest in the Dow Industrials on the first trading day of 1900, he would find himself with stocks valued at almost exactly the same amount in September 1921, over 21 years later.

The subsequent rise in stock values took place in three broad phases. The first, lasting from August 24, 1921, through October 21, 1926, boosted stock values (again, as measured by the Dow Industrials) by about 60 percent, which is a compound annual rate of about 10 percent. This was a steady, healthy rise in assets, largely uninterrupted by the kind of jolts that had been experienced in the two decades prior.

The next phase saw an acceleration in values, but not one which, in retrospect, could be viewed as a mania. Between October 1926 and June 1928, another 50 percent was added to stock values, representing an annual gain of approximately 20 percent. Thus, in this phase, the pace at which stocks were appreciating doubled.

The third and final phase of stock appreciation was between June 1928 and August 1929, a span of just over a year, in which the Dow Industrials lurched forward by about 90 percent, meaning annual gains were approaching a pace triple the prior period and ninefold what had been experienced from 1921 to 1926. It was during this phase that stocks caught the popular imagination, and those in leadership positions, such as Commerce Secretary Herbert Hoover, fretted over the "orgy of mad speculation" that he was witnessing.

The growth the market had seen from 1921 to 1927 was largely justified. America's economy was thriving, particularly in the automobile industry, and as the world recovered from the Great War that had taken place the prior decade, the unharmed American soil provided fertile ground for the widespread growth of a consumer economy. Except for the debacle of the Florida real estate speculation in 1926–1927, business was, on the whole, running smoothly.

The most notable exception was the agriculture sector, which, as commerce secretary, Hoover had sought to help through federal aid. However, Hoover had been consistently blocked by Coolidge, who embraced a far more *laissez-faire* role for the government. Farmers in the United States limped along for much of the 1920s, vastly separated from their prosperous urban countrymen and the growing mania on Wall Street (see Figure 12.2).

The funds powering the surge in stock prices came from many quarters, including corporate coffers and bank loans. As the nation turned away from more typical business ventures and devoted itself to stock and real estate ventures, the banks of the nation shifted their lending focus more and more

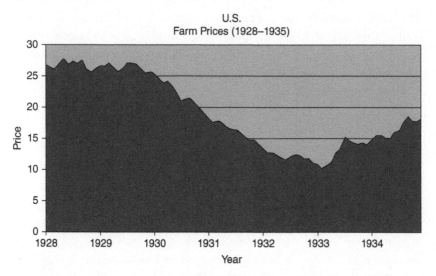

FIGURE 12.2 This graph of farmland prices in the United States shows that, after the 1928 peak, about 60 percent of the value was erased in the ensuing four years.

to financial speculation until, by 1929, more loans were dedicated to short-term investment bets than to regular commercial loans.

Herbert Hoover was certainly not the only politician or commentator to express concern about the market's dizzying rise, but most eschewed such concerns as the pointless admonitions of modern-day Cassandras. In an article from May 15, 1928, the *Wall Street Journal* wrote:

> It is to be feared that the agitation against speculation in Wall Street is very largely a case of sour grapes. It is felt that some people are making money with apparent ease and it is known that they are making it in Wall Street, which is always an object of distrust to the demagogue.

It is understandable, with the boundless optimism infused throughout the nation, why Coolidge would confidently proclaim in his final State of the Union address to Congress on December 4, 1928, that "In the domestic field there is tranquility and contentment.... [The nation should] regard the present with satisfaction and anticipate the future with optimism."

■ Stock Mania

In early 1929, some sober spirits were trying their best to calm what they perceived as markets that had become completely detached from economic reality. The Federal Reserve's own *Bulletin* in February 1929 stated that it would seek to restrain the use of "credit facilities in aid of the growth of speculative credit," since it had been one of the many spigots of liquidity that had fueled the mania to date.

The U.S. Senate in the spring of 1929 adopted a resolution supporting legislation "necessary to correct the evil complained of and prevent illegitimate and harmful speculation," and a member of the Federal Reserve Board early in 1929 railed against "... this period of optimism gone wild and cupidity gone drunk."

Even those in the business world who were the principal beneficiaries of the nation's largesse began to speak out. The head of U.S. Steel, Myron Taylor, stated that the stock market was "the folly of speculative frenzy that lifted securities to levels far beyond any warrant of supporting profits." And Mr. Trowbridge Callaway, the president of the Investment Bankers Association, told of "the orgy of speculation which clouded the country's vision."

From his own bully pulpit, the new U.S. President Hoover took the unusual step of trying to talk down the market. In later years he recalled, "I sent individually for the editors and publishers of major newspapers and magazine and requested them systematically to warn the country against speculation and the unduly high price of stocks." It is clear from these accounts that not everyone in the country was cheerleading the market higher.

However, many people were doing so, particularly in the popular press. Following are two excerpts from the media that help capture the spirit of the time, with some emphasis added by the author:

Millionaires have been made many times over with the unprecedented rise of certain individual stocks. Of a list of twenty well-known stocks which have increased from 600 to 6,000 percent during the last ten years, twelve famous names appear above the 1,000 percent mark, with one outstanding motor stock heading the list with a 6,493 percent increase. *No wonder our nation has gone stock market mad.*

The North American Review, December 1928

The common stocks of this country have in the past ten years increased enormously in value because the business of the country has increased. Ten thousand dollars invested ten years ago in the common stock of General Motors would now be worth more than a million and a half dollars. And General Motors is only one of many first-class industrial corporations. It may be said that this is a phenomenal increase and that conditions are going to be different in the next ten tears. That prophecy may be true, but it is not founded on experience. *In my opinion the wealth of the country is bound to increase at a very rapid rate.*

Ladies' Home Journal, August 1929

However, a respected economist of the day, Roger Babson, spoke at almost the exact peak of the market on September 5, 1929, in these prescient terms:

More people are borrowing and speculating today than ever in our history. *Sooner or later a crash is coming and it may be terrific.* Wise are those investors who now get out of debt and reef their sails This does not mean selling all you have, but it does mean paying up your loans and avoiding margin speculation.... *Sooner or later the stock market boom will collapse like the Florida boom.* Some day the time is coming when the market will begin to slide off, sellers will exceed buyers, and paper profits will begin to disappear. Then *there will immediately be a stampede to save what paper profits then exist.*

His words had an immediate effect on the market, which—floating in the ether as it was—was vulnerable to any harsh reality creeping in. The response from popular media was swift and almost universal in its dismissal of Babson's concerns. For example, the *Chicago Tribune* retorted on September 7, 1929:

> Roger Babson's dire predictions of an "inevitable crash" in the stock market, which would some time break the averages 60 to 80 points, evoked retorts today from economists, stock exchange houses, and others, most of whom took an opposite view or advised clients and the public not to be stampeded by Mr. Babson's forecast of a collapse that would rival that of the Florida land boom. Mr. Babson's view was directly controverted by Prof. Irving Fisher of Yale University, an economist of highest standing. Prof. Fisher flatly asserted that *"stock prices are not high and Wall Street will not experience anything in the nature of a crash."*

The Dow Jones Industrials peaked at 386.10 on September 3, 1929, and then begin to gently slide on an almost daily basis, but no day was severe enough to be construed as a panic. By October 22, about 15 percent of the market's value had been shaved away, prompting the *New York Times* to assert:

> *The stock market will see bigger gains in the immediate future than at any other period of its history,* and except for minor fluctuations the present high level of prices will be constant for years to come, according to a statement by Dr. Charles Amos Dice, professor of business organization at Ohio State University.... *"Among the yardsticks for predicting the behavior of stocks which have been rendered obsolete,"* Dr. Dice went on, "are the truism that what goes up must come down, ... that stock prices cannot safely exceed ten times the net earnings available for dividends on the common stock per share." *The day of the small investor is here.* Once despised and turned away, he is now sought day and night. The appeals come from the best banking houses as well as from the fly-by-night operator. *The wage earner is made aware of how easy it is to build up an estate by small installment payments.*

The mention of "small installment payments" is an interesting point, because at the time, an easy-money policy pervaded almost everything to do with stock speculation. Until 1928, the Federal Reserve had poured money into banks, which was increasingly used to fund speculation. The fat corporate profits of the late 1920s were increasingly turned away from additional business investment and instead put into gambling on the stock market.

One substantial source of credit were "call loans" from brokers, which allowed customers to buy stocks on as little as 10 percent margin. Offering call loans was an effortless, easy way to make money for banks, since they could borrow money at 3.5 percent and loan it out at 10 percent or more. Even large corporations recognized the opportunity and jumped into the call-loan business, with such titans as Standard Oil loaning $69 million a day at the peak of its lending.

■ The Market Cracks Wide Open

From the market's 386.10 peak on September 3, the drop to 325.20 on October 4, 1929, was meaningful but nothing to suggest panic. However, between the September 3 peak and the intermediate-term November 11 bottom, a full 50 percent of the value of the Dow Industrials would be erased, and the lion's share of this drop took place on three days: October 23 (market close: 305.90), October 28 (market close: 260.60), and October 29 (market close: 230.10).

These relatively small numbers might make it difficult for the modern reader to appreciate the severity of the drop, but imagining the present Dow 30 dropping from 14,000 to 7,000 in a two-month period might be of aid. In late 1929, the severity of the downturn was certainly not lost on the press. The *New York Evening Post* reported on October 30, 1929:

It is clear that *the Street is going through the greatest disaster in its history*. No fair words can gloss over that fact. Because there is no tightness of money we are without the most familiar feature of a bad [economic] time. Furthermore, *the stock market has been operating so independently of business* that we have not yet realized the larger results of its break. Nevertheless, *good must come even from this stern and cruel housecleaning. The country will go back to work....* That means here, as it meant in postwar Germany, *a revival of values.* How can any cool head fail to agree with Professor Irving Fisher's declaration that standard *American stocks have*

163

THE GREAT DEPRESSION

gone so much too low as to be crying to be bought? Such stocks are the bone and sinew of the country. *Not to believe in them is not to believe in America.* The world has so many things that must be done, and no one can do them better than our own people. *Our business strength has pulled us out of difficulties in days gone by. With faith it will do it again.*

Already, three themes are apparent that were pervasive in the popular culture of the day: (1) the values of the stock market were now better-aligned with reality; (2) the crash was a good thing, since the country could return to more productive endeavors than stock speculation; (3) business was basically sound and would continue to march on, unfettered by recent speculative excess.

This kind of all-will-be-well optimism was present in other dispatches on the same day:

No thoughtful person can regard what has taken place as less than good and hopeful. The country had gone speculation mad. It is worthwhile for the sake of the larger good that even so drastic a liquidation as has been witnessed should have taken place. There will be no panic because the United States has gotten beyond that stage in its economic development and because resources are available through the Federal Reserve System to prevent such a calamity.

Birmingham Age-Herald

The collapse was inevitable and has been predicted by careful observers for many weeks. *Prices of stocks have been boosted beyond all reason. ... The prices were purely artificial and speculative.* Now they have dropped to a more nearly normal figure, and while the experience has been costly to thousands of people, *in the long run it is much better to have the nation's securities on a business basis than upon a gambling and speculative basis.*

Montgomery Journal

Although losses suffered by the public have been enormous, a group of investors, numbering thousands, escaped uninjured and is now ready to take advantage of the break. *Thus is presented in the richest country in the world, with the most remarkable record of continuous prosperity in history, a bargain counter on which are offered shares in ownership of the rich industries that have led the way to progress in modern civilization.*

Chicago Herald and Examiner

Now that the inevitable deflation has come, *business conditions remain essentially sound with expanding demands throughout the world.* With market uncertainties virtually at an end and with credit being released from Wall Street for ordinary business uses, the way is prepared for a further advance in industry. *Once the adjustment is completed, the country will move forward to new levels of prosperity.*

Kansas City Star

Of course, little did any of these people know that the market would ultimately wipe out 90 percent of the Industrial Average in two years' time, and not merely 50 percent, when the ultimate nadir of 40.60 was reached on July 8, 1932.

■ Smoot-Hawley Tariff

Earlier, in the spring of 1929, when the stock market was still in its ascendency, there had been some growing concerns about subtle signs of slowdown in American business, certainly in the long-suffering farmland, and also in the important automobile sector. In April 1929, Congressman Willis Hawley introduced a bill that newly inaugurated President Herbert Hoover hoped would help the American farmer.

The bill, which was largely aimed at farmers when it was first conjured, was swiftly passed by the House, but over the course of the next year, it would grow into an unwieldy, all-encompassing law that would touch on 20,000 different goods. What would eventually be known as the Smoot-Hawley Tariff was formally known by the much longer and more cumbersome title:

An Act To provide revenue, to regulate commerce with foreign countries, to encourage the industries of the United States, to protect American labor, and for other purposes.

By the time the act was finalized and offered to the President, economists pleaded with Hoover not to sign it. A thousand economists signed a petition pleading with Hoover to veto the bill, with one of them, a J. P. Morgan partner named Thomas Lamont, recalled that "I almost went down on my knees to beg Herbert Hoover to veto the asinine Hawley-Smoot Tariff. That act intensified nationalism all over the world."

Historians now widely agree that the new tariffs were ruinous for the world economy of the early 1930s. Predictably, nations that traded with the United States erected their own retaliatory tariffs, and the already-suffering global economy was almost completely choked off. In what would become a theme for his efforts, Hoover's good intentions to turn the economy around ultimately turned disastrous.

■ Business Council

As an experienced and successful businessman himself, Hoover believed that the people best equipped to guide the nation out of the financial shock of the market crash were the business leaders of the nation, so he summoned them to the White House soon after the events of October. Hoover's Treasury secretary, famed banker Andrew Mellon, urged the president to simply leave things alone and let nature take its course.

Hoover vehemently disagreed, believing that "we should use the powers of government to cushion the situation ... the prime needs were to prevent bank panics such as had marked the earlier slumps, to mitigate the privation among the unemployed and the farmers which would certainly ensue ... we determined that the federal government should use all of its powers."

This was a surprisingly activist disposition for a Republican president of that era, but Hoover was not content to passively let events unfold before him. What was desperately needed in the nation was confidence, and throughout the month of November 1929, Hoover met with the captains of industry from manufacturing, the railways, the banks, and the great manufacturing firms to determine the best course ahead. Commensurate with this, both the president and the executives in session would offer the public regular pronouncements testifying to the basic soundness of the American economy.

On December 5, 1929, Hoover brought together 400 business leaders, many of them having conferred with him directly in the prior month, to review their collective findings and recommendations. He told the group that three actions had already been taken based on their discussions:

1. The Federal Reserve System had lowered its discount rate to member banks in an effort to spur money flow and lending.
2. If a bank were involved in the issuance of call loans to stock speculators, the Fed would refuse access to its discount window, thus providing a powerful disincentive from such loans.

3. The Fed had engaged in large-scale open market purchases of bonds in order to inject liquidity into the financial system

Hoover summarized the take-charge attitude of his administration by telling the gathering, "The very fact that you gentlemen come together for these broad purposes represents an advance in the whole conception of the relationship of business to public welfare. This is a far cry from the arbitrary and dog-eat-dog attitude of the business world of some 30 or 40 years ago."

It seems likely that Hoover had in mind the panic of 1891 with these remarks, and he sought to contrast the new world of Federal intervention versus the old world of businesses depending on the mercy of the likes of J. P. Morgan.

Hoover's request to the businesses of the nation was a simple one: don't cut wages just because you are worried about the financial health of the nation. His belief was that by maintaining current wage levels, the economy wouldn't suffer from a drop in consumer spending at such a fragile time.

In his own words, "the first shock must fall on profits and not on wages," and for a while, businesses complied. Here again, with hindsight, it can be seen that it would have been more beneficial to the nation's health if businesses had tried to avoid laying off employees, even if they paid lower wages, rather than artificially propping up the salaries being paid, particularly with the deflationary environment that lay ahead. Widespread employment at reduced wages is better than diminished employment at artificially high wages for those lucky enough to have jobs (see Figure 12.3).

Hoover also took the initiative of wiring every state's governor and the mayor of every major city to encourage them to commence whatever public works projects might be at hand, urging that every "road, street, public building, and other construction of this type could be speeded up and adjusted in such fashion as to further employment." Far from taking a passive role, Hoover endeavored to be as hands-on as possible in confronting the crisis and dispatching with whatever harm the stock market's shock had caused to the country's psyche.

At first, it seemed to work. The depths of the Dow Jones Industrials on November 13 were not revisited, and in the winter of 1929 and spring of 1930, the market steadily inched higher on almost a daily basis. By April 16, 1930, the market had increased in value a full 50 percent from its low six months prior, and although it was still about one-fourth lower than it had been the prior September, the nation seemed to understand that those peak price levels represented a complete break with reality, and there was no need to beat any prior records to contemplate a healed economy (see Figure 12.4).

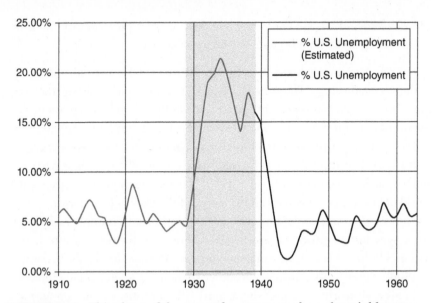

FIGURE 12.3 This chart of the unemployment rate shows how joblessness raced higher as the Great Depression started, peaking at nearly one-quarter of the nation's workforce.

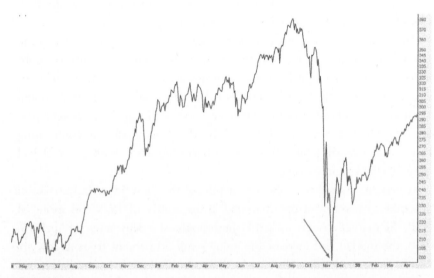

FIGURE 12.4 In late 1929 and early 1930, a large part of the damage to the stock market was reversed, indicating that perhaps the worst was already over.

On May 1, 1930, Hoover stated to the U.S. Chamber of Commerce that "I am convinced we have passed the worst and with continued effort we shall rapidly recover." In June of the same year, he assured the National Catholic Welfare Conference, in response to their request for an expansion of federal public works programs, that they were "… sixty days too late. The Depression is over."

■ The Slide Resumes

Although Hoover's actions in the six months following the crash, as well as the handsome 50 percent increase in stock price during the same time, suggested that the nation was on the mend, it was actually reaching an inflection point and about to descend into an abyss the country could not imagine. In 1930, a record 26,355 businesses failed, and the country's gross national product (GNP) dropped by 12.6 percent. There was no doubt that that economy was sick, although no one knew how badly or for how long.

The backbone of the economy, the bank system, was particularly vulnerable. The vast majority of banks in the country were established with little more financial stability than any other small business, such as a restaurant or grocery store. Most of them had no links to the Federal Reserve, and at the time there was no deposit insurance. This meant that if a bank failed as a business, it was likely that the money deposited within the bank would be diminished, if not wiped out altogether.

Hoover recognized this, writing later in *The Memoirs of Herbert Hoover* (Hollis & Crater, 1952) that "Our banking system was the weakest link in our whole economic system … the element most sensitive to fear … the worst part of the dismal tragedy with which I had to deal." Bank failures were not unusual, even before the Great Depression commenced: in 1929, 659 banks suspended their business, and in the first 10 months of 1930, a similar number of banks shut their doors. In November and December 1930, another 600 banks closed up shop, for a total of 1,352.

One bank in particular, the Bank of the United States (which was somewhat of a misnomer, since it was not a government entity) shut down on December 11, 1930, exacerbating the fear. This was, to date, the largest commercial bank failure in the history of the United States, with accounts from over 400,000 people approaching $300 million. Some overseas observers mistakenly took the name to mean more than it did, adding fuel to the fire of financial panic (see Figure 12.5).

FIGURE 12.5 Crowds are shown here gathering at the headquarters of the Bank of the United States, after it collapsed, taking $300 million of depositor funds with it.

Indeed, between 1929 and 1933, 10,763 out of 24,970 commercial banks in the country failed—a figure of over 43 percent. Some banks, desperate to stay in business, resorted to almost comic measures: one Utah bank manager instructed tellers to work as slowly as possibly, counting out small bills one by one, in order to reduce the pace at which money was being extracted by anxious account holders.

■ The Golden Lattice

For over a century leading up to the Great Depression, the world's economies had an interlinked, self-correcting system of currencies based on the gold standard. As national economies began to sink under the weight of the growing depression, which was most severe in the United States, the impetus to have this mechanism in place began to dissipate, since its presence caused a deflationary effect in the shrinking fortunes of individual countries.

The recognized reserve currency of the time, Britain's pound sterling, held tremendous sway over the global economy, which meant that the decision of Britain in September 1931 to abandon the gold standard was profound. The most stark metric to illustrate the effect this decision had was the collapse of global trade volume from $36 billion in 1929 to one-*third* that amount in 1932.

The cataclysmic effects of Britain's decision was felt most acutely by banks, 522 of which failed within a month of the announcement. In the whole of 1931, 2,294 banks in the United States closed their doors, double the amount of 1930, and yet another national record.

While Hoover's earlier actions in the earliest months of the crisis had been bold, decisive, and clear-headed, the worsening situation seemed to compel him to more desperate and less thoughtful acts. As the nation's balance sheet tipped from a surplus to a deficit, he decided to ask Congress for a sweeping tax increase in order to close the gap, the Revenue Act of 1932.

The tax act dramatically increased the number of citizens on the tax rolls, by way of eliminating most personal exemptions. The lowest rates zoomed from 1.125 percent to 4 percent, and the highest bracket went from 25 percent to 63 percent. Hoover wanted to keep the government's financial house in order, even with fiscal chaos swirling around him. His goal was to demonstrate to the rest of the world the nation's commitment to a stable, sound currency supported by tax revenues adequate to balance the expenses of the country. Of course, the real effect of this act was to cut even deeper into depressed consumer spending, making a bad situation even worse.

■ The Bonus Army

As the Depression ground on, Hoover made the most radical departure from his principal that "the government is best which governs least" by the creation of the Reconstruction Finance Corporation (RFC). Unprecedented in the country's history, the RFC poured taxpayer dollars directly into the balance sheets of private financial enterprises, with the goal of banks providing much-needed loans to the businesses of the country so they could get back on their feet again.

The initial capitalization of the RFC was $500 million, with an additional $1.5 billion authorized by Congress. The most liberal members of Congress were shocked at the boldness of Hoover's move, which not long before would have been tagged as outright Communist, but the longevity of the downturn begged for radical action. At the time, the magazine *Business Week* described the RFC as "the most powerful offensive force that governmental and business imagination has, so far, been able to command."

In spite of the RFC, business and bank failures continued to swamp the nation, and Hoover was increasingly pointed to as the man to blame. "Hoovervilles"—shanty towns of cardboard, tin sheets, and other scrap— dotted the landscape, and "Hoover flags"—the outturned, empty pants pockets of the nation's unemployed—were but two of the invented names attached to the beleaguered president. Although the depths of his situation couldn't seem to get much worse, Hoover was about to face the nadir of his presidency that summer.

It has been a tradition in the nation's history that veteran soldiers would be paid a "bonus" at the conclusion of the war equal to the difference in what they were paid for their service and what they would have been paid had they not enlisted in the first place. The veterans of the "Great War" were given a paltry $60 bonus, and after strong protestations, the veterans were finally granted by Congress relief in the form of a bill called the World War Adjusted Compensation Act.

This act, passed over Coolidge's veto in 1924, provided for $1 per day of domestic services, and $1.25 for each day of overseas service, up to a limit of $625. Sums smaller than $50 were paid immediately, but larger amounts—of which there were nearly 3.7 million recipients—were given a certificate instead. The certificate would come due in 1945, and the total value of these certificates was in excess of $43 billion (in inflation-adjusted terms).

During the prosperous 1920s, these certificates were in most cases thrown into drawers or safety deposit boxes as extra savings to be enjoyed in future retirement years. But eight years after their distribution, during the grinding poverty of the Depression, these certificates were seen as potentially vital sources of desperately needed cash. A growing chorus of veterans demanded their payment at once, as opposed to waiting another 13 years.

In January 1932, 25,000 out-of-work veterans from Pennsylvania marched to Washington, D.C., to demand their payments. Led by Father James Cox, a Catholic priest from Pittsburg, the group was dubbed "Cox's Army," and in the coming months, their ranks would swell with veterans from all over the country. They camped out all over Washington, including the grounds of the U.S. Capitol, but the majority of them set up a well-organized camp on the Anacostia Flats near the heart of D.C.

By June 15, the House of Representatives passed a bill that would have granted the veterans their accelerated cash payments, but the U.S. Senate resoundingly rejected the bill by a vote of 62–18, immediately dispiriting the veterans who thought a positive resolution was at hand. Many of these returned home, dejected, but several thousand of them remained, moving their camp to the U.S. Capitol, where they demanded that President Hoover take action to aid what was now referred to as the "Bonus Army."

On June 28, the attorney general of the United States ordered the local Washington police to evict the veterans from their camp. They did so, but the veterans soon returned. The police once again moved in to displace the men, but an altercation in one of the buildings compelled the officers to draw their guns and shoot two of the veterans, killing them both.

The enraged Bonus Army rioted, furious at the death of two of their comrades at the hands of fellow citizens, and the overwhelmed local police pleaded with Hoover to take action. Hoover ordered federal troops—led by none other than General Douglas MacArthur—to evict the Bonus Army from Washington, D.C., altogether. MacArthur assembled six battle tanks (commanded by no less a man than George Patton) and a column of infantry to proceed down Pennsylvania Avenue to confront the veterans.

The Bonus Army, seeing the troops in formation marching toward them, assumed that the troops were marching to honor the assembly of former soldiers, so hearty cheers erupted in support. Only when MacArthur ordered the soldiers to attack the veterans did they realize what was happening, and the terrified mob scattered in all directions.

In a foreshadowing of the kind of subordination he would exercise in the Korean War 20 years later, MacArthur exceeded the authority granted to him by the president and proceeded to the Anacostia camp. Hoover sent word, ordering the general to stop, but MacArthur ignored the direct command, thinking the veterans were bent on overthrowing the federal government.

MacArthur attacked the camp with bayonets, tear gas, and fire. The entire camp was set aflame, and dozens of the veterans were injured. One of MacArthur's aides, Major Dwight Eisenhower, recalled later of MacArthur's actions, "I told that dumb son-of-a-bitch not to go down there" (see Figure 12.6).

The news and images of United States troops burning encampments, threatening people with tanks and bayonets, and injuring and killing citizens, infuriated the deeply troubled nation. The entire ugly episode was decreed "The Battle of Anacostia Flats," and Hoover—already deeply unpopular—was vilified as never before in his political career, in spite of the deaths being at the hands of local police, and in spite of the mayhem that followed being largely the result of MacArthur's reckless behavior.

FIGURE 12.6 With the U.S. Capitol visible in the distance, the makeshift housing of the bonus army stood in flames, set ablaze by MacArthur and his men.

■ Regime Change

As the election approached in November 1932, it was widely (and correctly) believed that Hoover would be defeated by the popular governor of New York, Franklin Delano Roosevelt. Hoover had tried his best, but the nation seemed worse off than ever. The Dow Jones Industrials scraped the $40 mark in July 1932, a mere 10 percent of its peak value less than three years earlier, and unemployment was ubiquitous (see Figure 12.7).

Ten million people were out of work in early 1932, which was about a fifth of the potential labor force. Some large industrial cities like Detroit and Chicago had unemployment rates of nearly 50 percent. Those fortunate enough to still have jobs either had to accept part-time work or, in many cases, greatly reduced pay. Respected economists put forward the very believable fear that the millions without work would never again find employment, resulting in a nation permanently suffering from vast joblessness.

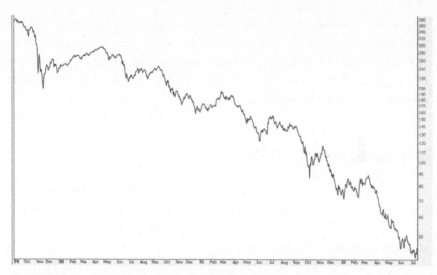

FIGURE 12.7 The slide of the Dow Jones Industrial Average from late 1929 to mid-1932 was relentless and terrifying. Nearly 90 percent of the peak value was erased in less than three years.

Roosevelt's victory over Hoover was extraordinarily lopsided. Roosevelt garnered 22.8 million votes compared to Hoover's 15.7 million, and Roosevelt's 472 electoral votes completely dwarfed the 59 Hoover managed to accrue (most of which were from a single state, Pennsylvania). Ironically, Roosevelt won much favor from the voters by lambasting Hoover for spending too *much* and leading the nation down a path of socialism. Whatever spending Hoover had overseen in his administration would of course be miniscule compared to the amounts the Roosevelt administration would later dispense.

In the months between the election and Roosevelt's March 1933 inauguration, the nation's spirit continued to be ground down by the heel of economic disaster. Although the stock market had bounced briefly from July to September, it resumed sinking for months afterward, threatening to break to an even worse low than before.

Political observers and commentators viewed with some envy the firm grip that Mussolini and Hitler had taken over their countries, unfettered by the need to please legislatures or constituents. Kansas's governor stated, "… even the iron hand of a national dictator is in preference to a paralytic stroke," hinting that an American dictator might be a preferable form of leadership in such dire circumstances.

Walter Lippmann, the popular newspaper columnist (who would in later years garner two Pulitzer Prizes for his writing) counseled the president-elect, "The situation is critical, Franklin. You may have no alternative but to assume dictatorial power." Never had the nation come so close to willingly handing itself over to one man as its overlord.

■ Grinding to a Halt

For nearly four years, the world, and particularly the United States, had been suffering under the travails of the Great Depression. Nearly 25 percent of the country was out of work; over 5,000 banks had failed; the government's attempts to change the direction of the economy had failed. It seemed as if the American way of life was slowly grinding to a permanent stop, perhaps soon to be replaced by the radical new structure of the Soviet Union, which was doing comparatively well.

In one final clumsy fumble in the last days of Hoover's administration, Congress decided to publish the names of the banks that were in receipt of loans from the RFC. What Congress hoped to gain from this is unclear, but the result was that the list was perceived as a handy and indisputable guide to which remaining banks in the country were weakest and therefore in need of government handouts.

Already shell-shocked by four years of a wretched economy, the public made use of this list immediately by rushing to the banks cited and removing their deposits. In states across the nation, governors were compelled to declare "banking holidays"—a euphemistic term meaning that the banks would be forcibly closed by government decree until such time as they were permitted to reopen—in a desperate effort to stop the hemorrhaging of cash from the almost completely spent financial bloodstream.

Out of the 48 states in the union, 32 of them had shut *all* of their banks, 6 more had virtually all their banks closed, and in the few states remaining, depositors were restricted to taking out only very small amounts of cash on a daily basis.

For example, Texas depositors were forbidden from removing more than $10 on any given day from their own accounts. It is helpful to remember that this was money ostensibly safeguarded by the banks and held in trust; the frustration of being forbidden from taking out one's own cash surely must have been maddening.

During these darkest of days between Roosevelt's election and his inauguration, President Hoover made repeated attempts to persuade Roosevelt to make some kind of reassuring pledge or announcement to the American people. Hoover well understood that his own credibility had been exhausted, but he was still president, and he knew what the nation needed far more than anything else was confidence.

Instilling confidence didn't necessary take money, guns, or new government programs; it simply needed the credible words of a recognized leader, and Hoover knew that Roosevelt probably had it within him to provide such a salve. Roosevelt shrewdly, if not cruelly, refused, holding back on any relief that could possibly be provided in Hoover's final days. Roosevelt, in the end, would make sure that he and he alone received all of the credit for the turnaround that would soon take place.

■ Shuttering the Banks

At long last, Saturday, March 4, 1933—Inauguration Day—had arrived. Appropriately for the dying capitalist economy, the New York Stock Exchange and the Chicago Board of Trade did not open as they normally would that Saturday, given the financial paralysis that had completely gripped the nation. Hoover and Roosevelt were driven to the Capitol—Hoover, stone-faced and obviously wanting to be anywhere else in the world at that moment, and Roosevelt, beaming. After that day, the two men would never see each other again (see Figure 12.8).

After being sworn in, Roosevelt took the podium for 20 minutes and uttered some of the most famous words of any inaugural address, as most of the nation listened to their radios to the historic event:

> So, first of all, let me assert my firm belief that the only thing we have to fear is ... fear itself—nameless, unreasoning, unjustified terror which paralyzes needed efforts to convert retreat into advance. In every dark hour of our national life a leadership of frankness and of vigor has met with that understanding and support of the people themselves which is essential to victory. And I am convinced that you will again give that support to leadership in these critical days.

Roosevelt also injected a thinly veiled reference to his willingness to take on what some might deem the same "dictatorial power" that

FIGURE 12.8 In March 1933, Hoover and Roosevelt sat in the same car prior to FDR's inauguration as president. Hoover was a weary, sullen figure next to the beaming president-elect.

Lippman had recommended if Congress was unwilling to submit to his firm leadership:

> I am prepared under my constitutional duty to recommend the measures that a stricken Nation in the midst of a stricken world may require. These measures, or such other measures as the Congress may build out of its experience and wisdom, I shall seek, within my constitutional authority, to bring to speedy adoption. But in the event that the Congress shall fail to take one of these two courses, and in the event that the national emergency is still critical, I shall not evade the clear course of duty that will then confront me. *I shall ask the Congress for the one remaining instrument to meet the crisis—broad Executive power to wage a war against the emergency, as great as the power that would be given to me if we were in fact invaded by a foreign foe.*

The first half-hour of Roosevelt's presidency, which would be followed by an unprecedented (and never-to-be-repeated) four terms in office, was already off to a bold, resolute start. But what was really needed was action, not words, and Roosevelt had already asked for an emergency meeting between himself and the leaders of all the major financial institutions in the country during the forthcoming week.

Prior to that, on Sunday, March 5, 1933, he took three important actions: (1) that transactions in gold be ceased immediately; (2) that a four-day nationwide banking holiday take place; and (3) that Congress should convene in a special session on the forthcoming Friday, March 9.

The plan was to spend Monday through Thursday putting together the necessary bill (for Congress to hopefully pass before the weekend) in order to right the nation's fiscal ship. The irony is that the vast majority of people would look back at these decisions as being exactly the kind of bold steps that Hoover failed to take, but it was in fact Hoover who had pleaded with Roosevelt to support precisely the same steps during the final weeks of Hoover's own presidency (which FDR refused to do).

With four days of breathing room, the nation's financial leaders understood that the stakes could not be higher for the nation, since this was perhaps their last opportunity to save the country's fiscal system before it got perhaps irreversibly worse. What they drafted during those four days was a bill called the Emergency Banking Relief Act, which would require any banks operating in the country to be approved by the Federal Reserve. The act was relatively short but gigantic in its impact; it read as follows (with some emphasis added by the author):

Title I
Section 1. To affirm any orders or regulations the President or Secretary of the Treasury had given since March 4, 1933.

Section 2. *To give the President the ability to declare a national emergency and have absolute control over the national finances and foreign exchange of the United States* in the event of such an emergency.

Section 3. *To authorize the Secretary of the Treasury to order any individual or organization in the United States to deliver any gold that they possess* or have custody of to the Treasury in return for "any other form of coin or currency coined or issued under the laws of the United States."

Section 4. To make it illegal for a bank to do business during a national emergency (per section 2) without the approval of the President.

Title II.
To enable the Comptroller of the Currency to take complete control of and operate any bank in the United States or its territories and to establish the terms and conditions under which bank is administered.

Title III
To allow banks to not allow debt to extinguish the use of stock.

Title IV
Section 401. To allow Federal Reserve banks to convert any U.S. debt obligation into cash at par value and any check, draft, banker acceptance, etc, into cash at 90 percent of its apparent value.

Section 402. To allow the Federal Reserve banks to make unsecured loans to any member bank at an interest rate of 1 percent over the prevailing discount rate.

Section 403. To allow Federal Reserve banks to make loans to anyone for up to 90 days if the loan is secured by a general obligation of the United States (such as a Treasury bond, for example).

Title V
Section 501. Appropriation of $2,000,000 to the President for carrying out this legislation.

On Friday, during the special session of Congress, the one existing typed copy of the bill was read, and most members of Congress didn't have the opportunity to even examine the bill with their own eyes before voting on it.

The House of Representatives took a voice vote, and with a roar of approval, the bill was immediately passed. It then went on to the Senate, where it was also passed against just a handful of no votes. By 8:36 that evening, FDR signed one of the most important pieces of legislation in the country's history, which had been presented to the legislative body for the first time only earlier that same afternoon.

The most important immediate aspect of the act was that the government had the power to supervise 100 percent of the nation's banks, and only with the government's approval based on proven solvency would each given bank be permitted to reopen. The banking holiday was extended past its original four days to last through Sunday, March 12.

That Sunday night, Roosevelt hosted his first "fireside chat," a radio address that would become a staple of his administration. Roosevelt correctly surmised that the mostly conservative newspapers of the land would distort and editorialize his actions, so he wisely chose to circumvent them altogether by directly communicating with the people through the relatively new medium of radio. Roosevelt told the tens of millions of listeners that "it is safer to keep your money in a reopened bank than under the mattress."

The people evidently understood and agreed. The next morning, March 13, the first time banks were open in the country since they had been shut down by emergency order over a week earlier, depositors around the nation lined up in front of their banks. But this time, unlike the many instances when they had lined up before during the preceding four years, they were in line to *deposit* their money, not take it out.

The flood of cash into the banks was unprecedented. Over half of all the cash that had been spirited out of bank accounts during the entire Depression was redeposited, and more important, the all-too-frequent national phenomenon of bank runs was brought to an abrupt end. With the introduction of federal supervision and deposit insurance, the public no longer feared that their deposit institution would go belly-up one morning, taking their savings with it. Faith in America's financial institutions had been restored.

The stock market responded just as enthusiastically. It had been closed even longer than the banks had, but when the New York Stock Exchange reopened on March 15, it enjoyed the largest single-day percentage gain in its entire history, vaulting 15.34 percent in one session. Although no one knew for sure at the time, the low price that had been set during the summer of 1932 would never been seen again. The vicious bear market in stocks was, at long last, over.

■ Putting People Back to Work

Now it was time for Roosevelt to attack a problem far more deeply entrenched: unemployment. Indeed, while the banking catastrophe was addressed head-on with magnificent results in less than two weeks' time, unemployment would become a persistent headache for almost another decade.

While modern public perception seems to perceive Hoover as a stingy, hands-off president and Roosevelt as the big-government spendthrift, it was actually Roosevelt who wanted to clamp down on the government spending that Hoover had engaged. On March 10, 1933, Roosevelt sent another emergency measure to Congress, asking for permission to remove half a billion dollars from the Federal budget. In words that would probably surprise most modern readers, Roosevelt described the federal government, by way of its profligate spending, to be "on the road toward bankruptcy."

He sought the immediate reduction in pay for members of Congress, federal employees, members of the military, and even veterans. In spite of some protestations by the affected parties, Congress passed this budget reduction, providing some fiscal relief to the badly strained national government's finances. Two days later, Roosevelt set in motion the end of prohibition by way of the Beer-Wine Revenue Act, which legalized those two classes of alcoholic beverages.

Having provided some financial prudence and some new revenue, Roosevelt began shaping new government programs to directly provide employment to millions of displaced citizens. The Civilian Conservation Corps (CCC) was designed from young men between the ages of 18 and 25 and was run in a style reminiscent of the military.

The young men would live in work camps around the nation and take part in conservation projects such as cleaning streams, building game sanctuaries, working on erosion projects, and planting trees. Paid about $30 per month, nearly two million young men took part in the CCC over the course of the 1930s.

A separate program, the Civil Works Administration (CWA), was created in November 1933 to employ men and women in highway repairs, digging ditches, and teaching classrooms, among other vocations. The CWA lasted only a few months and was later replaced by the Works Progress Administration (WPA), which was far more ambitious: like the CWA, it paid citizens to build schools, roads, airports, and building.

But it also oversaw subagencies such as the Federal Art Project, the Federal Writers Project, and the Federal Theater Project, each of which was aimed at providing work to those in the creative arts. Many murals and buildings created by the WPA are scattered around the nation to this day. When the WPA was finally shuttered in 1943 (thanks to the unemployment rate plunging to nearly zero), it had provided gainful employment to nine million Americans.

Of course, the largest and most lasting government creation of this era was the Social Security Act of 1935, which put in place an insurance for the old, the unemployed, and the disabled. For the first time in American history, there was a national program in place to provide a financial safety net to its citizens.

Although the United States was rather late in forming such a program compared to other industrialized nations, it was a political triumph for Roosevelt that such a profound shift in the government's role could win passage.

■ A Regulatory Framework

Although many of Roosevelt's newly created agencies would eventually be dismantled by the Supreme Court, some of them were core to the reshaping of American business and had profound effects on the economy lasting to the present day. Among these were:

National Labor Relations Act (known as Wagner Act of 1935) which encouraged collective bargaining and let to a greatly expanded union membership, peaking in the 1950s.

Securities and Exchange Commission in 1934, which was form to regular new stock issues and stock market trading practices, strictures that were seen as crucial given the debacle of the securities markets in 1929.

Banking Act of 1933 (also known as Glass-Steagall Act), which established deposit insurance and prohibited banks from underwriting or dealing in securities; this act was core to the stability of the financial system for the next seven decades, although the separation between commercial banks and investment banks was eliminated by Congress in 1999, and the weakening of the law contributed substantially to the financial crisis of 2008.

National Recovery Administration (NRA), which had several roles before the Supreme Court struck it down in 1935, including: (1) setting minimum prices and pages in almost all industries; (2) encouraging unions to increase the wages of its membership; and (3) cutting farm production in an effort to raise prices.

The transformation of the federal government from one primarily confined to military and diplomacy matters to one that injected itself into virtually every aspect of daily life was largely thanks to FDR's expansionary policies during his lengthy administration. This was in sharp contrast to the laissez-faire policies of the 1870s, when zero taxes and no meaningful regulation produced a bonanza for the nation's most successful capitalists but at a great collective cost to the majority of other Americans.

■ The Depressing Facts

As shown in Figure 12.9, the peak of the Dow Jones Industrial Average at the end of the Roaring Twenties would not be matched for decades. Although cold statistics can never capture the widespread human suffering, it is still instructive to appreciate the severity of the Great Depression with a smattering of salient figures:

- *Home ownership.* In 1930, 150,000 homeowners lost their property; in 1931, 200,000, and in 1932, 250,000.

- *Gross national product.* The GNP of the United States plummeted 50 percent between 1929 and 1933.

- *Auto manufacturing.* Production of automobiles dropped by 66 percent between 1929 and 1933.

- *Home construction.* Residential construction dropped 80 percent between 1929 and 1933.

- *Agriculture.* Farm income dropped two-thirds between 1929 to 1932, slumping from $6 billion to $2 billion.

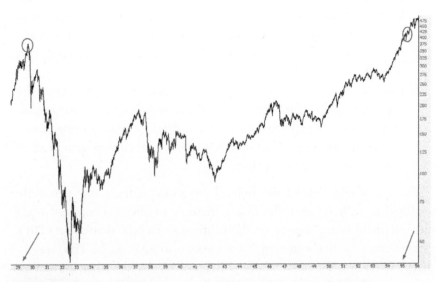

FIGURE 12.9 It would take over two decades for the stock market to return to the peak it experienced in 1929, as shown by this long-term chart of the Dow Jones Industrial Average.

- *Currency.* Demand for new currency was so feeble that the U.S. mint didn't have to mint any nickels in 1932 or 1933, any quarters in 1931 or 1933, any half dollars from 1930 to 1932, and any silver dollars from 1929 to 1933.

- *Income.* The average family income dropped from $2,300 a year to $1,500 a year, a decrease of 33 percent, between 1929 and 1932.

- *The poor.* Over 60 percent of Americans were categorized as "poor" by the federal government in 1933.

- *Deflation.* Wholesale prices declined 33 percent between 1929 and 1933.

Incredibly, one of the most promising prospects for out-of-work Americans was to seek employment in the Soviet Union, which was not suffering nearly as badly as the United States. One Russian trading corporation in New York had a steady flow of 350 applications per day.

■ A Double Dip

The recovery during Roosevelt's first term in office was consistent and powerful, although after years of steady growth, many metrics were still well below those seen in the late 1920s. Real gross domestic product rose on average 9 percent each year between 1933 and 1937, and the unemployment rate shriveled from 25 percent to 12 percent. While a 12 percent unemployment rate was not representative of a surging economy, it was at least a dramatic improvement from one-fourth of the nation's workface being idle.

The most fundamental reason for the resurgence in both the U.S. economy and those around the world can be expressed in a single word: devaluation. By unchaining itself from the gold standard, the United States permitted itself to grow its money supply, and the quantity of U.S. dollars pulsing through the economy grew 42 percent during FDR's first term in office. The economy had been choked off by a lack of credit, and the willingness to devalue the nation's currency permitted ample credit to return.

There was also the important side benefit of deflation's being reversed. During the early 1930s, it was well known that prices for just about everything were steadily going lower. In this environment, there is little reason to spend because the price will just be cheaper later, and there is even less incentive to borrow, since you'll just have to pay back the loan later with more valuable dollars. Thus, in a deflationary environment, the velocity of money slows to a crawl.

By embracing inflation, by way of a greatly enhanced money supply, the United States turned this psychology upside-down. In an environment of positive but contained price inflation, the incentive to buy and borrow returns. This creates the so-called virtuous cycle of an improving economy feeding into itself.

By 1937, a couple of circumstances took place that stopped the recovery in its tracks. First, greatly increased labor costs (brought on through a surge in union membership and potency) created a severe drag on profits and the economy in general; and second, the Federal Reserve decided it was time to clamp down on all the "easy money" flowing through the system and tighten their monetary policy.

The effects on the U.S. economy demonstrated just how fragile it still was: unemployment rose to 19.1 percent by 1938, and the negative effect on employment was so persistent that, even with another world war looming in 1940 (and its millions of job opportunities in the United States), the unemployment rate was still 14.6 percent

The "Roosevelt Recession" was relatively short lived, however, having extinguished itself in less than a year's time. The economy's downturn was modest compared to the ravages of 1929–1933, and the fundamental shift that had been put in place during 1933 and 1934 were still lifting the nation's economic strength for the rest of the decade.

■ The World Returns to War

By 1940, there were 1,042,420 federal employees in the United States, approximately twice the 553,000 employed by the national government during the 1920s. This one simple statistic illustrates just how profoundly the government's role had changed in America due to the Depression and its remedy.

The effects of the nation on the everyday lives of citizens was about to increase even more dramatically as the new decade of the 1940s dawned, since entering the conflicts that had been simmering in Europe and Asia in the final years of the 1930s was soon to become America's destiny.

With the newfound perspective that 10 years' time could provide, Frederick Lewis Allen looked back at the Roaring Twenties and captured the dreamy naiveté of the time in this passage from 1931's *Only Yesterday: An Informal History of the Nineteen Twenties* (Harper and Brothers):

Still the American could spin wonderful dreams of a romantic day when he would sell his Westinghouse common at a fabulous price and live in a great house and have a fleet of shining cars and loll at ease on the sands of Palm Beach.

And when he looked toward the future of his country, he could envision an America set free not from graft, nor from crime, nor from war, nor from control by Wall Street, nor from irreligion, nor from lust, for the utopias of an earlier day left him for the most part skeptical or indifferent; he envisioned an America set free from poverty and toil. He saw a magical order built on the new science and the new prosperity: roads swarming with millions upon millions of automobiles, airplanes darkening the skies, lines of high-tension wire carrying from hilltop to hilltop the power to give life to a thousand labor-saving machines, skyscrapers thrusting above one-time villages, vast cities rising in great geometrical masses of stone and concrete and roaring with perfectly mechanized traffic and smartly dressed men and women spending, spending, spending with the money they had won by being far-sighted enough to foresee, way back in 1929, what was going to happen.

CHAPTER 13

Postwar Prosperity

It is widely recognized that the event that lurched the United States out of its Great Depression was World War II. America has the distinct advantage of being flanked by two great oceans, which allowed it to participate in the war by way of both personnel and materials, but avoid the devastating physical destruction suffered in Europe and Asia. As the war neared its end, many people, intellectuals and average citizens alike, feared that their society would revert back to the misery of the 1930s. What happened instead was profoundly and wholly unexpected.

■ A Return to the Depression?

War is, by its nature, rife with uncertainty, and American was understandably anxious as it suffered through the early stages of World War II. By 1943, however, America had gained a foothold in both the European and Pacific theatres, and the prospect of a successful conclusion to the war began plausible.

At that time, famed economist Paul Samuelson spoke about postwar America. He stated in an article from 1943 entitled "Full Employment after the War," which appeared in Seymour E. Harris's *Postwar Economic Problems* (McGraw Hill):

> When this war comes to an end, more than one out of every two workers will depend directly or indirectly upon military orders. We

shall have some 10 million service men to throw on the labor market. *We shall have to face a difficult reconversion period during which current goods cannot be produced and layoffs may be great.* Nor will the technical necessity for reconversion necessarily generate much investment outlay in the critical period under discussion whatever its later potentialities.

The final conclusion to be drawn from our experience at the end of the last war is inescapable—were the war to end suddenly within the next 6 months, were we again planning to wind up our war effort in the greatest haste, to demobilize our armed forces, to liquidate price controls, to shift from astronomical deficits to even the large deficits of the thirties – then there would be ushered in the greatest period of unemployment and industrial dislocation which any economy has ever faced.

This does not deny that there may be a boom after the war. In this the experts may still be correct. For the release of controls upon demand coupled with plentiful amounts of monetary demand might well give rise to price increase, inventory buying, feverish speculation and all the superficial earmarks of a boom. But it would be the antithesis of a prosperity period, constituting instead a nightmarish combination of the worst features of inflation and deflation. Nor, having spent itself, could it be expected to evolve into healthier channels. *Instead, the final outcome would undoubtedly be a cumulative hyperdeflation from which, at best, we should lose a decade of progress and which, at worst, our democracy would not survive.* (Emphasis added)

This grim view was not held by a fringe element or trifling academic. Samuelson was one of the most foremost economists of the day, going on to be the first American to ever win the Nobel Prize in Economics, and he was described by the Swedish Royal Academy as doing "more than any other contemporary economist to raise the level of scientific analysis in economic theory."

Samuelson's pessimism was buttressed by Swedish economist Gunnar Myrdal, who warned in November 1944 in an article for the *Atlantic Monthly* (with emphasis again added by the author):

The economic uncertainty in America today centers in what is going to happen to this business boom when (1) the Federal demand for war materials diminishes and gradually disappears, and (2) the central control is replaced by free enterprise. Except for Nazi Germany and Communist Russia,—that is, for centrally planned economies,—we have no historical precedent for the stabilization of a boom. *In an unregulated capitalistic society it appears that a boom must always have an end and lapse into crisis and depression.*

... How can chaos be avoided once the enormous inflationary pressure and the balancing controls are simultaneously removed?

The article was titled "Is American Business Deluding Itself?," and the next year, as thrilled as Americans were about the end of a horrible conflict, there was widespread anxiety about just how the United States would transition from a wartime economy to a peacetime economy without plunging back into the despair of another Great Depression. The war, it was hoped, would not serve as simply a pause to the terrible experience of the 1930s.

■ The Great Transition

Naturally, once the war ended, the government cut back spending enormously. In 1944, government spending accounted for a full 44 percent of the nation's gross national product (GNP), but the government's share plunged to a mere 8.9 percent by 1948. It would be logical to assume in such an environment that the vacuum left by the disappearance of such a gargantuan portion of the GNP would cause horrendous economic turmoil, just as Samuelson and Myrdal predicted (see Figure 13.1).

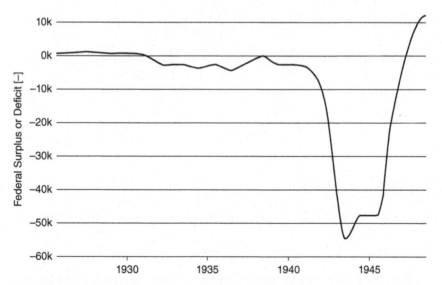

FIGURE 13.1 The drop in government spending was so great that Washington, D.C., actually enjoyed a budget surplus once the war was over.

The principal concern was unemployment. Once the war was over, 20 million people were released from the armed forces and munitions-related employment and flooded the private labor market. Unemployment did indeed rise, but only briefly, and only to a level of 3.9 percent, a rate any modern country's economy would be ecstatic to cite (see Figure 13.2).

So in a small way, the dire predictions came true in the form of a recession in 1946, as the GNP shrank by 12 percent. However, this figure is regarded as more of a statistical quirk than something representative of a genuinely moribund economy, and the United States was about to embark on what would later be considered the golden age of capitalism and by far its most prosperous era.

Investment spending, too, would soar. Consumption of durable goods more than doubled between just 1944 and 1947, and private investment ascended by 223 percent in the same time, with a 500 percent increase in consumer spending related to household items. After years of ascetic living, Americans were eager to catch up on years of spending, and a consumer society was born.

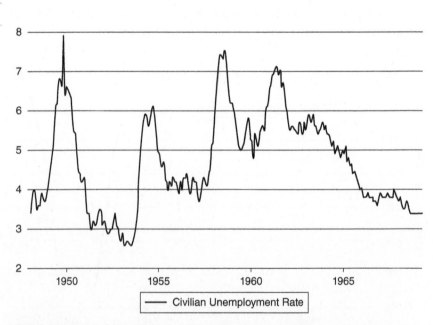

FIGURE 13.2 For decades after World War II, unemployment never got higher than the single digits, with most years enjoying a modest rate of about 4 to 5 percent.

■ Leader of the Free World

Congress wanted to do what it could to ease the transition of the many millions of soldiers shifting from military to civilian life. The keystone legislation passed was the Serviceman's Readjustment Act of 1944, more familiarly known as the GI Bill. The law provided funding for college education, employment, and housing assistance. Congress also provided cash for tuition, educational fees, textbooks, and living expenses for students. It also provided low-interest home loans. The GI Bill laid a solid foundation for the establishment of an educated, prosperous middle class that would fuel the economic boom of the 1950s and 1960s.

With a shortage of both labor and construction materials, homebuilding had been stagnant during the war, and with tens of millions of men coming back to the United States, there was a profound lack of housing. In Chicago, the situation was so dire that 250 old streetcars were auctioned off as temporary homes.

Companies sprang up to address the demand for housing, with the most famous being the Levitt brothers, Alfred and William. The Levitts endeavored to make homebuilding a mass-production affair, similar to the revolution Henry Ford had brought to automobiles by means of the assembly line.

The Levitts sought to control as much of the process as possible. They owned the forests where the wood was grown as well as the mills that turned trees into lumber; they created their own cement, manufactured their own nails, and otherwise absorbed whatever other industries they needed to provide them the components they needed to develop their Levittowns. They broke down the process of building a house into 27 precisely defined steps, and over time their firm became so adept at the mass production of homes that a new house could be constructed in an afternoon.

The Levitts didn't stop at just the homes, however. They built entire cities, complete with shopping centers, schools, churches, swimming pools, parks, and baseball fields. In the 1950s, the Levitts became synonymous with suburbs, and they were by far the largest homebuilders in the nation (see Figure 13.3).

The families living in those mass-produced houses started to mass-produce children as well. Between 1946 and 1964, the "baby boom" took place in America, with an average of 4.6 million babies being born every single year. The babies needed diapers, toys, educational products, school supplies, and many other consumer goods, and this preponderance of demand pulsed

FIGURE 13.3 Levittowns sprung up around the nation, defined by the homogeneity of the houses and the speed at which they were built.

through the American economy, fueling the nation's abundance and creating the most massive middle class any nation had ever witnessed.

The same year as the GI Bill was passed, the Federal Aid-Highway Act provided for government funding to greatly expand the nation's roads, which would be a critical part of the suburbanization of America and the ubiquity of cars in the nation. A total of 41,000 miles were slated to be constructed as a national highway system, and this infrastructure would create critical transportation arteries to support the growth of the country's economy as well as make the long commutes between workplaces in the city and homes in the suburbs feasible.

Two important facts from the wartime years helped make this mass consumption possible: a huge backlog of savings, and a legacy of rationing. During the wartime years, there weren't very many products to buy, so Americans had a record savings rate of 22 percent. By 1945, $1.3 trillion (as measured in modern dollars) had been socked away, and it was now ready to deploy into the economy.

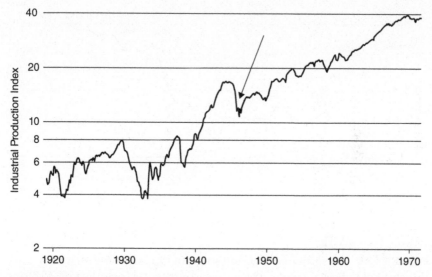

FIGURE 13.4 Except for a brief dip during the transition from a wartime to a peacetime economy, growth in the nation's gross domestic product was steady and robust.

Americans had been deprived of so much during World War II—sugar, meat, gasoline, shoes, bicycles, butter, food, appliances, radios, nylons, cars, housing—almost anything that a modern family would want to acquire had been rationed. Now that wartime privations were a thing of the past, American business lurched into action to satiate the American appetite for buying goods (see Figure 13.4).

■ Lifestyle Transition

The most apparent change taking place in the 1950s and 1960s was the suburbanization of the country. Between 1950 and 1970, 18 of the country's 25 largest cities shrank in population, in spite of the nation's having an explosive growth in citizens. However, the suburban population doubled from 37 million to 74 million.

Farms, too, saw their numbers shrink. In 1947, there were 7.9 million people working the land. A few decades later, only half that amount remained, thanks to the ability to produce far more agricultural products due to mechanization.

As Americans fled to the suburbs, they nurtured the new great American pastime: buying things. When the war ended, there were no more than eight

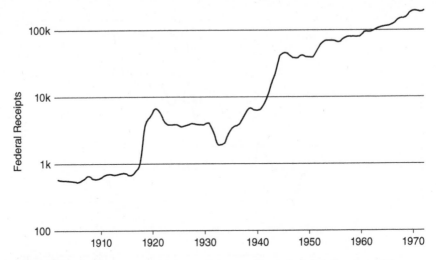

FIGURE 13.5 The economy's overall strength can be plainly seen with this chart of federal receipts, which grew consistently from the mid-1930s through the 1970s.

shopping centers in the entire country. By 1960, there were 3,840. During the same time span, the GNP leapt higher: $200 billion in 1940, $300 billion in 1950, and over half a trillion dollars by 1960. There may have been an ideological debate between communism and capitalism during the Cold War, but the numbers plainly showed which side was prospering (see Figure 13.5).

America was not the only capitalist nation in the world, of course, but it had the distinct advantage of suffering no damage from the war. Japan and Europe had to rebuild from the ashes and rubble of the conflict. America, however, merely had to convert their well-established military infrastructure into civilian manufacturing. For this reason, America took its place as the world's car maker, quadrupling its auto production in the 10 years from 1946 to 1955.

The nation's cars would enjoy even more places to go with the passage of the Highway Act of 1956, which allocated a $26 billion budget to the creation of 40,000 miles of interstate highway.

■ End of an Era

America's isolation from the rest of the world, and the relatively pristine state of its infrastructure at war's end, would not persist forever as an advantage. As difficult as it was for Japan and Europe to rebuild, in a way starting with a clean slate ultimately became an advantage for America's economic competition, and America's golden age of capitalism would swiftly wither away by 1970. The postwar prosperity was over.

A combination of factors came into play by this time. An oil embargo, a massive bear market in equities, and a worldwide energy crisis would all stifle the economic prosperity. America emerged from a costly, unpopular war in Vietnam, and the products from Japan and Germany—particularly automobiles—began to appeal to American consumers, who until that point had purchased American cars almost exclusively.

By the mid-1970s, America would begin to look like the has-been of the world. Its manufacturing states had become a rust belt; its economic surpluses had turned into shocking deficits; its dominance in innovation had been squandered. The sensational success of the 1950s and 1960s would give way to the gloomy malaise of the 1970s. Corporate America's day in the sun would eventually return, by after nearly a quarter-century of virtually unchallenged prosperity, it was time for America to suffer through a decade of doldrums.

CHAPTER 14

Energy, Politics, and War

N o other commodity in the modern age has affected the world stage as much as oil. As a basis for any modern economy, crude oil is second only to water as the liquid perceived as vital to life, and the global political stage—particularly since 1970—has been largely shaped by the price movement of oil in the financial markets. No wars have been fought over corn, pork bellies, or gold. In modern rhetoric, oil has been made the figurative equal of blood.

■ The Birth of OPEC

The popular perception of the Organization of the Petroleum Exporting Countries (OPEC) is that it is an all-powerful cartel of Middle Eastern countries that has unilaterally set the worldwide price of crude oil to maximize profits, to the chagrin of industrialized Western countries beholden to its decisions. The truth is far afield from this set of common assumptions.

The model for OPEC is actually an American creation called the Texas Railroad Commission (TRC), which was established late in the nineteenth century in order to, as the name suggests, regulate railroads. As the twentieth century dawned, and the decades passed, the domain of the TRC began to spread far beyond just rail lines, particularly with respect to energy resources. In spite of its name, the modern-day TRC holds sway over many local industries with one curious exception: railroads.

The TRC's control of production levels in the oil industry gave it tight control over oil prices for most of the twentieth century. Although it was established in Texas, the TRC was a crucial arbiter for the "Seven Sisters"—the big U.S. and Dutch oil producers—since no other body was so influential in controlling the price of crude oil. The countries outside of this domain closely studied the TRC's practices and effectiveness, since they had ambitions of their own about being bigger players in the global energy markets.

For much of the twentieth century, oil was a relatively cheap, plentiful commodity, and the focus of the TRC was to suppress production levels to avoid a repeat of the crash in oil prices that Texas suffered in the 1930s, when a barrel of oil could be had for as little as 25 cents. The principal oil-producing states of the United States (Texas, Louisiana, Oklahoma) had excess oil capacity, and the TRC had to regulate the flow in order to keep the price high enough for industry profitability. This was not always an easy task, since it is always tempting for any member of a cartel to break ranks and increase their own profits by selling more of the product in question, but the TRC had been a consistent enough enforcer of production ratios to garner the obedience of the oil producers in its domain.

From the end of World War II until the end of the 1960s, the nominal price for oil remained within a relatively narrow band of $2.50 to $3 per barrel, which in inflation-adjusted terms spans from $17 to $19. Oil and its by-products were typically American, and always cheap, which led to a boom in large, gas-guzzling American automobiles. There was little need for energy efficiency on either the road or in gas-heated households. America had more oil than it knew what to do with.

Around this time, in 1960, OPEC was founded by five member countries: Iran, Iraq, Saudi Arabia, Kuwait, and Venezuela. So even from its inception, OPEC was not an entirely Middle East entity. In the decade that followed its founding, other countries joined the OPEC organization: Algeria, Libya, Nigeria, Qatar, Indonesia, and the United Arab Emirates. So while OPEC had a strong Arab presence, it actually spanned three different continents (see Figure 14.1).

It was also not omnipotent. On the contrary, OPEC was itself largely at the mercy of the TRC's price-setting, and infighting among OPEC's own member nations did nothing to boost the selling price of their oil. Throughout the 1960s, a barrel of oil was very consistently about $3 per barrel in nominal terms, but taking inflation into account, OPEC members were getting less and less for their commodity.

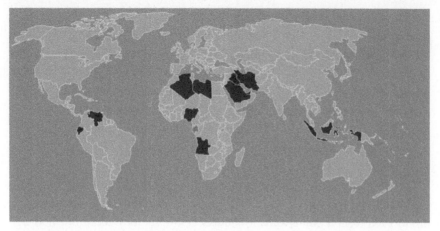

FIGURE 14.1 OPEC is not strictly within the Middle East, but instead has member countries on multiple continents.

As the 1960s came to a close, the United States had its own "peak oil" moment. The amount of oil that U.S. producers were able to take from the ground started dropping, and restricting the output from U.S. oil producers disappeared as a concern relevant to commodity pricing. In March 1971, the TRC made a surprising announcement: for the first time in its history, it would place no restrictions on the amount of oil that producers could sell.

The implication was clear: the United States was putting as much oil on the market as it could find, and the rest of the oil-producing world now had a golden opportunity to fulfill a need for the remaining demand.

■ War and Embargo

A series of unrelated events in the early 1970s conspired to send prices for oil skyrocketing to levels never seen, and at a pace no one could anticipate.

The first event was TRC's abandonment of production restrictions. It would render the TRC largely irrelevant to energy prices from that moment forward.

In 1971, the Nixon administration abandoned the direct convertibility of U.S. dollars into gold. This abandonment of the Bretton Woods gold standard meant the value of the U.S. dollar began to fall immediately, setting off asset inflation across the board. In just a couple of years after the decoupling of the dollar from gold, lumber prices increased 42 percent, food prices nearly doubled, and oil would make an ascent that would completely alter the geopolitical world stage.

When the Nixon administration took the United States off the gold standard, it also put into place a number of price controls, including a government-sanctioned selling price for domestic crude oil. One curious twist to this was that the U.S. enforced the pricing mechanism only for "old" domestic oil—that is, oil that had already been discovered. Newly discovered oil would be permitted to float in price with the rest of worldwide crude oil market. U.S. oil producers were thus compelled to simply not sell "old" oil, creating a scarcity in the market that normally would not have existed (see Figure 14.2).

Nixon's price controls distorted the normal mechanisms that allow a free market to function, and early in 1973, everyday Americans were already starting to have trouble filling their gas tanks. Some stations could not find any wholesale gasoline. As the *New York Times* reported on June 8 of that year:

> With more than 1,000 filling stations closed for lack of gasoline, according to a Government survey, and with thousands more rationing the amount a motorist may buy, the shortage is becoming a palpable fact of life for millions in this automobile-oriented country.

PANIC, PROSPERITY, AND PROGRESS

FIGURE 14.2 Americans started facing something they had never dealt with before: scarcity. Almost overnight, gas stations found themselves unable to supply a product they were expected to have in abundance.

Crude oil was about to get a shock much greater than what the United States had already inflicted upon itself with inflation: on October 6, 1973, Syria and Egypt commenced an attack on their neighbor, Israel. Not only was it a surprise attack, but it was scheduled on the holiest day of the Jewish calendar, Yom Kippur.

Israel frantically scrambled their aircraft, equipped their planes with bombs and missiles, and went on full nuclear alert. The United States voiced its support for Israel and made clear it would continue to supply Israel with the arms it needed to defend itself.

In retaliation, the Arab subset of OPEC, named OAPEC, announced an embargo on oil exports to specific countries that, in their opinion, supported the Israeli state. The sudden elimination of imported oil from these major producers meant that over 7 percent of regular oil output was now unavailable. This, coupled with the tension that surrounded the war, pushed crude oil prices much higher that autumn. Making the situation even worse, the Persian Gulf countries announced on January 1, 1974, that the price at which they would be selling their oil would be doubled.

It is no coincidence that the oil shock of the autumn of 1973 pushed the United States into a recession, which officially commenced in November 1973. Between October 1973 and January 1974—a mere four months—oil prices quadrupled. With worldwide economies depending on energy as the basis for day-to-day functioning, an unexpected 300 percent increase in a daily energy expense was a terrible blow.

The Yom Kippur War was very short lived, but its effects were long lasting. Secretary of State Henry Kissinger negotiated with Israel and got them to agree to withdraw from politically sensitive parts of Syria. Although negotiations were still ongoing in early 1974, the prospect of a settlement with Israel was sufficient for OAPEC to lift the oil embargo in March 1974.

Although the war itself was done, the impression that OPEC had made on the world—and, in turn, on itself—was permanent. Only recently had OPEC felt largely helpless in its role on the world energy scene. Now it found that it could singlehandedly cause a massive upward shift in oil prices and provide itself a powerful position at the bargaining table. The resentment Western countries and their citizens felt toward OPEC's actions would shape the political landscape for decades to come.

The stock market suffered from these actions as well. Early in 1973, the Dow had peaked at 1,067.20 on the 11th of January. By December 5, it reached 783.60, a loss of over one-quarter of its value. Indeed, for equities

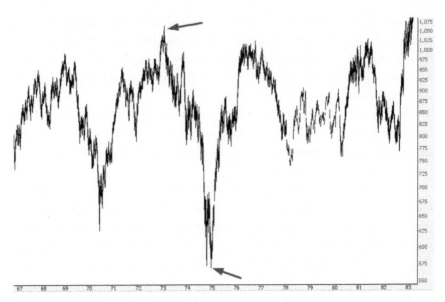

FIGURE 14.3 The Dow Jones in the 1970s swung wildly between about 600 and 1,000. During a single two-year period, marked with arrows, the Dow lost about 40 percent of its value, largely due to the energy crisis and its accompanying recession.

markets, most of the 1970s was a choppy, violent affair, with the Dow finally bottoming on December 9, 1974, at a low price of 570 (see Figure 14.3).

One of the best-known artifacts from the terrible stock market of the 1970s was the *Business Week* cover story of August 13, 1979, which proclaimed "The Death of Equities" (as is so often the case, the "cover curse" applies here, since *Business Week*'s cover preceded a sixteen-fold increase in equities over the next couple of decades in one of the most "alive" equity markets in financial history).

■ Don't Be "Fuelish"

The combination of rising prices for almost all goods (inflation) and a severe damper put on the economy by way of higher energy prices (stagnation) led to a new term that summed up much of the economic zeitgeist of the 1970s: *stagflation*.

The only good result from 1973's oil shock was that the Western world was finally forced to conserve energy. This conservation took many forms: smaller, more fuel-efficient vehicles; development of solar, wind, and geothermal power; increased insulation in buildings; lower speed limits on freeways; and increased public awareness about living a relatively energy-efficient lifestyle.

Lining up for gas was a relatively novel activity for citizens of the United States, who were for the most part wholly unfamiliar with rationing in a land that typically had so much abundance. "Odd/Even" rationing was put into place in some parts of the country, in which the last digit of a car's license plate would dictate whether or not one would be allowed to get gas on a given day (based on whether that digit was odd or even). In spite of such rationing, gas stations with nothing available to pump were relatively common. In late February 1974, about one-fifth of the nation's gas stations were completely out of fuel.

The federal government did not know how long such shortages would persist, so out of an abundance of caution, it designed gas-rationing coupons. The situation never got so bad as to require the distribution of such coupons, and the presence of the coupons as an official "currency" to make a purchase would surely have harmed the national psyche even more, so plans for such scrip were not revealed to the public at the time (see Figure 14.4).

The federal government also established the United States Strategic Petroleum Reserve in 1975 and, in a more sweeping move, it also created

FIGURE 14.4 Gas rationing coupons, as designed by the federal government, were never put into circulation.

an entirely new cabinet-level department called the Department of Energy. Daylight Savings Time, formerly used in various countries around the world only during times of war, was also brought back. In the United States, it was made a year-round affair from January 6, 1974, to February 23, 1975, as the country exercised any creative ways to curb its appetite for crude oil.

Energy shortages and nascent conservation efforts were not confined to the United States. Other industrialized nations had to find ways to reduce their own energy consumption. Switzerland, Norway, Germany, Italy, and the United Kingdom all banned the acts of boating, flying, or driving on Sundays. A resident of the Netherlands who used more than their government-allotted portion of electricity could face jail time. And, in the chill of Britain's winter, Prime Minister Heath asked that fellow Britons heat only a single room of their house and congregate there.

Things took a comic turn when a shortage of toilet paper took place in Japan and the United States. A rumor started going around that, since oil was required to run the machinery used in paper manufacturing, a wide variety of paper products including, importantly, toilet paper, would soon be in short supply. Widely watched television personality Johnny Carson inadvertently exacerbated the situation when, on December 19, 1973, he joked about this shortage. A three-week run on bathroom tissue swept the nation before people realized grocery shelves were in fact well stocked.

Although it would take years for people to change their habits, the alteration in buying patterns (toward more energy-efficient cars and products) and living habits (toward conservation) would become significant enough to make the entire economy far more fuel efficient. These efforts also made oil-importing neighbors less susceptible to interruptions of outside energy. The general shift from "gas-guzzling" U.S. cars to fuel-efficient imports, particularly from Japan, would also cause sweeping changes in the manufacturing world order, as it laid the groundwork for Japan's own global ascendency in the 1980s.

■ Iran and Iraq

High energy costs would be seen as a simple fact of life as the 1970s progressed, and prices were soon about to reach their highest levels (in inflation-adjusted terms) based on two new, related geopolitical events.

The first of these was centered in Iran, where the shah of the country, Mohammed Reza Pahlavi, fled a growing revolutionary uprising in early

1979. A new leader, the Ayatollah Khomeini, took his place, and the turmoil in the country severely disrupted what had previously been a smoothly operating energy producer. The regime change in the country, accompanied by the seizing of dozens of United States citizens as hostages, distressed both the citizens and the leadership of the United States.

President Jimmy Carter caused oil prices to move even higher by declaring that the United States would no longer accept oil from Iran. The combination of losing an important exporter of oil coupled with the still-active price controls on U.S.-produced oil made the bad situations of high oil prices even worse. Carter partly addressed this situation by introducing a phased deregulation of oil prices (which had been in place for eight years already), which would ultimately be wholly dismantled by Ronald Reason's first year in office.

Most automobile drivers in 1979 had been through the gas crisis of 1973–1974, and memories of rationing and long lines sent them rushing back to gas stations to fill their tanks. Thus, the American people once again found themselves using gas for no other reason than to idle their cars in a line of other cars waiting to get more fuel. The easing of price restrictions on U.S. producers eventually provided some relief, since it encouraged domestic exploration and refining of oil supplies, such as the massive oil reserves in Alaska.

Iran was directly involved in the second energy-related upheaval of this time by way of the Iran-Iraq war. Historically, the two countries had fallen on opposites sides of the Cold War, with the United States supporting Iran and the Soviet Union supporting Iraq. Alliances had weakened greatly by 1980, however, and the nations were fighting each other directly without any overt support from the Cold War rivals.

They were well equipped, however, with stockpiled munitions received over the years from their respective allies, and the United States, eager to avoid an Iraqi victory, did supply Iran with nonmilitary equipment as well as some important diplomatic concessions.

At this point, oil production from both Iran and Iraq had practically ceased. Prices for oil climbed from $15.85 in the spring of 1979 up to $39.50 in the spring of 1980. It was, in inflation-adjusted terms, a tremendous boon to revenue for the rest of OPEC, as income would reach levels that had never been seen and, even as of this writing, decades later, has not been witnessed since. Saudi Arabia in particular, far from the scourge of war, yet sitting on the largest oil reserves in the world, found itself flooded with cash from oil importers all over the world.

As it had in 1973, the *New York Times* reported on May 5 about a nervous and irritable public that lined up at U.S. gas stations across the country:

It's horrible; it's just like it was five years ago.... Throughout much of California today, and especially so in the Los Angeles area, there were scenes reminiscent of the nation's 1974 gas crisis. Lines of autos, vans, pickup trucks, and motor homes, some of the lines were a half mile or longer, backup up from service stations in a rush for gasoline that appeared to be the result of a moderately tight supply of fuel locally.

One irony of the gas lines was that Americans wasted about 150,000 barrels of oil per day just sitting in the line itself. The psychological panic about gas shortages was itself a contributor to the shortages.

American attitudes toward OPEC, the Middle East, and oil companies (both foreign and domestic) hardened into resentment and cynicism. A respected telephone poll from the Associated Press and NBC News indicated that over half the nation's adults thought the energy shortages were a hoax designed merely to boost oil company profits.

One section of the country that had no problem with high oil prices was the region that had plenty of oil under its own ground: Louisiana, Wyoming, Oklahoma, Texas, and Alaska. All of these states enjoyed sharply rising housing prices, booming downtown business districts, and overflowing tax coffers. As with OPEC, it was a boom-time for oil states in the United States, and with deregulation under way, it made much more business sense to seek out and extract as much oil as practical.

What these states and the OPEC did not anticipate was that the fantastic prices of 1980 were about to give way to plummeting oil values for years to come.

Several factors would come into play to diminish prices. First, with energy prices so high, oil explorers had unprecedented incentive to seek out new deposits, and as discoveries were made, increasingly large amounts of new oil would be made available to the market.

Second, a matrix of conservation efforts were beginning to pay off for energy consumers. Better-insulated homes and offices, smaller and more fuel-efficient cars, and more cost-conscious behavior conspired to significantly reduce the amount of energy any given economy, either a household or a nation, would need to function and grow.

As consumption began to dry up, prices started to fall, and Saudi Arabia took the lead in reducing its own production to try to halt the plunging prices. Between 1981 and 1985, Saudi Arabia shut down three-quarters of its production capacity, yet oil prices kept falling (although they surely would have fallen faster had the Saudis done nothing).

OPEC, however, is not a true cartel, because it cannot enforce production quotas on its members. The less affluent nations were increasingly desperate to garner as much revenue as they could, oversupply be damned, so they made no reductions in their output. Mexico and Venezuela, both of which had enjoyed brief periods of financial abundance, now found themselves heading toward sovereign bankruptcy. Thus, the Saudis were on their own in trying to keep oil supplies contained. The other nations were selling as much oil as they could extract from the ground (see Figure 14.5).

By August 1985, the Saudis were weary of singlehandedly trying to stem the plummeting price of oil by denying themselves export revenues, so they ramped up production again. This sent the already-depressed price of $27/barrel to beneath $10/barrel in 1986. OPEC countries as well as oil-producing districts in the United States were now part of a relatively depressed industry. In former boom towns such as Houston, "see-through" office buildings became the norm, and overbuilt downtowns were vacated by tenants that were no longer able or willing to pay the rent.

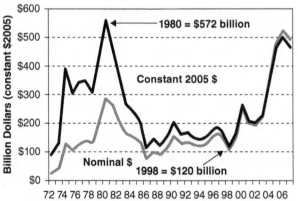

FIGURE 14.5 Oil revenues peaked in 1980, and once the trend of lower prices took hold, revenues both domestically and abroad began to plummet. Low prices for oil were the norm for much of the 1980s.

■ Invasion of Kuwait

The war between Iran and Iraq dragged on for almost the entire decade of the 1980s. A ceasefire was finally signed in August 1988, and both countries had suffered devastating losses in both life and property.

Iraq was deeply in debt with Kuwait and Saudi Arabia, who had each provided substantial financial support in Iraq's prosecution of the war. As battered as the country was, Iraq pleaded with its creditors to forgive the debt, but they refused to do so. Like Germany after World War I, Iraq found itself at war's end both badly damaged and deeply in debt to neighboring countries.

In 1989, Iraq turned its attention toward Kuwait, as it claimed that Kuwait itself should belong to Iraq. Its claim had some basis in history, as Kuwait had been part of the Ottoman Empire, but the United Kingdom concocted a new border for the independent nation in 1922, leaving Iraq with only a small sliver of land to provide access to the Persian Gulf. As such, Iraq was, now with Kuwait's borders defined, virtually a landlocked state. Kuwait enjoyed most of the coastline now, with its access to the Gulf and the corresponding ability to load oil tankers with the precious commodity (see Figure 14.6).

Iraq claimed that Kuwait was abusing its role as an oil producer in at least two ways. First, by overproducing beyond formerly agreed quotas, worsening the depressed price of oil (and, thus, Iraq's vital oil revenues); and, second, by "slant-drilling"—that is, drilling underground, at a sharp angle, so as to extract from oil wells that were beneath Iraqi land. This was, in Iraq's eyes, blatant theft of a crucial national resource.

As the world focused its attention on the massive changes happening in eastern Europe in 1989 (culminating in the removal of the Berlin Wall and the subsequent dismantling of the Soviet Union), relations in the Middle East were becoming sour between countries. Many non-Iraqis inside Iraq were subjected to bigotry and violence, and former allies such as Egypt took offense at Iraq's poor treatment of its expatriate citizens.

Iraq was not concerned about its reputation on the world stage with respect to human rights. It needed revenue, and it wanted to lay claim to the Kuwaiti state, so in July 1990, it threatened military action. Iraq moved 30,000 troops to the Kuwait border, and U.S. naval forces were placed on alert in the Persian Gulf. These events drew little in the way of attention from the general public at the time, although crude oil prices in futures markets began to move higher as tensions started to mount.

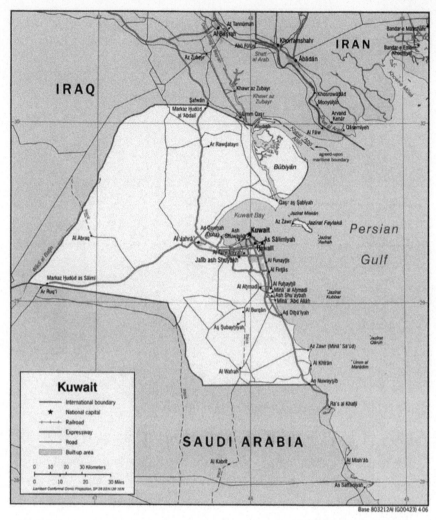

FIGURE 14.6 In spite of its tiny size, Kuwait had a far more substantial coastline than Iraq, which was virtually a landlocked country.

Diplomatic discussions were still being held between Iraq and its neighbors, and in spite of Iraq's saber rattling, it seemed that a diplomatic solution could be found. Late in July 1990, Saddam Hussein, the leader of Iraq, met with U.S. Ambassador April Glaspie. She told the Iraqi delegation, "We have no opinion on these Arab affairs." Hussein took this as an implicit pledge that the United States would not interfere with any action Iraq took against Kuwait (see Figure 14.7).

FIGURE 14.7 Saddam Hussein, former leader of Iraq.

Before taking action, Hussein demanded $10 billion from Kuwait as payment for the oil it believed had been stolen via slant oil drilling. Kuwait was willing to negotiate on this point, and it came close to matching the demand by offering $9 billion.

However, it would seem Iraq was not genuinely interested in reaching a financial settlement, because in spite of the relatively small distance between the positions of the two parties, Iraq ordered an immediate invasion. On August 2, 1990, Iraq commenced the bombing of Kuwait City.

The tiny nation of Kuwait was no match for Iraq's gigantic military machine, battle-hardened by eight years of war with Iran. Besides the small size of Kuwait's army and air force, it had—incredibly—decided to stand down its military forces on July 19, in spite of Iraq's obvious troop movements and belligerent posturing. Iraq had an army of nearly a million men, versus Kuwait's 16,000. Iraq also had 4,500 tanks, hundreds of military aircraft and helicopters, and 20 brigades of special-forces units.

It took only 12 hours for Iraq to overrun Kuwait's defenses. The Kuwaiti royal family fled their country, and most of the ministers and cabinet members had fled south of the border to the safety of Saudi Arabia. Iraq was now firmly in control of Kuwait, and it moved its massive army to the border dividing Saudi Arabia and Kuwait, suggesting that perhaps even the oil-rich giant to the South might be next to be invaded by Hussein's forces.

The world's reaction, both diplomatically and financially, was swift. Equity markets slumped, while crude oil prices shot higher. The capture of Kuwait was worrisome enough, but the prospect of any diminishment of Saudi oil was far worse. The United Nations Security Council acted with unusual resolve and alacrity, passing Resolution 660 (condemning the invasion and demanding the withdrawal of troops), 661 (placing economic sanctions on Iraq), and 665 (authorizing a naval blockade in the Persian Gulf) within days of the invasion (see Figure 14.8).

Hussein, perhaps surprised at the reaction of the West, took to the radio airwaves on August 12, suggesting that Iraq would be willing to withdraw

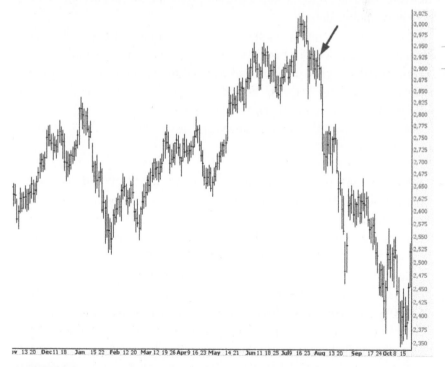

213

ENERGY, POLITICS, AND WAR

FIGURE 14.8 After the invasion of Kuwait, marked with an arrow, the Dow Jones Industrial Average lost over 20 percent of its value in only about three months.

in troops, but only in exchange for the withdrawal of Israel from Palestine, Syria, and Lebanon. He also stated that the United States would need to withdraw troops from Saudi Arabia. The United States refused, making clear that the demand for Iraq to leave Kuwait was conditioned on nothing, and that they would not make concessions to see Iraq leave Kuwait.

Apprehension grew about Westerners that were being held inside Iraq. The Iraqi government was known for its use of "human shields"—that is, placing civilians in militarily important locations as a disincentive to attack. There were about 350 Japanese inside Iraq, as well as, famously, a young British boy who appeared on television with Saddam Hussein.

The boy was obviously nervous as Hussein tousled his hair and said, "We hope your presence as guests here will not be for too long. Your presence here, and in other places, is meant to prevent the scourge of war." The insinuation Hussein was making on worldwide television was clear.

As preparations for war began, financial markets continued to be very nervous. The last major war America had been involved with had been in Vietnam, and painful memories from that war, and its conclusion, loomed large in the public debate.

Newspapers and nightly reports were filled with unsettling stories about the size and aptitude of Hussein's military forces. Iraq was said to store chemical and biological weapons and was said to have no reservations about using them. America began to consider the prospect of being at war for years with a powerful, deeply entrenched enemy.

An account from the Reuters newswire of October 26, 1990, captures some of the angst:

> Renewed fears of a Persian Gulf war swept world oil and financial markets today after the U.S. signaled readiness to almost double its forces against Iraq to more than 400,000 troops.... Concern grew over reports that Kuwait's oil fields have been mined by Iraq's occupation forces, which Washington says have been heavily reinforced.... U.S. officials say they are moving hundreds of Abrams main battle tanks from German bases to the Gulf in the next few weeks.... Iraq, with nearly 5,000 Soviet tanks, has a five-to-one advantage over the Americans so far. Military experts say devastating air power gives the U.S. a strike edge, but tanks would be decisive in holding desert territory.... The Financial Times reported that Iraqi military engineers have attached explosives to 300 of Kuwait's 1,000 oil wells as a precaution against any attacks by the U.S.-led multinational force....

The news wire went on to account for the discomfort the West was feeling with respect to facing a vicious enemy:

Former British Prime Minster Edwin Heath was quoted as saying Iraqi President Saddam Hussein would use chemical weapons and would mistreat foreign captives if attacked. Iraq has one of the world's deadliest arsenals of poison gas and still holds 2,000 hostages, Western and Japanese men, some as "human shields" at strategic targets. U.S. intelligence chief William Webster said there was evidence that Iraqi troops had protective equipment to operate in a chemical war.

Thus, in the months leading up to the war, the prospect of a muscular and unscrupulous enemy armed with long-outlawed weapons gnawed at the psyche of the United States and its coalition partners.

The Gulf War was unique in a number of respects, but one of them was that the United States stated early on that those who would benefit most from the war—principally, Saudi Arabia—would also be the ones to bankroll it. The Saudis did not hesitate to pledge the billions of dollars necessary to repel a threat like Hussein and his army from their border.

It was also unique in that the United States was not acting alone; it assembled armed forces from 34 different countries, ranging from Australia to the United Kingdom. Countries without standing armies, such as Japan and Germany, instead contributed financially ($10 billion and $6.6 billion, respectively). Although the United States was the public face of the coalition, and accounted of nearly three-quarters of the soldiers, it was getting a lot of help, both financially and militarily.

On November 29, 1990, Iraq was put on notice via UN Resolution 678 that it had until January 15, 1991, to get out of Kuwait. If it did not, it would be removed by force. In the meantime, the Coalition forces would maintain the military operation Desert Shield, which was meant to ensure the defense of Saudi Arabia and its precious oil fields.

■ The Hundred-Hour War

The deadline came and went, and Iraq had not budged from Kuwait. On January 17, 1991, the aerial bombardment against Iraq commenced. The coalition executed 100,000 individual sorties, dumping nearly 100,000 tons of bombs on Iraq. Desert Shield had now given way to Desert Storm, and the U.S.-led forces sought to batter the country for weeks prior to a ground invasion, to "soften up" the resistance as much as possible.

The air attacks were executed in three specific phases, each with different goals: the first was targeted at Iraqi's Air Force and anti-aircraft firepower; the second was against command and communications facilities, in order to break up the chain of command and the ability of the military machine to stay in contact; and the third was against various naval facilities, weapons research centers, and Scud missile launchers. The last of these, the Scud missiles, had been used periodically against Israel, and the concern was that Iraq might launch a substantial attack against America's ally with the remaining Scuds.

In the days leading up to the January 15 deadline, traders in the energy markets feared that, in the event of a shooting war, oil would ascend to heights never seen before. Although oil had bolted from about $17 to $46 in 1990 following the invasion, there was now talk of oil trading over $100 per barrel, since a major Middle East conflict could cause widespread shortages. The uncertainty of the weeks and months ahead led to rampant speculation about just how serious the oil price spike could be.

On the contrary, at virtually the moment coalition aircraft began bombing Iraq, oil prices went into a free-fall. It was swiftly apparent that Iraq was going to be pummeled, at least during these initial stages of the war, and the coalition was suffering virtually no damage in counterattacks. On January 18, the day after the attacks began, the *Los Angeles Times* reported on equities registering their second-largest point gain in market history:

> Hopes that the Persian Gulf War would be brief sent Wall Street stocks soaring Thursday. The Dow Jones Industrial average closed up 114.60, or 4.6% ... today's Nikkei index soared 1,004.11, or 4.5% ... in Frankfurt, the DAX index jumped 99.99 points, a record 7.6% ... gold stocks were pummeled ... gold for February delivery plunged $30.10 on New York's Commodity Exchange, to $374.40 an ounce, as President Bush called the initial phase of the Persian Gulf war a success. It was one of the largest one-day declines in gold prices in the market's history.

Weeks of aerial bombardment continued, and finally, on February 24, 1991, operation Desert Saber began: the ground attack. Two Marine divisions and an Army Battalion moved toward Kuwait City. The shell-shocked Iraqi troops that they encountered put up half-hearted resistance, having

FIGURE 14.9 General Norman Schwarzkopf, flanked by Colin Powel and Paul Wolfowitz.

been pummeled by bombs for over a month and now apparently eager to surrender (see Figure 14.9).

Instead of facing years of ground warfare, the Americans completed their liberation of Kuwait in the span of 100 hours. Hussein ordered a retreat on February 27, 1991, and President Bush declared Kuwait to be liberated. During its retreat, the Iraqi forces employed a "scorched earth" policy, setting nearly 700 oil wells ablaze, and surrounding the blazes with mines to make them difficult to extinguish. Having lost Kuwait, Hussein decided to create an environmental disaster in its wake.

■ An Uneasy Partnership

Until the day arrives that the principal energy source is something other than oil, it seems like that the volatility and political gamesmanship surrounding crude oil will continue indefinitely. The curious combination of ancient religious schisms, political alliances, economic dependencies, and environment sensitivities all combine to make for an extremely dynamic, and at times toxic, combination on the world stage.

From the perspective of the financial markets, it is interesting to note how significant events are sometimes telegraphed weeks before they are brought to the attention of the general public. The Iraqi invasion of Kuwait, for example, was perceived as a shocking surprise to the world when it happened on August 2, 1990. An examination of movements in the futures markets for crude oil, however, show a strong upsurge in prices, accompanied by significantly higher volume, several weeks before the attack actually took place.

There is little doubt that crude oil will continue to hold a singular place among commodities for the foreseeable future. Its importance to industrialized economies will give it powerful sway in global politics that other financial instruments simply cannot possess. If the day comes that cheap, reliable, alternate energy sources are made widely available, a sea change is likely to take place on the world stage that will undo many of the political structures and alliances that were formed in the last half of the twentieth century.

CHAPTER 15

Precious Metals and the Destruction of a Billionaire

The stunning bull market in precious metals in the late 1970s, followed by its swift collapse, has a fascinating and remarkable history. The roots of the event date back to the dark days of the Great Depression, when President Roosevelt issued Executive Order 6102, which outlawed the "hoarding" (that is, the ownership in almost any form) of gold by any person or other entity within the United States.

Prior to this order, gold was intricately intertwined in the nation's currency. U.S. dollars were convertible into gold on demand, and this convertibility had helped constrict the velocity of money severely. Roosevelt recognized that inflating the money supply was essential to turning the economy around, so he took the extraordinary step of criminalizing private ownership of gold as one of the steps to decouple the precious metal from the nation's currency.

The president signed the order on April 5, 1933, only weeks after his first term in office began, and it gave the nation's citizens until May 1 to turn in all their gold in exchange for $20.67 per ounce in cash. This seems like an extraordinarily low price today, but in inflated-adjusted dollars, it equals about $400 per ounce. Some exceptions were made to the order: those who used gold as a component of a professional service (such as artists, dentists, and jewelers) could buy and use gold, and rare, collectible coins were spared the melt-down process that other coins would undergo.

Although they were supposed to obediently turn in their coins, the wealthier citizens of America who had meaningful amounts of gold simply stored it away overseas, usually in Switzerland. In spite of the severe penalties sanctioned in the order, there actually wasn't a single successful prosecution of anyone in the country for violating the President's edict.

■ Melting Down Saint-Gaudens

The U.S. Mint had been producing gold coins, as it had for many years, including a $20 gold coin designed in 1907 by famed sculptor August Saint-Gaudens. The coin was called a Double Eagle, and it is considered to this day the most beautiful coin ever minted by the United States. It was 90 percent gold and 10 percent copper, and its gold content was equal to its $20 face value (see Figure 15.1).

Many of the coins had been minted since the design was completed in 1907, and they were still being produced by the U.S. Mint even after the executive order banning gold had been signed by the president. The new coins were not distributed, however, and by late 1934 all but two of the coins had been ordered to be melted down. The two officially saved coins were presented to the U.S. National Numismatic Collection and, as far as the U.S. Mint knew, those were the only 1933 Saint-Gaudens Double Eagle coins in existence, as the others had been assumed melted back into gold bars already.

After May 1 passed and the Treasury had paid everyone their $20.67/ounce for the gold that was turned in, the Treasury ratcheted up the official price of the metal to $35 per ounce, an increase of 70 percent. This had two immediate effects: first, it meant that all the citizens who had dutifully turned in their gold found themselves with paper money that was suddenly worth a lot less, and second, the government had an instant 70 percent profit on all the gold it had bought from the citizens. The profits were used to fund the Exchange Stabilization Fund that was sanctioned by the Gold Reserve Act of 1934.

One individual who failed to submit his substantial gold holdings (5,000 ounces) to the government was an attorney named Frederick Campbell. The federal government charged Campbell for failing to turn in his gold, but the judge refused to prosecute Campbell with the crime based on a

FIGURE 15.1   The face of the famed Saint-Gaudens gold coin, originally minted in 1907.

technicality: since the order was signed the President Roosevelt, as opposed to the secretary of the Treasury, it was deemed invalid. Campbell did ultimately have to sell his gold to the Treasury, but he did not have to endure a criminal prosecution for his initial failure to do so.

As for the Saint-Gaudens coins, those will return to our story later in this chapter, and many years after 1934 was over.

■ The Hunt Fortune

Not that many years before the Great Depression, the seeds of a great American family fortune were being planted. Haroldson Lafayette (H. L.) Hunt was born in 1889 in Illinois, and although his father provided a very comfortable existence to H. L. in his teenage years, the boy decided to strike out on his own. So, at only 16 years of age, he headed west and took up whatever jobs he could find. H.L. was a logger, a farm worker, and even a mule team driver—but all the while, he was developing his real proficiency: playing poker.

H. L. was intellectually sharp and had a successful gambler's instinct for risk and reward. He was fearless about betting big, whether early in his life when he had very little money, or later in his life when he was fabulously wealthy. He also seemed to have extraordinarily good luck for most of his business life, which was an excellent attribute for someone inclined to taking large risks. Only six years after he left home, H. L. got word that his father had died, so after receiving his inheritance, he decided he could finally become more ambitious and start his own business.

His first enterprise, cotton farming in Southeast Arkansas, didn't hold his attention very long, and he reverted back to gambling: both the kind with cards and, with his inheritance, land speculation. He met his first wife, Lyda, and they moved to El Dorado, Arkansas, where there was word of newly found oil.

In what would become consistent with his usual good luck, H. L. struck oil with his very first well, and he expanded his new enterprise, the Poor Boy Drilling Company. He sold the firm at a handsome profit in 1925 and proceeded to Florida and its well-publicized land boom. There he met and fell in love with another woman and, not to be inconvenienced by the fact he was already married, got married to her as well. He managed to emerge from Florida's land speculation successfully, avoiding the collapse, and he and his second wife established a home in Shreveport, Louisiana, about 100 miles away from his first family.

H. L. then got word from a friend of a promising oil lease in East Texas, so he ventured out there to try his luck at some Texas drilling. With typical Hunt luck, not only did the drilling prove successful, but Hunt Oil, his new firm, would soon find itself to be the leading independent producer of crude oil in the nation, having located itself on one of the biggest oil fields ever found.

Crude oil was only a dollar a barrel in those days, and once the Great Depression had fully gripped the country, and the ocean of oil from East Texas began flooding the market, the price dropped to an almost incomprehensible 15 cents per barrel. In spite of the low value for the commodity, Hunt Oil thrived, and H. L. moved his first family—the one in El Dorado, Arkansas—down to Dallas, Texas.

In 1955 Lyda died, and H.L. married Ruth Ray, with whom he already had four illegitimate children. Thus, with three different women, H. L. Hunt had 15 children, which, in his mind, would be beneficial to the world, as he was spreading his "genius gene" to all of his offspring.

■ The Hunt Children

As his various children reached adulthood, H. L. looked to them to help grow the family business. His first son from his first marriage, Hassie, seemed to have his father's knack for finding oil and making shrewd deals. By the age of 25, he already was a successful oil entrepreneur in his own right, but due to an onset of severe psychological problems, he was sent to a variety of treatment centers to remedy the malady. Unfortunately, the most forward-thinking approach to the problem at the time was a full frontal lobotomy, which, once complete, rendered Hassie largely incapacitated for the rest of his life.

Thus, H. L.'s second son, Bunker, also from the first marriage, found himself in the lead role. Unfortunately, H. L. didn't have the fondness for Bunker that he had for Hassie, and he made his feelings abundantly clear to anyone who would listen.

Bunker was desperate to prove himself to his father, but his luck seemed just as bad as his father's seemed good: as he traveled around the globe, looking for promising oil discoveries, he hit dry hole after dry hole. He was losing millions of dollars of the family fortune, and his failings only amplified his father's distaste for Bunker.

That all changed with the Sarir Field in Libya. Bunker had secured leases on two tracts in Libya designated simply as Concession #2 and Concession #65. Out of a need for cash, he sold half his interest in #65 to British Petroleum, and it was subsequently discovered that the area in question contained the largest oil field ever discovered in history: somewhere between 11 and 13 billion barrels of oil. Bunker suddenly found himself with a $5 billion asset, and his father's grousing about his stupid son came to an immediate and very understandable halt.

■ The Next Best Thing to Gold

Even with oil priced at a mere $2 per barrel in 1961, Bunker was now the world's richest man. Bunker parlayed his newfound fortune into many other businesses over the years, including cattle, sugar, restaurants, and millions of acres of real estate. By 1970, both his father and Bunker himself were breathtakingly rich.

Around this time, Bunker got a visit from a commodities broker who asked him one simple but thought-provoking question, as he gestured to various objects sitting around his house: "Bunker, do you believe you're going to have to pay more for these things next year than you did this year?" When Bunker acknowledged the prices would probably be higher, the dealer suggested a solution to the problem at hand: silver.

The notion of precious metals as a store of value goes back for thousands of years in human history, but the most obvious choice, gold, was off limits. FDR's 1934 prohibition of gold from private ownership in the United States was still in place in 1970, even though most of the people who lived when the order was established had long since died. Silver, however, the "poor man's gold," was an interesting alternate candidate.

For one thing, silver was cheap. An ounce of pure silver could be had for less than a barrel of crude oil, and it had many industrial uses. Besides its utility in jewelry and industrial applications, it also was a stable, simple investment tool. If inflation was going to get worse, as Bunker was convinced it would, what better place to allocate paper dollars than the "hard money" of silver?

There were other factors in the world that made purchasing silver sound sensible. In 1970, the world seemed to be a mess, and it looked like it was going to get a lot messier. There was a war raging in Vietnam, the United States was full of protesting hippies, and there was the persistently unstable Middle East. From Bunker's lofty vantage point, the world looked like it was on a very bad path, and he wanted to protect his fabulous fortune from the wretched road the world seemed to be traveling.

Thus, Bunker and his younger brother Herbert started accumulating silver, buying 200,000 ounces in the first few years of the 1970s. This represented a minuscule fraction of a percent of their wealth, but it was the start of what would ultimately become a vast accumulation of the metal.

■ Muammar Gaddafi

Around this time, a radical military man named Colonel Muammar Gaddafi seized power in Libya and nationalized the country's oil wells. Of course, Bunker's successful operation was one of these, and the arch-conservative Bunker expected the United States to take ferocious action against this thief.

The United States did nothing of the sort, and Armand Hammer (the interestingly named CEO of Occidental Petroleum) agreed to give Gaddafi a 51 percent "royalty" in exchange for continuing operations in Libya.

Bunker was incensed at this thinly veiled extortion payment. The Hunts had a grave distrust of many parties, including East Coast oil companies (led, they believed, by the Rockefeller clan), and Occidental's capitulation to this lunatic Colonel was just more proof that the Hunts' worldview was correct.

One by one, all the other oil companies followed Occidental's lead, pledging over half their oil revenues to the Libyan government. The other oil-producing countries took note as to how successful this form of extortion was, and OPEC, discussed in the prior chapter, was formed soon thereafter, since it was clear that the oil-thirsty West could be pushed around at will (see Figure 15.2).

FIGURE 15.2 Colonel Gaddafi, pictured in the mid-1970s, who successfully captured a gigantic revenue stream from the oil companies whose drilling operations he nationalized.

■ The Accumulation Accelerates

Bunker's suspicions about the world going to hell in a handbasket seemed affirmed as never before by what happened in Libya, and he greatly accelerated his purchases of silver. In 1971, President Nixon destroyed the last vestige of America's tie with gold by eliminating the convertibility of dollars into the yellow metal (at a fixed rate of $35 per ounce), and it seemed that at last precious metals were going to be allowed to find their true value. In 1973 and 1974, the Hunts had acquired futures contracts to obtain 55 million ounces of silver, about 8 percent of the world's entire supply.

The Hunts, however, were not executing the futures contracts the same way that 99 percent of the other traders were. Most traders sought speculative profits based on the appreciation of the price of the paper contract during the brief life span of the contract itself. The Hunts, however, actually wanted to take *possession* of the physical silver, paying for it in full upon delivery. For them, the paper contracts were not a speculative tool; they were instead a vehicle to lock in the price of a commodity that they wanted to own in unprecedented quantities.

Bunker had no intention of letting this mountain of silver sit around at one of his ranches, however. He feared that Nixon or some other future president would do to silver what Roosevelt had done to gold and, at some future date, seize it. He thus sought to transport his holdings, and all future acquisitions, to safe warehouses in Switzerland, where the U.S. government couldn't get its hands on it.

One does not simply ship 55 million ounces of silver via United Parcel Service, though. Bunker chartered a fleet of 707 planes for the sole purpose of jetting the hoard of silver overseas, and he needed some serious security to ride with the jets to ensure their safe passage.

To this end, the Hunts held a shooting contest at their Circle K Range, hosting a multitude of cowboys to prove their sharpshooting skills. The dozen most proficient of them were hired as marksmen to accompany the armored trucks and jets that were hired to deliver the silver to its safe Swiss storehouse.

The amount of silver was so vast that six different storage facilities had to be employed to hold all the metal. Even though it cost three million dollars per year just to store the silver, and transporting it to Switzerland was a $200,000 expense by itself, the Hunts thought it was well worth it to get the metal out of the reach of the hands of the United States.

The storage fees and transportation costs were an insurance expense, in a way. Now that the three 707s had delivered their payload, and the dozen armed cowboys had seen it safely to Zurich, the mission thus far had been accomplished.

■ A Rising Asset

As inflation gripped the country in the early 1970s, precious metals did indeed begin to rise in price. What had started out as a way to preserve value turned into a remarkably profitable investment for the Hunts. Silver climbed from $1.50 per ounce to $2, then $3, and, by the spring of 1974, to $6. Word was beginning to get out that Nelson Bunker Hunt was behind all the buying, and he might be trying to corner the market.

Although that wasn't his intent, Bunker definitely wanted to keep accumulating silver, and he was interested in bringing in some major partners to help him with his efforts to sweep up as much of the world's silver as possible and keep the price appreciating. He set his sights on the wealthiest men in the Middle East, which had in common with Bunker both the source of their wealth (oil) and the scope of their wealth (billions).

Bunker first sought to partner with the Shah of Iran, but efforts to do so seemed to be going nowhere. He then set up a meeting with King Faisal of Saudi Arabia, to be held in April 1974. The king, however, was assassinated by none other than his own nephew just a few weeks prior to the meeting. It seemed the Hunt luck was not working in finding a Middle East partner yet, so he focused on other ventures (see Figure 15.3).

For one, silver was not the only commodity enjoying price appreciation, and the Hunt brothers endeavored in a variety of other commodity plays to take advantage of the price inflation happening around them. They decided to target soybeans, and faced with a limit of only 3 million bushels per trader, they brought in other Hunt family members to amass a 22 million bushel portfolio.

The exchange was none too pleased at the workaround the Hunt had employed to garner a position of that size, and the Commodity Futures Trading Commission (CFTC) filed suit against the Hunts for the violation. In the end, it didn't really matter, because the Hunts scored a $40 million profit from their gigantic long position in soybeans (see Figure 15.4).

FIGURE 15.3 King Faisal, during a trip to the United States. Bunker Hunt wanted to partner with him in his silver venture, but the King was assassinated before that could happen.

Since the general investing thesis of the Hunts in the mid-1970s was that the prices of just about everything would be going higher, they spread their wealth to holdings in cattle, property, other oil concerns, sugar, and just about anything else they felt would be adversely affected by inflationary forces. As Bunker himself said, "Any fool can run a printing press," and just about anything was better to own than paper.

Another venture was far more closely aligned with their grand silver scheme. The exchanges on which they were buying silver had limits on position size, similar to what the Hunts had encountered with their soybeans trade. However, for organizations involved in the actual *mining* of metals, no such positions existed, because it would be inappropriate to forbid a large miner to make use of futures contracts for hedging.

Thus, the Hunts realized that if they owned a mine, they wouldn't have to be concerned with meddling exchange regulators and the CFTC with

FIGURE 15.4 The price of soybeans rocketed higher in 1972 through 1974, as delighted traders spoke ambitiously of "beans in the teens" as a hopeful target price.

respect to their growing silver ambitions. Thus, the Hunts sought to purchase the largest silver mine in the country, Big Creek, owned by a public firm named Sunshine Mining.

The Hunts bought 28 percent of the firm in the open market and secured an option to buy the rest at a later date. Not only would owning the mine allow the Hunts to acquire unlimited amounts of silver, but the mine itself was a prodigious producer of the metal, with reserves of over 30 million ounces.

■ Hostile Management and Friendly Arabs

Even though the Hunts had installed a handpicked CEO, G. Michael Boswell, to run Sunshine on their behalf, they soon found themselves with a problem: Boswell and his crew refused to sell the remainder of the company at the $15/share price that had been discussed before. While the Hunts perceived the price as a ceiling, the firm's management saw it as a floor. With the price of silver on the move higher, the assets Sunshine owned were certainly more valuable, and the old purchase price seemed insufficient to Boswell and his team.

Boswell wrote to the company's shareholders and urged them to not sell their stock to the Hunts, and a flurry of litigation was unleashed. In the end, the Hunts were unable to complete their scheme to acquire the remainder of the firm, and they ended up selling back the 28 percent they did own. Their dreams of owning a silver mine were dashed, and they elected to return to more conventional methods of amassing a silver fortune.

Around this time, the Hunts received some positive responses to 50 letters they had sent out to various sheiks in the Middle East. A new enterprise, International Metals, was formed to consolidate the efforts of the Hunts and the likewise wealthy participants from the Arabian participants to acquire silver at ever-increasing prices. The Hunts had a 50-50 partnership with the Saudis, and together they intended on building a war chest of cash adequate to secure 90 million more ounces of silver bullion.

As rich as the Hunts were, they did not have the hundreds of millions of dollars of cash idly lying around to hold up their end of the deal, since their assets were tied up in a variety of other ventures and investments. Therefore, they attained loans from a number of large U.S. banks to fund their purchases in International Metals. In the summer of 1979, the partnership was funded and ready for action, and they swiftly accumulated futures contracts calling for delivery of 43 million ounces of silver.

Throughout the 1970s, silver had more or less steadily climbed from $1.5 to $6, but by the autumn of 1979, its rise began to resemble that of a market in a manic state. The price climbed from $6 to $16, and then it stabilized for several months. With silver now settled around the $17 level, the exchanges were concerned that the rich investors doing all the buying were trying to corner the silver market. The two exchanges that traded silver had 120 million ounces collectively, and at the rate buying was taking place, it seemed conceivable that International Metals could empty out both warehouses within a matter of weeks (see Figure 15.5).

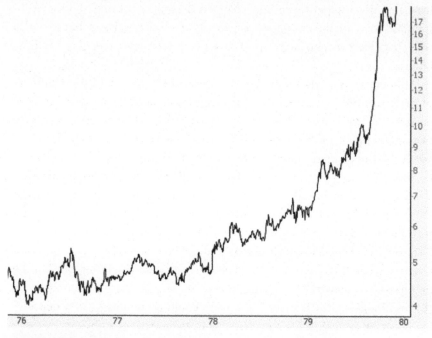

FIGURE 15.5 Silver's gentle rise in the early and mid-1970s picked up pace dramatically in 1979, and once it broke into the double digits, the price ascent became parabolic.

■ Changing the Rules of the Game

Officials from the Commodity Futures Trading Commission and the two exchanges had a meeting with the Hunts to ask about their intentions and to see if, at the lofty prices silver had achieved, they might be interested in being net sellers instead of buyers of the metal. After all, the profits they had achieved were already sensational. The Hunts told them they had no interest in selling, not only because they didn't want to deal with the substantial taxes such profit-taking would incur, but also because they actually did want to permanently retain as much silver as they could acquire.

Taking delivery of the commodity promised in silver contracts was certainly not illegal; far from it, because even if the vast majority of traders never took delivery, the fact that the Hunts were choosing to pay cash for the product represented by the paper contracts was, of course, wholly appropriate.

Thus, even though the CFTC had no legal case to pursue, the Chicago Board of Trade had reached the end of its patience with the Hunts and their insatiable silver appetite, so they changed the rules: not only did they substantially increase the margin requirement for silver purchases, but they also set a strict limit that no party could have silver contracts exceeding 3 million ounces.

Although it was not public knowledge at the time, 23 of the members of the board on the Commodity Exchange were short a total of 38 million ounces of silver. For every dollar silver moved up, the members collectively lost another $38 million, and the unprecedented rally in the bullion was putting some of these members at risk of ruin. In retrospect, it's clear to see that the board members were far from disinterested and objective parties when it came to suddenly changing the rules governing silver trading. With this extraordinary conflict of interest, they wanted the Hunts to be restrained, and they wanted the price of silver, in turn, to drop.

Silver did indeed languish between about $16 and $18 for a couple of months, while the Hunts and the exchange officials were facing off. On the one hand, (a) constricting buying power by way of margin increases and (b) limiting how much silver big buyers could accumulate had a depressing effect on the price. On the other hand, the exchange's obvious concern about running out of silver and the fact that the richest man on the planet, flanked by extraordinarily wealthy Arabs, made clear they wanted to buy up as much silver as they could, balanced out the bearish news. The price had reached equilibrium for a while, and it was unclear whether the bulls or bears would finally break the price out of its range.

By October, the Hunts and their associates were sitting on 192 million ounces of silver, making them substantially larger owners of the metal than the exchanges themselves.

As the winter of 1979 approached, it became clear who was going to win the battle, as silver commenced lurching higher, moving in limit-up spurts on an almost daily basis. ("Limit-up" meaning that the exchange would not permit the price to move any higher than a certain fixed amount, which invariably meant the market was willing to pay more, but it was *allowed* to until the next trading day). The price soared to $20, $30, $40, and beyond (see Figure 15.6).

As 1980 began, silver streaked to its highest level in history, $49, which in inflation-adjusted terms is about three times that amount. The Hunts and their partners had profits in the billions of dollars, and the futures exchanges were becoming frantic with worry about what was going to happen next.

Whereas a stock exchange would have been delighted with a bull market in equities, the circumstances are different with commodities. The hyperbolic

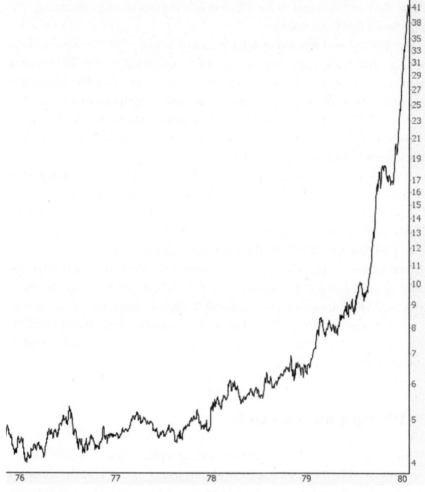

41
38
35
33
31
29
27
25
23
21
19
17
16
15
14
13
12
11
10
9
8
7
6
5
4

76   77   78   79   80

FIGURE 15.6 Silver's already-incredible performance became manic later in the year, with silver breaking into the 20s, 30s, and 40s, with no plausible limit in sight.

rise in silver was no cause for celebration at the exchanges. They were facing very real limits as to whether or not they could honor the futures contracts that were being traded, so they had to act even more aggressively this time.

The exchanges, backed by the CFTC, declared new and even more restrictive limits on how much silver futures investors could acquire. Bunker Hunt became the public face of the silver bull market and declared that, given these new draconian measures, "... *the market will move to Europe.... The silver market in this country is a thing of the past.*" It seems that Bunker's paranoia about the East Coast and its meddling in free enterprise were becoming true in an awful and rapid fashion.

Even at the extraordinarily lofty prices of January 1980, the Hunts kept buying, with Bunker agreeing to take on an additional 32.5 million ounces of silver that spring. At this point, the mountain of silver the Hunts had acquired was worth about $4.5 billion, the vast majority of which was pure profit. Although the Hunts had borrowed money and leveraged their positions to accrue such an unprecedented cache, the fact is that, on paper, their investment had paid off spectacularly.

Commercial consumers of silver were none-too-pleased that the cost of their raw material had soared so dramatically. The famed jeweler Tiffany & Co. paid for a full-page advertisement in the *New York Times* condemning the Hunts for their silver acquisitions and the effect it was having on prices.

In part, the ad stated, "We think it is unconscionable for anyone to hoard several billion—yes, billion—dollars' worth of silver and thus drive the price up so high that others must pay artificially high prices for articles made of silver." Of course, there was nothing "artificial" about the price—it was a reflection of market reality—but such expensive silver would certainly make it harder for Tiffany's to sell its wares at attractive prices to the nonbillionaire public.

■ Putting an End to It

At this point, the exchanges did something extraordinary: simply stated, they outlawed buying. More specifically, on January 21, 1980, the COMEX said that the only orders they would accept would be liquidation orders. No one could buy. They could only sell.

The market was past the point of shrugging off news like this. With no buyers permitted, the price went into a free-fall. The day after the announcement, silver plunged to $34. To add to the selling pressure, the everyday people of the American middle class finally woke up to silver's sensationally high price and began selling everything they might possess with silver content, from heirloom silverware to coins jingling in canvas bags.

In the first couple of months of 1980, it was reported that 16 million ounces of silver coins and 6 million ounces of scrap silver (including more than a few silver tea sets from little old ladies across the nation) were dumped into the silver market, causing prices to shrink that much faster (see Figure 15.7).

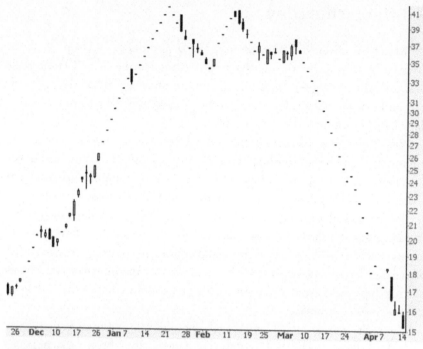

FIGURE 15.7 The "limit up" days of silver soon gave way to "limit-down" days, in which markets were instantly quoted at the start of each trading day as the lowest possible prices permitted. A normal price bar has a high and a low for the day, but with limit-up and limit-down days, a simple dash represents the entire day's activity of a single price quote, during which virtually no trading would have taken place.

In spite of seeing his profits vanishing by hundreds of millions of dollars on a daily basis, Bunker kept a stiff upper lip and stated, *"Why would anyone want to sell silver to get [paper] dollars? I guess they got tired of polishing it."* As nonchalant as he may have appeared in the press, his billions of dollars of silver were suddenly lurching limit-down in price, day after day.

Bunker Hunt kept behaving in the same fashion as he had before, confident that the recent downturn was just a blip in silver's inevitable rise higher. He continued taking delivery of bullion, buying up more contracts, and taking up a multimillion-dollar stake in another silver mine.

He even announced that his employees would be given their bonuses in silver or gold, instead of cash, if the metals were more valuable when the bonuses were due. Bunker was, in sum, trying to give silver whatever positive press it could garner, given the unfortunate circumstances.

■ Silver Thursday

By March 3, silver had slipped to $35.20 per ounce, a drop of about 30 percent from just two months before. Although the overall Hunt position was still profitable, a meaningful amount of the gains had disappeared. The bull market was clearly over, and the price kept getting hammered on a daily basis, reaching $21 by March 14.

Paul Volcker, the chairman of the Federal Reserve, had declared open war on inflation, and he was pushing interest rates to levels the nation had never seen before. The fantastically high interest rates were mopping up cash from around the world and drawing it away from such alternatives as silver.

The Hunts had many expenses related to their silver holdings, such as the storage costs. But the biggest cash drain of all was the making of margin payments, because as the price of the metal continued to drop, the exchanges demanded larger and larger cash payments so that the International Metals partnership could avoid a margin call, which would compel the selling of their futures contracts.

Although the margin calls had been paid obediently during the collapse, that all changed on March 25, 1980. The Hunts' silver broker, Bache, contacted the partnership with a $135 million margin call. The Hunts stoically informed Bache that they couldn't make the payment. The game was at an end.

Bache started dumping the Hunt silver, and they likewise notified the CFTC about the margin call and its consequences. Bache warned the CFTC that the Hunts would be facing more calls, given the ongoing plunge in silver's price, and that they would likely have an account with a significant negative balance. Word of the dire situation quickly leaked out, and full-scale panic took hold of the precious metals markets.

In a last-ditch effort, Bunker made an announcement from Paris that he and four Arab partners had completed the acquisition of more than 200 million ounces of silver, and they would be issuing silver bonds to investors, both small and large, that were backed by the metal. In a way, Bunker was going to distribute his own metal-backed currency, returning to the tradition that national governments had long ago abandoned.

One aspect of the announcement that was visibly lacking was the name of *any* large banks that would be participating in such a venture. The public swiftly concluded that Hunt was just announcing a *hoped*-for plan, not an actual public offering of silver-backed bonds, and that he hadn't even found any credible banks to partner with him.

Although Bunker hoped to shore up silver's price with such a bold announcement, it had precisely the opposite effect. On March 27, 1980, the day after

Bunker's announcement, the silver market went into an unmitigated free-fall. It opened at $15.80, and frantic trading flooded the pits. Unfounded rumors begin to circulate, such as that the Hunts were facing a billion-dollar margin call they couldn't meet, and that their broker was about to shutter its doors.

Silver's plunge had not gone unnoticed by the equity markets. The Dow Jones Industrial Average had been above 900 early in the year, but the pummeling that both gold and silver had been taking had a wasting effect on equity prices, particularly since there were rumors that the Hunts would need to dump vast quantities of their own public holdings in order to meet their silver market requirements. The Dow was trading at about 760, a 15 percent drop, during what would be known as "Silver Thursday" (see Figure 15.8).

FIGURE 15.8 The Dow Jones Industrial Average suffered alongside silver, as massive selling flooded precious metals markets. Silver Thursday created a climactic bottom in the market that, in retrospect, was a superb buying opportunity in equities.

As the trading day wore on, the damage was becoming extraordinary. Silver was trading at $10.80 an ounce, nearly 80 percent lower than it had been just a couple of months before. The Dow was showing a loss of 25.43 points, a fall of over 3 percent in a single day and the lowest price it had seen in five years.

The investing public was beginning to perceive the Hunts as having created a financial debacle that reached far beyond their beloved silver. Before the closing bell rang, bargain hunters bucked up equity prices and reversed almost all the losses for the day, although silver was still hammered down to its $10.80 bid.

On January 17, the Hunts had $4.5 billion in silver, $3.5 billion of which was profit. By the closing bell of Silver Thursday, the picture had changed dramatically: now the Hunts' silver misadventure had $1.5 billion in assets (the bullion itself) and $2.5 billion in liabilities. The Hunts were presented with just about the last thing they wanted to see: *another* margin call, this one for $100 million.

Just about the only people happy with the events of Silver Thursday were those fortunate enough to have sold silver short at higher prices. Armand Hammer—the same man who infuriated the Hunts by being the first to bend to the will of Gadaffi—locked in a gain of $119 million with silver's collapse, since he had the foresight to see that silver's parabolic rise would soon come to an end.

■ The Bailout

Because the Hunts had started purchasing silver when it was much cheaper, the cost basis of their bullion was only about $10, which meant that even with the complete devastation that had been leveled against silver prices in the first couple months of 1980, they still had a small profit on their holdings. Their trouble wasn't with the bullion but with the massive number of futures contracts they had secured with an average price of about $35 per ounce.

The debts they owed on these obligations were enormous and so complex that no one was sure what the exact figure was, but the damage was in the neighborhood of $1.5 billion. On top of this, they already had an obligation to take delivery of silver to the tune of $665 million to add to their already staggering pile of bullion. The Hunts had acquired much of their silver with leverage, which worked fabulously during silver's unrelenting ascent, but had a devastating effect now that prices had fallen so hard.

On the Sunday following Silver Thursday, Bunker met in Dallas with some principals of his organization as well as the Engelhard organization to which they owed $665 million for a looming silver delivery. The Hunts notified Engelhard that they didn't have the cash to take the delivery and that their tremendous holdings of silver stored abroad had already been pledged as collateral for other loans. Bunker Hunt, when contemplating their monstrous losses, uttered a phrase that would achieve some lasting notoriety: "A billion dollars isn't what it used to be."

The tremors that the Hunts had caused on the nation's financial markets required the most senior attention, so that afternoon they flew to Boca Raton to meet with the leaders of the largest banks in the United States as well as the chairman of the Federal Reserve, Paul Volcker. Volcker normally frowned on providing any assistance to speculative ventures, but in this instance he happened to be in town to give a speech, and he decided to get involved in the negotiations that the Hunts and Engelhard were having with the banks.

The negotiations dragged on through the night and into the early morning, with a rumpled and weary Volcker occasionally showing up in his night clothes with a dress shirt haphazardly thrown over his pajama top.

The negotiations were complex and difficult, but by Monday morning, an arrangement had been made: the Hunts would hand over 8.5 million ounces of silver to Engelhard as well as a 20 percent interest in several oil properties. The oil interests were untapped, and the Hunts didn't know if they were giving away an ungodly sum to get out of the mess they were in, but given the circumstances, they had little room to negotiate.

Since the Hunts and Engelhard had reached an arrangement about their own financial relationship, the Hunts now turned to the gathered bankers to get a loan that could cover all the existing debt obligations. Led by First National Bank of Dallas and Morgan Guaranty of New York, a group of banks assembled $1.1 billion in loans to the Hunt interests so that they could honor their debt obligations.

Among the terms of the deal was a pledge that the Hunts not speculate in the silver market until everything had been paid off—given the situation, it seems unlikely that the Hunts would need to be restricted from having anything to do with silver again in their entire lives.

What was shocking to the rest of Hunt clan was how much of the family's assets had to be pledged as collateral for the bailout. The rest of the Hunt children, most of whom had absolutely nothing to do with the silver debacle, found their coins, jewelry, cars, oil interests, paintings, furs, racehorses, and other valuable assets suddenly collateralized.

Although the other Hunts didn't partake of the splendid (albeit fleeting) gains that had been enjoyed by the participating Hunt brothers, they did find themselves having to help pay for these financial risks across almost all their asset classes.

■ Gold Riding Shotgun

Throughout all the Hunts' silver drama, gold likewise participated in its own highly correlated bull market. Unlike silver, gold was not the beneficiary of a very focused buying spree by the richest men in the world, but it had its own reasons for moving higher.

In May 1973, gold was pegged at $42.22 per ounce by the government, but by January 1980—the same month silver peaked—gold hit a lifetime record of $850 per ounce, a 20-fold increase. Besides the surging inflation of the late 1970s, political unrest in Afghanistan (specifically, the Soviet invasion) as well as the turmoil in Iran with the taking of American hostages fueled the flames of international worry. Such fears often drive money into historically safe assets, and in this case, the safest asset of all was perceived as gold.

Although gold had enjoyed a spectacular run during the final years of the 1970s, once the price peaked in January 1980, gold would enter a grueling, seemingly interminable bear market of its own for nearly 20 years. It would finally bottom at $251.70 in August 1999, near the height of Internet stock mania. In inflation-adjusted terms, the peak price of gold in early 1980 was well over $2,000 per ounce, a price that, as of this writing, has never been matched (see Figure 15.9).

■ The Double Eagle Returns

The Double Eagle gold coins from 1933, described much earlier in this chapter, should have been completely lost to history, having been melted down by government order, with the exception of the two specimens saved by the U.S. government. It turns out, however, that a small number of the coins found their way out of the U.S. Mint, and one of those eventually become the most expensive coin sold in history.

The circuitous, multidecade route of the "escaped" coins is an interesting tale in itself. It seems that someone at the U.S. Mint with access to the gold coins—perhaps the mint cashier, although no one will ever know for

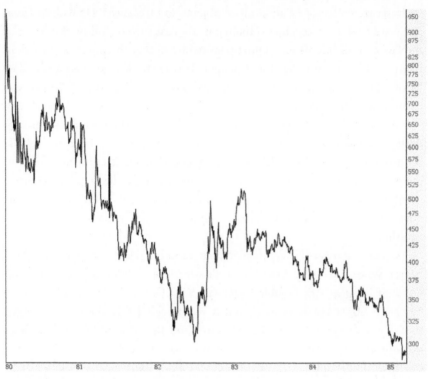

FIGURE 15.9 Gold's gains in the 1970s were spectacular, like silver's, but in the 1980s and 1990s, gold was a catastrophically bad investment.

sure—pilfered at least 20 coins and got them into the hands of Israel Swift, a jeweler in Philadelphia. This went unnoticed for years, until one of the coins appeared at a coin auction.

A reporter was intrigued by the appearance of this coin that wasn't supposed to exist, so he contacted the U.S. Mint as part of his research. In turn, the Mint notified the Secret Service, which opened up a case to investigate the matter.

One would normally think that a single coin from over a decade ago would not have been a matter of national interest, but the Secret Service took the matter very seriously and wound up tracking down seven different coins, each of which were, once retrieved, doomed to be melted at the Mint, as they should have been 10 years earlier. Because so many years had gone by since the theft, Israel Swift had the statute of limitations to thank, since he could not be prosecuted.

Unknown to the Secret Service, there was another 1933 Double Eagle sitting in Egypt, owned by none other than King Farouk, who was an enthusiastic collector of all kinds of objects and treasures. He had, in 1944, purchased the coin and had actually taken great care to follow the letter of the law and fill out all the export paperwork so that the purchase and shipment of the coin was legal and proper. This all took place just a few days before the Israel Swift matter came to light, and the export license was granted without incident.

Although the Treasury Department tried to get the coin back through diplomatic channels, the king saw no reason to hand over his legally acquired property. In 1952, he was deposed from his throne, with his many treasures seized and put up for public auction. The Treasury Department asked the new Egyptian government to hand over the coin, and the government agreed that it would. Strangely, however, the coin once again vanished.

Decades later, at the Waldorf-Astoria Hotel in New York City, the U.S. Secret Service arrested British coin dealer Stephen Fenton, and among his holdings was the very Double Eagle that King Farouk had possessed so long before. A court battle ensued, and it was decided that the coin belonged to the government of the United States and that it could be sold at auction. In an interesting settlement, it was also decided that, unlike all the other Double Eagles, this one would be made into legal tender (that is, monetized), as originally intended in 1933.

The story of this small, single coin becomes more interesting still: when deciding where to store this singularly valuable coin, the Treasury officials settled on the vaults of the World Trade Center. In July 2001, only a few months before terrorist attacks would destroy the building complex, the coin was moved to Fort Knox.

Finally, on July 30, 2002, the coin was put up for auction at Sotheby's and sold for $6,600,000. A 15 percent surcharge was tacked on by Sotheby's plus—almost comically—a $20 fee in exchange for the intrinsic $20 "monetized" value of the coin as legal tender (although it can safely be said the coin would never be spent in exchange for $20 in goods or services).

Thus, $7,590,020 was the final bill for the coin, with half the cash (plus the intrinsic value of $20) going to the U.S. Treasury and the other half going to coin dealer Stephen Fenton. After over 70 years of making its way all over the world, the coin finally found a permanent home with an anonymous buyer after only nine minutes of bidding.

Finally, it should be noted that 10 more Double Eagles have been uncovered—again, emanating from the actions of Israel Swift—but that lengthy litigation has determined that these too are the property of the U.S.

government. They remain securely stored at Fort Knox and, as of this writing, their fate has not been determined.

■ Bankrupt Billionaires

The inflationary 1970s had been very kind to the Hunts and their businesses. Surging prices in soybeans, crude oil, silver, Texas real estate, and many other commodities augmented the family fortune by billions.

The 1980s were a mirror image for the family's assets. Texas real estate fell in value precipitously, and crude oil collapsed from about $32/barrel in late 1985 to about $10 in early 1986. The Hunts found themselves with $1.48 billion in assets, and debts of $2.43 billion. The Hunts had grown from the richest people in the world to some of the world's most indebted (see Figure 15.10).

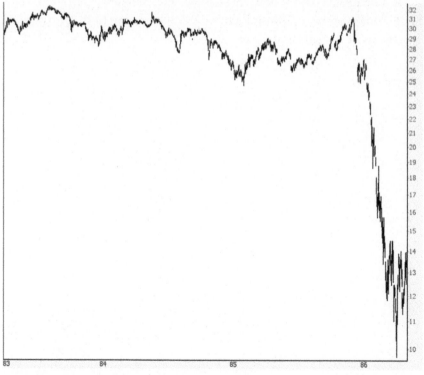

FIGURE 15.10 Crude oil, the basis for the Hunt family fortune for most of the twentieth century, had its own precipitous drop in the mid-1980s, exacerbating an already-remarkable turn of fortune for the Hunt clan.

In 1987, the Hunts had as many lawyers working on their financial legal battles—15 in all—as there were children in the family. The banks fighting the Hunts on the other side of the table hired 50 *times* that many attorneys to wage war against them, and by 1988, the war was over, and the banks had won.

Adding to the financial pain being brought by their creditors, the Hunts also faced another unexpected nemesis: a mineral company from Peru. During the run-up in silver prices, a rogue trader inside the company sold short the metal, ultimately suffering terrible losses for the firm. In 1988, a court awarded $134 million damages to the Peruvian firm, payable by the Hunt brothers.

Bunker Hunt filed for personal bankruptcy in 1988, and he emerged from the formalities with several million dollars in assets but a bill to the IRS for $90 million that had to be repaid over the ensuing 15 years. It was the largest personal bankruptcy in Texas history, and a coda that would have seemed preposterous had one predicted it a few years earlier.

The remarkable tale of the Hunt saga can, at its simplest, illustrate vividly that leverage can be a powerful ally or a deadly enemy to the fortunes of even the most storied family dynasties.

CHAPTER 16

Latin American Debt Crisis

L atin American countries have a long history of economic booms and busts, accompanied by foreign lending which has helped fuel the growth of the developing economies of South America. There have been multiple instances of widespread defaults on these debts, but no crisis was more severe or widespread than that which occurred in the 1980s, threatening to bring down some of the world's biggest banks.

■ A Healthy Development

Prior to the debt crisis of the 1980s, the last major economic shock suffered in Latin America was during the Great Depression. The worldwide departure from the gold standard in the early 1930s, as well as the ubiquitous economic cataclysm occurring around the globe, compelled most developing countries to simply default on their loans. By 1935, 97.7 percent of bonds issued by Latin American countries (with the exception of Argentina) were in default. Even by the end of World War II, a decade later, two-thirds of Latin American debt had gone unpaid.

Following such a financial debacle, the financial world had scant interest in providing funding to the nations of South America following the war. However, economies in Latin America starting improving on their own. The region had healthy growth in both agricultural exports as well as industrial manufacturing, and between 1950 and 1980, overall gross domestic product quintupled.

Manufacturing enjoyed a healthy 7 percent annual growth rate through the 1960s, and exports between South American countries as well as to overseas customers increased markedly. Export growth grew at an average of 12 percent per year, and trade between countries in South America grew at an even healthier 16 percent annually.

■ Oil Money Hunts for a Home

In the early 1970s, banks were running into an unfamiliar problem: a dearth of large commercial customers who wanted to take out loans. One of the principal profit centers for banks had been the working capital loan, but as the commercial paper market provided a convenient, short-term loan source for creditworthy corporations, businesses didn't need to turn to their banks for such financing.

Contemporaneous with this was the growth of the Eurodollar market. The term *Eurodollar* is somewhat misleading, since it implies something to do with Europe. In fact, it is merely a term to describe U.S. dollar deposits housed somewhere outside the United States and, thus, outside the jurisdiction of the United States Federal Reserve.

After World War II's conclusion, there was a steady increase in the value of Eurodollar deposits around the world (the term *Eurodollar* applied irrespective of the bank's location, including deposits in Asia). By the end of 1970, $385 billion in Eurodollar deposits existed, and with the growth of oil wealth in the 1970s, this figure would grow significantly. The inflow of these funds to banks would create an enviable problem for these institutions, since they would seek to deposit these funds into safe investments with superior yields. Sovereign debt was seen as one of the better choices.

Because Latin America had been largely ignored by the banking world after the Great Depression, there was relatively little debt outstanding even by the end of 1970. Total debt in all the countries was only about $29 billion, but as South America gathered the interest and attention of commercial banks, an ocean of funds was offered to the nations of the region. By the end of 1978, the loans outstanding increased to $159 billion, which equals an annual growth rate of about 24 percent.

During the mid-1970s, the influx of capital was seen as healthy for all the parties involved. For banks, it provided a presumably safe destination for billions of dollars that threw off healthy interest payments; for countries, it provided massive amounts of capital that could be used for building out infrastructure and funding increasingly expensive energy projects; and for oil-producing countries, it completed a virtuous financial circle in which petroleum-based revenue could be "recycled" back into the developing countries that needed the cash to make further oil purchases.

As crude oil became more expensive, the continued flow of loans into Latin America became less of a way to build out productive infrastructure and more of a way to bridge the gap between expense and financial resources. Countries in the region were becoming increasingly indebted and dependent on the persistent rollover of the short-term debt that was coming due at increasingly high interest rates.

Servicing the debt became more difficult for borrowers, as the annual funds required for such servicing mushroomed from $12 billion in 1975 to $66 billion in 1982. As early as 1977, the largest U.S. banks were beginning to reconsider the wisdom of pouring money into Latin America and began pulling back on the size and quantity of loans being made. Banks from other nations filled this vacuum, however, as commercial banks from Japan, Europe, and the Middle East increased credit lines for Mexico, Argentina, Brazil, and other nations of the zone.

Between 1976 and 1980, nearly 70 new banks were opening up each year in the region. These were the greatest boom years for OPEC nations, particularly as oil revenues reached a historic peak in 1979, and the balance of payments problem in South American countries was most easily remedied by the continued recycling of petrodollars from the Middle East.

By 1981, however, even non-U.S. banks began to curtail their enthusiasm for Latin American lending, as the strains of servicing the debt by the nations of the region was becoming apparent. Some simple data points illustrate the sea change that had taken place in the finances of the region. The ratio of debt to gross national product (GNP) between 1970 and 1982 increased:

- For Argentina, from 8.8 percent to 29.1 percent

- For Brazil, from 7.7 percent to 18.6 percent

- For Venezuela, from 8.8 percent to 29.1 percent

Overall debt had made great leaps during the 1970s, and by the early 1980s, new loan disbursements were persistently high:

1970: $1.4 billion
1975: $8 billion
1978: $24.6 billion

1980: $23.1 billion
1981: $28.1 billion
1982: $24.6 billion

■ Interest Rate Shock

The fundamental problem with all of the debt that had been issued to Latin America was that it was short term. This meant that as the debt came due, it was rolled over into new debt, which, given the inflationary environment, was almost always at a higher interest rate. Developing countries found themselves in a position similar to someone who bought a house they could barely afford and whose monthly payments doubled due to climbing bank rates.

Inflation, particularly due to energy cost increases, was bad enough of a problem, but when U.S. Federal Reserve chairman Paul Volcker committed himself to "breaking inflation's back" with substantially higher interest rates, the burden on developing nations would get much worse. The industrialized world was committed to getting inflation under control, and this was doubly bad for some countries, since it meant not only higher interest rates but also, over time, much lower prices for their exports (particularly energy exports).

The severity of the situation can be illustrated with one simple fact: in 1982, the bank debt outstanding in Latin America grew by 10 percent. However, the interest rate being charged was 16 percent. What that meant was that every cent of new debt was being used simply to pay back interest, plus an additional 6 percent was being extracted from the reserves of the debtor nations just to keep up with the debt servicing. In a sense, the developing nations were beginning to drown in their own debt.

The situation reached a breaking point on August 12, 1982, when Mexico's minister of finance told the U.S. Treasury secretary, the chairman of the Federal Reserve, and the managing director of the International Monetary Fund (IMF) that Mexico would not be making its payment due on August 16. Mexico's debt was $80 billion, and it was declaring a moratorium on its payments.

Mexico's move emboldened other nations to stop making payments on their own debts. By October 1983, payments were in arrears on nearly a quarter-trillion dollars in debt, and 27 different countries had ceased making regular payments on their sovereign obligations. Not all of these developing countries were in South America, but 16 of them were, with the largest debtors being Mexico, Brazil, Argentina, and Venezuela. These four countries alone accounted for $176 billion of the debt outstanding.

The largest banks in the United States faced an extraordinary risk at this point, since the tens of billions of dollars owed them by these four nations was a sum larger than the bank's own capital reserves. As J. Paul Getty famously said, "If you owe the bank $100, that's your problem. If you owe the bank $100 million, that's the bank's problem." The banks did indeed have a problem, and they were compelled to practice patience so that they did not incite a greater financial catastrophe.

Although 1983 was not a banner year for the worldwide economy, most nations were still relatively healthy, but Latin America was suffering a crisis even worse than it had experienced during the Great Depression. All 18 countries in the region were enveloped in the crisis this time, and unlike the years of the Depression, there was not yet an acceptance that the debts could simply be written off as uncollectible. The debt load that Latin America had taken on was staggering, with a 1,000 percent increase between 1970 and 1980.

The IMF intervened, offering to help restructure the debt payments in return for the countries agreeing to draconian austerity programs. The reduced spending in Latin American nations exacerbated an already-bad situation with the region's economy. The gap between rich and poor widened, unemployment increased, and poverty compelled some of the lower classes to a life of crime. Murders and drug trafficking increased, and the once-robust growth of the 1960s and 1970s gave way to stagnation and lowered standards of living.

The lack of capital caused a domino effect on the economies of the area. A lack of capital meant the production capacity of the nations was underutilized. This, in turn, meant lower employment, lower taxes, and an even more difficult situation for the indebted governments. Widespread macroeconomic problems characterized what would later be known as the "lost decade" for the entire Latin American region, commencing in 1982.

Oil-producing nations such as Mexico and Venezuela, which had enjoyed a boom period in the late 1970s thanks to the extraordinary price of crude oil, were especially hard-hit, as the real price of energy exports withered away throughout the decade. The austerity programs of the IMF—an entity that many citizens in South America were coming to deeply resent—would not be a lasting solution to the debt problem the nations faced.

■ Baker and Brady

In September 1985, U.S. Treasury Secretary James Baker met with the IMF and World Bank in South Korea where he announced a new plan to address the Latin American debt crisis that he summarized as "structural adjustment with growth." The plan called for rescheduling debt payments to make them more manageable and an issuance of new loans totaling $29 billion to help shore up the economies and their ability to meet their obligations.

The shot in the arm was insufficient to jump-start the economies, however, so the Baker Plan was augmented the next year with a further restructuring of $176 billion in debt with an additional $14 billion in new loan assistance. This enhancement, however, still did not adequately address the crisis.

Around this time, a new but growing secondary market for Latin American debt had sprung up, and given the circumstances, the prices being paid for the bonds were substantially discounted from their par value. Although both the debtor nations and the IMF were behaving as if all the bonds were going to be paid back at par, the more realistic secondary market was pricing the bonds at levels other parties were willing to pay, which compelled debtors to point out that there was no point in them being required to service the debt at face value when it could be purchased on the open market at a meaningful discount.

Therefore, in 1987, yet another enhancement to the Baker Plan was put into place that allowed for the retirement of debt at a discount. This was the first time in five years that the organizations formally charged with addressing the crisis tacitly admitted that there was no realistic way the debt could be expected to be repaid in full.

A new presidential administration brought with it a new Treasury secretary, Nicholas Brady, who in 1989 offered up a plan of his own. The Brady Plan invoked a more meaningful cash infusion to provide assistance to countries buying back their discounted debts, with $24 billion in loans from the World Bank and IMF and $6 billion from the Japanese government. With debt-reduction mechanisms and sufficient wherewithal for the countries to take advantage of their buyback opportunities, the crisis was finally beginning to abate.

An important element of the Brady Plan was an agreement by the participating nations to introduce economic reforms to promote internal economic growth and, in turn, give themselves the capacity to continue paying down their debts. About one-third of the $191 billion in outstanding loans was forgiven, and these losses were absorbed by the issuing banks (see Figure 16.1).

This damage to bank balance sheets did not go unnoticed by ratings agencies. Between 1977 and 1988, long-term debt ratings for Bank of America

FIGURE 16.1 Large financial organizations like Bank of America suffered declining share prices through the 1970s as the burden of massive South American debts weighed on their prospects.

declined from Aaa to Ba3, for Chemical Bank from Aaa to Baa1, and for Manufacturers Hanover from Aaa to Baa3. Share prices suffered as well, although a failure to adequately address the massive problem would surely have been more deleterious to the fortune of the bank shareholders than it had been with the Brady Plan in place.

■ Hyperinflation

Although the issue of the massive overhang of debt had finally been addressed as the 1980s came to a close, a new problem in the form of inflation began to take hold in some South American countries. Prior to 1972, inflation had been extremely modest in most of Latin America, averaging between 2 percent and 4 percent back to the mid-1950s.

The median rate of inflation picked up markedly throughout the 1980s, however, peaking at about 40 percent in 1990 before commencing a steady and persistent drop. By the end of the 1990s, inflation had returned to a median of about 5 percent. Before it did, hyperinflation briefly ravaged the economies of Bolivia, Brazil, Peru, Nicaragua, and Argentina, with three other nations—Mexico, Uruguay, and Venezuela—briefly going through a bout of triple-digit inflation.

The early 1990s were a healing time for the region, however, since the debt problem and inflationary woes were being addressed in an organized fashion by a consortium of international interests. Gross domestic product (GDP) growth grew from negative 2.1 percent in 1990 to 0.8 percent in 1991, 0.6 percent in 1992, and 2.1 percent in 1993. At the same time, inflation dropped from 648.3 percent in 1990 to 162.5 percent in 1991, 140 percent in 1992, and 25.3 percent in 1993.

As confidence in the region was restored, capital began to flow back in, whereas it had been cut off almost completely following the Mexico announcement in 1982. Comparing 1989 to 1991, capital inflows increased from $5 billion to $40 billion.

This is not to say that the turmoil came without costs. Poverty increased substantially between 1980 and 1990, growing from 40.5 percent of the population to 48.3 percent, and for those still working, real wages dropped by up to 40 percent. It would take 14 years of economic healing for poverty levels to drop to where they had been in 1980.

▪ Subprime Parallels

The debt crisis was by far the most serious and far-reaching in Latin America's history. In a sense, the situation had strong parallels with the players and circumstances of the subprime crisis that would take place in the United States two decades later. To compare the players in the late 1970s with those in the early 2000s:

- The OPEC nations, rich investors seeking a good return on their money, were played by (that is, took the role of) the pool of fixed-income capital buying derivatives instruments.

- The developing countries, poor credit risks seeking funding, were played by subprime home buyers.

- The commercial banks were played by the investment banks.

- The short-term, automatically rolling loans were played by the adjustable rate mortgages.

- The rising interest rates were, once again, played by rising interest rates, with similar effects on debtors in both scenarios.

In both circumstances, something that was *assumed* to be AAA rated (in the 1970s, sovereign debt, and in the 2000s, mortgage-backed collateralized debt instruments) turned out to be prone to failure, and likewise in both time periods, those who were borrowing money found themselves unable to meet their obligations and having to rely on a government bailout.

CHAPTER 17

The Reagan Revolution and Crash

Entering the 1980s, the United States could be forgiven for viewing its future with a healthy amount of skepticism. The past two decades had been wearisome for the nation, as it had gone through civil unrest, presidential assassination, surging inflation, a stagnant economy, an outdated "rust belt" industrial sector, the disaster of Vietnam, the first presidential resignation, and a persistent cold war.

The leadership of the United States in the form of Nixon, Ford, and Carter hardly inspired the public, either. The nation exited the 1970s with a sense of malaise, and although it was still a superpower, the United States and its population could plausibly accept the prospect that its best days were behind it.

In this environment, the country was ready for a new direction, and it found it in the form of Ronald Reagan. America wanted to be told that it could be a great nation again, and Reagan's assurances that a smaller government, lower taxes, and a new respect for business and the good it could do resonated with the voting public. Jimmy Carter lost his bid for a second term in office, and Reagan began in early 1981 what would be an eight-year stint in the White House.

■ The Death of Inflation

If there was one aspect of the economy that characterized the 1970s, it was inflation. It had persisted for most of the decade, and as long as it was an economic reality, it would continue to choke off any meaningful growth in the nation's business.

Paul Volcker was the chairman of the Federal Reserve when Reagan took office, and he was determined to "slay the inflationary dragon" by constricting the money supply. This action by the Fed would be painful and prolonged, but it was effective. As money tightened, interest rates soared, and everyday Americans saw their home payments dramatically escalate as some mortgage rates approached 20 percent (see Figure 17.1).

The surge in interest rates threw America into a deep recession, which occupied two years of Reagan's first term, and the citizens who voted him into office began to have serious doubts about their choice. Although inflation was dropping, joblessness soared to over 10 percent and high borrowing rates made it more difficult for the middle class to meet their financial obligations. Reagan's popularity plummeted, but the bitter pill the Fed had forced the nation to swallow would eventually cure the patient. Inflation was slashed from 13.5 percent in 1980 to 3.2 percent in 1983.

The country now had a decent foundation on which to build the economic success story of the 1980s and 1990s. This foundation would lead to an ascent in capitalism that the nation hadn't seen since the gilded age, and it would positively affect asset prices almost uninterrupted for the next 20 years.

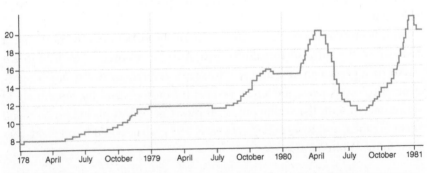

FIGURE 17.1 The prime rate was increased in steps from 8 percent to over 20 percent in an effort to break inflation's grip on the economy.

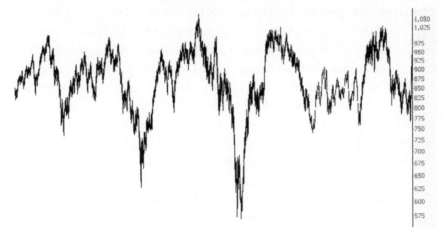

FIGURE 17.2 The stock market, represented here with the S&P 500 index, meandered aimlessly for 15 years, and the nominal price data does not reflect the erosion in equity value that was taking place because of inflation.

■ Rebirth of the Stock Market

Just as the 1960s and 1970s had been an overall dismal era for the United States socially and economically, likewise it was a moribund period of the stock market. Adjusted for inflation, the return on stocks from 1967 to 1982 was negative 70 percent. The fact that someone could invest their money into American business and, after fifteen years of waiting, have lost nearly three-quarters of their investment's value, speaks volumes about the state of U.S. equities during those years (see Figure 17.2).

Stocks continued to perform poorly during the 1981–1982 recession, but on August 12, 1982, they would finally mark an inflation-adjusted bottom of 776.92 as measured by the Dow Jones Industrial Average. Not long before, in April 1982, interest rates peaked, with even the "prime rate" (the lowest rate banks offer their safest, most credit-worthy customers) exceeding 20 percent. With stocks so battered and interest-bearing accounts paying so much, it is easy to see why there was so little interest in the stock market, but starting in the summer of 1982, equities would begin a climb that would persist for decades.

■ A Business-Friendly Nation

The so-called Reagan Revolution had several important tenets: lower taxes, deregulation, and growing employment.

Earlier in the twentieth century, some income tax rates exceeded 90 percent, and when Reagan entered office, the top tax rate was still 70 percent. Reagan had adopted the theory of the Laffer curve, which contended that, after a certain threshold of taxation, people would simply choose not to work rather than remit most of their marginal earnings to the government.

The Laffer curve posited that by *lowering* tax rates, a government could actually enjoy *higher* revenue by way of more taxable income on the whole. In other words, the government would have a smaller slice of a much bigger pie, and therefore could have the best of both worlds: more revenue (good for the government) yet lower taxes (popular with the public).

Thus, in a series of steps, Reagan cut the top tax rate from 70 percent to 28 percent. He also significantly reduced the capital gains tax, which meant that investors would forgo a smaller piece of their investment gains to the government. Naturally, this meant that the bulk of tax cuts would be enjoyed by those at the upper ends of wealth and income.

In spite of this redistribution of wealth, the economy did grow, and it provided an engine for job creation. From November 1982 to November 1989, nearly nineteen million new jobs were created in America. No other country had ever generated such a large quantity of jobs in a period of only seven years. In turn, the unemployment rate (which had reached almost 11 percent during the recession of Reagan's first time) shrank to 5 percent, which most economists consider quite close to "full employment" in the United States (see Figure 17.3).

The thriving economy was a boon to productivity: during the Reagan years, $30 trillion of goods and services, and a corresponding increase of $5 trillion in personal wealth, was created. Although most of the asset gains

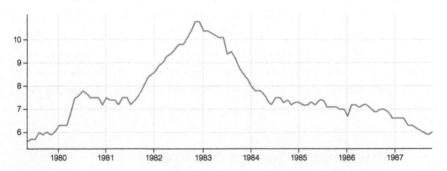

FIGURE 17.3 The unemployment rate went into the double-digits halfway into Reagan's first term, but then begin declining steadily to half the peak rate.

were enjoyed by the upper echelon, the growth in both jobs and living standards was spread out among all the classes.

Reagan was shrewd (or lucky, or both) to inflict the economic pain the nation required during the first two years of his first term, because by the end of 1984, the economy was doing well enough to provide him surging popularity and a landslide election victory. During his second term, the economy continued to thrive, as did the stock market, but well into Reagan's second term of office, a financial disaster was looming.

■ Bonds and Inflation Signal a Change

The investing public had become accustomed to a steadily rising market in the 1980s, which was a welcome change from the two decades prior. From August 1982 through August 1987, the most severe retracement in the S&P 500 was only about 13 percent, which took place late in 1983 and early 1984. Such a subdued dip in the course of a multi–hundred percent rise in the market was relatively painless for most investors. Indeed, throughout the course of the entire history of the U.S. stock market, there had never been such a consistent rise unhampered by a more severe downturn (see Figure 17.4).

Late in 1986, however, interest rates started inching up, signaling concerns about asset inflation. The thriving economy was starting to diminish bond prices, and the cost that businesses and consumers were having to pay in interest were on the rise. The stock market paid little heed to interest rates, and it continued to push higher in the first half of 1987 (see Figure 17.5).

The bond market, whose weakness often precedes that of equity markets, was starting to weaken badly, and although the investing public had no way of knowing it at the time, the market would reach a peak that it would not see again for two years on August 25, when it closed at 2,722, a nearly 2,000 point rise from the bottom just five years earlier.

Some fundamental economic data began to suggest caution. Most people are familiar with the price-to-earnings ratio as a simple way to measure fundamental value. For example, a $50 stock which represents $5 per share in earnings for a company has a price/earnings ratio of 10. The reciprocal of this is the earnings/price ratio, which is a way of comparing the "yield" of earnings for a stock versus other yield-bearing instruments. In this example, the earnings-to-price ratio would be 10 percent.

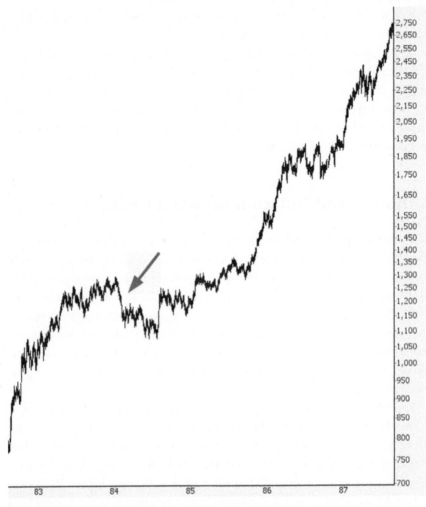

FIGURE 17.4 The stock market rose steadily from 1982 to 1987, with only a modest downturn, marked here by an arrow, briefly interrupting years of gains.

By the middle of 1987, the average earnings-to-price ratio was 4.75 percent, which was the lowest it had been in nearly 30 years. At the same time, the interest a person could earn on risk-free bonds was 9.4 percent. The "spread" between the earnings-to-price ratio and risk-free bond yields was therefore 4.65, which was a 35-year record. Simply stated, people were being paid much better in a risk-free bonds than they were being "paid" by the earnings from common stocks. Staying in common stocks didn't make rational economic sense any more.

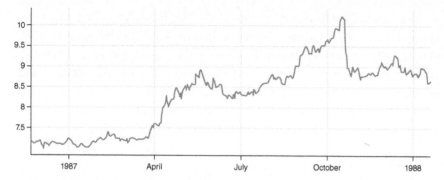

FIGURE 17.5 In the spring of 1987, interest rates started accelerating their climb, which in turn depressed bond prices.

■ Three Days in October

Between the market's peak in late August and October 13, 1987, the market shed about 10 percent of its value. The drops were not substantial, but they were fairly steady, although even with this diminishment the Dow was still up over 25 percent for the year.

Each month, the government's report of the trade deficit would be released, and for most of 1987, the reports had been disappointing. For month after month, the expectations for the trade deficit were smaller than the reported figure, and investors became concerned that the economic engine of the United States might be slowing down. More overseas goods were being purchased by U.S. consumers than U.S. goods were being purchased by foreign customers, and the outward flow of money was acute.

The latest trade deficit report was slated for October 14, and expectations were for a figure of about $14 billion. When the official figure of $15.68 billion was reported, the Dow slumped by 95 points, a drop of about 4 percent and, at the time, a record point drop for the index. The combination of rising interest rates and consistently disappointing deficit figures were beginning to tamp down the multiyear optimism surrounding equities.

There was another reason for the selloff, which was legislative. The U.S. Congress had put together a bill that would eliminate the tax benefits associated with debt-based corporate mergers. The "merger-mania" of the 1980s had been an important component in the ascent of stock prices, and a reduction in the attractiveness of corporate mergers would surely eliminate a key source of demand for shares.

The market's weakness persisted into the next day, when the Dow slipped another 58 points. The day following that, Friday, October 16, was an options expiration day. Expiration days often add extra volatility to an equity market's session, and this Friday was no exception—the market beat its record for a point-drop on the Dow 30, set only two days before, by falling another 108.35 points. It also set a new record for trading volume. The S&P 500 lost a full 9 percent just during that one week.

■ A Worrisome Weekend

The weekend following such a harrowing drop was infused with tension for investors. Treasury Secretary James Baker augmented this unease by announcing over the weekend his desire for the U.S. dollar to lose value versus other currencies, as a way to address the mounting trade deficits. A cheaper dollar, he reasoned, would increase demand for U.S. products and would shrink the gap. Overseas investors, however, sought to dump U.S.-denominated assets based on this pledge from the secretary.

More subtly, there was a growing awareness about disturbing similarities between the pattern of the stock market in 1929 and that of 1987. Some important investors, such as hedge fund manager Paul Tudor Jones, had honed in on this analog many months before. The similarities between the respective years in the market were virtually identical on a day-by-day basis, and as Tudor stated after the crash:

> The week of the crash was one of the most exciting periods of my life. We had been expecting a major stock market collapse since mid-1986 and had contingency plans drawn up because of the possibility we foresaw for a financial meltdown. When we came in on Monday, October 19, we knew that the market was going to crash that day.

Some money managers did not catch on to the analog as early. During the weekend of October 17–18, money manager Stanley Druckenmiller visited the legendary fund manager George Soros who showed him the 1929/1987 analog that Paul Tudor Jones had put together. As Druckenmiller recalled in Jack Schwager's 2008 book *The New Market Wizards*, "I was sick to my stomach when I went home that evening. I realized that I had blown it and that the market was about to crash."

■ Black Monday

Before the market opened on Monday, the *Wall Street Journal* published its own chart, overlaying the 1929 stock chart with 1987's and pointing out the alarming similarities. To an investing public that was already on edge, being informed by none other than the *Wall Street Journal* that the market had all the makings of another calamitous crash was a shock to the system.

Along with this, there were reports of two United States war ships bombing an Iranian oil platform in the Persian Gulf in retaliation for Iran's missile attack on a U.S. ship. As markets began opening in the Far East, equity prices began to slump badly, and everyone braced for what seemed like another bad day in the U.S. stock market.

At the opening bell, the market was already down another 8 percent, but there were so many orders to sell stocks that even the already-depressed indexes did not reflect the damage underneath the surface.

When stock specialists have far more orders to sell than to buy, there is an order imbalance, and some specialists did not begin executing trades at the opening bell. The price quotes were "stale" price points from the prior close. Many specialists for large stocks on the New York Stock Exchange did not begin trading until a full hour had already passed.

Even among the giant Dow 30 stocks, 11 of them were not open for trading at the opening bell, and a full 30 percent of the market capitalization of the S&P 500 had no trades during the first half hour on Monday, October 19. Thus, the price quotes used to calculate the indexes were artificially high.

This arithmetical circumstance led to a puzzling spread between the index prices that were quoted by the New York exchanges and the futures prices being quoted from Chicago. Arbitrage traders sought to take advantage of this ostensible spread by *buying* futures and placing equal orders to *sell* stocks when they opened. The belief was that the spread between the actual stocks and the futures contracts would compress back to zero, where it belonged, and the traders could profit from that compression. What they did not realize was that the quotes they were seeing for stocks did not reflect reality.

When the stocks did finally begin trading, the executed prices were dramatically lower than the speculators had been quoted, generating instant and substantial losses for the arbitrage traders. Even with stocks now finally open, the sheer volume pulsing through the exchange was more than the computers could handle, and quotations were typically an hour behind. Therefore, traders could not place bets with real information, since they had no idea what the actual price for a security was. They were unwittingly

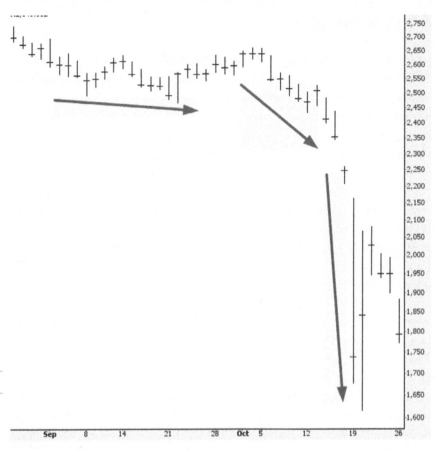

FIGURE 17.6 September and October 1987 witnessed an increasingly sharp decline in U.S. equity prices.

witnessing historical price data, basing decisions on quotes that were extraordinarily stale, instead of real-time quotes (see Figure 17.6).

As the trading day continued, and the Dow's drop worsened, the chairman of the Securities and Exchange Commission (SEC), who was making a speech, off-handedly commented after the speech that "there is some point, and I don't know what point that is, that I would be interested in talking to the New York Stock Exchange about a temporary, very temporary, halt in trading." Word swiftly got around that the exchange might close, which only added to the panic, since traders did not want to be stuck in positions with no market in which to liquidate them.

By the closing bell, the Dow had lost 508 points and closed at 1738.74, which represented a record-breaking drop of 22.61 percent in a single day.

The top news story on television and in newspapers around the world was of the stock market crash, and given how eerily the 1929 analog had played itself out, esteemed economists began to speak of the prospect of another major depression sweeping the nation, similar to the one experienced in the 1930s.

■ Turnaround Tuesday

In order to bring some calm to the markets, the U.S. Federal Reserve issued a brief statement before the opening bell, which read: "The Federal Reserve, consistent with its responsibilities as the Nation's central bank, affirmed today its readiness to serve as a source of liquidity to support the economic and financial system." This single sentence was the entire announcement.

Although the statement had absolutely no specifics at all, the explicit "support" of the Fed gave the market some much-needed confidence at the opening bell.

The buying was relatively short lived, however, as stocks began to weaken again, and order imbalances began cropping in once more. About 7 percent of all the stocks were closed for trading altogether, since the specialists could not adequately match buyers and sellers.

Panic began to break out in the Chicago futures market, and the S&P 500 contract fell to 181, a price far below the actual stock prices in New York. The futures were briefly selling at a 22 percent discount to the actual stocks in New York, when in reality the spread between the two should have been virtually zero.

The confusion with respect to stale quotes, now in its second day, compelled the futures exchange to halt stock index futures for the only time in its history during October 20 at 11:45 A.M. at the Chicago Board Options Exchange and at 12:15 P.M. at the Chicago Mercantile Exchange. These exchanges reopened a little more than an hour later, and with a large number of major corporations announcing stock buyback programs, the stock market finally got back on its feet and ended the day with a gain. The Dow Jones Industrials had a 400-point trading range on Tuesday, which, relative to the size of the index, was enormous.

■ Sorting Out the Reasons

The damage from the 1987 crash was severe. The Dow Jones Industrials fell 36 percent in just seven weeks, and the S&P 500 futures contract fell over 47 percent in the same time span (although a portion of this drop was due to the contracts selling at a substantial discount from the cash price, due to a combination of panic and stale stock quotes).

As with any financial panic's aftermath, people wanted someone or something to blame. As far as the public could tell, the market crashed with virtually no warning, and the entire year's gains had been wiped out in just a few days. Worse, the media was filled with fearsome stories about how a new Great Depression might be looming, just like the one that transpired after 1929's plunge in equities.

Portfolio insurance was the first stated culprit. This "insurance" was an investment strategy that had come into popular use by which computer models would calculate the optimal equity allocation for a given portfolio and use stock index futures to increase or reduce risk exposure.

In a normal market in which the alignment between underlying assets and futures prices was very close, portfolio insurance had been a useful tool, but in the mayhem of October 1987 when wild disparities between real value (stock prices) and theoretical value (futures contracts) took place, portfolio insurance only made the situation worse. Far from moderating portfolio allocations, the rapid-fire selling from portfolio insurance models greatly exacerbated the selling pressure.

The *Wall Street Journal* was prescient on this topic, as it noted on October 12, precisely a week before the crash, that portfolio insurance could "snowball into a stunning rout for stocks." Paul Tudor Jones, the fund manager who would profit so handsomely from the stock market debacle, described portfolio insurance as "an accident waiting to happen."

Changing economics, such as the yawning trade deficit gap and the steady climb in interest rates, were a more fundamental reason for the support being removed from the lofty equity prices in the summer of 1987. One interesting aspect of this period is how investor sentiment peaked just when the fundamentals were beginning to erode most severely.

In May 1987, according to the Drexel Burnham Lambert Decision-Makers Poll, institutional sentiment to the stock market was 40.2 percent bullish and 27.1 percent bearish. As the market extended its climb, sentiment toward stocks sweetened even further, with 57.2 percent bullish in August 1987 versus 19.6 percent bearish. Stock market bears were virtually nonexistent at what was actually the ideal time to be bearish on the stock market.

After the crash, these figures changed sharply, with bulls registering only 12.4 percent in January 1988 versus 48.2 percent bears. In spite of this pessimism, equities cautiously but consistently started their ascent again, although it would be nearly two years before prices on the Dow would match those seen in August 1987.

A depression did not occur, although investors got another quick scare in October 1989, almost exactly two years after the crash, when the Dow plunged by nearly 7 percent in a single day after a Japanese-led leveraged buyout of United Airlines fell through. The *Barron's* cover story that weekend was titled, "Oh, No, Not Again!" in a nod to the fears people had that, after two years of recovery, another crash was about to unfold (see Figure 17.7).

The drop in the market in 1989 was short lived, however, particularly since "circuit breakers" had been put in place on the exchanges to curtail

FIGURE 17.7   A severe drop in October 1989 turned out to be a single-day phenomenon, as equities did not continue crumbling as they had two years before.

unrelenting selling. Given certain thresholds in stock market losses, the exchange would be required to shut down either temporarily or for the remainder of the day, depending on the severity of the drop. Having these circuit breakers in place gave some comfort to traders that a runaway crash like the one in 1987 would not be permitted to happen again.

The jolt that U.S. equities felt when the Japanese investment group seeking to purchase United Airlines failed was a warning shot, however, from a much larger crisis developing overseas. In the next chapter, we will explore the economic miracle that took place in Japan and the bear market which followed, which would dwarf anything that had happened in the United States during the 1980s.

CHAPTER 18

The Rising and Setting Sun of Japan

A s the summer came to a close in 1945, Japan lay in ruins. It had spent the past five years at war, and the nation had been assaulted by an unrelenting fire-bombing campaign, climaxed, of course, by the only two nuclear weapons ever dropped on humans in world history. Japan, once with dreams of Pacific-wide domination, was now one of the poorest and most devastated nations on Earth.

269

The United States, Japan's fiercest opponent during the war, now turned its attention to rebuilding a country in which 25 percent of housing had been laid waste and whose power grid and industrial infrastructure were effectively non-existent. What would happen over the next half-century would become one of the most astonishing economic miracles—as well as one of history's greatest collapses—ever recorded.

■ The Early Economic Structure

As an island-nation, Japan for centuries had been isolated from the rest of the world, at first by the surrounding sea, and later by deliberate cultural choice. Japan was a nation that, as far as possible, practiced self-reliance. In the late nineteenth century, there existed a world of difference between

FIGURE 18.1   Until the middle of the twentieth century, the majority of Japanese occupied themselves with agricultural jobs.

highly developed industrialized nations—such as the United States and Britain—when compared to Japan.

As a largely agricultural society, Japan focused its modernization efforts on improving mechanization and modernization of farming. From the 1880s to the beginning of the twentieth century, Japan made great improvements in its ability to produce large amounts of foodstuffs, which expanded its ability to trade with other nations for the natural resources and other goods it lacked (see Figure 18.1).

During this time, several important characteristics developed in the Japanese mindset with respect to business. First, as an island that needed goods from other nations to feed and provide for its own population, Japan became an adept and active trader with other nations overseas; second, as a country that benefited from the inventiveness of those same nations, it became quite proficient at adopting and *improving* technologies and techniques from its trading partners; and third, as a culture, Japan was clearly divided between landowners (a tiny percentage of the population) and those who actually worked the land.

In a way, Japan was, even during the early twentieth century, operating within the same agricultural feudalism that Europe had during the Middle

Ages, hundreds of years before. The majority of the population was working in agricultural, and almost all of them toiled on the land with little in the way of rights or profits.

■ The Aftershocks of War

World War II took most able-bodied men off the farms and put them into battle. At the war's conclusion, the reversal of this flow of bodies meant that nearly 8 million people left the military and were expected to return to civilian life. This was coupled with the fact that all those formerly employed creating the weapons, transportation, and other necessary products for wartime were no longer needed, and over a million and a half Japanese citizens returned from overseas to their native land. In all, over 13 million people who wanted to work needed jobs after the war ended.

Japan's need for food was greater than ever, so the vast agricultural industry was still awaiting all those workers. Farming provided work for 18 million citizens, but, as before, the work did not pay well, and even those employed found themselves underemployed. The country was reduced to subsistence living, as millions toiled in the fields just to have something to eat each night.

There was another big problem for Japan, and that was a lack of energy. Even though Japan had abundant coal resources, the people who had been forcibly made to extract those resources—Korean and Chinese prisoners of war—had returned to their own countries, and there was a lack of skilled workers and necessary equipment to extract the necessary coal for the nation's energy requirements.

In short, Japan had millions of people without enough work, enough food, or enough energy, and it was widely feared that the winter of 1945–1946 would usher in widespread starvation throughout a country that had already lived through years of horror.

It was during this era that another deep-set cultural principal was embraced: small families. In a country with too many mouths to feed, it was decided the only reasonable long-term solution was to reduce the birthrate.

■ The United States Rebuilds

The United States understood that a healthy, prosperous ally in the Asia region would be far more valuable than a ruined nation, and it sought to rebuild and feed Japan to help the country get back on its feet. To this end, it put into motion three policy reforms that would rework the cultural and economic fabric of the nation for decades to come.

The first reform was to break up what were known as the *zaibatsu*, which were the business conglomerates that were given favorable treatment by the government and enjoyed great advantage over any competition. These conglomerates were granted lower taxes, large government loans and subsidies, and favored selection during government contract provision. A cozy and corrupt relationship existed between the government and these firms, and it would be impossible for the healing force of capitalism to exist side-by-side with this feudalistic relic.

The dismantling of *zaibatsu* power took several forms, many of which had the goal of establishing a more equal relationship between the public and the management of an organization. The companies would be required to sell their stock to the public and, where necessary, break up into smaller, independent units as opposed to operate as a huge monopoly. The groundwork was put in place for real competition, and the Anti-Monopoly Law would ensure that no large firm was permitted to achieve a stranglehold on the recovery.

The second reform, which was especially important for an agrarian culture like Japan's, was land reform. Here too, the general goal was to democratize the business entity, ending the landlord-serf relationship. The government bought the large land holdings of the farmers and put this land, divided into much smaller lots, into the hands of those working the soil.

A farmer working his own land not only is going to be much more proficient at the task than a distant and detached owner, but will also maximize the use of the land since he has the opportunity for personal profit.

The land reform which was put into place swiftly transformed the agribusiness of the nation, as the percentage of farmers who owned the land on which they worked went from only about 50 percent up to 90 percent just a few years later. This reinvigorated farming in the country and eliminated the prospect of potential starvation that the country feared at war's end.

Finally, the nature of what it meant to be an employee in Japan was changed with a series of laws that led to substantial growth of labor unions. Unions had been virtually nonexistent in Japan until the end of World War II, and workers had no meaningful rights. Once workers were giving the opportunity to organize, bargain, and strike, unions became prominent with amazing swiftness: membership in labor unions grew from essentially 0 percent in 1945 to 60 percent in 1949.

Now workers had a voice they never had before: they could organize themselves, collectively bargain, or protest any management practices viewed as dangerous or unfair. Beyond this, Japanese business took on the rather unusual pledge of lifetime employment. As long as an employee was willing to work hard for a company, he in turn was told he could expect gainful employment until retirement. Thus, workers in Japan went from having almost no rights at all to enjoying some of the most generous rights of any employees in the world.

Besides all of these important reforms, there is one other critical aspect to remember about the new Japan: they were forbidden from having a military. Although this may have seemed like a devastating concession at the time, extracted from a humiliated and defeated nation, it turned out to be a tremendous economic blessing. A country that is forbidden from having its own military is also relieved of the huge and nonproductive expense. The United States was going to provide whatever military protection the Japanese might have otherwise enjoyed, all without having to fund it.

■ From Dodge to Independence

In the late 1940s, it was quite clear to the United States that they had a new war on their hands—a Cold War—and that a strong ally in Asia was more important than ever. Although Japan was recovering, the United States wanted to accelerate the recovery and sought the help of Detroit banker Joseph Dodge to focus on the currency and economy of the nascent government.

Inflation was starting to get out of control in Japan, so the Dodge plan (known as the "Dodge Line") set out three laws to address the problem: (1) require a balanced government budget; (2) cease the loans from the Reconstruction Finance Bank, since the flood of cash had already set the nation's recovery in motion and was actually starting to cause economic harm; and (3) eliminate subsidies being handed out by the government, since they were interfering with natural business growth.

Dodge's guidance helped stabilize the Japanese economy and its currency, and his economic leadership was, in the years to come, recognized as invaluable. Empower Hirohito himself would, in 1962, award Dodge a medal in recognition of his work during this period of economic recovery.

A greater blessing came to Japan from the most ironic of sources: another war. In 1950, when the Korean War began, Japan found itself with two great

FIGURE 18.2 The Korean War was an unexpected blessing to the Japanese economy, much as World War II had saved the United States from falling back into another economic depression in 1939.

economic advantages: (1) it had rebuilt itself to the point that it was a proficient and capable industrial resource; and (2) it was geographically situated at a strategically important place relative to the Korean peninsula (see Figure 18.2).

Just as the U.S. economy was saved from another depression when World War II began, the Japanese economy was saved by the Korean War. Japan was so firmly on its feet by 1952 that the United States ended its occupation of the country. In just a few years, Japan was changed from the most ferocious enemy of the United States to a reliable base for its ships and planes.

■ Thing-Making

In the early 1950s, Japan focused on what it called "priority production," which meant a focus on basics such as coal mining, steel production, and shipbuilding. It was creating a solid foundation for the widespread industrialization that would come years later, and it helped move the country away from its former focus on farming. In the modern world, becoming proficient at industries such as steel would be more valuable than another marginal increase in rice output.

The Japanese recognized they had a special talent for *monozukuri* ("thing-making"), and throughout the country, one- and two-man businesses set up shops in spare bedrooms, garages, and extra offices to manufacture whatever they think they could sell.

At first, "Made in Japan" was synonymous with cheap, shoddy, copycat products (see Figure 18.3). Japan did not yet have the experience or infrastructure to create high-quality products, but what the rest of the world did not realize is that, in steps, Japan was working its way up to becoming a formidable competitor. Although Japan's resources were limited, the ability of its citizens to learn from and, more important, *improve* upon the ideas, products, and techniques of other countries would become its greatest asset.

Even though the years after war's end had saved Japan from starvation, it was still a very poor country, and almost all its citizens struggled just to get by.

FIGURE 18.3 Most Japanese products from the 1950s were inexpensive toys and very simple consumer electronics. "Made in Japan" was, at the time, synonymous with "Cheap."

In 1950, an average Japanese citizen had the same income as a person living in Ethiopia or Somalia. It was fortunate for Japan that a war was taking place that was close enough to be economically helpful but not so close as to be dangerous, but once the war ended, it was unclear how Japan could thrive on the world scene on nothing but cheap knock-offs from the great economic powers.

This reality was summed up succinctly by none other than U.S. Secretary of State John Foster Dulles, who said of the Japanese that they *"... should not expect to find a big U.S. market, because the Japanese don't make things we want."* It may have been true at the moment, but that statement would soon face a very different reality.

■ The Soaring Sixties

The Korean War gave Japan the resources and the reason to build up a more substantial industrial infrastructure, compelling the nation to invest in factories and equipment. In what would become a theme for decades to come, the Japanese would visit and learn from factories in other, more developed parts of the world and bring those techniques back to Japan. Subsequent improvements would, in time, make Japan a more efficient and cost-effective producer than whomever they copied in the first place (see Figure 18.4).

By the early 1960s, Japan's recovery and reputation had made such progress that it was honored to be the host of the 1964 Olympic Games in Tokyo. In fewer than 20 years, the country had gone from a devastated wasteland to a relatively prosperous and recognized global participant.

The economic growth of Japan in the 1960s was astonishing. Whereas most industrialized nations considered a growth rate of perhaps 2.5 percent or 3 percent per year to be healthy, Japan was experiencing annual economic growth that reached into the double digits. The growth rate by the late 1960s was nearly 11 percent annually and, in an event that no one would have dared predicted just a decade before, Japan was the second-largest economy in the world by 1968. Only the United States, its former opponent that had restored Japan to economic health, was larger.

In spite of the divorce between government and business that the United States had demanded at war's end, the Japanese government had reestablished a variety of healthy and largely beneficial ties between its national government and the companies within its borders. Perhaps the most important of these was the Ministry of International Trade and Industry (MITI), which acted as a brain trust, finance arm, and adviser for the important industries of the country.

FIGURE 18.4 Japan began to develop a good reputation in the worlds of photographic equipment and consumer electronics, such as this early transistor radio.

At the same time, in spite of the elimination of *zaibatsu*, a somewhat new form called *keiretsu* was conjured up, which promoted integration among related companies. Companies in strategic industries (namely power, coal production, steel production, and shipbuilding) were supported and guided by MITI, and cross-ownership among key companies in these fields was actively encouraged.

The *keiretsu* were also encouraged to eschew the short-term focus of their Western competitors and focus on long-term economic growth and profits. The "long view" became the desired view as far as the MITI was concerned, and—as with lifetime employment and widespread employee unionization—a focus on long-term profits instead of short-term results became a relatively unique aspect of the Japanese economy on the world scene.

■ OPEC and Little Japanese Cars

As the Korean War had provided unexpected benefits to Japan in the early 1950s, two decades later, a different crisis would again been a boon to Japan: the energy crisis. When the Organization of the Petroleum Exporting Countries (OPEC) exercised its muscle during the early 1970s, the price of crude oil (and, in turn, gasoline) shot higher. Detroit, which since the inception of the automobile had been the world leader in car production, was still producing millions of oversized, overweight, gas-guzzling cars that were instantly less attractive to the buying public (see Figure 18.5).

FIGURE 18.5 The gas crisis of 1973 was a shock to both the American public as well as its automakers. Gas rationing, long gas lines, and sharply higher energy prices became the norm.

There was an alternative, of course, in the form of Japanese cars. The small, low-cost, gas-efficient cars from Japan had never become very popular in the United States, but the gas crisis gave them a new reason to be attractive. Datsun (known today as Nissan), Honda, and other Japanese car makers latched on the opportunity to sell their relatively fuel efficient vehicles to overseas markets that were confronted with much higher gas prices.

As Americans began to embrace Japanese autos, they discovered other advantages. For one thing, Japanese manufacturers were very progressive in their use of robot technology in their plants. Robots don't go on strike and, by definition, they don't make human errors. Thus, the cars tended to be of higher quality than similar U.S. offerings. In addition, because of Japanese manufacturing efficiencies, makers such as Honda were more economically priced than Ford or General Motors products (see Figure 18.6).

The rising success of Japan was mirrored by the demise of the United States. Once-proud industries such as steel and autos began to decline

FIGURE 18.6 Early Japanese cars were peculiar, but as automakers such as Datsun and Honda gained proficiency and insight into the American market, their cars would outstrip their American rivals and pose a serious threat to Detroit.

with alarming speed in the United States, and terms like the *rust belt* were used to describe sections of the United States that had formerly been areas of widespread middle-class employment. Resentment started to grow that the Japanese were somehow being "unfair" by offering attractively priced products that were more efficient and popular than the American equivalents.

■ Electronics Giant

Alongside Japan's success with cars was its growing dominance in electronics. Sony had offered its first transistor radio to the market back in 1955, but by the late 1970s, the most respected and innovative makers of consumer electronics were the Japanese. When Sony introduced its Walkman, for example, it became an international sensation, much like the Apple iPod that would be introduced a quarter-century later.

Japan started to get a reputation as a kind of modern-day utopia, with content workers, an unstoppable manufacturing base, and the world's longest life expectancy. It became easy to speculate that the United States and the Japan would eventually switch roles: that is, with the United States on the decline, with its overpaid workforce, inferior products, and shrinking industries, it would soon found itself in the number 2 economic spot that Japan had occupied for so long.

The late 1970s and early 1980s provided Japan a tremendous growth in the variety and popularity of consumer electronics. Old standbys like televisions, speakers, and radios were still popular, but new products such as the Betamax and VHS video recorders, video cameras, and personal computers were introduced (see Figure 18.7).

Japan made important inroads in virtually all aspects of electronics, particularly semiconductors, computer components, and printed circuits boards. Just about the only two areas in which Japan hadn't achieved domination were integrated circuits (led by the U.S. firm Intel) and software. It was widely believed that it would not be long before Japan captured those areas as well, since it had proven so adept at everything else.

American firms became envious of the remarkable prosperity in Japan, and organizations in the United States tried to ape the behavior of their overseas competitors in ways that, in retrospect, seem comic. Many blue-collar workers in Japan would begin their workday with calisthenics, for example, so some American firms, in a stellar example of confusing

FIGURE 18.7 The video cassette recorder had been used professionally for a number of years, but models affordable for the home became popular in the late 1970s, giving Japan a whole new category of electronics to create and sell.

correlation with causation, told their workers to start performing calisthenics as well. Not surprisingly, this did not create any kind of miraculous turnaround in America.

Meanwhile, Japan's coffers continued to bulge. Japan was the number 1 creditor nation on the planet, and it was consistently the largest exporter. The Japanese economic miracle was studied, discussed, and imitated, and although the end of the twentieth century was still years away, academics discussed the very real possibility that the "American Century" (the twentieth) would yield to the "Japanese Century" (the twenty-first), just as America had closed the door on the "British Century" of the 1900s. It was an alluring and easy-to-believe narrative.

■ The Bubble Swells

Japan's economic growth did not, of course, go unnoticed by its stock market. The Nikkei 225 index, which stood at 1929 on May 31, 1970, grew steadily to 5,359 by January 31, 1973, an expansion of 177 percent. By August 31, 1981, the Nikkei stood at 8,019, a growth of about 315 percent from the 1970 level. As tremendous as those returns are, looking at the long-term chart of the Nikkei, the growth was relatively steady and, in light of the bubble to come, quite muted.

The U.S. stock market was in the doldrums for much of that time, and the long-term bull market in U.S. equities did not begin until around 1982. During the 1980s, both the United States and Japan would enjoy spectacular rises in their equity markets, although Japan's growth would overshadow that of the United States. By October 31, 1987, even with the worldwide crash in stock prices, the Nikkei was at 26,646, a value 1,200 percent above where it began in 1970.

Businessmen, scholars, and politicians all paid attention to Japan with increasing admiration and, in some cases, alarm. Lawrence Summers, who would in forthcoming years have a variety of senior roles in academia and the federal government, said in December 1989:

> Today, Japan is the world's second largest economy ... an Asian economic bloc with Japan at its apex ... is clearly in the making. This all raises the possibility that the majority of American people feel that Japan is a greater threat to the U.S. than the Soviet Union are right now.

The stock market in Japan, by December 1989, had a value of $4 trillion, which was 50 percent higher than the value of the entire U.S. stock market. Although as a country Japan was much smaller in terms of size, population, and economy than the United States, it sported an equity market valuation substantially higher than the United States, and Japanese stocks likewise accounted for nearly 50 percent of the entire world's stock market valuation.

As with many bubbles, attempts plausible "reasons" were offered to explain away the extraordinary price levels. The most common was that

Japanese accounting practices were extremely conservative and thus substantially understated earnings. On the contrary, Japanese accounting took great liberties, using a variety of gimmicks to mask any weakness.

The euphemism created for this was *zaitech* or "financial engineering," in which positive financial information (such as profits from stock trading and other risk endeavors) flowed right to the profit statement, whereas negative information (like assets whose values had declined) would be sequestered to an off-the-books balance sheet. As the stock market kept climbing, corporations who otherwise had no connection to investing would seek out gigantic, low-interest loans to invest in the Nikkei with the hope of padding their profits with speculative equity gains.

On the surface, the fundamental numbers were very elevated: the price-to-earnings ratio was, on average, 60, which was quadruple the similar metric for U.S. stocks. The valuation of individual companies was, in some cases, breathtaking as well. NTT Corporation, the equivalent of America's AT&T, was itself worth most than AT&T, General Motors, General Electric, Exxon, *and* IBM all put together.

For a single telephone company in a relatively small nation to have a value greater than five of the largest, best-known corporations in the world was, of course, astonishing, but very few people were willing to declare a "bubble" of what had been such the long-running success story known colloquially as Japan, Inc.

■ Unparalleled Property Prosperity

As amazing as the Nikkei 225 was, it paled next to the growth in real estate prices. The value of property in Japan, spurred on by generous lending by Japanese financial institutions, became parabolic. In particular, the land in Tokyo, particularly certain coveted districts downtown, reached valuations that would have been unthinkable even a few years prior.

By 1990, the total value of property in Japan was estimated at $20 trillion, which was double the value of all the stock markets in the world. Thinking of this another way, the market was declaring at the time that the land in Japan was worth double what every public company on the planet was worth, including the very richly-valued companies of Japan itself (which, one could surmise, *already owned* a meaningful part of the aforementioned real estate).

Comparing property-to-property produces other surprising figures. The United States, for example, is 25 times larger than Japan, but its estimated real estate value in 1990 was just one-*fifth* that of Japan's. In other words, Japan soil had a value 125 times greater than U.S. soil.

Lenders became more generous with those seeking credit, and the time-lines for required payment stretched farther and farther into the future. Whereas 15- and 30-year loans are the standard in the United States, "multigeneration" loans became commonplace in Japan, with 90- and even 100-year payback periods. A family could buy into a house with every expectation that their grandchildren, two unborn generations in the future, would still be making payments.

In 1989 and 1990, when gawking over both equity and property valuations in Japan became commonplace in the media, one of the most frequently cited anecdotes was that the land on which the Japanese Imperial Palace sat was worth as much as the entire state of California. And if Japan was feeling that California was not enough, it theoretically could have bought the entire country of the United States in exchange for the city of Tokyo, whose values were at that time equivalent.

Golf courses, too, became a peculiar and particularly coveted form of real estate by the Japanese. The golf courses in Japan alone, at their peak, were valued at half a trillion dollars. And because land in Japan's cities became so exorbitantly priced, builders had to become increasingly inventive about how to create a useful building on smaller and smaller plots of land. So-called "pencil buildings" began springing up, buildings so small that they could house only one office per floor.

One can grow numb to all the superlatives about Japanese land at this time, but one other anecdote illustrates how manic the situation had become: in the most coveted section of Tokyo's downtown, the Ginza shopping district, a minuscule three-square-meter bit of land, unfit for absolutely any commercial purpose, sold for $600,000. It was large enough for a person to comfortably place a sleeping bag and lay down, but little else (see Figure 18.8).

The desire to buy up assets spilled outside of Japan's own borders. Real estate in Hawaii and the continental United States was acquired with increasing fervor, as were extraordinarily expensive works of art. Records were set as Van Gogh's "Dr. Gachet" painting sold for $82.5 million. The buyer admitted he paid $30 million more than he intended, but as easy as money was to make, particularly for this Japanese billionaire, the extra $30 million was worth winning the auction.

Americans began to have increasing angst about wildly wealthy Japanese companies buying up such icons as Rockefeller Center, the Empire State

FIGURE 18.8 The famed Ginza shopping district in downtown Tokyo enjoyed real estate prices never seen before anywhere in the world.

Building, Pebble Beach Golf Course, and Paramount Studios, to say nothing of the hundreds of smaller, lesser-known properties and companies that Japan was acquiring. It began to seem that Japan wasn't just going to pass in front of the United States economically; it was going to take it over in the process of doing so.

■ The Japan That Can Say No

One with a contrarian mindset often looks to peaks in social awareness about a particular phenomenon or circumstances in order to speculate about the likelihood of a reversal. The "cover curse" is a simple example of this: that is, when a particular social movement, or personality, or other cultural phenomenon begins making the cover story of widely read publications, a reversal of fortune or at least popularity is often at hand.

An extreme example of this came in the form not of a cover story, but of an entire book. In 1989, at the very height of Japan's economic, equity, and property bubbles, *The Japan That Can Say No* was written and published. It was coauthored by Shintaro Ishihara, the minister of transportation and an important legislative figure, and Akio Morita, the cofounder of Sony Corporation.

The book was an instant sensation, and it was considered quite controversial because one of the prominent points it made was that lazy, dim-witted American workers had been beaten by hardworking, educated Japanese competitors and, thus, would soon find themselves in a permanent second place.

It was a book full of defiance to the United States—the country to which the authors felt the Japanese should say "no" to—which was extraordinary considering that America had laid all the groundwork for Japan's prosperity in the preceding 40 years.

Among other things, the book made arguments that:

- The United States dropped the atomic bomb on Japan out of racism, since they otherwise would have dropped the bomb on Germany (this conveniently leaves out the fact that the atomic bomb wasn't ready or tested while the European theatre was still active, and America's intended target for the atomic bomb was, in fact, originally Germany).

- American businesses focus too much on financial engineering and mergers as opposed to the creation of quality manufactured products.

- The United States doesn't make desirable products, which is why it runs a constant trade deficit.

- Japanese character is superior to that of Americans.

- U.S. product quality is low because U.S. laborer quality is low, particularly compared to the highly educated Japanese worker.

- Japan should use its technology superiority as a strategic negotiating weapon; for example, Japan could threaten to provide the Soviet Union with important new technology unless the United States agreed to a given set of demands.

A book with these kinds of assertions would naturally lead to some backlash, particularly considering how uncomfortable Americans already were with Japan as an unstoppable economic force. These worries would soon be abated, however, and the United States wouldn't have to do anything to make the bravado in *The Japan That Can Say No* a moot point. Japan was poised for a long and devastating reversal of fortune.

■ The Big Crash

Equities in Japan peaked on the last trading day of the year in 1989. The Nikkei ended the year with a crescendo, and the majority of market observers agreed that the market was not overvalued. There was no reason they should not have expected 1990 to bring in more profits, since the trend had been so strong, so persistent, and so long-lived.

The Bank of Japan, however, had been eyeing the exploding stock and property values with increasing concern, and in January 1990, it took action by raising interest rates. The effect on stocks was swift, and in 1990, instead of padding the already-incredible profits of stock owners, equities went into a free-fall, losing nearly half their value by the end of the year.

A stock market drop that severe is bad news in any market, but in Japan, due to the highly leveraged and deeply intertwined corporations, banks, and cross-holdings of stock, the effect was far worse. Just as the creative financial engineering had supercharged the gains of all asset classes during the rise, the exact opposite effect took hold now that the principal fuel for asset appreciation—the Nikkei 225—was shrinking.

Property values had a delayed reaction to the sudden increase in interest rates. For most of 1990, the extraordinary property values stayed aloft. (A very similar phenomenon took place a decade later in the Silicon Valley, since the extremely high prices for homes and, even more so, office space did not follow the Nasdaq downward until half a year after the bubble first popped.)

The pain to property owners would not be long in coming, however, and given the 100-fold increase in values that had been enjoyed over the years, it is not surprising that such a large portion of asset values were at risk of disappearing. By August 1992, the Nikkei was down to 14,309, a loss of about $2 trillion in Japanese equity prices (with more to follow), and, at the same time, real estate assets had dropped by $8 trillion from their peak.

The Bank of Japan did not reverse its decision, even given the clearly negative effect it was having on asset values. On the contrary, it kept increasing rates, and it did not resume easing until July 1991, once the horrendous effects were already in full swing.

■ Damaging Demographics

As the core assets of equities and property values plunged in Japan, concerns about worldwide Japanese domination vanished, and speculation turned to what challenges, as opposed to opportunities, the country might be facing.

Because of Japan's low birthrate, a tradition initially sewn into the cultural fabric in the days after the war to stave off national hunger, the simple demographic fact was that fewer and fewer wage earners would be available to support a larger and larger retired population. The median age in Japan was relatively high, and it was moving higher, and the trends looked very negative for supporting the national welfare system. Similar projections were calculated for the United States, but the Japanese situation was much worse.

On top of this, the decades-old guarantee of lifetime employment started to fray at the edges, as companies found it to be fiscally impossible to maintain full employment in an environment of falling demand and shrinking prices. The unemployment rate in Japan had been essentially zero for many years, but a million manufacturing jobs were eliminated between 1992 and 1996, pushing the unemployment rate from 2.1 percent to double that amount in the same time span. By 2001, unemployment would stand at 5.6 percent, a remarkably high rate for a country long accustomed to assured gainful employment.

There was a subtle cultural reason for the longevity of Japan's economic problems as well: a deep-set desire to avoid losing face. The huge corporations were, in a sense, anthropomorphized expressions of Japanese culture, and a refusal to admit serious mistakes, declare extraordinarily severe losses, and begin the lengthy healing process was avoided (and, as of this writing, decades later, is still being avoided).

No less a figure than Alan Greenspan wrote in his 2008 book *The Age of Turbulence* (Penguin) that "[t]he Japanese purposely accepted hugely expensive economic stagnation to avoid massive loss of face for many companies and individuals." Banks, for example, would move bad loans on the books to subsidiaries, thus erasing the liabilities on paper but failing to confront the reality of the situation, which is that the loans would almost certainly never be repaid.

Just as accounting gimmicks were used to pad profits on the ascent of assets, so, too, were different techniques used to tuck away "bad" assets with the hope that they would somehow be remedied at an undetermined point in the future.

At the Tokyo office of Germany's Deutsche Bank, chief economist Ken Courtis succinctly summed up the financial configuration of Japanese finances as having "Himalayan balance sheets and Saharan returns." In other words, the meager profits still being thrown off from enterprise were dwarfed by the monstrous debts that had been accrued to fund the stratospheric climb in the first place.

■ The Lost Decades

Predictions from the late 1980s about Japan's becoming the world's largest economy were swiftly rendered out of the question. Instead, in the 20 years from 1990 to 2010, the gross domestic product (GDP) of the country remained unchanged at about $5.7 trillion. During the same time, the United States (which certainly was not spared its own share of financial and political problems) saw its economy leap from about $7 trillion to nearly $15 trillion. By 2010, the Asian country occupying the second spot on the economic leader board was not Japan, but China.

Although the bulk of the Nikkei's collapse was in the first several years of its bear market, the losses continued over the years, and in October 2008, the Nikkei printed a value of less than 7,000, an 82 percent drop from its approximate value in 39,000 almost two decades earlier. Just as the U.S. stock market took almost 30 years to beat its valuations from 1929, after its own Great Depression, Japan likewise would almost certainly not see 1989-level valuations on the Nikkei until well into the future (see Figure 18.9).

Even though the accounting departments of Japanese corporations were avoiding putting the unseemly fiscal realities on paper, some companies and

FIGURE 18.9 The Nikkei, shown here over a nearly 40-year period. The climb from about 2,000 to nearly 40,000 took 20 years, whereas the collapse to about 7,500 took only about 13 years. Even with a partial recovery already in place, it could be decades before the Nikkei ever beats its late 1989 high.

individuals had no choice but to sell, at great losses, assets they had acquired only a few years earlier.

Hawaii's Westin Maui resort, purchased for $290 million, was sold in 2000 for less than half that price. Another Hawaiian trophy property, the Grand Wailea, produced a similar 50 percent loss when it was sold for $300 million in 2000, sharply in contrast with the $600 million paid during the peak of Japan's prosperity a decade earlier. On the continental United States, the famed Pebble Beach golf course was likewise liquidated at a modest percentage of its purchase price.

Corporate acquisitions by Japanese conglomerates fared no better. When the Rockefeller Center, one of New York's most famous and iconic properties, was bought by Mitsubishi, it was just another piece of evidence that Japan was taking over America. When Mitsubishi unloaded the property in 1996, it took a $2 billion loss. Sony suffered even worse from its ill-fated purchase of Columbia Pictures, as $2.7 billion was written off the corporate books.

No matter what accounting games may have been going on in Japan, the government's financial situation was more straightforward and far more alarming. Whereas the government used to enjoy surpluses, it now found itself having to borrow increasingly large amounts of money through bond issuances in order to support the nation's welfare system as well as the multitudinous projects created to shore up the country's employment.

Japan's percentage of debt compared to its GDP was about 60 percent in 1990; 15 years later, it was nearly 200 percent, and as of this writing, the figure is 230 percent and growing, requiring the use of the term "quadrillion" to express the debt in terms of yen.

One might think that with the trillions of dollars of currency generated by the Japanese government to address its economic woes, inflation would be rampant. On the contrary, the astronomically large debts in the country act as a metaphorical black hole for all the new currency, and deflation has persisted in Japan steadily for over two decades. Those many years of plunging asset values, weak growth, and deflationary pressures led to the term *lost decades,* used by Japanese to describe the era.

■ A Perpetual State of Recovery

Central bankers are persistently fearful of two negative outcomes: inflation and deflation. An inflationary environment yields shrinking buying power, the wage/price spiral, and public frustration at the rising cost of goods and services. A hike in interest rates, such as the suffocating increases by the Fed in the early 1980s, usually curtails these problems.

Deflation, however, is far more nettlesome. While the notion of goods and services getting perpetually cheaper might sound appealing to the everyday public, deflation is far more a curse than a blessing. Such an environment creates a harmful desire to hoard cash, since it is usually the only thing that gains value over time. This means that the flow of money in an economy is sharply curtailed, harming employment, wages, and growth. After all, why pay $2,000 for a new television when it is likely the same product will cost $1,000 in a year?

This kind of deflationary environment is precisely what Japan has experienced, not for months or years but decades. The public has grown accustomed to a feeling of resignation about job prospects, salaries, and the future. Long-term deflation has a gruesome effect on the public psyche with respect to the economy, and people resort to a combination of fatalism and pessimism.

This is not to say that the Japanese, particularly the government, haven't made many efforts to turn the situation around, but many of these projects have led to nowhere. One example is the MITI's "Fifth Generation" computing project, which in the 1980s convinced some industry professionals that Japan would, once and for all, finally own the entire computer industry, from semiconductors to memory to hardware.

The Japanese computer industry poured $450 million into the ill-fated project, which promised to leapfrog the rest of the world by producing breakthrough supercomputing technology and artificial intelligence. Instead, the project produced absolutely nothing, and MITI wound up offering whatever was developed during the project to anyone in the world who wanted it for free. American software and hardware companies could rest easy that Japan would continue to be relegated to making chips and circuit boards, and they would lose a lot of that business to Korea and China in any case (see Figure 18.10).

The lifetime employment pledge of Japanese employers was rendered a historical footnote, and increasing numbers of businesses replaced permanent workers with temporary hires that could easily be dismissed and didn't come with the burden of employee benefits. By 2009, a full third of the Japanese labor force were "temps."

These everyday citizens had problems of their own left over from the asset bubble. Many of them got caught up in the real estate frenzy and bought residential property on credit. With the bubble fully deflated, a family that

FIGURE 18.10 Japan excelled at several areas of component manufacturing for high technology, but it never found success with personal computers or software on the world stage.

paid, for example, $500,000 for a small condominium in 1990 would see its value diminish to about $140,000 a decade later. As of this writing, residential properties are worth only 10 percent what they were at the peak of the asset bubble, and families are making payments on mortgages that vastly exceed the value of the property.

A 90 percent drop in residential real estate is potentially ruinous, but the damage done to commercial real estate values was even more extraordinary. The choicest commercial real estate in Tokyo was fetching $139,000 per square foot in 1990, but a quarter-century later, the same square footage had a value of 1 percent the peak price. Altogether, stock and property owners in Japan witnessed a mind-boggling $20 *trillion* drop in value to their holdings between 1990 and 2010.

Japan's insistence on "saving face" and not making the necessary write-offs and readjustments in the wake of the asset bubble provided nearby Asian countries with superb business opportunities. Even though the 1990s were horrible for Japan, they were fantastic years for most of the rest of the industrialized world, and Korean firms like Samsung left former leaders like Sony far behind in the electronics race.

Meanwhile, the Japanese government would continue to prop up banks and businesses with virtually unlimited amounts of cash, thus creating a nation full of "zombie" companies that, by honest accounting, should have declared bankruptcy years ago. The Japanese government also spent $10 trillion on various public works projects between 1991 and 2001 which, while effective at keeping the unemployment rate relatively low, still sank Japan ever-deeper into a national debt for projects that were, in some cases, absolutely unnecessary "make-work."

The recovery Japan enjoyed in the 1950s, 1960s, and 1970s was one of the most amazing success stories in the history of business. A nearly-ruined nation literally rose from its own ashes and threatened, for a while, to become the indomitable leader of all the economies of the world.

However, the country's hubris at its peak, as well as its reckless lending and overly cozy relationship between banks, businesses, and the government conspired together to make a bubble whose popping created shock waves that are still keenly felt a quarter-century later.

The last decade of the twentieth century and the first decade of the twenty-first were humbling for Japan as a country and as a people. As the United States struggles with its own fiscal problems and future welfare obligations, Japan has mutated from a country that threatened to take America's number 1 spot on the world stage into something closer to an object lesson in how a country's finances should not be managed after such a devastating blow. In the halls of U.S. Congress, lawmakers point to Japan as an example of the kind of path the United States should refuse to take. Only the future will show how either country untangles itself from its self-made problems.

CHAPTER 19

The Savings and Loan Debacle

The savings and loan crisis of the late 1980s was, at the time, the greatest financial calamity to hit the United States since the Great Depression. A confluence of interest rate changes, well-intended government initiatives, and a deliberately lax regulatory environment combined into one of the largest bungles in the history of the U.S. government, which wound up costing taxpayers hundreds of billions of dollars.

Once all the dust settled, nearly half of the thrift institutions in the United States were gone, and the financial framework of the nation would be permanently altered.

■ Good Intentions and Honest Growth

Most Americans in modern times know that the split between those who own their residences and those who rent them is about two-thirds to one-third. At the beginning of the Great Depression, however, these figures were reversed. Home ownership was seen as largely the venue of the solidly middle class and above, and only about a third of Americans owned their residence.

The FDR administration sought to promote home ownership and, as a result, also the home construction industry. What made purchasing a home difficult for most people was that mortgages were only five years in length, climaxing in a substantial balloon payment at the end, and these obligations were beyond the reach of the working man. The federal government established a number of agencies, notably the Federal Housing Administration, to facilitate a much larger market for mortgages, including a new class of instrument that had terms of up to 30 years.

A 30-year, fixed-rate mortgage represented a huge change in the real estate market, and millions of Americans who would not have considered buying a home could now weigh its benefits. At the conclusion of World War II, the market for homes and their attendant mortgages rose dramatically, and many working-class families turned to their local thrift institutions for mortgages.

Thrifts, also known as savings and loan (S&L) organizations, had emerged from what were then known as the building and loan (B&L) organizations of late eighteenth-century Britain. These early organizations were cooperatives, formed by neighbors as a means of pooling savings and making home loans available to their fellow neighbors. The goal of these cooperatives was not profit, but instead was seen as a mean of promoting the cooperation, responsibility, and thrift of the working classes, as well as providing them a means to purchase their own living quarters. It was seen as a social good, not a moneymaking opportunity.

America's own version of B&Ls grew slowly in the nineteenth century, but the Great Depression wiped out many of these institutions. After 1945, however, a surging middle class in America, coupled with a blossoming residential construction industry, provided fertile ground for the growth of U.S. thrifts.

The business model of S&Ls was simple. They acted as depositories for their members, and they used these funds for home mortgages for the same constituents. As with commercial banks, the deposits were backed by the federal government, although the insurance organization was not the Federal Deposit Insurance Corporation (FDIC) but the FSLIC, which stood for Federal Savings and Loan Insurance Corporation (see Figure 19.1).

The cliché about S&L bankers was that they had a "3-6-3" business: that is, they would pay 3 percent on deposits, charged 6 percent on mortgages, and be on the golf course by 3 P.M.

In order to attract depositors, thrifts would often engage in "interest rate wars" in which they would try to offer slightly superior rates than their competition. With both commercial banks and thrifts trying to outdo each other with respect to how much interest they were willing to pay depositors, the federal government put in place what would be the first element in the debacle that was to come: they enacted a law forbidding banks from offering rates over a certain amount. The interest rate

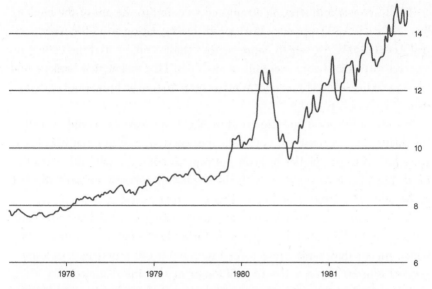

FIGURE 19.1 The federal government guaranteed deposits, which provided comfort to customers they did not enjoy prior to the Great Depression.

wars were over, and thrifts no longer had their principal differentiator to try to attract new deposits.

■ Loaning to Lose

Because of the growing popularity of the commercial paper and money markets, commercial banks were facing problems of their own attracting deposits. New opportunities for fixed-income savers meant that commercial banks were less attractive, and these new vehicles pulled money away from both regular banks as well as thrifts.

Because thrifts were very limited in what they could do with their deposits, they were also very vulnerable to changes in interest rates. For the 1950s and 1960s, this was largely irrelevant, but as inflation started to increase in the 1970s, the thrifts found themselves in a worrisome position.

The practice of "borrowing short to lend long" meant that the revenue of the bank (interest from fixed-rate mortgages) might not keep pace with expense (the interest paid out to depositors). The industry term for this situation was maturity mismatching, since the maturity different between savings (very short-term) and mortgages (30 years) was so great.

The Carter administration attempted to come to the aid of the banking business with the Depository Institutions Deregulation and Monetary Control Act (DIDMCA), which, among other things, eliminated the ceiling on interest rates that banks were allowed to pay. This meant that banks could once again use interest rates as a way to compete for the finite pool of deposits in their market.

In spite of the good intentions of DIDMCA, it created a terrible situation for thrifts. The expense side of the ledger increased substantially, as banks were forced to pay higher interest not only to compete with other institutions, but also to keep pace with the exploding interest rates of the late 1970s and early 1980s (see Figure 19.2).

At the same time, the revenue side of the ledger was relatively stagnant. Indeed, adjustable-rate mortgages were forbidden by federal law until 1981, which meant that banks were forced to rely on old mortgages yielding 5 percent interest, irrespective of inflation or market interest rates.

The spread between interest rates being paid (for deposits) and interest rates being charged (for mortgages) was the basis for banks to exist in the first place, since the difference in these rates was the bank's operating profit.

In the interest rate environment of the early 1980s, however, this spread disappeared and went negative, yielding an average of –1.0 percent in 1981 and –0.7 percent in 1982. There was no way these businesses could sustain themselves, since they were paying more for money than they were taking in.

In 1981 and 1982, S&Ls collectively reported $9 billion in losses, and when assessed from an objective accounting standpoint, the entire industry was not only valueless, but actually had a negative net worth. What had once

FIGURE 19.2 Interest rates soared in the late 1970s and early 1980s, peaking with a prime rate that exceeded 21 percent

been a socially progressive effort to promote home ownership among the working classes now found itself as a multibillion-dollar debacle.

■ Overly Deregulating

By the federal laws and accounting standards of the time, what should have happened is for the government to shutter a large number of the thrifts, since the institutions were technically insolvent. The losses on customer deposits would have bankrupted the FSLIC, however, and the bureaucrats in charge did not want to confront the disaster on their hands head-on. In addition, senior management at the big S&Ls had a close relationship with their regulators, and government authorities failed to act as diligent executors of the regulations in place.

Instead, federal regulators permitted banks to bridge the difference between their assets and their liabilities with a bookkeeping entry known as goodwill. This supposedly represented the value of the bank's expertise in a particular area of business. What it was in actuality was a thinly veiled accounting gimmick used to pretend that the firm was still solvent and that the books were in good order.

The view from Washington, D.C., was that the S&L industry just needed time to heal itself within the framework of a less regulated environment. In fact, thrifts had been lightly regulated for decades, the interest-rate cap notwithstanding, but with the passage of the DIDMCA and, in 1982, the Garn–St. Germain Depository Institutions Act, the thrift industry was going to be operating in a complete different framework than before.

Thrifts were now far more at liberty to do with their funds almost anything they chose. Whereas before they were confined to making residential home mortgages at fixed interest rates, now they could put money into commercial real estate, speculative land deals, new business ventures, and even junk bonds.

Around the same time, major tax reform had been passed by Congress that providing generous tax benefits to real estate investors, making demand for loans, particularly for commercial real estate, surge.

To ease financial pressure on the S&Ls, regulators reduced the amount of funds they had to keep on hand from their deposits. The rate had been 5 percent, but in November 1980 it was reduced to 4 percent, and in January 1982 yet again to 3 percent. This freed up substantially more capital for thrifts to lend, but also made them more vulnerable to downturns, since they were effectively increasing their leverage.

The antiregulation philosophy of the Reagan administration led to the weakening of the already-flaccid regulatory bodies dedicated to policing S&Ls. Bank examiners from the federal government were poorly paid—the starting salary in 1983 was $14,000 per year—and poorly trained. The Federal Home Loan Bank Board was also badly understaffed as well, so much so that hundreds of thrifts escaped even the most basic examination for years.

Another relaxation in standards was the elimination of the 400-shareholder requirement for S&Ls. The genesis of thrifts had been the organization of hundreds of neighbors putting together a not-for-profit cooperative and using those deposits for home loans. By law, these cooperatives had to have at least 400 shareholders, 125 of whom had to be from the local community and no individual with more than 10 percent of the entire stake.

The new regulations permitted ownership with as little as one owner, which made acquiring and controlling thrifts dramatically easier for people and companies that wanted to take advantage of the new environment. The entire philosophy of an S&L's being a community-based cooperative of neighbors was tossed onto the ashbin of history.

The thrifts themselves also could now choose whether they wanted to be federally chartered or state chartered. Just as thrifts had competing for deposits by offering increasingly tempting interest rates, now states began competing for thrifts themselves to set up shop in their state, in order to benefit from the fees the banks would pay in to the state government.

California, for example, passed the Nolan Bill in December 1982, which created a framework for thrifts that was even more liberal than the new federal rules. With this bill in place, California-chartered S&Ls would be permitted to invest up to 100 percent of their deposits in anything they wanted.

For depositors, whether the bank was state or federally chartered made little difference, as their deposit was now insured for $100,000 by the federal government (up from the $40,000 limit prior to Reagan's new laws).

The moral hazard created by this situation is quite clear: thrifts were now in a position to take in whatever deposits they wanted, with customers assured that nothing could possibly be lost up to $100,000 in an account, while at the same time the banks were permitted to use these funds in whatever venture, no matter how speculative, they desired.

It became the ideal combination for any ambitious businessperson (or charlatan), since the source of funds had no fear of loss, and the owner of the thrift could walk away from any potential disaster, confident that the federal government would make the depositors whole.

■ The Real Estate Boom Goes Bust

The fortunes of the S&L industry began to turn around. Whereas the industry had lost $4.6 billion in 1981 and $4.1 billion in 1982, it made $1.9 billion of profits in 1983, $1 billion in 1984, and $3.7 billion in 1985. On the surface, it would seem that deregulation had saved the entire thrift industry and had turned a potentially sweeping disaster into a new chance for an important part of American finance.

The problems that were evident in the early 1980s, however, were still present under the veneer of the business-friendly environment of the mid-1980s, and the festering financial fundamentals would reemerge soon. There were already some substantial failures taking place, such as the $300 million collapse of Empire Savings in Mesquite, Texas (a state that was legendary for its lax banking regulation and above-average interest rates, known colloquially as the "Texas premium.")

In 1986, new tax laws from Washington, D.C., had a chilling effect on the real estate industry, as many of the advantages of commercial and residential speculation from the 1981 bill were eliminated. The boom in real estate halted at once, and Texas thrifts, particularly dependent on both real estate and oil, suffered as both assets dropped precipitously in value.

In 1987, half of all the nation's losses from S&Ls were from just 1 of the 50 states—Texas—and "see-through" offices became the norm. Vacancy rates ran over 30 percent in Texas, and of the 20 largest dollar losses in the thrift industry, 14 of them emanated from the Lone Star State.

One of the remarkable things about this new environment in banking was just how little capital it took. An average American might think that hundreds of millions of dollars are required to start something as impressive as a new bank, but very little capital was actually required.

People who had no experience in banking at all recognized the opportunity that a thrift represented: access to capital with a federal guarantee and the permission to put those funds into any venture—including one's own ventures—that one chose.

It was certainly far more attractive than trying to raise money from hard-nosed investors who would demand a substantial portion of any upside from an entrepreneur. In a sense, it was like the federal government had created a risk-free pool of billions of dollars into which any businessman could dip his fiscal ladle.

The investments that thrifts made moved far away from the staid and predictable residential mortgage market that had been their *raison d'être* before.

Now thrifts had stakes in ski resorts, hamburger franchises, junk bonds, and alternate-energy ventures, such as a company trying to convert cow manure into methane gas.

The states with some of the most outlandish investments were naturally those with the softest regulation—California, Florida, and Texas. But the location of the bank that would become the most infamous in the entire S&L fiasco was in a different state altogether: Arizona.

■ Keating's Lincoln

In the mid-1970s, Charles Keating was a senior executive at American Financial Corporation. Keating came under suspicion by his shareholders, and several lawsuits were filed against him by the company's investors. The Securities and Exchange Commission (SEC) initiated their own investigation, charging Keating and other senior staff members with falsifying SEC reports and defrauding the company's investors.

Keating resigned in August 1976, arranging as part of his departure agreement the right to buy an unsuccessful homebuilder in Phoenix, Arizona, called American Continental Homes for $300,000. Although American Continental was doing poorly as a business, Keating was determined to turn the organization around and become an important real estate developer in the rapidly growing Phoenix area.

Keating was an adept manager, and by the 1980s, American Continental was the biggest homebuilder in both Phoenix and Denver, and its bottom line no longer reflected losses but instead millions of dollars in profits. Keating staffed senior positions with family members, and he enjoyed the perquisites of successful corporate life, including three corporate jets and a helicopter.

An unflattering profile in *Fortune* magazine quoted one person as stating, "It seems almost impossible to find anyone who actually likes Charles Keating." Protective of his reputation, Keating had 5,000 buttons printed up with the declaration "I Like Charles Keating" and had them handed out to any employees or customers willing to pin it on.

Keating was a shrewd businessman, and with the sweeping deregulation of the Reagan administration, he saw that purchasing an S&L was a golden opportunity. He was later quoted by author Kathleen Day in her *S&L Hell* (Norton, 1993), stating, "I know the business inside out, and I always felt that an S&L, if they'd relax the rules, was the biggest moneymaker in the world."

There was an organization available for sale called Lincoln Savings & Loan, which, particularly given the standards of the time, was still a cautiously run organization. It had stuck to the traditional realm of home mortgages, and it had slowly grown over the years, oscillating recently between modest annual gains and losses.

Keating arranged for American Continental Corporation to buy Lincoln for $50 million. In spite of his pledge to regulators to keep existing management, he fired them within days of the acquisition and, as with American Continental, installed his own relatives and friends in senior management.

Lincoln turned its back on the boring and predictable world of home loans and plunged into real estate development projects and junk bonds, quintupling its asset base from $1.1 billion to $5.5 billion in a span of four years.

In spite of the weak regulatory environment, Lincoln's growth and practices were aggressive enough to attract even the attention of the National Bank Board. The board found that Lincoln had $135 million losses that it failed to report and had greatly exceeded the liberal limits the federal government had imposed on thrift investments.

Keating, who was already accomplished at buying the loyalty of local politicians with generous campaign contributions, tried to similarly ingratiate himself to whatever influencers could be of aid. He paid Alan Greenspan, at the time a private economist, to write a paper supporting Lincoln and its investments, and he made employment offers to members of the National Bank Board as well as their spouses.

These efforts did not succeed in getting regulators to drop their examination of Lincoln, so Keating went higher up the political food chain and made $1.3 million in donations to five U.S. senators: Alan Cranston of California, John McCain and Dennis DeConcini of Arizona, John Glenn of Ohio, and Donald Riegle of Missouri.

These senators, who would later be known as the "Keating Five," were the focus of Keating's homespun lobbying effort to get the National Bank Board to leave Lincoln alone (see Figure 19.3).

Keating lobbied McCain particularly hard, providing him and his family multiple trips on the corporate jet to Keating's Bahamas retreat, but McCain's reluctance to aggressively push back against Federal examination irked Keating, who called McCain a "wimp" behind his back.

The five senators did meet with the National Bank Board to suggest they back off of Lincoln, and whether or not the meeting made any material

FIGURE 19.3 John McCain, one of the Keating Five, would find his political future badly damaged by his involvement with Lincoln Savings.

difference to Lincoln's short-term future, the damage to the political capital of the five Senators in future years would be substantial.

Lincoln continued to grow, establishing a byzantine network of dozens of interconnected businesses and developments. In October 1988, Keating embarked on his largest real estate venture to date, a $300 million project called the Phoenician Resort. He also began, although never commenced in a meaningful way, a gargantuan project called Estrella, which was a 20,000-acre development of houses, office buildings, industrial plants, schools, shopping centers, a resort, and a hospital. Estrella would house 200,000 people, had it been completed.

An interesting counterweight to Keating's aggressive (and some would say unethical) business practices and political maneuverings were his conservative moral proclamations. He had made the fight against pornography a crusade for much of his adult life, and he crafted rules for residents of the Estrella project that would forbid inhabitants from ever having an abortion or ever watching pornography. He had these covenants removed from the real estate documents only when his legal team told him they were unenforceable.

As Lincoln's financial situation became more precarious, Keating's attempts to shore up capital became increasingly desperate. Lincoln's accounting firm, Arthur Young, expressed concerns about some of the practices going on in the firm, but instead of addressing their concerns, Keating had them fired and replaced by Touche Ross.

Far worse, Lincoln branch managers were told to encourage their depositors to exchange their federally insured certificates of deposit with American Continental's own bonds. A sales document blatantly told staff to "always remember the weak, meek and ignorant are always good targets."

Therefore, people who had money in Lincoln that was backed by the federal government were encouraged to abandon this safe store of value and move the cash into bonds that were, unknown to them, already judged to be insolvent by an independent assessor.

Because the depositors were executing this transfer within the confines of a federally insured back, many of them falsely assumed that the bonds would likewise be safe from failure. Many of these depositors were elderly and uninformed about the risk they were taking, and in the end, the bonds would be rendered worthless. FDIC Chairman William Seidman would later state that this switch was "one of the most heartless and cruel frauds in modern memory."

Keating even tried his hand at foreign currency trading to create speculative trading profits, but he instead managed to lose $11 million more of the firm's money in a single month. The cash crunch at the bank was getting worse, and in spite of Keating's attempts at influence peddling, regulators were not backing down anymore.

In April 1989, American Continental Corporation declared bankruptcy, and Lincoln Savings was placed in receivership by the Federal Home Loan Bank Board. Incredibly, a full 23,000 depositors had been convinced to put their savings into American Continental bonds, which were not federally insured, and newspapers were rife with tales of senior citizens whose life savings had been damaged or wiped out altogether. One widely circulated photo showed an elderly woman angrily confronting Keating in a courtroom. The bondholders saw nearly $300 million vanish.

American taxpayers would be on the hook for $3.4 billion to cover losses for Lincoln depositors. Keating had spent $50 million of the firm's money just fighting regulators, but in the end, the day of reckoning for Lincoln arrived. Not that he was ashamed of his attempts to buy off senators: in April 1989, Keating told reporters, "One question, among many raised in recent weeks, had to do with whether my financial support in any way influenced several political figures to take up my cause. I want to say in the most forceful way I can: I certainly hope so."

The criminal charges and lawsuits began piling up swiftly. In September 1989, Keating was subjected to a $1.1 billion fraud and racketeering suit from the federal government. He was brought in front of Congress in November to answer questions, but he pled the Fifth Amendment to each question.

California charged Keating with 42 different counts in September 1990, and he was convicted in December 1991 of fraud, racketeering, and conspiracy. He was sentenced in April 1992 by Judge Lance Ito (who would become nationally famous for residing over the O. J. Simpson trial several years later) to 10 years in a maximum-security prison.

This sentence was augmented in January 1993 by a federal conviction based on 73 different counts of fraud, conspiracy, and racketeering. In July 1993, Keating was sentenced to 12 and a half years in a federal penitentiary. He was further ordered to pay $122 million in restitution to the government. The Resolution Trust Corporation also received a summary judgment in the amount of $4.3 billion against Keating, which was the largest judgment against an individual in history.

Keating took on the role of a victim, declaring himself a "political prisoner" of the United States and stating that if the regulators had never gotten involved, all the investors in his organization would "be rich."

In spite of the mountain of convictions against him, Keating's luck changed in his favor in 1996 as the famously liberal Ninth U.S. Circuit Court of Appeals in San Francisco overturned multiple convictions. In the end, there were no felonies on Keating's record, and he was a free man after serving only 4 and a half years in prison.

■ A New Foundation

By 1986, it was obvious that the S&L industry was in serious trouble, but the federal government was still not putting forth adequate measures to address the situation. The Reagan administration sought $15 billion in funds to address the crisis, even though a sum three times that amount was probably needed, but Congress did not approve even that request. It instead injected $10.8 billion into the badly strained FSLIC, and no reform in regulation took place, given the cozy relationship S&L executives had with the political leadership.

By the end of 1988, where were about 250 S&Ls with nearly $81 billion in assets that were technically insolvent. With a new president inaugurated, on February 6, 1989, George H. W. Bush announced a new program to attack the S&L crisis. This proposal would culminate in the Financial Institutions Reform Recovery and Enforcement Act (FIRREA).

At last, the government had taken serious action to address the crisis: the Federal Home Loan Bank Board and FSLIC would be eliminated, having completely botched their duties to the taxpayers. Their role would be served instead by the much stronger FDIC. There would also be a new organization created called the Resolution Trust Corporation, which would be charged with the task of liquidating the hundreds of billions of dollars of real estate owned by the defunct S&Ls.

FIRREA effectively turned the calendar back to the regulations of the 1970s, eliminating the liberal reforms introduced in the early 1980s. The capital requirement was substantially increased from 3 percent back to 8 percent, and thrifts would now be subjected to the same capital standards as commercial banks. The freewheeling days of S&Ls were over.

The Resolution Trust Corporation (RTC) had a Herculean task before it. Between 1989 and 1995, it managed to sell off nearly $400 billion in assets from the 747 thrifts that were shuttered. At first, RTC sought simply to sell off parcels of land and developments in the open market, but the prices it received were deeply discounted. RTC took on a new, far more successful approach, when it instead created equity partnerships that bundled properties and were partially sold off.

These partnerships would be partly sold to investors, with the RTC maintaining a stake, and as the investors were able to sell off the properties at genuine market values, both the investors and the RTC participated in the profits from the proceeds.

Taking this approach was a better way to align the interests of the RTC with the investors who wanted to take advantage of the mountain of properties that were made available. Given the fiasco that the federal government had a major hand in creating with the S&L crisis, the creation and execution of the RTC was a welcome contrast, since the disposition of assets was handled successfully and to the general benefit of taxpayers.

Between 1986 and 1996, the number of S&Ls dropped from 3,234 to 1,645, a nearly 50 percent reduction. The industry had survived seven years of government-mandated madness at a cost of $160 billion. The nation had surely learned its lesson, but at a tremendous financial cost.

CHAPTER 20

Fall of the Soviet Union

The collapse of the Soviet Union in 1991 had almost no effect on financial markets at the time. However, the story of this event is critically important to the years that follow, because no other international event so profoundly changed the landscape of global politics and, parallel to this change, worldwide capitalism.

For 70 years, Russia had been in the grip of a Communist regime, and for nearly half a century, the dominant theme of world affairs was the Cold War between the USSR and the United States. With breathtaking speed, events took place that swept away this old world order in a way that not even prominent experts predicted.

■ Back in the USSR

The Soviet Union had been a looming presence for so much of the twentieth century, that most people in the 1980s had never known a world without it. The USSR enveloped a substantial portion of Earth's land and population, and for decades it had faced off in a stalemate with the United States as its ideological opposite.

There had, of course, been conflicts during the twentieth century that were proxy wars between the two superpowers, most notably the Korean and Vietnam wars. But the United States and the USSR had never engaged in direct war with one another. The threat of World War III and its "MAD" (mutually assured destruction) outcome prevented the leadership of either superpower from going too far.

The totalitarian regime of the USSR effectively suppressed dissent in Russia and the many satellite nations of the Soviet Union. The press was controlled, free speech was quashed, and the economy was rigidly, if ineffectively, planned. There had been attempts at uprisings—strangely, taking place at regularly 12-year internals—in Hungary in 1956, Czechoslovakia in 1968, and Poland in 1980—but none of these allowed the countries to break free of the USSR's grip (see Figure 20.1).

The Soviet Union was a powerful and stable political force, and the buildup of nuclear arms between the two superpowers kept the world on edge from the 1950s through the 1980s. As proficient as the Soviet Union was at going nose-to-nose with the United States in the arms race, over the course of decades, communism's innate inefficiencies would catch up with it. The economy of Russia was weak, and it was getting weaker.

By the 1980s, a huge portion of the Russian economy was dedicated to the military. Seventy percent of industrial output was directed to military purposes, and with Ronald Reagan redoubling America's own efforts, including a space-based missile defense system, Russia was compelled to spend even more of its strained resources on arms. Although the leadership of the USSR was cognizant of the strain the military was putting on the economy, it seemed to be a necessity for survival.

West Berlin   East Berlin

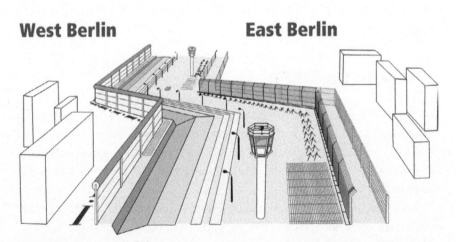

FIGURE 20.1 Nothing was more symbolic of the division between east and west than the Berlin Wall, which for a quarter-century had split the German capital of Berlin into two.

Ronald Reagan's July 1983 speech which declared the Soviet Union an "evil empire" was a boon for those in the Russian military, as they could count on the financial spigot being turned on to an even greater volume. In a strange way, Ronald Reagan was one of the best things that could have happened to those with an interest in the Russian military machine.

An important revenue source for Russia was the sale of natural resources, particularly crude oil. In the latter portion of the 1980s, the price for crude oil spiraled downward, putting a severe crimp in the Soviet budget. Russia was forced to borrow funds from Western banks to purchase the grain needed to feed its own people. The USSR, through its own flawed system, was in the process of starving itself.

■ Gorbachev

In the early 1980s, the Soviet Union went through a series of leadership changes which eventually produced someone who, for the Communist regime, was a relatively forward-thinking change agent: Mikhail Gorbachev. After the death of Brezhnev in November 1982, Yuri Andropov took the senior post of general secretary of the Soviet Union. Andropov reigned at the same time of the "evil empire" speech, which elicited a response from the official Russian press agency stating Reagan was "thinking only in terms of confrontation and bellicose, lunatic anti-communism."

The elderly Andropov was dead by February 1984, and he was succeeded by the 71-year old Konstantin Chernenko, who himself was already in bad health. Relations between the Soviet Union and the United States were still very chilly, with the USSR boycotting the 1984 Summer Olympics held in Los Angeles as payback for the United States' boycott of the 1980 games in Moscow. Andropov's time in office, like his predecessor, was brief; he died in March 1985, allowing Gorbachev to assume power.

Mikhail Sergeyevich Gorbachev (see Figure 20.2) was a dynamic force in the Soviet Union, seeking to bring a fresh morality to a system he viewed an intrinsically corrupt. He was not a naïve man, understanding that he had to operate within the confines of the Soviet system to effect change. His assertion of the need for *glasnost* (openness) and *perestroika* (reform) were demanded by a change he described as "a new moral atmosphere is taking shape in the country ... a reappraisal of values and their creative rethinking is under way."

FIGURE 20.2 The two most prominent world leaders of the mid-1980s, Mikhail Gorbachev and Ronald Reagan.

What Gorbachev saw around him was distressing: bribery, poverty, corruption, food shortages, long lines, and a labor ethic that, in one oft-repeated quotation, was summed up as "we pretend to work and they pretend to pay us." The Soviet system was sick, and Gorbachev sought to return it to health. He made no claims to wanting the Soviet Union to undergo a radical metamorphosis; he simply wanted to right the Soviet ship, which was listing badly.

China was undergoing its own subtle change, but the approach to the change was a polar opposite to Russia's: China was seeking economic liberalization while preserving political strength, whereas Gorbachev was loosening the political grip on his people while preserving the economic structure.

Gorbachev sensed the waste of human capital that was taking place in the present system, and he reflected years later in the publication *Foreign Policy* that "our society, our people, the most educated, the most intellectual, rejected that model on the cultural level because it does not respect the man, oppresses him spiritually and politically."

Gorbachev's own prime minister, Nikolai Ryzhkov, buttressed this sentiment by stating in 1985 for the American Enteprise Institute, "We stole from ourselves, took and gave bribes, lied in the reports, in newspapers, from high podiums, wallowed in our lies, hung medals on one another, and all of this—from top to bottom and from bottom to top." Gorbachev sought to save Russia's spirit from the system that had been put in place in 1917.

Gorbachev tended his reforms to the economy with the Law of Cooperatives, which beginning in May 1989 allowed private ownership of businesses in services, manufacturing, and foreign trade. Entrepreneurs, after decades of being impotent in the Soviet system, were finally able to open stores, restaurants, import/export exchanges, manufacturing plants, and other businesses.

Free speech also was allowed to emerge again. Public opinion polls were permitted, and their results—even if they were embarrassing to the government—were published for all to see. Countless political prisoners were released from their incarceration, and a widespread sense was taking hold that lasting and important change was possible.

Given the decades of corruption and hypocrisy in the Soviet Union, a free press found a treasure trove of stories and exposes that proved awkward for the leadership to acknowledge. The country's widespread problems of alcoholism, drug abuse, and poverty were brought to light. The 1986 nuclear disaster in Chernobyl also tarnished the reputation of the Soviet leadership.

Even CNN was permitted to broadcast into what had been only recently a tightly controlled police state. In 1989, CNN was the first unofficial news broadcaster allowed to send programs to Moscow. The destination for these broadcasts was minuscule—just foreign guests residing at Moscow's Savoy Hotel—but enterprising Muscovites were able to figure out how to pick up the signal, and Russians were now able to watch an uncensored news broadcast for the first time in their lives.

The liberalization taking place in Russia did not go unnoticed by the satellite states. The populations in eastern Europe saw an opportunity to assert their own desire for freedom, and although the Russian leadership did not condone it, it likewise refrained from suppressing it. Bulgaria,

FIGURE 20.3 These guards in East Germany, who in months before would have been ordered to shoot, watched amused as crowds begin to dismantle the Berlin Wall.

Czechoslovakia, East Germany, Poland, Romania, and Poland had all broken free from their Communist governments by 1991.

As early as 1987, the Baltic region asserted its desire to break away from the Soviet giant. Estonia, Georgia, Moldova, Ukraine, and other republics began agitating for their own independence. Country by country, the Soviet Union was breaking up, and Gorbachev appeared to be passively allowing it to happen (see Figure 20.3).

■ The August Coup

Hard-liners in the Soviet government were outraged at Gorbachev's reforms and the disintegration of the Soviet empire that was taking place. Gorbachev had put a proposal into motion that would have formalized the dismantling of the old union into a collection of independent republics, and he declared Russia itself a sovereign state on June 12, 1990. The treaty to transform the old USSR into a federation of republics was set to be signed on August 20, 1991.

Several hard-liners formed their own group called the State Committee on the State of Emergency, and they confronted Gorbachev, demanding that he himself declare a state of emergency and a call to restore order. Gorbachev refused, and he left on a planned vacation on August 4, planning to return for the treaty signing on August 20.

The conspirators wanted to prevent the treaty's signing, as they correctly surmised that the elimination of the old Soviet system would be bad for their own personal interests, so on August 18, they met with Gorbachev at his vacation retreat and insisted again that he declare a state of emergency. When he refused once more, the hard-line conspirators cut off his communications lines, ordered him to remain on vacation, and told the KGB guards that no one was to leave the compound.

The conspirators planned to oppose by force anyone sympathetic to Gorbachev, so they ordered up a quarter-million pairs of handcuffs and 300,000 arrest forms. KGB personnel were all summoned for active duty, and Gorbachev's lieutenant—Gennady Yanayev—declared himself acting president of the USSR due to Gorbachev's being "ill." Gorbachev was not ill, of course—he was simply being held captive.

The self-ordained emergency committee ordered all newspapers banned in Moscow, except for those controlled by the party. It seemed that the years of reform Gorbachev had put in place were being overturned in a matter of hours. Armored tank units rolled into Moscow, and paratroopers prepared for any ensuing battle in the Russian capital.

One man that the emergency committee had failed to imprison during the coup was Boris Yeltsin, who arrived at Russia's parliament building—the so-called "white house"—on August 19. Yeltsin declared that what was going on was a coup, and he urged the military to not participate. He demanded that Gorbachev be allowed to address his people, and he had fliers distributed around the city declaring the actions of the emergency committee to be blatantly illegal.

Thousands of citizens gathered at the white house, erecting makeshift barricades and urging soldiers and tank commanders to disobey the emergency committee. Yeltsin famously stood on a tank to speak to the gathered masses. Three citizens were killed by the gathering military, and these three were heralded as martyrs for the democratic cause, prompting a huge funeral and protest by the residents of Moscow (see Figure 20.4).

Yanayev continued to lie about Gorbachev, stating that the president was simply "resting" and that "over these years he has got very tired and needs some time to get his health back." Hardly anyone believed such a declaration, however, and once it was clear the military wasn't going to participate in the coup, the conspirators gave up.

FIGURE 20.4 Recently elected as Russia's president and now facing down a coup, Boris Yeltsin makes a triumphant gesture to the people in Moscow.

They tried to speak with Gorbachev, but he refused. He was able to contact Moscow again, and he announced to an eager audience that the coup members were all dismissed from their posts and that all the actions they had taken were illegal and thus void. The coup had sputtered into a failure.

It was obvious to everyone, including Gorbachev, that the days of the Soviet Union were rapidly coming to an end. The hard-liners' attempt at a coup was the last desperate gasp of the fetid leadership to maintain a hold on power, but the small freedoms that Russian citizens had been allowed to enjoy would not be permitted to be reversed.

On Christmas Day, 1991, Mikhail Gorbachev announced his resignation as the president of the Soviet Union. The hammer-and-sickle flag flying over the Kremlin was lowered, and the next day, a new flag—one of the Russian republic—was hoisted in its place.

■ Private Enterprise

As much as Russians craved freedom and a thriving economy, they were ill-prepared to be thrown instantly into capitalism after decades of Communist stagnation. The deeply entrenched ruling class from the days of the USSR took advantage of their positions and either seized state assets for themselves or sold them off to friends or cronies. The merely powerful within the Communist state became the rich and powerful of the post-Communist state (see Figure 20.5).

The state apparatus did make some attempts to allocate the wealth of Russia somewhat democratically. An organization was set up by the government called the State Committee for State Property Management of the Russian Federation. The Committee established a voucher system, entitling Russian citizens to a small stake in the formerly state-owned enterprise of its choosing. Virtually the entire population was granted vouchers to partake in their share of the nation's wealth.

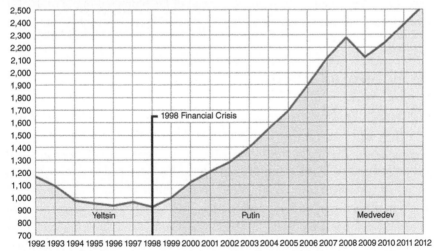

FIGURE 20.5 The Russian economy thrived after the fall of communism.

With poverty so widespread, many of the recipients had no interest in a piece of paper that gave them a tiny interest in the future profits of a business. Their needs were more immediate, such as putting food on the table.

Thus, millions of Russians sold their vouchers at cut-rate prices to shrewd businessmen who knew they could acquire them at a deep discount. The senior management of the corporations, well aware of the value that the vouchers ultimately might have, relieved their fellow citizens of their claims in exchange for some immediate spending money.

The tremendous dislocation of the economy created widespread problems in the first half of the 1990s for the Russian people. Far from being in a thriving free-enterprise paradise, Russians began to miss the days of state-controlled predictability. A quarter of the population lived beneath the poverty line, and the country's productive output fell sharply as the country's businesses retooled and reorganized. Economic problems became so acute that by 1996, Boris Yeltsin's reelection as president was seriously threatened by a Communist rival.

What eventually turned the economy around was the rising value of commodity prices. Russia was rich with industrial metals, crude oil, precious metals, and gemstones. Moscow came one of the most expensive cities in the world to live, and the handful of oligarchs that had benefited from the suddenly shift from communism to capitalism were now some of the richest men in the world.

The gap between rich and poor in Russia was huge, and in a 2006 poll, two-thirds of Russians regretted that the Soviet Union ever failed. The liberation of the country's resources, instead of becoming an opportunity for the masses, instead became asset heist for those in positions of power.

■ Satellites Adrift

The biggest losers of all from the USSR's demise were the satellite states that depended on the largesse of a Soviet sponsor to make up for the shortcomings in their own economies. Once the Soviet Union disintegrated, Cuba lost 80 percent of both its import and export business, and the nation's gross domestic product (GDP) fell by more than a third.

Whereas the United States had tried to choke off the Cuban economy with a short-lived naval blockade in 1962, the results were far more sweeping when ships simply stopped showing up from Russia 40 years later. Imports of Russian crude oil ceased, and Cuba's ability to sell its own principal exports—sugar, fruit, and industrial metals—was greatly impaired for want of willing buyers.

The situation was much worse in North Korea. Whereas Cuba at least had warm sun all year and fertile ground in which to grow crops, North Korea was profoundly isolated and subject to much harsher conditions. The already-tiny GDP of North Korea fell from $2,800 per capita in 1988 (in the final era of USSR support) to a mere $1,200 per capita a decade later. Up to two million people are estimated to have starved to death in a famine that almost certainly would have been avoided in the days of Soviet assistance.

Former allies of the Soviet Union that had once been bitter enemies of the United States began to reshape themselves into thriving capitalist nations. Vietnam, the locus of the most recent proxy war between the superpowers, gradually displaced its Communist ideology with thousands of independent businesses, a stock market, and a growing export business.

Now that the Cold War was over, the world could turn its collective attention to a principal activity of the 1990s: making money. Capitalism had, by all popular accounts, won the war, and many nations besides the United States were prepared to embrace an entrepreneurial spirit.

The old saw that one should be careful what one wishes, as they just might get it, could have been applied to the United States: with the face-off between the United States and the Soviet Union a thing of the past, the competition that American enterprise would be facing would be far more powerful and successful than before.

CHAPTER 21

The Asian Contagion

The phenomenal rebuilding of Japan after World War II into the world's second-largest economy is the stuff of business legend, and from the 1960s forward, Japan dominated the region as the richest and most powerful nation in Asia (at least until the turn of the millennium, when China had moved into the number 2 spot).

What was just as unexpected, however, was the ascendency of such countries as Singapore and Malaysia, which were third-world backwaters in the 1950s yet became some of the fastest-growing economies in the world. The Asian region, particularly the so-called "Asian Tigers," enjoyed phenomenal growth for decades until it was suddenly and unexpectedly interrupted by a sweeping currency and financial crisis in 1997.

■ The Booming Decades

From the early 1960s through the 1990s, a number of countries in Asia exhibited astonishing growth and a collective transformation into some of the most dynamic economies in the world. Four in particular—Singapore, Taiwan, South Korea, and Hong Kong—were such standouts in their development as economic forces that they were dubbed the "Asian Tigers" (see Figure 21.1).

Whereas most developed countries are content with a 2 percent or 3 percent annual growth rate, the Asian Tigers enjoyed growth rates in excess of 7 percent, year after year, for decades. Formerly considered little more than third-world ex-colonies, Hong Kong and Singapore established themselves

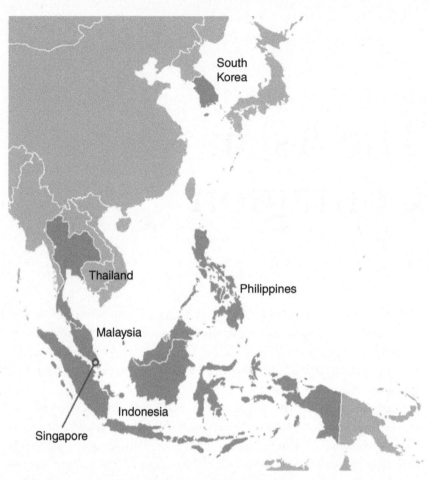

FIGURE 21.1 The Asian Tigers, highlighted here on a map of the region along with a few other rapidly growing economies.

as world-class financial centers, and all four Asian Tigers were recognized as manufacturing powerhouses, particularly in the field of high-end electronics with such prominent firms as Samsung Electronics.

Tiny countries like Singapore could not grow a meaningful economy based on their own small population. Instead, these developing countries focused on exports. All of the countries in Asia that sought a major presence on the global economic scene emphasized a consistent set of values:

- A focus on exports.

- A business-friendly government featuring low taxes and an accommodating regulatory environment.

- Government leadership that took an active part in providing financing and strategic guidance for key industries.

- Relatively heavy investment in education, with a recognition that an educated workforce was critical to long-term prosperity.

Although not sanctioned by government decree, another common element across the thriving Asian economies was a high savings rate among the public. Coupled with this was a widespread acceptance of the importance of educational opportunities that the government was providing the nation's children.

Ironically, the Asian Miracle was made possible by what many in America would recognize as "American values"—specifically, the value of getting a good education, working hard, and saving as much as possible. The Asian Tigers were, in a sense, beating America at its own game, and the consistently surging annual growth proved that the formula was working. The economies were thriving, lifespans were getting longer, and the citizens of these countries were healthier than ever.

■ Liberal Lending

Given the prosperity of the region, banks all around the world were eager to lend money to the growing economies of Asia. Banks in Japan and Europe were particularly anxious to loan tens of billions of dollars to banks in Hong Kong, Singapore, Indonesia, Malaysia, and other growing Asian economies. These local banks would, in turn, lend billions out to enterprises in their own countries.

The governments of these nations recognized that the investing world would be hesitant to put money into a country that had outsized currency risk, so the central banks of these nations tended to peg their currencies to the U.S. dollar, the globally recognized reserve currency.

The Asian banks helped themselves to extra profit by borrowing from overseas banks in U.S. dollars but making loans to local businesses in the local currency. In this way, the bank could enjoy the higher interest rates that loans denominated in ringgits, won, pesos, or other local currencies enjoyed while having to pay out the lower interest rates of the U.S dollar–denominated loans from Europe, Japan, or the United States. The spread between these two rates constituted an important profit center for the banks.

After the 1985 Plaza Accord, at which it was agreed that the U.S. dollar should come down in value relative to other currencies, the Japanese yen began a steady ascent in value. Japanese banks took advantage of this by investing heavily in neighboring nations, such as Malaysia, Thailand, and Indonesia.

There was a widely cited report from the World Bank that stated a trillion dollars of infrastructure was needed throughout the developing economies of Asia, and Japanese banks in particular wanted to participate in a portion of the lucrative funding that evidently was needed to support the area's build-out.

Although pouring tens of billions of dollars into developing economies is, by definition, somewhat risky, the banks doing so took comfort in the fact that global financial backstops—notably the International Monetary Fund (IMF) and World Bank—seemed dedicated to preventing financial catastrophe. Relatively recent events such as the Latin American debt crisis of the 1980s and the Mexico currency debacle of 1994 were both remedied with massive financial support from the IMF and World Bank, and private bankers were justifiably confident that, even if a country fell on hard times, a financial debacle would not ensue.

Another important aspect of lending in the region was the cozy relationship banks had with both national governments as well as the largest industrial clients. Banks were firmly compelled by governments to pour lending into industries that were seen as strategically important to the government, and varying degrees of what was termed *crony capitalism* ensured that well-connected businessmen received whatever loans they required, irrespective of risk or fundamental economic soundness. There was, in short, far more money in search of a home than the economies of the region actually warranted by any rational measure.

■ A Subtle Slowdown

Under the surface of all the growth, however, there were some fundamental misallocations of resources taking place. An inordinate amount of capital had gone into real estate development, and some overly ambitious industrial projects, including one of the world's largest dams and one of the world's most expensive steel mills, also received funding from commercial banks.

Even though external evidence, such as the equity markets and the amounts being loaned out by banks, seemed to suggest abundant prosperity, there were subtle signs as early as 1993 that things were slowing down. For such export-oriented economies, there was one economic figure to watch more important than any other: the current account balance.

The private and public parties within a nation import and export a certain value of goods and services over the course of a given time period. If, on the whole, they export more than they import, the wealth of the nation increases, and it runs a current account *surplus* for that time period.

Alternately, if they import more than they export—in other words, if they are spending more than they are taking in, they run a current account *deficit*, and the nation as a whole is less wealthy.

Nations than run regular deficits don't necessarily find themselves impoverished. The United States has had trade deficits countless times, and it is deeply in debt for having done so, but it also happens to be the basis of the world's reserve currency and is also one of the world's most creditworthy borrowers, so it has the luxury of running a regular deficit. The developing economies of Asia, however, had no such advantages.

If a nation is consistently bleeding its economy with a current account deficit, and its currency is pegged to an external value, it will become increasingly difficult to justify that peg. It would be loosely similar to Dell's stating that its shares were redeemable on a one-for-one basis with Apple shares in March 2005. At the time, that would be briefly rational, since the shares had the same value. But as Apple grew wealthier, and Dell stagnated, any such "peg" would be considered ridiculous.

In this far-fetched example, Apple is analogous to the United States (a relatively stable entity growing in value), and Dell is analogous to any of the stated Asian economies whose currencies were pegged to the U.S. dollar. For the latter, the underlying economies were beginning to weaken due to persistent current account deficits. In the early part of the 1990s, the export market for the various Asian economies had been spectacular: 18 percent per year for Malaysia, 16 percent for Thailand, 14 percent for Hong Kong, and 15 percent for Singapore.

These exports had also grown in quality as well as quantity, as there was a shift away from older manufactured goods like textiles and toward more expensive goods with higher barriers to entry like semiconductors, high-end televisions, computers, and memory chips.

Thailand was one of the first to see the fortunes of its current account begin to change. In 1993 the current account deficit was 5.7 percent, increasing to 6.4 percent in 1994, 8.4 percent in 1995 and 8.5 percent in 1996. As this was taking place, it caught the attention of currency traders, who sought to profit in large changes of currency values.

Because the currency of the nation, the Thai baht, was pegged to the U.S. dollar, there was a growing strain between the stated value of the baht (that is, the official peg) and the objective economic assessment of its real value.

Had the baht been a free-floating currency, there would have been no such strain, since its market value would have been updated in real time on a pip-by-pip basis. It was a pegged currency, though, and speculators began selling baht and buying U.S. dollars with a view that eventually the peg would have to be reset.

Malaysia was also beginning to feel the pinch of its own deficits, which stood at 8.8 percent of the country's gross domestic product (GDP) by 1995. In spite of the economic fundamentals weakening, Malaysia's leader, Prime Minister Mahathir Mohamad, had laid out an ambitious plan to grow Malaysia from a developing economy to a globally recognized industrialized nation by the year 2020, which he dubbed "Vision 2020."

Much like the building booms of the southwestern United States in the late 1970s and the U.S. housing bubble of 2005, there was a deluge of both residential and commercial building happening throughout Asia in the early 1990s. Property values were increasing 25 percent per year in some areas, and with attractive tax incentives put in place by growth-oriented governments, banks had all the more reason to keep pouring funds into real estate, in spite of the slowdown in exports.

Overbuilding was the natural outcome, and by early 1997, there were over 365,000 new apartments in Bangkok alone, sitting unoccupied. Even with so much unneeded housing, there were still projects in motion to build another 100,000 apartments.

Construction projects were not limited to homes and warehouses. Huge industrial initiatives were also undertaken, such as the new government center in Malaysia, which cost US$8 billion, or the Bakun Dam, the most ambitious power-generation project the country had ever attempted.

Neighboring Indonesia had likewise enjoyed solid growth, although most of the benefits of the growth flowed to the first family, led by Indonesian President Suharto, widely recognized as a corrupt and self-serving dictator.

He controlled a network of *hundreds* of interlinked businesses in Indonesia, strategically doled out among family and friends, and he ensured that his government would grant whatever monopolies, tax breaks, or protective tariffs were necessary to benefit his businesses. Indonesian banks were compliant with the wishes of the president, as he directed them to put hundreds of millions of dollars into whatever business required the cash for growth (see Figure 21.2).

FIGURE 21.2 Indonesian President Suharto manipulated the government he led for the maximum benefit of the hundreds of businesses he and his family and friends controlled in the 1990s.

■ The Thai Baht Bomb

The first serious warning sign of trouble was on February 5, 1997. Although the stock market in Bangkok had been declining for months already, there had not been any serious commercial failures or currency troubles. This all changed on February 5, when Somprasong Land, a prominent developer of property in Thailand, announced it was unable to make its $3.1 million interest payment on an $80 billion loan. The company was defaulting on the loan, and the stock market—already down 45 percent since its peak the prior year—tumbled 2.7 percent.

Once Somprasong defaulted, other Thai property developers were less hesitant to come forward with their own bad news. Individual property developers did not pose any severe risk to the Thai economy, but the health of one of its largest banks—Finance One—did.

Finance One was the key intermediary between property developers and international banks. Finance One borrowed from overseas banks in dollars and make loans in baht, which had been a profitable strategy during more prosperous times, but as developers began to cease making payments, Finance One found it increasingly difficult to fulfill its own obligations. The number of nonperforming loans in Finance One's portfolio had doubled during 1996, and in the first quarter of 1997, the quantity of these bad loans doubled once more.

The disposition of currency traders toward the baht began to appear well founded. For the past 13 years, the baht had been pegged to the value of the U.S. dollar at a fixed exchange rate of about $1 equaling 25 baht (that is, a baht equaled about four U.S. cents). As the economic news about Thailand worsened, short sellers took on larger positions betting against the baht currency.

The Thai government sought to shore up confidence in its currency and began to use its own U.S. dollar reserves to support the baht's value. Thailand began buying baht with the U.S. dollars it held in its treasury, deploying 5 billion of the country's dollars to try to beat back the short sellers. The country's reserves were not infinite, of course, and the officially reported balance of U.S. dollar reserves dropped to $33 billion, the lowest level in two years.

Although it had been reluctant to do so, since it would harm domestic businesses, the Thai government also raised interest rates by 25 percent, in order to make the baht more attractive to investors. It is a hazardous game to raise interest rates to support a currency that is weakening due to a faltering economy, since the act of raising interest rates will only harm the economy further. But the Thai government wanted to use whatever tools it had in its arsenal to combat the attack against the baht.

Unknown to everyone except a few government insiders, the Thai government was being deliberately deceptive about their reserves. Although the admission that they had spent their way down to $33 billion was troublesome enough, the real truth was that the government had just over $1 billion in reserves. The other $32 billion was committed to futures contracts, having already been deployed in an effort to stabilize the currency. The government was out of ammunition.

On July 2, 1997, the Thai government announced that it had "discovered" it had only $1 billion left in U.S. dollars, and it was forced to let the baht

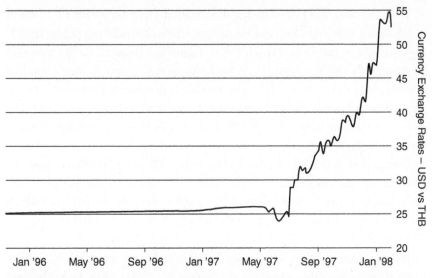

FIGURE 21.3 The number of Thai baht required to purchase one U.S. dollar soared from the official peg of about 25 to more than double that amount, once the Baht was allowed to float freely against other currencies.

float freely. Those with short positions against the baht were overjoyed, as it plunged 18 percent instantly, and its slide would continue for months to come (see Figure 21.3).

■ Instantly Expensive

The core problem for debtor banks in a country whose currency is depreciating is that the mechanism they have to pay their debts—their local money—is less valuable than it was before. If a currency falls 25 percent, it effectively increases how much one is in debt by one-third, since it takes one-third more of the currency to pay the debt. If a currency falls by 50 percent, it *doubles* the effective debt, even if the nominal amount hasn't budged.

This is exactly the situation in which the Thai government and the national banks found themselves. The baht was plunging, and the already-weakened economy was facing a catastrophe. On July 28, the Thai government asked the IMF for an emergency injection of capital. It did this knowing full well that the IMF had a habit of insisting on major changes in government spending, taxation, and business behavior before such a loan would be granted.

True to form, the IMF stated it would assist Thailand with $17.2 billion in loans, but it would only do so if the government would cut public spending, raise taxes, raise interest rates, and shutter any financial institutions that were judged to be insolvent. Many banks in the developing Asian nations had been given a free pass by their governments, in spite of their shaky financial conditions, since the government believed it would be more harmful to close down major banks than simply make the necessary accounting adjustments to simulate solvency.

Compelled by the IMF terms, by December 1997, Thailand had closed 56 different financial organizations (which, in turn, added 16,000 people to the unemployment lines) and saw its stock market drop by 57 percent, which was even worse than the year prior in which the same market dropped 45 percent.

Just as Somprasong's admission that it was having financial difficulties made it easier for other property developers to do the same, once Thailand had devalued the baht, other Asian nations whose currencies were straining at present peg levels likely felt empowered to do likewise, as painful as it would be. The Indonesian rupiah, the Malaysian ringgit, and the Singapore dollar all had their pegs substantially lowered by their governments.

The drops in these currencies was massive. The Indonesian rupiah, for example, went from an exchange rate of 2,400 to 1 (versus the U.S. dollar) to 10,000 to 1 in the space of just the four months between August 1997 and January 1998. Such a drop effectively more than quadrupled the debts owed to overseas banks (see Figure 21.4).

Now that years of overbuilding, political corruption, and crony capitalism were beginning to catch up with the region, embarrassed government officials began resorting to conspiracy theories and accusations of racism as they lashed out at the world about their situation.

Malaysia's Prime Minister, Dr. Mahathir Mohamad, pointed to famed money managed George Soros as the leader of those attacking the currencies. The prime minister claimed that the plunges in value of both the currency and the stock market were due to racist short-sellers and a "Jewish agenda" that wanted to see harm befall the country.

Mahathir proclaimed those spreading negative information about Malaysia were liars and should be shot as rumor-mongers that were conspiring against a country whose economic fundamentals, in his opinion, were still sound. As so many governments had tried in the past, Mahathir also outlawed short-selling, which failed to stop the slide. (Short-sellers actually provide a vital balance to any market, and when a bottom is finally hit, the shorts covering

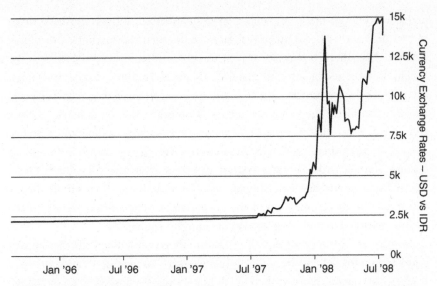

FIGURE 21.4 The Indonesian rupiah's exchange rate versus the U.S. dollar.

their positions are just about the only ones placing "buy" orders. The banning of short-selling was just as ineffective as it had been during most other points in financial history.)

Indonesia's corrupt government was in need of a bailout as well, and it would require a cash injection even larger than Thailand's. On October 31, 1997, the IMF and World Bank announced a $37 billion rescue package for Indonesia, which was contemporaneous with the shuttering of a number of troubled financial institutions, a pledge to balance the budget, a promise to reduce public spending, and a commitment to bring transparency to the business dealings of Suharto and his family.

Suharto was never seen as a shining example of integrity, and as doubts began to creep in about all the pledges and promises that had been set forth, the bounce that the rupiah and Indonesian stock market had experienced faded away. By December, Moody's downgraded Indonesia's credit to junk status.

Weeks later, on January 5, 1998, President Suharto provided the press with the country's 1998–1999 budget, which was based on rosy assumptions that those familiar with the Indonesian economy found implausible. For the budget's numbers to actually work, the GDP would have to suddenly grow a full 4 percent, inflation would need to plunge from 20 percent to less than half that amount, and the rupiah would need to experience a 20 percent appreciation against the dollar. For a struggling economy's government to propose a budget made on such a large quantity of unlikely positive turns of fortune met with instant punishment in the financial markets: the rupiah crumbled another 50 percent against the U.S. dollar.

The person second-in-command at the U.S. Treasury, Larry Summers, accompanied a contingent of IMF personnel on an emergency trip to Jakarta in order to address the worsening crisis. Soon thereafter, on January 15, they announced a plan that was plausible and had the backing of the United States.

In particular, there were specific measures designed to move Indonesia to a more genuinely democratic system and away from the corrupt dictatorship of Suharto and his clan. Budget cuts, deregulation, reforms in the financial sector, and a cleaning-up of the government's corruption were greeted by international finance as positive, meaningful reform.

In spite of all the turmoil, Suharto announced on January 20 that he was going to run for yet another term—his seventh—as president, and currency traders once again dumped the rupiah in volume. It plunged to an exchange ratio of 14,500 rupiah to 1 U.S. dollar, since the assumption that Suharto would finally be leaving the political scene was clearly misplaced. Suharto's association with Indonesia had become, given the circumstances, a negative for the nation's reputation and economy.

■ The Big Economies Join the Drop

It is one thing for a relatively small emerging economy such as Malaysia's to be undergoing a financial crisis; it is quite another when globally important nations such as Korea and Japan do. These much larger economies were not insulated from the travails of their smaller neighbors. The signs of strain came a little later for them, but they came nonetheless.

South Korean businesses, particularly the largest, multi-industry conglomerates, had been the recipients of tens of billions in loans from banks around the world. The majority of this debt was short term (that is, no more than a year until maturity), but loans coming due more often than not would simply be rolled over into another loan of a similar term. These were short-term loans in name only.

Having the vast majority of loans on a short-term basis poses one significant risk, however, which is that the lenders are not *required* to roll over the loans at all; they can simply demand payment in full.

One large Korean firm that was buried by such loans was Hanbo Steel Corporation, which had debt of five trillion won, equal at the time to about

$5.8 billion. Hanbo was the fifth-largest steelmaker in the world and the second largest in Korea, but in late January 1997, it announced that it would be freezing payments on all of its debt.

There was more bad news to come. That summer, in July, auto manufacturer Kia stated it would need an emergency loan to continue operations. Had Kia needed money two years earlier, it would have probably been deluged with offers, but in an environment of increasing financial anxiety, there were no loans proposed. In October, the Korean government itself put Kia into receivership, much as the U.S. government would do with General Motors during the 2008 financial crisis.

Korea's takeover of Kia had an unintended consequence, as Standard & Poor's immediately downgraded Korean sovereign debt, compelling the Korean equities market to drop over 5 percent in a single day and plunging the Korean won to a new crisis low (about 1,000 won to one U.S. dollar).

Just as Malaysia turned to its U.S. dollar reserves to try to shore up its beleaguered currency, so, too, did Korea extract billions of U.S. dollars from its $30 billion reserve. By selling dollars into the open market in exchange for won, Korea helped stave off a collapse briefly, but $15 billion in expenditures later, Korea had failed to turn the tide in any meaningful way.

The situation in Korea was complicated by the fact that a national election was going to take place that December, and three major candidates were vying for the top spot to replace the current president, Kim Young-sam, who was constitutionally foreclosed from seeking another term.

Smaller countries were desperate for IMF help, but national pride held Korea back from making such a request. On November 13, 1997, the government stated it did not need any assistance from the IMF, since it believed Japan and the United States could provide assistance directly. Only a few days later, when it was clear that neither country was going to be leaping to Korea's aid on its own, the won plunged further, and by November 21, Korea set aside national pride and made a formal appeal to the IMF for a $20 billion financial lifeline.

Upon examining the country's situation, it was clear to the IMF that even a loan of that size was nowhere near the amount needed to stem the bleeding. By December 3, the IMF and the Korean leadership had brokered a deal for nearly three times the requested amount—$55 billion—that would require, among other things, an economy more accessible to international participation and ownership. The announcement of the deal sent Korea stocks soaring 7 percent, the largest single-day gain in the history of the exchange.

The three candidates for Korea's presidency were each asked to sign a pledge that they would abide by the terms of the IMF deal. Two of them did, but Kim Dae-jung decided to get some political mileage out of the situation and publicly stated he would sign no such document, because the deal with the IMF "violated national pride." He further stated that he would renegotiate the deal with the IMF to avoid the kinds of job cuts the agreement was seeking.

Such threats from a leading candidate spooked the financial markets again, and this time the Korean won collapsed to a 2,000-to-1 ratio with the dollar. Korean debtors, like their Malaysian debtors, now owed over twice the debt they did before, based on the greatly reduced value of their local currency.

Kim Dae-jung was troubled how his assertions had caused so much damage and uncertainty within the markets, so he relented and said that he was agreeable to the IMF terms, and he would comply with them if he won the presidency. On December 18, he did in fact edge out the other two candidates, and he made the debt issue in Korea his more urgent priority.

With a new president in place who was apparently willing to abide by the IMF's reforms, the financial world began to accommodate Korea's needs. Late in January 1998, 13 overseas banks agreed to delay the repayment requirements on Korea's short-term debt. The government raised interest rates to attract foreign investors, and the government said that in order to protect jobs, Korean businesses would have to become more internationally competitive instead of relying on government protection.

Korea's reforms marked an essential turning point for the country. Its U.S. dollar reserves had dwindled to under $9 billion, but a decade after the depths of the crisis, these reserves would amount to over a quarter-*trillion* U.S. dollars.

Across the Sea of Japan, Japanese banks were nervously eyeing all the troubles happening in Malaysia, Indonesia, South Korea, and the various other countries roiling from currency troubles, oversupply of real estate, and weakening industries.

Japanese banks had loaned out tens of billions to various other Asian countries (in Thailand alone, fully half the loans were from Japanese banks), and having been struggling with its own shaky financial system since 1989, it could not withstand another major financial shock without sending further tremors to other industrial nations in Europe and North America.

On November 3, 1997, Sanyo Securities announced it would be filing for bankruptcy. Sanyo was no juggernaut on the world financial scene, but it was

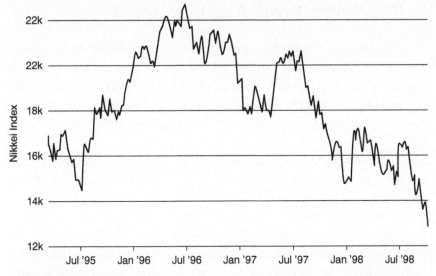

FIGURE 21.5 The Japanese stock market, represented by the Nikkei 225, plainly showed the troubles of the 1997 Asian crisis were felt by the region's largest economy.

still the seventh-largest stock brokerage in Japan, and only one week later the tenth-largest bank, Hokkaido Takushoku, likewise announced its own bankruptcy. Less than two weeks later, a larger securities firm—Yamaichi—joined the others in line at bankruptcy court (see Figure 21.5).

Although most of the nations in the region had troubles, the source of those troubles have different origins: Thailand's was from overbuilding real estate; South Korea's was from overly ambitious industrial plans; Indonesia's was from political corruption.

In Japan, years of "papering over" deep troubles in the banking system was the root cause, since property values across Japan had plunged. Had the banks been subjected to rigorous and honest accounting, they would have been recognized as insolvent. Adjoined to this, the country was burdened with the massive loans Japanese banks had issued to all these nearby nations and the systemic risk it was facing if defaults became widespread.

The one risk Japan did *not* share with the others was an attack on its currency. Japan had exceptionally deep pockets, having accrued a massive war chest of U.S. dollars during decades of trading surpluses. In spite of its other problems, Japan was still in the leadership role in the Asian region, and it was the least susceptible to its currency's taking the plunge suffered by the others.

■ The World Turns Another Corner

As 1997 came to a close, the damage suffered by stockholders of the Asian region was severe. Some markets were down 75 percent, and some individual equities had lost 100 percent of their value. Citizens faced higher interest rates, a radically weakened currency, and more uncertainty about the economic future than some of them had known in their lifetimes (see Figure 21.6).

The "see-through" buildings made famous by Houston of the early 1980s suddenly appeared to have new homes: Jakarta had a 10 percent vacancy rate, Bangkok 15 percent, and Shanghai 30 percent. The myth and mystique about "Asian Capitalism"—particularly the powerful synergy created by governmental partnership with private industry—was swiftly dispelled. The close relationship between business owners, politicians, and central bankers had instead yielded gross amounts of debt, overbuilding, and unnecessary infrastructure. Waste, not efficient capital allocation, was the result.

The IMF was put in the role of regional savior. Its overall purpose was to serve as a temporary aid to countries that were experiencing balance of payment problems, and that purpose was successfully executed repeatedly in 1997 and 1998 during the Asian crisis. One hundred ten billion dollars

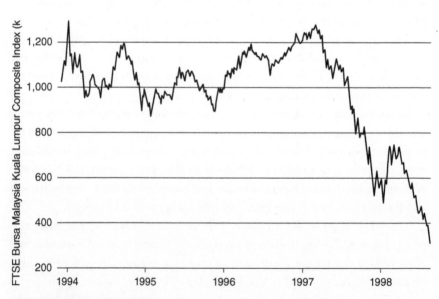

FIGURE 21.6 The Kuala Lumpur stock exchange had lost three-quarters of its value in just over a year's time.

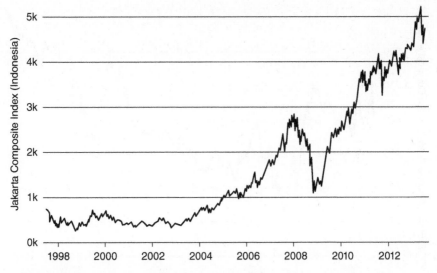

FIGURE 21.7 From the depths of the crisis, the Indonesian stock market would go on to grow by more than 10-fold.

in loans were deployed in three countries alone—Indonesia, Thailand, and South Korea—and in each case, the economies and the currencies eventually recovered and the loans were repaid (see Figure 21.7).

By the start of 1998, the IMF had provided loans to 75 different countries in the world, and in each case, various edicts for government reform, alterations in operating procedures for the local economy, taxes, interest rates, and other economic levers were exercised.

Perhaps the most positive outcome of the crisis was a region-wide cleansing took place with respect to politics and practices. Formerly insular industries were required to open up to outside investment and participation, and the worst aspects of "crony capitalism" were shut down.

By virtue of the IMF's intervention, however, the lingering risk of moral hazard now loomed larger than ever. The banks, builders, and businesses had all, to varying degrees, acting irresponsibly, and when economic disaster finally emerged, the IMF and World Bank bailed out the parties from the crisis they had created. The temptation to behave recklessly in the future, cognizant of the IMF safety net, would certainly be an understandable outcome.

For the time being, however, the recovery had a firm footing in the region. Interest rates, which had escalated horribly during the crisis, began to return to precrisis levels. Equity markets strengthened and, in the years to come, would return triple-digit gains for some of the smaller countries. And

FIGURE 21.8 It would take nearly a decade, but Malaysia's stock market eventually pushed past its precrisis levels.

by 1999, the shrinking GDPs changed course and begin yielding positive figures again, showing growth had returned (see Figure 21.8).

As with so many financial crises that had taken place in world history, the root of Asia's problems had to do with too much money chasing too few genuinely worthy opportunities. The Asian miracle had produced sensational economic gains for many years, but even in the best of circumstances, there must at some point be a reversion to the mean. The Asian Tigers got theirs in early 1997, and the memories of the financial scars would persist for years to come.

CHAPTER 22

Russian Crisis of 1998

A fter the collapse of the Soviet Union, the capitalist world viewed Russia not as a defeated enemy but instead as a potentially powerful partner in business. The Asian miracle (such as in Japan) as well as the European miracle (such as in Germany) had created widespread prosperity from the ashes of World War II, so it was likewise hoped that a Russian miracle of some kind might emerge from the cessation of the Cold War.

The core difference between the robust economies of Japan, Germany, South Korea, Singapore, and all of the rest of them versus Russia was this: Russia was not starting with a clean slate. Instead, it faced the challenge not of building something from scratch, but trying to alter the nature of a deeply entrenched economic failure. The industries that had lumbered and groaned from year to year in the time of communism were still there, and a path had to be laid out to shape the Russian economy into something that could in the world's playing field based on free enterprise instead of central planning.

■ After the Fall

The disintegration of the Soviet Union was chaotic and confusing for its former member-states. The countries of the former Union of Soviet Socialist Republics (USSR) outside of Russia were exhilarated at their new freedom, and these satellite nations were in many cases small and nimble enough to carve out a place for themselves in the global economy. Their fortunes varied based on their own natural resources, their proximity to trading nations, and their own economic infrastructure, but after decades living under rule from Moscow, they each started the 1990s with a sense of opportunity.

Russia was a somewhat different story, since it began its new life as an independent republic that was deeply in debt from the Soviet years. The International Monetary Fund (IMF), the World Bank, and the governments of the United States and Japan each recognized that Russia would need financial assistance and guidance to undergo the metamorphosis from centrally planned economy to a market economy.

The nascent success of the former Soviet states in eastern Europe was encouraging, and Boris Yeltsin—riding high in popularity from his facing-down of the conspirators during the failed Russian coup—occupied the president's seat with firm control of the government. Russia had a massive welfare state, a large elderly population, and a very narrow economy, based largely on the export of energy products. There was not much time to address the deep economic challenges facing the very new country that had a lot of very old problems.

■ Loans Instead of Growth

In a developing economy, strength comes from growth. As businesses grow, the financial segment of the economy strengthens, tax revenues increase, the government's currency reserves grow, and over time a nation establishes creditworthiness and a reputation as a good risk. There are some essential foundational elements to this kind of prosperity, including a system of law in which there is a relatively level playing field, availability of capital, and an environment in which business agreements can be honored and enforced.

Such an environment bore little resemblance to Russia in the early 1990s. A handful of men with close ties to the Kremlin were able to secure valuable assets in the chaos and confusion of Russia's early days as an independent state, and in spite of attempts to "spread the wealth" through the widespread distribution of vouchers to all the citizens of Russia, it did not create the even distribution of wealth that was envisioned.

Instead, business insiders bought up the vouchers cheaply from fellow countrymen and were able to consolidate wealth and power. Russia was shaping up as a nation with a tiny number of fabulously rich people contrasted with an overwhelming majority of citizens who were just able to scrape by.

The IMF provided an important substitute for genuine economic growth in the form of loans. However, the IMF's normal role of providing short-term cash injections to countries facing payment imbalances was not the nature of its relationship with Russia. Instead, global entities like the IMF viewed the new Russian state as a once-in-a-generation opportunity to get a potentially vital free-market force on its feet, and it would loans billions in an effort to do so.

The first loan was for $1 billion, issued by the IMF in April 1992. The next year, a loan for $1.5 billion was issued, and a year after that, another disbursement of the same amount. The loans kept coming, crossing the $10 billion mark by the end of 1995, and just a few months later, on March 26, 1996, a new loan package of $10.2 billion was announced, more than doubling all the prior obligations. It was the second-largest single disbursement made in IMF history.

Atypically for the IMF, there were no demands for financial reforms, a strengthening of the legal framework for business, a pledge to enforce tax collection, or any of the other adjustments the IMF would be in a position to demand with so much money at stake. The managing director of the IMF brushed off such concerns by stating, "It is our duty and moral obligation to support this country."

The principal force behind all these loans was the Clinton administration, which was urging the IMF to be generous in its support of Russia. The stability and success of the Russian Federation would ultimately be good for the United States, and as the most important member of the IMF (as well as the only nation with veto power), the United States was in a position to compel obligation-free loans that would have been unthinkable for other nations.

■ Welcome to the Club

This is not to suggest that Russia had made no progress in efforts to privatize its economy and get its commercial house in order. Russia expressed its commitment to eventually retiring old Soviet debt, and in spite of occasional bouts of near-hyperinflation, it had made substantial progress by 1995 in getting inflation to moderate.

The primary goal in addressing Soviet debt was to establish the new Russia as a creditworthy business partner whose sovereign debt, even one from an old regime, could be trusted. Russia sought to avoid the disaster that the Weimar Republic had suffered in the 1920s trying to simply print up cash to pay debts, which led to devastating hyperinflation, so Russian leadership repeatedly made clear that monetizing its debt was not a viable option. Partly for this reason, inflation dropped from 131 percent in 1995 to 22 percent in 1996 and 11 percent in 1997. In a short span of time, Russia appeared to be conquering some very serious fiscal flaws.

Based on its progress, Russia was invited to the Paris Club, an informal collection of nations that regularly met to address problems of debtor nations. This was a proud moment for Russia, since its inclusion was an affirmation that the nation's plan to pay over $60 billion in Soviet debts was evidently viewed as tenable. Russia also opened up its debt markets to overseas lenders, including its short-term debt market known as the GKO.

The good news came at a time when several principal problems loomed:

- *Tax collection.* The federal government was not collecting anywhere near the taxes it was due, and part of the reason was the fractured nature of tax collection. In an effort to combat corruption, the tax system had been deliberately set up as a collection of local offices instead of one central revenue bureau. These local offices were charged with collection of provincial taxes as well as federal, and it was their task to remit federal taxes to Moscow. A widely practiced scheme, however, would be for tax officials to work with local businesses to underreport their revenues, and thus lower their federal tax bill, in exchange for extra payments to the local government. On the whole, this would save the business tax expenses and help local states with their own revenues, but the central government would be denied its correct tax income, creating a worsening deficit for Moscow. Some estimates held that the federal government was only getting half of the tax revenue that it was truly owed.

- *Nonpayment of wages.* Many people in both the public and private sector were working but were getting paid either only partially or not at all, due to the inability of their employers or governments to make payroll. The old Soviet joke that "we pretend to work and they pretend to pay us" now seemed only half-true for many citizens, as work was actually getting done, but paychecks were being held in arrears. This was obviously a source of discontent, as it became increasingly difficult for ordinary Russians to buy what they needed to live.

- *Narrow revenue sources.* Russia was a very resource-rich nation. During times of high energy and metal prices, such as the first half of 2008, this would mean a bonanza for the country, since revenues would soar along with elevated commodity prices. However, it also left the country vulnerable to depressed prices, and the lack of diversification in its exports put Russia at the mercy of global commodity prices over which it had little control.

In spite of these issues, Russia was perceived as a country with a potentially bright future, and investors in emerging markets turned their attention to the former Soviet state and begin bidding up its stock market. Prices began ascending rapidly, and as impossible as it would have seemed just a few years earlier, Russia became the top-performing stock market in the world as broad indexes ascended by triple-digit percentage gains.

The GKO (which stands for "state short-term obligations" when translated into English) market was also increasingly popular with non-Russians. It paid extraordinarily high interest rates which, given Russia's modest inflation, provided a moneymaking opportunity for Russians and non-Russians alike. The interest being paid on GKO notes reached the triple digits by the middle of 1997, which created a sizable strain on the Russian government, which was having trouble collecting tax revenue to pay for such expenses in the first place.

■ Strains in the Kremlin

As 1997 drew to a close, Russia's export income was beginning to crumble, as prices for metals and oil dropped substantially. Between the weakness in exports and its trouble collecting tax revenue, the Russian government drafted a new tax code that was built as a simpler, fairer, and easier-to-enforce system of government income. This tax plan was submitted to the Duma, Russia's legislative body, and it was approved.

President Yeltsin shocked the nation soon thereafter by firing his prime minister, Viktor Chernomyrdin, over accusations of corruption. He simultaneously fired the entire cabinet and, to head the new team, Yeltsin appointed Sergei Kiriyenko.

The appointment of Kiriyenko as prime minister of Russia was perplexing to observers, since he was very young—only 35—and had less than a year of experience in the government, having spent most of his working life in banking and energy companies. The Duma stalled on its approval of the appointment, but after Yeltsin threatened to dissolve them as well, they relented and gave their blessing to the young man who now occupied the prime minister's office.

During this time, the spring of 1998, a series of communications blunders unnerved investors. First, the chairman of the Central Bank of Russia (CBR) met with a number of government ministers and stated that the government might be facing a debt crisis within several years if it did not make positive steps to close its income and expense gap. The CBR chairman didn't know it at the time, but there were reporters in the room listening, and word quickly spread in the media that that CBR was concerned about a debt crisis. Since the widespread Asian crisis had only abated weeks beforehand, global investors were very nervous about any developing economy whose debt might be called into question.

Prime Minister Kiriyenko's inexperience with public relations revealed itself soon thereafter, and he mentioned during an interview that tax revenues were 26 percent beneath plan and that the government was "quite poor now." He used this as the jumping-off point to discuss his plans to reduce government spending and boost revenue with the new tax plan in place, but the principal point expressed in the media focused on how "poor" the government was, not the plans it was undertaking to remedy the situation.

A third foible ensued when Deputy Treasury of the Secretary Larry Summers visited Moscow. He went to the office of Prime Minster Kiriyenko and requested a meeting. An aide, unfamiliar with Summers and suspicious of the importance of a mere deputy secretary, said he would not be able to meet the prime minister. This was an unwise move, considering the vital political support the United States represented to Russia, including its close ties with the IMF.

This critical mass of blunders gave investors an ugly impression of what was happening in Moscow, and talk about currency devaluation and debt default began to spread. Russian stocks and bonds slumped badly, and prices on Russian bonds were so depressed that they were soon yielding 47 percent.

As the Russian ruble continued to lose value, the CBR took two steps to slow the drop: it boosted interest rates from 30 percent to 50 percent, and it bought a billion dollars' worth of rubles in the open market using its foreign currency reserves.

Unrelated to these moves, but even more damaging to the economy, crude oil had dropped to prices that hadn't been seen in decades, with levels threatening to break into the single digits per barrel. The wealthy owners of Russian energy interests agitated for Moscow to devalue the ruble, but on the contrary, CBR chairman Sergei Dubinin told the press on May 20, "When you hear talk of devaluation, spit in the eye of whoever is talking about it." Dubinin increased the lending rate once more, tripling it to 150 percent (see Figure 22.1).

FIGURE 22.1 The lending rate from the Russian Central Bank soared in 1998, spiking to 150 percent in the summer.

More bad news came when coal miners, weary of not getting paid, went on strike and blocked the Trans-Siberian Railway. Russian workers were owed $12.5 billion in unpaid wages, and poverty was becoming widespread not so much from lack of work as lack of a paycheck.

In less than a year, Russia had moved from burgeoning prosperity to nationwide crisis, and Yeltsin made nightly television appearances urging the nation's business leadership to have faith in Russia and bolster their investments in the country.

It was difficult for businesses to thrive in an environment where the central bank was charging 150 percent for loans. The bonds issued by the government were paying extremely high rates as well, but even with such outsized returns, the bonds were not selling, because there was too much fear they would never been paid back upon reaching maturity.

■ Moratorium

The IMF sought to address the growing crisis, and on July 16, 1998, Russia, the IMF, the World Bank, and Japan collectively announced a $17.1 billion infusion of cash, which was to be augmented with $5.5 billion of overseas loans for an overall federal loan package of $22.6 billion. This time, the IMF made demands in exchange for the loan, which included a severe reduction in budget deficits.

The size of the deal was a positive shock to the financial markets, and Russian equities ascended 17 percent in a single day, which was a new record. Excitement about the loan deal dissipated quickly, however, and a new record for a single-day move in the stock market—this time to the downside—was made when equities lost 9 percent on July 27.

The tension and uncertainty about Russia's situation was resolved on August 17, 1998, when Russia announced that it was not only devaluing the ruble but also suspending payments on its debts, which totaled $45 billion. It also announced a 90-day moratorium on payments of private external debt.

Reaction to the news was very negative, and the stock market's plunge accelerated. The dumping of stocks became so acute that, on multiple occasions, the stock exchange had to suspend trading to restore order (see Figure 22.2). As the *Wall Street Journal* reported the following day, "Facing a choice between two economic evils to fight its financial woes, Russian chose both."

What was more outrageous to everyday citizens was that much of the IMF money that had been poured into Russia recently was allocated to

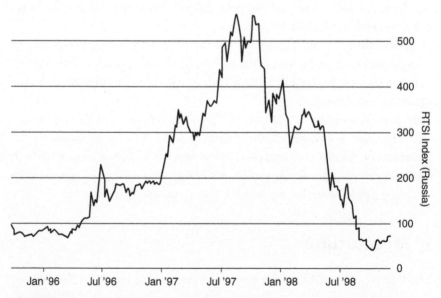

FIGURE 22.2 The Russian stock market, which had soared in 1996 and 1997, quickly lost all of its prior gains.

well-placed Russian elite to exchange their ruble-based bonds for U.S. dollars. The rich had found an escape hatch, by way of the IMF cash infusion, and the well-connected were able to avoid disaster while the vast majority of citizens were struggling just to survive.

U.S. President Bill Clinton had a meeting scheduled in Moscow that September, so he dispatched a senior Treasury official to Moscow to help address the crisis and avoid an awkward and embarrassing leadership summit. The new prime minister, Kiriyenko, and his cabinet resigned on August 23 after a mere five months in office.

■ The Have-Nots

With pressure on the ruble continuing, the CBR announced on September 2 that it would no longer maintain a "peg" and instead would allow the currency to float freely in the open market. In just a few weeks, the ruble crumbled to an exchange rate of 21 to 1 versus the U.S. dollar, a loss of two-thirds of its value from the already-diminished values of the prior month.

While inflation had largely been beaten back by 1997, it returned with force during the ruble's collapse. Store owners were posting new, higher prices on a daily—sometimes several times a day—basis, and retail prices rose 36 percent in just the first week of September when the ruble was allowed to float freely.

Russian banks severely restricted the ability of depositors to withdraw funds. Customers were allowed to withdraw only rubles, even if their accounts were based on U.S. dollars, and they could only take out a small amount of cash each day. With the value of the ruble falling precipitously, depositors helplessly saw the true worth of their imprisoned deposits drop on a daily basis.

These were the lucky ones, however, as millions of depositors at the banks that did not survive the crisis had their entire savings wiped out. One elderly man, who had spread his money at three different banks as a precaution, was stunned to find that all three banks had failed, and the entirety of his savings was simply gone.

The number of people living beneath the poverty line (which, by Russian standards, was a genuinely low level) soared to 40 percent. Those in rural areas were at least able to grow their own food to survive. Those in the cities, particularly the elderly, had to rely on the charity of others to get by.

Public health problems grew along with the financial despair. Alcoholism, long a problem in Russia even before the financial crisis, became epidemic. Deaths from alcohol consumption were cited as 35,000 per year, versus 300 a year in the United States, a country with over twice the population of Russia. Drug use, too, became severe, with Russia's own Ministry of Interior reporting 3 million Russians (about 2 percent of the population) as habitual drug users.

Prices for everything were going up, but imported items had substantially higher increases due to the plunge in the ruble's value. Whereas inflation for 1998 as a whole was 84 percent, imported items quadrupled in price. Even if a citizen could afford the essentials, shortages were widespread, with such basics as cooking oil, sugar, cleaning detergent, and food staples being snapped up from near-empty store shelves.

After weeks of worsening turmoil, protestors took to the streets. On October 7, 1998, 100,000 people marched on the streets of Moscow, with similar but smaller demonstrations taking place in other Russian cities on the same day. By October 20, Yeltsin issued a presidential decree banning mass protests between 10 P.M. and 7 A.M. and forbidding any protests from lasting longer than five days.

Citizens, particularly older ones who had lived for decades under Soviet rule, were accustomed to long lines, shortages, and cash problems. Some resorted to the more primitive economic system of bartering, since the value of exchanging rubles for goods and services had been so badly damaged.

Even employers that owed their workers for labor resorted to creative means of issuing payments: teachers in one town were paid with cemetery headstones, and one textile manufacturer in Kostroma settled its tax bill with the local police by means of 6,000 new pairs of socks.

In such a crisis, public health suffered as well, with shortages of drugs and supplies becoming severe. Medicine had to be rationed, and patients were restricted to a maximum of five days in the hospital. More generally, Russia's population was shrinking due to a combination of economic hardship, an aging population, and rising divorce rates.

The population had been dropping each year since 1992, and in the year following the crash of the ruble, there were 784,000 more deaths than births in the country. In spite of Russia's enormous size, the population was not even half that of the United States, and it was on a pathway to a shrinking population.

■ LTCM in America

The financial turmoil in Russia was not confined to its borders. Overseas holders of bonds and Russian stocks suffered, as the financial instruments became either worthless or greatly diminished in value. The entire surge in the Russian stock market had reversed, and in percentage terms it lost as much in less than one year as the U.S. stock market had lost during the entire Great Depression.

One high-profile casualty of the Russian financial disaster was Long-Term Capital Management (LTCM), founded in 1994 by Salomon Brothers' former vice chairman John Meriwether. Meriwether recruited to his hedge fund's board of directors Nobel laureates Myron Scholes and Robert Merton, as well as a number of other Wall Street luminaries. Meriwether wanted his new fund to begin with a sizable asset base, and such financial star power was effective at bringing in deposits. On the day the fund launched, it had over $1 billion under management.

LTCM took a highly leveraged approach to its trading, as it exploited minute differences between financial instruments whose divergences were projected to close. The company traded mostly in bonds from the United States, Japan, and Europe, and its intensely mathematical strategy paid off handsomely for investors, yielding returns of 40 percent during each of the first few years. The asset base grew thanks to such gains as well as new deposits, swelling to almost $5 billion before the Russian crisis hit.

The fund was positioned early in 1998 to take advantage of an anticipated diminishment in the spread between Russian bonds and the bonds of industrialized nations such as the United States. If troubles in Russia were abated, the perceived risk of Russian debt would diminish, interest rates would fall, the spread would likewise fall, and LTCM would log yet another year of outsized profits.

Instead, the positions started moving against the firm. In May 1998, the fund was down 6.42 percent; in June, it lost another 10.14 percent. The losses worsened substantially once the Russian crisis was in full swing, with the fund accumulating $1.85 billion in losses by the end of August. On one day alone, August 21, LTCM lost over a half billion dollars on its positions.

Investors began exiting the fund in a panic, and over the first three weeks of September, via a combination of redemptions and losses, equity dropped from $2.3 billion to $400 million. With many highly leveraged derivatives positions still on the books, the firm now had a equity-to-position ratio of

1 to 250, meaning even the smallest additional move against the firm's positions would wipe it out and cause a cascade of defaults.

With assets under management of just $400 million, LTCM was no longer a substantial hedge fund, but the nature of its positions made its failure a systemic risk, so much so that the U.S. Treasury organized a bailout to inject $3.75 billion of capital into the firm and unwind its positions in less adverse circumstances. Most of the money came from large investment banks, such as Goldman Sachs and J. P. Morgan. Indeed, with the exception of Bear Stearns (which itself would be wiped out in 2008), almost all the big names of Wall Street finance were participating.

The losses for LTCM's investors totaled $4.6 billion, spread among swaps, emerging market debt, arbitrage, junk bonds, and other directional trades. The bailout was a success, only insofar as the positions were sold at a small profit from the distressed prices at which they were acquired, and the fund was able to be wound down in an organized fashion in 2000.

■ Russian Resurgence

What saved Russia after its horrendous 1998 crisis was not deft internal leadership or global bailout; it was simply the fortuitous circumstance that energy prices rebounded sharply in 1999 and 2000, which substantially increased the nation's import revenue. In both years, Russia enjoyed a healthy trade surplus and was able to help restore its depleted foreign reserves (see Figure 22.3).

The cheapening of the ruble had also benefited domestic industries, as it made imports far more expensive than domestically made alternatives. Russia enjoyed the same benefits as if it had erected trade barriers, but without the geopolitical consequences of doing so. As the financial sector slowly restored itself, and domestic balance sheets improved, back-wages were paid out to workers, who in turn were able to put the cash back into the local economy. In short, the seizing-up of financial flows had abated, and the economy was returning to normalcy now that the velocity of money within it had accelerated.

Most of the 1990s had been difficult years of transition for Russians. From 1993 to 1998, unemployment climbed each year, ascending from 5.5 percent in 1993 to 11.5 percent in 1998. However, during those same years, inflation was brought under control, decreasing from an 844 percent increase in consumer prices in 1993 to the single digits by 1998 (see Figure 22.4).

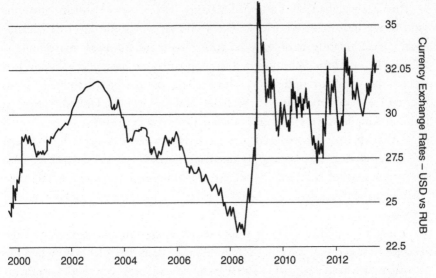

FIGURE 22.3 After the crisis, the ruble was still volatile, but it remained within a trading band of about 25 to 35 rubles to the U.S. dollar.

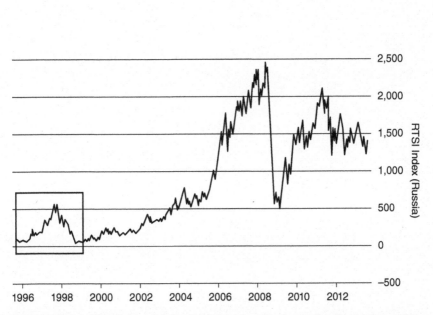

FIGURE 22.4 The rise and fall of the Russian stock market in the late 1990s, highlighted on the left side of this chart, is dwarfed by its subsequent ascent prior to the 2008 global financial crisis.

Russia never had the luxury of starting with a clean slate. Its oligarchs and heavy industries were deeply embedded, and some level of corruption was an innate part of both the government and business environments. The basic legal foundation needed to support sound business practices. In a recent survey of corruption levels for each nation, Russia still ranked 133rd, beneath such countries as Iran, Vietnam, and Egypt. (The United States and United Kingdom were ranked 19th and 17th, respectively).

Although Russia recovered from its crisis to some degree, the damage to its reputation was lasting. Its financial markets remained volatile, with the stock market resuming its ascent, this time even more incredible than the one in 1997, only to lose years of gains during the 2008 global financial crisis.

Russia's economic advantages and disadvantages in the beginning of the twenty-first century were not much different than they had been when the Russian state first emerged in 1991. It can be said, however, that the reforms compelled by its 1998 financial crisis were at least a positive step on the path to normalizing Russia's place on the global economic stage.

CHAPTER 23

Captured by the Net

The Internet bubble, which inflated throughout the late 1990s and peaked early in 2000, was unique in several ways: first, unlike so many bubbles of centuries past, it involved not hundreds but instead millions of people. It was not confined to a small geographic region or the machinations of a crafty confidence man; instead, it revolved around what was, in fact, an important technological advancement whose promises were in many ways fulfilled later but whose early attempts were often misguided.

A few of the world's largest and most successful company emerged from the bubble, but in the process, trillions of dollars of wealth were destroyed and millions of people were gravely disappointed at the difference between what was promised and what was actually realized. Many of these people suffered substantial financial losses along the way.

In just two years, from 2000 to 2002, technology companies alone accounted for a $5 trillion loss in shareholder value. The top 10 failed dot-com start-ups—not public companies, but just the privately funded small businesses—accounted for $2.7 billion in losses for their investors.

A few notable examples of the so-called "dot-bombs" of the era include:

- Pets.com—a loss of $300 million, and whose sock puppet became emblematic of the Internet collapse.

- eToys.com—a $247 million loss.

- Kozmo.com, which delivered, usually by bicycle, whatever a person at home might want brought to their home—$280 million loss.

- Go.com, which was Disney's mammoth effort to insert itself into the Internet space—$790 million loss.

- WebVan, which was nothing more than a way to order groceries for delivery to your house—$800 million loss, and one of the largest and most conspicuous failures.

The emergence of the Internet and the businesses that sprang up around it did become an important part of both culture and commerce in the years after the bubble burst, but the mania surrounding the early days of the commercial Internet—particularly with respect to the retail investor's participation in the public markets for these firms—was unprecedented (see Figure 23.1).

FIGURE 23.1 This chart of the Nasdaq Composite Index illustrates the astonishing ascent of stock values during the Internet bubble of the 1990s.

■ Living History

Unless one is writing an autobiography, it is atypical for an author to insert himself into a book about history. I would like to make an exception in this chapter, however, as the Internet boom (and subsequent crash) was an integral part of my own personal experience.

My life intersected with the Internet bubble in three ways: first, my longevity online; second, my own start-up business located in the heart of the Silicon Valley; and third, the nature of my business, which was financial information.

I have been online for a very long time, relatively speaking. I got my first modem in 1981 and wrote my first book, *The World Connection*, in 1982. The book was itself about online communities, and it was published a dozen years before commercial browsers were widely available. The introduction of the Internet, therefore, was for me simply a new way to access online content, which I had been doing for a dozen years already.

My business, Prophet Financial Systems, was founded on July 1, 1992, long before anyone outside the U.S. Defense Department was even aware of the existence of anything called the Internet. I founded the business in Palo Alto, the very nexus of all things related to high-tech start-ups, where it remained until it was sold 13 years later. The business itself was given "angel" funding by Andy Bechtolsheim, who himself is a famed entrepreneur and had the foresight to be Google's first investor.

Finally, the very nature of the business—financial information for retail investors—put me and my colleagues very close to the growth, psychology, and mania related to the stock market. Because of this triad of circumstances, I personally had an especially acute experience with the technology-driven stock market of the 1990s, so I will interrupt the normal flow of this chapter from time to time in sections denoted as "Living History" to share the state of my own business and how it compared to what was going on all around us.

■ Fuel for the Fire

The United States experienced a recession around 1991 and 1992, and although it wasn't particularly severe or long lived, it was bad enough to compel Americans to change presidents. George Bush lost his bid for a second term, and a young new leader, Bill Clinton, took office. There was no way anyone could tell at the time, but Clinton's two terms would run parallel with not only a widespread economic boom but also the most pervasive investing mania in American history.

The Internet itself wasn't introduced to the world with fanfare. On the contrary, the computer network had been in place since the first two nodes were connected in October 1969, and a growing web of military, academic, and research sites were plugged into the system throughout the 1970s and 1980s. Early in the 1990s, the federal government decided to turn the network over to public management and commercialization, allowing for a much larger and more diverse application of the network (see Figure 23.2).

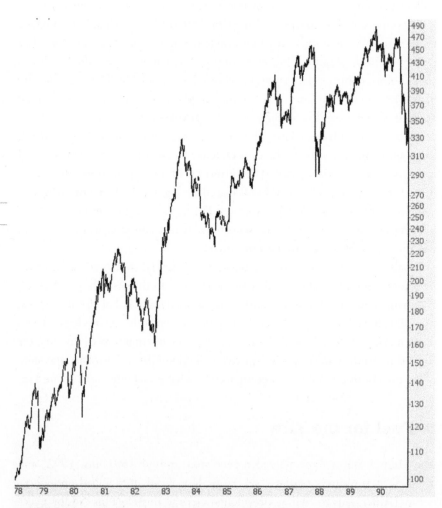

FIGURE 23.2 For the dozen years before Clinton took office, the Nasdaq moved generally higher, but in the more normal up-and-down pattern of typical equity markets. The very broad trend was up, but the growth was in stages and took many years to transpire.

The technical and economic soil in the early 1990s was fertile ground for what would become the dot-com boom for several reasons:

- *Cold War victory.* After decades of an expensive Cold War, the United States emerged as the de facto winner and the world's only remaining superpower. In addition to America's "victory" over the Soviet Union, it also had successfully prosecuted an actual war, the first Gulf War, faster and more effectively than anyone had dared imagine. American seemed nearly invincible from a military perspective and looked forward to a "peace dividend" made possible by the absence of any major enemy. It also continued to enjoy a geographic isolation, flanked by two vast oceans, that would continue to provide a placid sanctuary from whatever political flare-ups were bound to happen in the years ahead.

- *Online investing.* Stock investing had been, even until the early 1980s, something in which relatively few Americans participated. The bull market from 1982 to 1987 helped spur some people to trade, and early discount brokers (such as Charles Schwab) made trading more accessible and inexpensive for the public.

  However, it was not until the early 1990s that this trend became more widespread. More online brokerages opened their doors, and commission wars between them drove prices down from several hundred dollars per trade (which was typical in the early 1970s) to a near-ubiquitous $9.95 per trade. The low transaction cost and convenience of trading through a computer was instantly appealing to a whole new generation of investors.

  The media, too, would play a huge part in the 1990s of popularizing trading. One cable channel, originally created as a consumer television station, was called the Consumer News and Business Channel (or, simply, CNBC). Aware of the growing popularity of retail trading, CNBC repositioned itself away from consumer advocacy and toward the world of active stock traders.

- *A credible arrative.* In the latter half of the 1990s, as Internet-based businesses began springing up as an increasingly swift pace, the fundamental template for many of the businesses formed had a ring of credibility and authenticity to it: that is, the Internet was a new business frontier, start-ups were involved in a "land grab," and the most important objective was to Get Big Fast, irrespective of huge short-term losses.

The losses, investors were assured, would all pay off later in big profits once a firm had achieved dominance. Millions of people became entranced and seduced by the prospect of easy profits, and for a while, it seemed like the only foolish folks were those that chose to sit out the mania. No less a person than Warren Buffett, who shied away from the Internet madness, was chastised as being sadly behind the times as his firm Berkshire Hathaway lagged the red-hot performance of tech-laden stock indexes in the late 1990s.

■ The Foundation is Laid

It should be noted early on that many equity markets around the world in dozens of different industries thrived in the 1990s. The stock market boom was by no means confined to just high-tech stocks in the United States. However, the most extreme amounts of price appreciation, press attention, and cultural effects took place in this one industry (the Internet) and one country (the United States).

The timetable of most financial bubbles follows four time-worn phases:

- *Disruption and displacement.* This is when something new appears on the scene that is so important that an entire way of business is subjected to disruption and transformation. History has given us examples that are small (like the cotton gin) and large (like the locomotive), but they all produced a sea change in how people go about working, moving, or living.

- At first, the change is rarely given much attention; for example, the invention of the transistor, arguably one of the most important inventions of the twentieth century, barely merited a small mention deep inside the pages of the *New York Times* when it was introduced. Those who participate (either as investors, business owners, or inventors) at this earliest stage usually benefit the most later, since their stake was acquired cheaply, before the public was even aware of the new product or service.

- *Growth.* This is when the more observant or well-read members of the public become aware of whatever is taking place. These are the "early adopters," in marketing parlance, and people buying stock in America Online, Yahoo!, or Netscape during their public offerings in the first half of the 1990s could be included in this category.

- *Exuberance.* Here is the phase of the bubble when participating investors often think to themselves, "This is easy." Profitable trading seems to be almost a foregone conclusion, and it appears the entire public is participating in the newfound market, both as consumers and as speculators. Traders in this stage are, consciously or not, functioning within the *Greater Fool* paradigm: that is, the hope that, in spite of whatever high price is paid for a given financial instrument, someone else (a "greater fool") will come along and be willing to pay an even *higher* price.

- *Reality.* The least favorite part of a bubble (except for those who are short the market), this is when reversion to the mean takes place and, often, when frauds are exposed. In the famous words of Warren Buffett after the tech bubble finally popped, "Only when the tide goes out do you discover who's been swimming naked."

If a date had to be assigned to the beginning of the first phase, "disruption," it would probably be January 23, 1993. It was on this day that 21-year-old Marc Lowell Andreessen released his first public version of the Mosaic web browser. The Internet had only recently become accessible to the general public, but the software that existed for web "browsing" was awkward, hard-to-use, and buggy.

Although Andreessen's first effort was relatively primitive, it was the first browser that casual computer users could use to easily explore what was, at the time, the small number of websites that existed around the world.

There had been plenty of other online communities before the World Wide Web. Electronic bulletin board systems had been running for decades, and computers had long been able to exchange files, host chat sessions, provide e-mail services, and act as file archives. But the ability to use a graphical browser to "surf" content was novel, and the Mosaic browser's features and fame quickly spread throughout the world of savvy and curious computer users.

Living History

What the world knows as the Silicon Valley initially gained fame in the 1970s because of semiconductors and memory and in the 1980s because of personal computers and video games. California's Santa Clara Valley was the locus of thousands of new successful technology companies during those years, but in those days, a "start-up" was typically something that (1) was physical and had to be manufactured and, thus (2) required a meaningful amount of start-up capital.

(Continued)

Businesses that offered services and software could be started with little working capital, and my own start-up was one such enterprise. I named the company Prophet, and I started it after leaving a nine-person company that sold historical financial data and daily updates to retail stock and commodity traders. My partner and I wanted to create a better product to compete with that of our former employer, and with a small amount of seed capital from a local investor, we rented an office, bought some computers, and went to work.

This was during the summer of 1992, and although by then the personal computer industry was quite mature, there was relatively little going on with computer-to-computer communications. The most innovative and interesting company that provided online services was called America Online, and I had some prior interactions with the founder of this company when I worked at Apple Computer in the late 1980s.

As an intern at Apple, I was involved in a strategic planning group that spend its time researching and writing about what we called Worldwide Channel Systems (WWCS), which was a proposed computer network to connect our customers, vendors, and resellers to Apple itself. The thick document we put together was, in retrospect, quite prescient about the huge import that electronic networks would have on business, but at the time, our work went wholly ignored by a senior management that was more interested in more immediate matters, such as product pricing.

During my assignment with WWCS, however, I was asked to work with a tiny outfit in Virginia called Quantum Computer Services, founded by a fellow named Steve Case. Since I had been using online systems for a decade already, I was quite interested in this new firm and what it was doing, and Quantum—which had an agreement with Apple to provide their newest software for a couple of our computer platforms—viewed Apple as an important strategic partner.

The software that Quantum (which later renamed itself America Online) had created was far more sophisticated and easy to use than anything else I had tried before, so I was not surprised to see the company thriving as the nation's fastest-growing online service. AOL went public in 1992, the same year I started Prophet, and its stock would spend most of the 1990s ascending.

As for Prophet, what we were doing wasn't especially advanced: we were simply storing thousands of years of historical financial data in a large database and proving modem-based access to individual subscribers. Our stack of modems would sit idle most of the day, but after the market closed, the lights on the modems would sparkle as individual traders from around the country would, one by one, establish a telephone-based connection with our server and download their price updates for the day. Seeing those modem lights flicker with customer activity was the most gratifying part of the day.

There is very little else that compares to the excitement of starting a new business. You have before you a sheet of white paper on which anything can be written. The possibilities seem endless, and the freedom you feel, particularly after having been simply an employee somewhere else, is exhilarating.

Amidst all this excitement, of course, there's a lot of work to do. Prophet started off as a two-person company, that is, an engineer who had done the programming at our former employer, and I, who took care of everything else. The "everything else" guy takes care of anything that isn't actual programming. I dealt with the legal paperwork, getting advertising and marketing plans together, acquiring data sources, and getting our first office.

The business we were putting together wasn't terribly complex from a technical standpoint. We acquired a large amount of historical price data on stocks, futures, and other financial instruments, and stored them in a database. We set up a live data feed so that at the end of each day, we could update all that daily financial data with the latest information. And we set about creating a program, with the rather humdrum name of "Access," to give individuals the ability to download the data that they wanted.

These customers, in turn, would look at the data using charting programs that other companies made. Now, the market for historical financial data wasn't very big in 1992. Even the largest companies in the industry had a customer base measured merely in the thousands,

(Continued)

and the biggest firm out there probably had no more than $5 million in sales. So Prophet wasn't in the kind of industry that would merit venture capital funding, but for two young men putting together something new, the prospect of building even a million dollar business was energizing.

Just a few months after we got our office, we actually had a product to sell, thanks to the programming efforts of my partner. Marketing the product was simple enough, since there were some well-established venues to promote something like Prophet in a niche market like ours. There were trade shows that popped up every couple of months in different parts of the country, and there were a few major magazines in which we could advertise.

Our little business was doing pretty well. A year into it, we were able to pay our rent, pay our salaries, pay for marketing, and cover all the other odds and ends that go into running a small enterprise. We were starting to feel a little cramped in our first office, so we started looking around for something a little larger and more professional looking, and I found a nice place on the first floor of an office building on the other side of Palo Alto.

Now, moving into our first office when we were just beginning was exciting because of the novelty of the situation. Moving into a nicer, larger office was exciting in a different way, since it affirmed that we were actually starting to succeed and could enjoy some of the fruits of our labor.

After all, we were able to pay for a respectable space with decent salaries all based on the revenues we were generating, and we recognized that if we could keep growing, we actually might be onto something. So in early August, 1993, we moved into this building and got ready for a new chapter in our history.

After a couple of weeks, we were settled in to our nice new office and continuing to nurse the business along. I went home on Friday, August 13, 1993, after a long day. Late that night—again, this was Friday the 13th, so bad luck was in the air—the huge glass window into my office was smashed, and someone broke in and took everything of value. All our computers, monitors, and—worst of all—backup drives were stolen.

I was unaware of this, of course, since we didn't have an alarm system in place, and I was puzzled early on Saturday morning when the phone rang with my office number showing on the caller ID. The policemen on the scene looked at my office phone and saw one of the buttons marked "Home," so he pushed that one and got me. After they explained who they were and why they were calling, I rushed to the office and, once there, saw the mess. Our business, in a very literal sense, has been stolen away.

We weren't sure who had done this, or why. Was it some drug addict desperate for something he could sell for cash? Was it our former employer looking for an opportunity to wipe out a growing competitor? It did seem suspicious to us that whoever broke in stole our backup tapes, of all things.

But on that horrible Saturday, it didn't take long for us to realize that the entire year we had spent building the business had just been destroyed. The computers could easily be replaced. The programming code and customer database, however, could not, and our reputation was going to be irreversibly damaged. We were back at square one.

■ Raging Bulls

The two most basic businesses in the early commercial Internet were service providers and browser companies. Internet service providers (known as ISPs) were firms that would create a means for an individual to access the Internet.

In the old days of online communications, a person might use a modem to dial in to a dedicated information services, such as CompuServe, The Source, or a local electronic bulletin board, but the user was confined to whatever information and services were within the confines of that system. Internet service providers, on the other hand, allowed the person to dial in to a modem as well, but once connected, that person was linked up to the much wider array of interconnected systems instead of a single computer.

America Online was, in spite of its novelty, much closer as a business model to the old-fashioned services like CompuServe, since its content and features were within the "walled garden" of AOL. In spite of this, the company was a marvelous business success.

America Online had gone public in 1992 and, from March 1992 to March 1996, it enjoyed a spectacular increase in the value of its stock, from a total market value of $70 million at the initial public offering increasing to $6.5 *billion* four years later. The early investors in the company had sensational profits, and the investing public was delighted at the returns this new business was creating for their portfolios.

The larger of the new ISPs sought a public market for their firms as well. PSINet and UUNet both went public, and as a harbinger of the reliable first day "pops" so many future Internet-related companies would have, both firms saw their stock prices double on their first day of trading. Another ISP, Netcom, offered its stock at an initial price of $13, and it doubled as well, although it took a couple of months to do so.

What was remarkable about these firms and their valuations was that none of them were particularly large businesses. Netcom, for example, had a mere 41,500 subscribers when it went public (as opposed to the millions AOL had), and each of those subscribers paid the $20/month that was typical of ISPs.

The valuations given to these firms, even at their initial offering price, suggested that every single existing customer was worth at least a couple of thousand dollars in value, which was much higher than other companies that enjoyed much higher recurring revenues from subscribers (such as cable television businesses). The market was clearly assigning a value that assumed a huge amount of prospective growth in the customer base.

Living History

Computer modems aren't often associated with human emotions, but I can tell you from personal experience that one of the saddest things I've ever seen is a tall stack of modems that didn't have computers connected to them lighting up with customers on the other end.

During the weekend just after we were burglarized, none of our customers had any idea there was anything wrong at Prophet. This was before people even used e-mail, so there wasn't any way to get the word out quickly. From the customer's point of view, it simply seemed that our product was broken, and knowing how our hard-won reputation was collapsing was sheer torture for me.

Our insurance coverage replaced simple things like the computers and other hardware, but even with all this technology around me, I attained a deep appreciation for paper. That is, even though our customer database was stolen, every single sale we had ever made had originally been written on order forms, allowing us to piece back our customer information, sheet by sheet. And for me, job number one was getting the word out to these people about what had happened and what we were going to do about it.

Given that there was no website to put up an alert and no e-mail addresses to send a notice, we had to rely on the written word to get our urgent message out. I mailed out a letter to all our customers explaining very directly what had happened and stating that, even though it would be a couple of months before our data service would be back online, we would mail them a disk at the end of every week with all the financial updates at no charge.

Although some of our customers decided to leave, most of them were appreciate, supportive, and wanted us to get through this, so they stuck with us. It was a good lesson in the importance of swift and honest communications with customers.

While my partner took on the unenviable task of creating a product from scratch that he had already completed before the burglary, I spent my time preserving as many customers as I could and trying to think of other ways to grow our damaged business. An idea occurred to me that requires a little background to explain.

A few years earlier, back in 1990, I was a relatively new employee at Apple who had been given the assignment of managing the relationship between Apple and an interesting new business from Virginia called Quantum Communications. Quantum was an online business run by a fellow named Steve Case, and they were offering a high-quality dial-up service with a lot of custom content and services. The fact that Apple assigned Quantum to a nobody like me illustrates that they didn't think very much of the relationship.

I recognized Quantum as having a really cool product, and I enjoyed working with the people on their team. During the course of our relationship, they changed their name to America Online, and they began to get increasingly popular with the growing base of

(*Continued*)

computer owners who also had modems. You probably have a pretty good understanding of the history of AOL, so I'll leave it at that.

With my new business, it occurred to me that a company like AOL might need data like ours, so I wrote an e-mail to none other than Steve Case, reminding him of our work together and hoping that he would remember me. He wrote back that same day stating that, yes, they just happened to be putting together something called AOL Finance, and he would have one of his people, Bill Youstra, get in touch with me.

In retrospect, it seems kind of amazing that I would write to Steve Case and get a response so quickly, but AOL hadn't become the international sensation that it was to be in the late 1990s, and it was simply good fortune that I happened to know Steve Case in the first place. Bill Youstra got in touch with me and set up a face-to-face meeting. He was considering several providers of data, such as the giant firm Standard & Poors, so I really wasn't sure what our chances were going to be.

He came out and met with our four-person staff, and I told him earnestly what our business did and what its goals were. Bill and I really hit it off, and before he left, he said something to me that made an impression: "I really like your corporate culture." Even with hindsight, I have no idea what "culture" could be gleaned from a handful of people in a small office, but it meant the world to me that we even had a fighting chance at having our first commercial customer.

Within a few weeks, I got word from America Online that they were going to sign us up for a contract that would pay us to use our data, depending on how many charts they delivered to their own customers. They warned us it would be nearly a year before their charts were up and running, but for us, this was a huge victory. Not only did we have our first business account, but it was with a firm that seemed like it could be going places. And, best of all, the more successful they were, the more money we would be paid. I was thrilled.

But big hopes about the future don't pay the bills, and with our revenue at $0 per month, we were starting to hurt. We didn't have big expenses, but there were expenses nonetheless. We had to pay office rent, the phone bill, insurance premiums and, most of all, salaries. Any small business owner knows that personnel is by far the biggest cost, and even though there were just a few of us, paying salaries from a company that had no revenue and no serious funding was difficult. We cut our salaries to the bone, paying ourselves just enough to scrape by. I've never made so little in my life.

We finally did get back online, and although about half our customers had given up and moved elsewhere, we at least finally had some money coming in. But things weren't really taking off. We were still adding customers day to day, but this was a specialized business, and it was in an era that really didn't have a world of interconnected computers to exploit. We were growing our business the old-fashioned way; organically, and with face-to-face selling at trade shows and on the phone. It was slow going.

After about a year of this, my partner had reached his limit. The thrill of starting a business had been replaced by the mental drudgery of going through the burglary and its recovery and, now, the day-to-day task of trying to hold things together. He also made it pretty clear to me that I was probably wasting my time by sticking around. In his own words, he stated that if I were able to save Prophet, the pope himself would fly out, decree that I had performed three miracles, and grant me sainthood. It was hardly a parting word of encouragement. But I was on my own.

So now I had my own decision to make. Do I give up like my partner did, go out and find a real job, and leave behind the frustration of being paid almost nothing to work my tail off? Or do I keep trying? Well, the prospect of going back to the workaday world of scheduled meetings, business trips, and annual reviews had absolutely no allure for me, and I still loved the world of charts and trading as much as ever. I was going to keep going.

The lease to our office was up for renewal, so I made another decision. I was going to pull up the stakes and move my struggling little business into my house. After all, the business was really just down to me and one technical support person. What did we need an office for? She agreed that she would work from her home—which for her was great news, since it meant no commute—and I would do the same. Since we only dealt with customers on the phone, it

(*Continued*)

wouldn't make any difference, and we could save the precious capital we had left by not shelling it out to a landlord.

The prospect of starting over on my own from home reenergized me in a way I hadn't felt since two years ago when I started Prophet in the first place. I felt it gave me a certain fresh start, and even though I didn't have an engineer, I had enough basic programming skills to hold things together, so I was going to do the best I could. Prophet was going to continue, and I was going to nurse it back to health right from my own house.

■ Netscape

As for browser makers, by far the most dominant leader was Netscape, the firm which Jim Clark (cofounder of Silicon Graphics) had founded and which had hired Internet wunderkind Marc Andreessen as its lead developer. The browser that Andreessen had created (as a replacement for the Mosaic browser he had initially built) was called Navigator, and it enjoyed a 60 percent market share in 1995.

If there was one day that should be marked as the kick-off to Internet stock mania, it would be Netscape's IPO. On August 9, 1995, Netscape held its initial public offering. The starting price for the stock was set at $28, but the buying interest in the stock was so strong that no trading in the stock took place for the first two hours of the day. The stock finally opened at $71, making Jim Clark's initial investment in his business worth two-thirds of a billion dollars.

Netscape's offering was far larger and more widely covered than the various smaller IPOs that had taken place in the preceding months, and the short span of time from incorporation to public ownership surprised veterans of both the financial services and high-technology industries.

What was especially stunning to the public was that Netscape attained such a substantial valuation without ever making a penny of profit. In years past, a firm would have had to prove itself with several years of steadily uptrending profits before a public market was made. In the new world of Internet start-ups, it appeared that profits could be merely prospective as opposed to actual. Forthcoming revenues and profits were, it would seem, good enough for investors in this new economy.

As exemplary as the initial offering was, the stock price of NSCP continued to increase as 1995 continued. By December the price would reach $170 per share, valuing the small and unprofitable start-up at $6.5 billion and giving Jim Clark a $1.5 billion stake based on his initial investment of a few million dollars. He was now, based largely on his gamble on the young Marc Andreessen (who himself received a relatively small amount of stock), one of the richest men in the world.

Netscape's market share and sensational stock price did not go unnoticed by Microsoft, which had been surprisingly absent from the nascent Internet revolution. Microsoft announced that it would be getting "very serious" about the Internet, and the statement alone shaved $30 off Netscape's share price on the day Bill Gates uttered it.

In the months to come, Microsoft would be relentless about its inclusion of the Microsoft Internet Explorer browser into its Windows operating system (an action that would eventually come back to haunt the company). By June of 1996, Microsoft's actions in the so-called browser wars managed to eliminate half the value of Netscape's peak stock price.

At the same time this was going on, the popularity of electronic bulletin boards pertaining to stock trading was increasing. Websites dedicated to the discussion of stocks—particularly high-technology stocks—were springing up overnight, and a couple of the most popular included Silicon Investor and Raging Bull.

CAPTURED BY THE NET

These electronic gathering places would, over the next five years, become the nexus for hype, rumors, and elation as a growing sea of day traders focused entirely on markets. An entire Internet ecosystem based on venture capital, start-up businesses, stock trading, high-tech talent, and intellectual property was blossoming, and most of it was located in a 15-mile radius within the Santa Clara Valley.

For some reason, one stock in particular—Iomega—achieved a cultlike following on the message boards. The company wasn't an ISP or a content provider; instead, it sold an inexpensive backup device for computers called the zip drive, and between May 1995 and May 1996 the symbol IOMG vaulted from $5 to more than 10 times that amount.

Long before the Internet bubble burst, Iomega had a "burst" of its own as the stock lost half of its value just one month after it peaked. In the years ahead, the stock would proceed to lose almost all the multithousand percent gains it had made from the largely mania-fueled, stock-discussion-board-driven ascent in its price.

When I started Prophet, it had the two most crucial people any computer-based business needs—a business guy, me, and a technical guy, my partner. After my partner quit, the only help I had left was customer support person. I was, when it came to the technology side of the company, very much on my own.

Having paying customers is very motivating, however, and not only did I want to help the business survive, I didn't want to let those customers down. After all, they had stuck with us through all our downtime after our business was ransacked, and if they weren't going to give up on Prophet, neither was I. But where was I going to start?

Well, just as necessity is the mother of invention, it is also the mother of education. I taught myself as much about databases, modem protocols, and data formats as I could. There was one and one person only holding the systems together, and that was me. I taught myself a programming language called REXX and a database system called DB2, and in the waning days of 1995, I became increasingly confident that my little financial data business was actually going to pull through.

Now, even though being at home meant no impressive office, it also meant no impressive rent to pay each month. I also had no extra utility bill, insurance bill, furniture to pay for, or many of the other incidental expenses of running a business. Except for me and my inexpensive customer support person, there were really no expenses to pay, so my little company found itself very profitable very quickly.

On top of that, for a person like me, being at home focusing on a business can be really satisfying. When I'm interested in a project, there's nothing I love more than working, and the better I made the product, the more positive feedback I got from our customers. When you are starting a small business, you can't help but be close to the customers, and there's no purer form of feedback and ideas than being in touch with real users day after day.

Now even though the Internet had started to come on the public scene in 1994, I really didn't know what it was or how it worked, even though I had been online longer than just about anyone. But my experience with modems and bulletin board services starting back in 1982 really didn't mean I was going to comprehend what the

Internet was or how important the Web would be to our future, so I
remained willfully ignorant for a surprisingly long time.

With all the excitement about the Netscape IPO in August of
1995, however, that all changed. I taught myself HTML and learned
the basics of Web servers and browsers. Now that I had my feet
wet in the world of programming and databases, I was able to put
together my first website.

It was, as you might expect, nothing more sophisticated than an
online catalog of the data products Prophet offered, but I was proud
to at least be on the Web. Little did I know, within a few years the
notion of people downloading data via modem would be completely
subsumed by the technology I had just tried out.

Although plenty of my time was occupied with building our
product's code and tending to customers, I also had time to brainstorm
about new ideas. A friend of mine who was a patent attorney offered to
write up the patent applications for many of these ideas in exchange for
a small piece of the company. I agreed to this, and these user interface
patents would later be both a blessing and a curse to the business.

I also had developed my coding skills enough that I had written
our first charting program. It was extremely simple, able to do little
more than create an image of daily stock chart data with some very
basic studies, but to me it meant a couple of big things: first, I was
proficient enough with coding that I could actually make a product
worth selling, and second, I had put Prophet into the business of
charting content, as opposed to just numeric data.

By this time, around 1998, I got in touch with a business associate
that had his own business called Investools, to see if he would be
interested in my Web-based stock charts on his site. He agreed to
this, and in addition to paying Prophet a small monthly fee, he also
gave the company a block of warrants to buy stock in his company at
a fixed price. I put the warrant agreement into the same file folder
as the charting agreement, and I was delighted that my little charts
would not only be on my site but another firm's as well.

A few months later, Investools got in touch with me and said
that they actually would be interested in talking about acquiring my

371

(*Continued*)

business. Investools was bigger than Prophet—they had a couple dozen employees versus just the two at mine, and they had venture capital backing and a widely used product. I was excited about the prospect of actually getting some money for my business, since I had until recently been scraping by on almost no salary.

So I got in touch with my angel investor, Andy Bechtolsheim, and told him the good news—that his investment was about to pay off, and it would do so far more swiftly than anticipated. His answer surprised me—he said that instead of selling out, he'd be more interested in putting more cash into the business and making it, in his words, "a real company."

To me, this seemed to prove the maxim that you can only get money easily when you don't need any, so after a couple days of thought, I excitedly told Andy that I would be glad to go his way and take Prophet from a little two-person outfit at my house into a genuine start-up organization.

■ Yahoo! and Irrational Exuberance

The next category of Internet business to capture the public imagination was the search engine. The public, both as investors and as Web users, was still becoming accustomed to the nuances of the Web, but it was clear that people needed an easy-to-use gateway—a "portal" in the parlance of the day—to get to what they wanted. A search engine seemed the most logical mechanism for accomplishing this goal.

The first search engine to have an initial public offering was a Canadian firm which had sprung from a project at the University of Waterloo. The business called itself OpenText, and Montgomery Securities of San Francisco engineered a $61 million public offering of the stock in January of 1996. It was well received, and other start-up search engines in the San Francisco Bay Area took note of the successful IPO and immediately scheduled public offerings of their own. Lycos, Excite, and Yahoo! all made arrangements to execute their IPOs in April.

Lycos was the first one to go out, on April 2, soon followed by Excite two days later. A cursory examination of Excite's business at the time of its

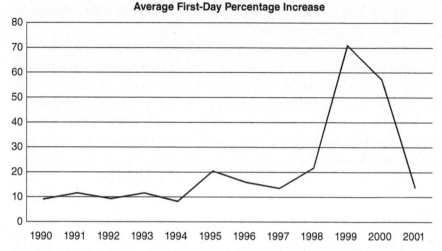

Average First-Day Percentage Increase

FIGURE 23.3 Yahoo! had a very successful public offering, and during its entire run in the 1990s, it would experience a virtual uninterrupted rise of many thousands of percentage points.

public offering illustrates how eager the public was to put money into what was, in fact, a very small enterprise. For the entirety of 1995, its most recent full year, Excite had revenues of $434,000 (and, obviously, no profits). Even at just the starting IPO price, Excite was given a valuation of $175 million.

The far more popular and well-known search engine, however, was Yahoo!, and its IPO was scheduled for April 12, 1996. The stock was priced at $13, but it opened at $25, rose to $43 during its first day, and closed at $33, an increase of about 150 percent from its offering price. At the time, it was the second-biggest increase in IPO-day price in Nasdaq history, and it gave Yahoo! a market capitalization of $850 million. Yahoo!'s young founders, David Filo and Jerry Yang, were both centimillionaires at the end of Yahoo!'s first day as a public company (see Figure 23.3).

The "pop" that would take place in so many Internet stocks warrants a brief explanation. Normally, when an investment bank determines at which price a given security should be priced, it tries to make a reasoned judgment as to the approximate price the public will buy the shares. The investment bank itself purchases the shares at the offering price, and in turn it sells these shares to other parties, such as retail traders.

A bank would not want to price a security too high, particularly since a price drop on a company's first trading day has a damaging effect on the reputation of the company. It is also typically a mistake for a bank to price a security too low, because the company going public doesn't directly benefit from the instant price appreciation.

For example, if a company sells $100 million in stock to its underwriting bank, and the bank is able to sell that same stock for $300 million on the day of the company's public offering, the bank enjoys $200 million in trading profits. More colloquially, the company going public has left "money on the table", and although the publicity surrounding such a successful event may benefit the company in the short run, it is almost certainly not worth the vast fortune that the investment bank was allowed to pocket (see Figure 23.4).

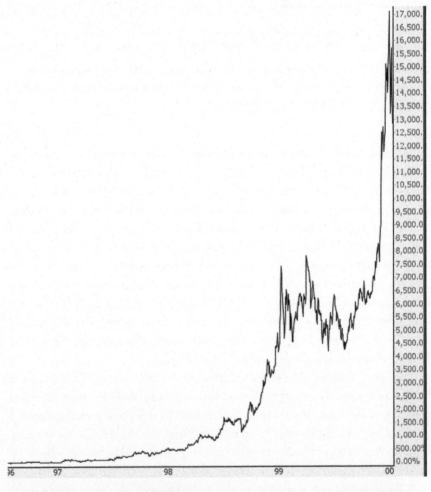

FIGURE 23.4 The average first-day "pop" for U.S. IPOs was elevated, but relatively muted until 1998, but it would explode to never-before-seen levels shortly before the bubble burst.

Although Internet mania would still have over three years to run, on December 5, 1996, Alan Greenspan remarked in a speech that an atmosphere of "irrational exuberance" might be affecting asset prices and pushing them to levels that were perhaps not based on solid economic sensibilities.

Stock markets around the world almost instantly sold off on nothing more than the utterance of that two-word phrase, and it is likely that Greenspan took that as a cue to keep his mouth shut with respect to the asset valuations he was witnessing. He would remain largely mute on the topic for the balance of the Internet bubble, since diminishing asset values is rarely an effective way of maintaining one's popularity in the midst of an economic boom.

■ The Cackle Heard around the World

One of the very few Internet companies created during the 1990s that continued into the next century as a thriving business with a much higher stock price was Amazon. The company was founded in 1994 by Jeff Bezos, who had earlier been asked by his employer to research what a good business would be to start on the Internet. Bezos concluded that books would be a good product to sell via the Web, but his employer decided against it.

Bezos was so convinced of the opportunity that he left his job, as well as its high salary, to venture across the country and start the business himself. He and his wife flew to Texas and, from there, drove to Seattle, where he intended to begin the company. According to corporate legend, his wife drove most of the way while he worked on the business plan in the passenger seat. Once settled in Seattle, he and a few initial employees set up shop in a garage and began their venture.

One fortuitous event around this time was that the U.S. Supreme Court ruled that consumers would not have to pay sales tax when purchasing a product from a company that did not have a presence (or, in legal terms, a "nexus") in the consumer's own state. Being able to sell books (and soon other products) without the burden of sales tax would give Amazon an immediate advantage over local retailers. This was one of Amazon's earliest advantages that brick-and-mortar booksellers didn't have.

Bezos originally called his site Cadabra (as in the magic word *abracadabra*) but, in 1995, opted for the name Amazon instead, since he wanted an easily recognizable name associated with something large and impressive. Similar to Apple Computer's founders, he also liked the fact it was at the beginning of the alphabet. The Amazon site sold its first book in July 1995, and in its first two months of business, Amazon shipped orders to every state in the United States as well as dozens of other countries.

Even though its website was just a few months old, Amazon announced its intent to go public in October 1995. From an early press release, Amazon succinctly summed up the benefits their service was able to offer book buyers:

> At a time when pundits are questioning the advantages of shopping online, Amazon.com offers consumers a shopping experience that would be impossible without the Internet. A physical bookstore as big as Amazon.com is economically impossible because no single metropolitan area is large enough to support such a mammoth store. Were Amazon.com to print a catalog of all of its titles, it would be the size of 7 New York City phone books.

Bezos made no secret of the fact his company was unprofitable and would be so for years to come. He asserted that a focus to "get big fast" was the way to achieve and maintain dominance on the Web, and he intended to build out the product lines offered on Amazon.com far beyond just books. Over time, Amazon would offer virtually everything that a large store like Target might carry, all available for no sales tax and, in many cases, free shipping.

On May 15, 1997, Amazon went public. Its offering price was $18, and the opening trade was at $27. The stock closed at $23.50 that day for a rise of 33 percent. While a one-third increase was respectable, it did not grab headlines for having a huge first-day "pop." Unlike virtually every firm that would go public in the late 1990s, Amazon's great stock gains would come years after the bubble actually burst. In the meantime, Amazon would enjoy the ascent and, for a while, a descent similar to that which would ultimately confront every public Internet company in the country.

A few months later, the first serious rupture in what had been an unrelenting bull market took place. Before the market opened in New York on October 27, 1997, an Asian currency crisis was affecting markets around the world. The Hong Kong Hang Seng Index fell by 6 percent, and the markets in Japan, London, and Germany each fell about 2 percent. The Dow opened lower, and by 2:36 P.M., the Dow Jones Industrial Average had lost 350 points, prompting an exchange-mandated curb on trading.

By the rules established after the 1987 market crash, trading was halted for 30 minutes and resumed at 3:06 P.M., at which time the drop in prices gained momentum. The trading curb, intended to allow investors to calmly assess the situation, instead created a sense of panic and desperation to dump positions, which traders did swiftly once they were again able to do so. By 3:35 P.M. EST, the Dow was down 550 points, and based on the same set of "circuit breakers," trading was halted for the remainder of the day.

The substantial drop in U.S. stock prices increased the unrest in Asian markets, and on October 28, the Hang Seng index fell another 14 percent, more than twice the drop from the prior session. All the Asian and European markets fell, and when U.S. trading opened on the 28th, stocks fell there, too.

However, buying strength was substantial enough to quickly reverse the downtrend, and by the end of the trading session, the Dow was up over 337 points on extremely strong volume. Indeed, it was the first time in the history of the exchange that over a billion shares had traded hands.

So while the 27th of October reminded people that stocks were still vulnerable to sell-offs, the 28th emboldened investors with the belief that the bull market so was so strong that even a currency crisis and international stock market rout could be shaken off with a single trading session. In retrospect, it was an important first tremor in the bull market, but stocks still had over two years of strength before a sustained bear market actually commenced.

| Living History |

Around this time, I was visiting a friend's house one evening, and as I was thumbing through the *Wall Street Journal,* I saw a blurb that Telescan, a public company in Texas, had purchased Investools, a Menlo Park company. As I sat there, I had a vague recollection that part of the agreement to provide my simple charts to their website included some stock warrants.

I rushed home, pulled the contract out of my file cabinet, and soon calculated these warrants were worth a million and a half dollars. Getting those warrants included in our agreement was a very good business decision; I wish I could claim it was my own idea.

Having gone from having very little money to having well over a million dollars was a tremendous change for my start-up, and I was finally in a position to make Prophet a real business, with a real office, and actual employees who came in every morning and left every night—it was going to be quite a change.

(Continued)

It may seem obvious, but there is nothing more important to the future of a new business than the people it hires. This is particularly true in high-tech start-ups, because the rules of arithmetic do not apply. One great engineer is not the same as two good engineers. More likely, one great engineer is the same as 6, 10, or even 20 decent engineers. Just as a room full of composers couldn't have written the music of Mozart, a room full of competent programmers cannot make the superior code from one genius that distinguishes a start-up.

What Prophet needed most were talented engineers. And, let me assure you, finding a good software engineer in 1999 was no easy task. All the talent started getting sucked up once the Internet craze started four years earlier, and the talent that was left was (1) really expensive and (2) not at all talented.

So we scoured, as best we could, to find someone—anyone—decent. By chance we located a consulting firm in Boston that had some engineers from the former Soviet bloc, and they were more than glad to find placement for their consultants on the West Coast.

When it comes to the resumes of software engineers, 98 percent of them look identical; I actually got pretty good at just eyeballing a resume and seeing who was decent and who wasn't. One person in particular, Alex Dobrovolskiy, stood out as quite promising. I noticed that he even had taken the second-place prize in a nationwide contest in mathematics back in the Ukraine, so evidently he was very smart.

We asked to speak with Alex on the phone. It was a difficult conversation because his English was pretty limited, but even over the phone he seemed smart and likable, so we decided to take a chance and devote some of our cash to this new engineer.

Like many transplanted engineers from the former Soviet Union, Alex was in this country without his family. He came here because he could earn much better money and, hopefully, eventually bring his family over. As I got to know Alex, he told me he had a wife, Eugenia, and a son of about 12 years.

It was rapidly apparent that Alex wasn't just bright—he was brilliant. Prophet had very, very little when he started, and our charting code—heaven help us—was written by me. This is the equivalent of having an ambitious eight-year-old boy construct a house for you to live in.

Even over a period of months, our communication remained difficult since we didn't speak the same language, although using the written word, he did just fine. So there were dozens of instances where I'd come over to his desk, start to explain something, and then just fire up Notepad on his computer and type to him what I was trying to say. I could type English much faster than I could get him to understand the spoken word, so we had this curiously silent way of communicating. He would type right back, with me sitting next to him.

Of course, there were other folks besides Alex at the office. Including myself, there were now 10 people at Prophet. As with any small business staffed with young people eager to succeed, we worked very hard and had a lot of fun while doing it. Most days would begin at about 8 A.M. and continue on until 10 at night. We ate together, made hiring decisions together, brainstormed together—it was quite a change from the several years of working in solitude without any true engineer available to me. We put together a good website, expanded our products, and even had the homey touch (later adopted by giants like Google) of welcoming dogs into the office.

The outside world started to take notice. Our first break was being included in *Forbes* magazine's "Best of the Web" survey, soon followed by inclusion in the *Barron's* annual awards for best websites for traders. This was at the height of the Internet boom, and as swiftly as it felt like we were moving, Prophet was dwarfed by competitors that had received $20 million in venture funding, which made our accidental $1.5 million seem puny.

As modest as that $1.5 million might have seemed in comparison to the huge venture rounds occurring with other firms, it changed Prophet, and it changed how I spent money. Beforehand, I would watch every dime. I would scrape and scrounge to get used equipment on the cheap. I would only pay for projects I knew were vital to the company's growth. In a word, I was prudent.

(Continued)

After our bank account got fat, all that prudence went out the window. I hired a public relations firm at $15,000 a month. I snapped up consultants for experimental programming projects that didn't bring new revenue into the business. I bought expensive computing equipment without really thinking it through.

And this experience finally answered for me a question I had always wondered about the Silicon Valley—how could companies that got a $20 million check from venture capital firms ever burn through all that cash? The fact is that, no matter how big the figure is, it isn't as big as you think, and the world is absolutely packed with vendors that are happy to relieve you of all that extra weight in your wallet. I had greatly increased our burn rate, and it wasn't long before I realized that we would soon go through all that cash and I had to regain my boring but absolutely essential sense of prudence.

■ The Madness Goes Exponential

As 1998 began, the fervor around Internet stocks began ramp up for what would be a two-year climax in Internet mania. The near-ubiquitous presence of online stock accounts, new IPOs, and breathless press coverage about Internet companies combined to create a nation whose citizens believed that there was no reason that everyone couldn't become wealthy from the stock market.

The major Web companies provided their shareholders with astonishing gains: AOL was up 593 percent in 1998, and the search engine Yahoo! was up a very similar 584 percent. Online retailer Amazon bested both of these with a gain of 970 percent.

Run-of-the-mill companies that until the 1990s had absolutely nothing to do with high-technology discovered that anything suggestive of "dot-com" was beneficial to both their public image and their stock price. One example was a firm called K-Tel International, which for decades had sold musical compilations on television. Anyone who watched television in the United States during the 1970s saw K-Tel's ads hundreds of times, but the days of mailing vinyl records prompted by a person's toll-free telephone call seemed a distant relic by 1998.

K-Tel, however, announced their intent to sell music on the Internet, and that press release (which was merely a reflection of a future plan, and not a reality with actual financial results) was enough to quadruple the company's stock price in just a couple of weeks. As the stock price soared, the company made another announcement: that they would split the stock to make it "more available" to the investing public. Here again, in spite of an absence of anything actually material to the company's financial results, the stock leaped $12 based on nothing more than an announcement of a stock split.

Even though by 1998 the Internet and its IPOs had been around for a few years, the public was still very naive about what announcements were important and what announcements was mere fluff, so almost everything was assumed to be positive.

One good example is the Amazon Associates program, which was an affiliate program that Amazon introduced that would allow anyone to promote Amazon products on their own website and, in return, get a small cut of the sale. If, for instance, someone had a website that specialized in classic cars, and they featured a $40 book from Amazon about those cars, the person who ran the site could earn perhaps $1 for each of those books that was sold.

Even though anyone at all could sign up for the program, from a housewife with a simple homemade website all the way up to large public companies, the mere mention that a firm was "partnering" with Amazon was enough to make that stock price source.

Public companies would issue press releases announcing their new "partnership" with Amazon which, while technically true, would represent nothing more than the fact that someone at the company took a few minutes to sign up for the Amazon Associates program, which would almost certainly be immaterial to the own company's bottom line.

Amazon itself was attracting an enormous amount of positive press, and when the company announced plans to sell music CDs, the stock zoomed up to $100 per share, and shortly thereafter vaulted to $140. Around the same time, another media-related website, Broadcast.com, went public on July 17, 1998. Broadcast.com had revenues of about $6.9 million at the time, but far from being profitable, it showed losses equal in size to its revenue. In other words, for every $1 the company was taking in, about $2 was going out. In spite of this, the stock had an issue price of $18, and it closed its first day at nearly $63, a gain of 250 percent.

Just as the stock market experienced a severe shudder in October of the prior year, it hit another nasty bump about 10 months later. On August 31, 1998, another currency crisis—this one emanating from Russia—sent another shock wave into equity markets. The Dow fell 513 points, and the Nasdaq, in its largest point drop thus far in its history, lost 140.43 points.

High-flying Internet companies lost larger percentages, such as Excite and Amazon, each of which lost about 20 percent in a single day. Instead of a one-day turnaround, the turmoil in the stock market persisted for weeks, and newer firms like GeoCities saw their stock prices lose about three-quarters of their prior peak value. The steady flow of IPOs was brought to almost a complete halt.

■ A Las Vegas in Every Home

The popularity of retail trading had grown in stages. Discount brokers like Schwab and Fidelity brought the first wave of traders in during the 1980s; online brokers like E*Trade and Datek drew in many more traders during the early 1990s; and by the second half of the 1990s, an entirely new form of trader—the "hyper-active" or "day" trader—burst on to the scene.

Day traders were not especially numerous compared to other classes of traders, but the frequency of their trading activity made up for their small population. Schwab alone had six million customers online, and TD Waterhouse had another two million, with hundreds of thousands of new customers joining online brokerages each month. But while one of these regular investors might place a few trades each year, if even that much, a day trader might place hundreds, or even thousands, of shares on any given day that the market was open.

The beneficiaries of all this activity were usually not the ones doing the trading but, instead, were the firms getting the commissions. Day-trading firms would provide the office space, the desk, the trading software, and access to the market, and in return they were paid commissions for each trade executed. The vast majority of traders lost money, but the day-trading firms raked in generous commissions from all that buying and selling. It was a form of legalized gambling that could give people the thrill of chasing profits without bothering to fly to Las Vegas. Metaphorically, the day-trading rooms were the new casinos, and the traders were the tourists, eager to place bets.

Day-trading rooms were springing up in cities and towns across the United States, backed by about 60 different businesses with suggestive names as Momentum Securities and All-Tech Investments Group. One estimate put the number of full-time day traders at around 6,000, but their activity accounted for up to 15 percent of the entire volume on the Nasdaq (and, for some high-flying dot-com companies, day traders would account for most of the day's volume).

As with the kind of gambling found in Las Vegas and Atlantic City, there was a dark side to day trading in the form of addiction. Some day traders allocated irresponsible portions of their funds to this highly speculative, very risky endeavor, and most traders had to struggle just to keep a positive account balance. Those who, in the parlance of the business, "blew up" their accounts could choose to either return to their normal day jobs or, if possible, scrounge up additional funds and hope their luck would turn around for future trades.

One such struggling day trader was Mark Barton, a 44-year-old man living near Atlanta, Georgia. He lived with his second wife (his first having died under mysterious circumstances) and two children. Bitten by the day-trading bug, Barton quit his job and dedicated himself to full-time stock trading.

In eight weeks, he lost $105,000. On Tuesday, July 27, 1999, his brokerage, Momentum, issued a margin call, which meant that he would be required to give them a check to bring his account back to a positive balance if he wanted to continue trading there.

That night, he battered his wife to death with a hammer. The next day, the $50,000 check he had given to Momentum bounced, and he went home and murdered his daughter and son. As if in a scene recreated from *In Cold Blood,* he placed the children's bodies in their beds with their toys beside them and wrote a suicide note to be discovered later.

On Thursday, July 29, he drove to Momentum, walked to the trading floor and said, "It's a bad trading day, and it's about to get worse," and started shooting. He killed four people and wounded several others. He then went to All-Tech, another brokerage, shot the manager, went to the trading floor, and shot dead another four people. A few hours later, he pulled up at a gas station, hid behind his van from the police, and shot himself dead in the head.

The note he had left at his home reads, in part, as follows:

Leigh Ann is in the master bedroom closet under a blanket. I killed her on Tuesday night. I killed Matthew and Mychelle Wednesday night. There may be similarities between these deaths and the death of my first wife, Debra Spivey. However, I deny killing her and her mother. There is no reason for me to lie now. It just seemed like a quiet way to kill and a relatively painless way to die. There was little pain. All of them were dead in less than five minutes. I hit them with the hammer in their sleep and then put them face-down in the bathtub to make sure they did not wake up in pain, to make sure they were dead.

I'm so sorry. I wish I didn't. Words cannot tell the agony. Why did I? I have been dying since October. Wake up at night so afraid, so terrified that I couldn't be that afraid while awake. It has taken its toll. I have come to hate this life and this system of things. I have come to have no hope. I killed the children to exchange them for five minutes of pain or a lifetime of pain. I forced myself to do it to keep them from suffering so much later. No mother, no father, no relatives. The fears of the father are transferred to the son. It was from my father to me and from me to my son. He already had it. And now to be left alone. I had to take him with me.

I killed Leigh Ann because she was one of the main reasons for my demise.... I know that Jehovah will take care of all of them in the next life. I'm sure the details don't matter. There is no excuse, no good reason I am sure no one will understand. If they could I wouldn't want them to. I just write these things to say why. Please know that I love Leigh Ann, Matthew and Mychelle with all my heart. If Jehovah's willing I would like to see them all again in the resurrection to have a second chance. I don't plan to live very much longer, just long enough to kill as many of the people that greedily sought my destruction.

News of the Barton killings swept through the country, both due to its horror and its connection to the nation's new fascination with high-stakes online trading. It was a grim reminder that not everyone was getting rich off the mania, and that the extreme emotions conjured up by such risky endeavors could have tragic consequences.

■ Century's End

As the stock market stabilized in the autumn of 1998, confidence began to return among the trading public. An important element of the positive atmosphere surrounding trading was new media. CNBC, of course, had for the entirety of the 1990s been a consistent cheerleader for the bull market, but the printed word was just as important in promoting a positive and risk-embracing disposition toward capitalism and investing.

Appearing on bestseller lists were such books such as *Dow 36,000* (whose title revealed its prediction) and *The Roaring 2000s* (which itself projected a value of 41,000 on the Dow by the year 2009, which turned out to be off by about 80 percent). Not to be outdone, an author named Charles Kadlec wrote *Dow 100,000: Fact or Fiction*.

New magazines, too, served the need for more timely material about business trends and breakthroughs, such as *Business 2.0, The Industry Standard, Red Herring,* and *Upside.* As the mania around investing and Web technology continued, each of these magazines became thick with advertisements. The correlation between the weight of these magazines and the stock market averages was probably very close, as they would find their page counts plunging in later years, the magazines reduced to sizes that would blow away with a mild breeze.

In the meantime, however, the public felt they had little to fear except for the much-discussed Y2K event. The supposition about Y2K was that, as the infrastructure of the modern world had become so dependent on computers, and since some computer programs had not anticipated having to deal with dates by 1999, there might be chaos at banks, airports, utility companies, and other important points that relied on software.

It would later become one of history's ironies that of the many problems that appeared on the world stage in 2000 and 2001, some of them tremendous, the Y2K problem would be a complete nonevent and would render virtually no problems to anyone.

Investor confidence was affirmed sensationally on November 13, 1998, with the public offering of a small website named TheGlobe.com, created by a couple of Cornell students. As with so many other firms, the revenues of the company were modest, and the losses were substantial, but the public was still hungry for shares of new Internet companies.

TheGlobe's share price was $9, but the first public trade was at $87, and the stock climbed as high as $97 that day before closing at $63.50. The 606 percent increase in price was a new record for an IPO, and the market capitalization for the tiny firm was $840 million, making both of the young founders, still in their mid-20s, centimillionaires.

One of them, some weeks later, was filmed with his model girlfriend by a television show shouting at the camera, "Got the girl. Got the money. Now I'm ready to live a disgusting, frivolous life." The statement neatly captured the zeitgeist of early 1999, as young people envied what was seen as an easy path to riches (see Figure 23.5).

What TheGlobe's two founders would soon find, however, is that $100 million on paper is not the same as $100 million in the bank. Although investment bankers were able to sell stock, company insiders were typically foreclosed from selling any stock for a period of 12 to 18 months. TheGlobe was a money-losing business, with revenue of $2.7 million in the first nine months of 1998 and losses of $11.5 million. Losing $4.25 for every $1 of

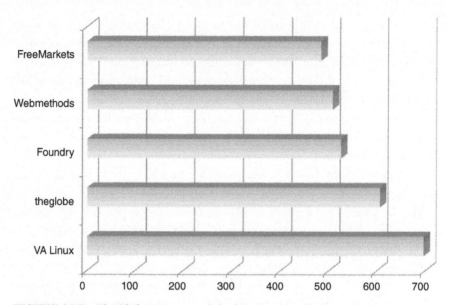

FIGURE 23.5 TheGlobe was one of the biggest first-day pops in Internet IPO history, with the top five represented in this chart.

revenue was a very bad business even by Internet standards, and eventually these metrics would catch up with the highly elevated stock price.

Around the same time, a much larger company held its IPO, and it was a business that actually was slightly profitable: on September 24, 1998, eBay went public with a target price of $18, but it opened at $53.50 per share and closed at almost $48, generating a first-day return of 163 percent.

Whereas many Web companies were, as businesses, not particularly novel, eBay had an opportunity that was both large and unique to the Internet. It was a company that didn't have to manufacture or warehouse anything. Instead, it acted as a marketplace for buyers and sellers, extracting a tiny portion from each transaction, and thus was able to garner profits even in the 1990s (in the first half of 1999, the company had $215,000 of profit from $14.9 million in revenue).

■ Analysts as Oracles

After eBay's successful offering, an investment bank stock analyst projected that, within a year, the stock could climb as high as $100. The stock did so within 10 *days* of the prediction. Following this, another analyst stated that the stock may well climb to $150. Based on nothing more than this prediction, the stock leaped to $130 the same day.

The increasing frenzy about IPOs became so acute that investors began to make careless and even comic mistakes. In a two-week span, no fewer than six Internet companies went public: AboveNet, InfoSpace, audiohighway.com, Internet America, uBid, and Xoom. When Xoom went public, its ticker symbol was XMXM, but a completely unrelated firm with the ticker symbol ZOOM enjoyed high volume and a very strong price movement on the day XMXM came public, almost certainly due to confusion about what Xoom's stock symbol was.

Ideas for new websites were becoming challenging, since almost every conceivable specialty, market, and interest seemed to already have an abundance of dedicated websites. The largest site devoted specifically to women was iVillage.com, with such "channels" (as the site dubbed them) as Astrology and Relationships. The company had already burned through $65 million of its funding and had lost $43.7 million in 1998 alone, based on revenues of $15 million.

A week before the planned iVillage IPO, the chief financial officer (CFO) quit and made a statement that, based on what she had seen with respect to the company's accounting, she would not be comfortable being associated with the organization. The resignation of a company's CFO—to say nothing of a statement casting dispersion on the company's accounting practices— would normally stop any IPO dead in its tracks.

In iVillage's case, the continuously ascending stock market created an especially forgiving public, and the IPO proceeded as planned. Goldman Sachs took the company out at an initial price of $24 per share but, of course, the first trade was much higher: $80. At day's end, the money-losing outfit was valued at $1.9 billion, and its stock sported a first-day gain of 233 percent.

Henry Blodget, the Merrill Lynch analyst who had achieved notoriety for forecasting what was, at the time, an outlandish target for Amazon's stock price (only to see it achieved within weeks) was, along with Mary Meeker, a favorite personality for business interviews. When asked by his management in early 1999 whether the sensational returns in Internet stocks was merely a bubble, he replied in an internal report:

> The overall Internet stock phenomenon may well be a bubble, but in at least one respect it is very different from other bubbles: there are great fundamental reasons for own these stocks. ... The companies

underneath these stocks are (1) growing amazingly quickly and (2) threatening the status quo in multiple sectors of the economy.=

In his reply, Blodget conveniently ignored the fact the firms in question were losing money hand over fist in exchange for that growth. Henry Blodget, in his interview, was stating, in a sense, that "it's different this time," which history has clearly shown are the most dangerous words to investors.

Blodget was far from the only analyst touting the magnificence of the market. The stock market bears had long been shamed out of public speaking, and the media wasn't interested in giving them a forum in any case. On March 29, 1999, as the Dow crossed the 10,000 mark for the first time in history, well-known trader Ralph Acampora stated of the 10,000 mark in a March 1999 Washington Post article, "It's no longer a ceiling, it's a floor … As time goes by, we'll be looking down at it

No one can know if Acampora was conscious of it at the time, but with this statement, he was harkening the famed quote from economist Irving Fisher who, at the peak of the stock market in September 1929, stated, "Stock prices have reached what looks like a permanently high plateau." It was a soothing platitude that history has not since forgotten.

■ Mountains of Money

Broadcast.com, cofounded by Mark Cuban, had sported a $300 million market capitalization in the summer of 1998, which was about 50 times the revenues of the firm. As astonishing as that valuation was, by April 1, 1999, Yahoo! announced it would be paying $6.1 billion for the company.

Due to the date of the announcement, some people thought it was an elaborate April Fool's Day prank, but it was, in fact, the truth. Broadcast.com's latest results showed sales of $22.3 million and a loss of $16.4 million. Yahoo! was paying 275 times the company's revenue to own the site. (Wisely, Mark Cuban thereafter executed an options position to profit from the fall in Yahoo!'s stock he was sure would come.)

On the other side of the United States, having gained fame from CNBC, Jim Cramer had put together a subscriber-based website called TheStreet.com. Although it seemed like the whole country was spending its time trading, the number of active investors who were willing to pay a monthly fee for a site like TheStreet was actually quite small. Even the most successful stock-oriented websites had just a few tens of thousands of paying members.

In spite of this, the combination of Jim Cramer's celebrity, the stock-investing focus of the site, and the rampant Internet mania, made for another winning public offering. TheStreet.com went public on May 10, 1999, at a price of $19, shooting up to $73, and closing its first day at $60, a gain of 216 percent. TheStreet.com, with just a few million dollars in annual revenue, had a market capitalization of $1.5 billion making Jim Cramer, for the time being, a very rich and delighted entrepreneur (see Figure 23.6).

FIGURE 23.6 TheStreet.com's price movement from its IPO to this writing is illustrated here. The stock price at the company's initial offering has never been matched, and for the first couple of years as a public company, TheStreet's stock price spent most of its time going lower.

As the number of start-ups increased, the companies funding those start-ups increased in quantity as well. In late 1996, when the Internet frenzy was already quite strong, there were 458 firms managing $52 billion in assets. Just three years later, there were 779 firms—a 70 percent increase—managing $164 billion—a 215 percent increase.

Thus, a form of inflation was taking place, as a much larger supply of money was chasing a relatively fixed number of deals. The quality of investments, by the nature of these changing dynamics, was bound to decrease, while the funding for those deals, for the same reasons, was prone to increase.

In 1996, venture capital (VC) firms invested $11.2 billion in 2,123 different ventures. In 1999, VC firms put $59.4 billion into 3,957 firms, indicating that the size of the deals had tripled. One firm alone, a consumer drug seller named PlanetRX, raised $59.3 million for its start-up. Gone, it seemed, were the days when a giant like Apple Computer had been started with the $1,300 of proceeds from selling an old VW van and an HP calculator.

■ The WebVan Peak

The biggest funding of all was committed to the most pedestrian of activities: groceries. If there was any consistent task that nearly everyone in the country could be relied upon to perform, it was shopping for food. Louis Borders, the founder of the bookstore of the same name, determined that the most promising opportunity for the new world of the Internet was to provide people a way to go grocery shopping without leaving their home. His new company was called WebVan, and it received initial funding of $275 million. In exchange for this, the investors received a mere 6.5 percent of the company, valuing the start-up at over $4 billion.

Unlike eBay, which could be a "pure" Internet company, acting as a go-between for buyers and sellers, WebVan had to invest in substantial physical infrastructure and product purchases in order to execute its vision. WebVan would need to stock all the items a person might expect from a grocery store—many of them perishable—and it would need to do so all over the United States.

As large an idea as it was, the notion of providing an online system for people to place grocery orders wasn't new. Peapod, for example, had already spent 10 years building up a similar business, and in that time it had only serviced 100,000 customers (many of them just once, since they just wanted to try it out). In spite of this lackluster performance from a similar business model, WebVan moved forward with ambitious plans to build warehouses around the country and stock them with groceries for sale.

The first warehouse was, appropriately, built in the San Francisco Bay Area, near where all the high-tech and Web excitement was going on. It was built in Oakland, and it had the capacity to handle 8,000 orders per day. Webvan launched its website to great fanfare, but the reception was tepid. Even though many people were curious about WebVan and wanted to try the service, if nothing else out of curiosity, the Oakland facility was never challenged with more than a few hundred orders per day.

WebVan pushed forward, signing a half-billion dollar construction deal with manufacturing giant Bechtel. The deal called for the construction of 26 warehouses all over the United States, each with the same efficiency and capacity of the Oakland facility.

Only two months after their first delivery of groceries, WebVan filed for its own IPO under the symbol WBVN. In the first half of 1999, it had total revenue of $395,000 (in contrast, a *single* Whole Foods grocery store has about $25 million in annual revenue) with losses of $35 million. Future projections were hardly comforting, calling for a total loss of $78.03 million in 1999, $154.3 million in 2000, and $302 million in 2001. Even when surrounded by a swarm of money-losing Internet companies, WebVan was a particularly severe money loser.

But, once again, the public ignored these grim projections and consumed the company's public offering. WebVan went public on November 2, 1999, at $15, opened at $26 and closed the day at 24 7/8, giving the firm a value of $8 billion. Initial investors had doubled the value of their stake in very short order, and WebVan held itself out as the new model for grocery-shopping convenience in America.

A similar "convenience" play on a smaller scale was in the form of Kozmo.com, which itself raised $100 million. Instead of bringing groceries to a customer's house, Komzo would bring just about anything that could be transported by a bicycle messenger. If a person wanted someone to pick them up a pack of cigarettes and a *New York Times,* they could log in to Kozmo. If they needed an extra six-pack of beer for a party, they could use Komzo. If they had a craving for a pack of gum, they could do it through Komzo.

Of course, the existence of the Internet didn't bring any real efficiency to this business model. Komzo could just as well have set itself up in 1950 with a team of bike messengers and a telephone. The only difference was that customers issued their requests by a browser page instead of a phone conversation. The average order Kozmo customers placed was $12, and whatever slim profit could be garnered from orders of that size did not come close to covering the substantial expenses of such a human-intensive operation.

■ An Adoring Press

The media continued to feed the frenzy of the Internet fire, which partly explains why the investing public was still receptive to companies with such fundamentally poor prospects. *Wired* magazine was particularly enthusiastic about the "new economy" that had graced the world. The featured story in July 1999 was titled "The Roaring Zeroes," and its subtitle stated "The good news is, you'll be a millionaire soon. The bad news is, so will everybody else." The article brings forth the concerns in the back of the minds of those enjoying the phenomenal growth of the late 1990s but beats them back with some extraordinary optimism:

> We have rehearsed this downfall in our minds over and over again. Each of us has clever friends who mutter about tulipmania and the madness of crowds. Any one of us can fill in the gory details. The Crash is effortless to imagine.
>
> But what if we face, instead, a decade or more of continued good times? What if the digital bubble is made of Kevlar? What if the Dow doesn't fall to 3,000, but zooms to 30,000 in four years? What if we are just at the beginning of the beginning of a long wave of ultraprosperity?
>
> Picture 20 more years of full employment, continued stock-market highs, and improving living standards. Two more decades of inventions as disruptive as cell phones, mammal cloning, and the Web. Twenty more years of Quake, index funds, and help-wanted signs. Prosperity not just for CEOs, but for ex-pipe fitters, nursing students, and social workers as well. The market will fluctuate daily, but by 2010, the Dow will soar past the 50,000 mark.

The logic behind such stories seemed sound at the time. After all, business prosperity and equity strength had continued uninterrupted for almost the entire decade, and there were few people who could offer a plausible reason why there should be any reversal in the current prosperity. Extrapolating the positive trends seemed sensible, even if it did result in articles speculating quite seriously that by 2020 the average citizen would have an income of $150,000, the Dow would be over 50,000 (and on its way to 100,000), and everyday people would enjoy the services of personal chefs.

Wired also featured an interview with favored trend guru George Gilder, an oft-quoted analyst of the time. In the interview, Gilder stated that projections called for a "thousand-fold increase in Internet traffic over the next five years" and, thus, in another five years, "there would be a million-fold increase." Gilder's logic, apparently, was that since a thousand times a thousand equals a million, the world could anticipate a million-fold increase in Internet users over the next decade, in spite of the fact that such growth would suggest a population of 150 trillion people on the planet.

As the end of 1999 drew near, the most spectacular public offering (at least in terms of same-day gain) was about to launch. The Linux operating system was seen as the most viable competition to the Microsoft platform, and in spite of the operating system's being free, it was also seen as an intriguing business opportunity. One firm that had built itself around Linux, bundling together the operating system with some off-the-shelf computer hardware, was named VA Linux, and on December 9, 1999, its stock went public.

Before the stock's opening price was shown on quote screens, reporters were so stunned with the bids being posted on the Nasdaq that they weren't even comfortable uttering them. The offering price was $30, but trading didn't open until the first print went across at $299. The price peak at $320, over 10 times the offering price, before closing the day at $239.25, a 698 percent same-day return and, even as of this writing, the biggest IPO "pop' in history.

It would also be the highest price the stock would ever reach, and although the elated founders had no way of knowing it, the stock's value would sink beneath that of a pack of chewing gum by middle of 2002. (Sadly, there would be no Kozmo around by that time to deliver it).

The stock market was in an absolutely frenzy, and as the world focused on "the end of the century" (even though a few picayune souls pointed out that century's end didn't really happen for another year), *Time* captured the spirit of the era by naming none other than Jeff Bezos as their 1999 Man of the Year.

It is easy to note, with the benefit of hindsight, what an evident sign this was to exit the stock market. After all, the "cover curse" is so well-known as to be a cliché, but as frenetic as the market was, the Nasdaq was still about 10 weeks away from its ultimate peak.

On December 31, 1999, Muhammad Ali rang the opening bell at the New York Stock Exchange, commencing the last trading day of the 1990s.

When the closing bell rang, the Nasdaq market registered an 85.6 percent gain, the most impressive annual gain for any major U.S. stock index in history.

More narrow indexes had even more amazing gains, particularly the Dow Jones Internet Composite, which garnered a 167 percent rise. The cover of *Fortune* magazine summed up the attitude of many Americans, which featured a cartoon drawing of a man grimacing and stating, "Why is everyone getting rich except me?" Even though money seemed to be everywhere, very few people felt that they had enough for themselves.

■ Peak and Fall

The lofty equity markets were partly justified by the healthy American economy. The U.S. federal government was running a budget surplus, something it hadn't done in decades, and at the renomination of Alan Greenspan, Clinton revealed he was just as caught up in the Internet mania as the rest of the nation when he stated, "I've been thinking of taking Alan.com public; then, we can pay the debt off even before 2015." (It should be noted that that U.S. debt will not, in fact, be paid off in 2015, owing to the fact that Bill Clinton was off in his estimate by the amount of $24.5 *trillion* dollars).

The first few days of trading saw a little weakness, but stock buying resumed as the world breathed a sigh of relief that the Y2K risk was a phantom menace. Then, on January 10, one of the most astonishing business announcements in corporate history was made when Steve Case said that AOL would be buying Time Warner, the largest media company in the world, for $165 billion.

The fact that a company whose principal business was selling dial-up access to home computer users was in a position to acquire the world's biggest media company plainly shows how different "old" and "new" media companies were being valued. The two leaders of the companies, oddly, appeared at the announcement wearing their "uniforms" somewhat backwards, Case wearing an expensive suit and Gerald Levin sporting khakis and an open-necked shirt.

Although the stock market had been going up universally for years, a divergence took place on January 14, 2000, which is when the Dow Jones Industrial Average reached an intraday peak of 11,908.50 and closed at 11,722.98. It would be the peak of the Dow Jones for years to come, although the Nasdaq wasn't done climbing.

The Fed had already started inching up interest rates (and would do so six times between late 1999 and early 2000), but until January 14, stocks simply kept going up. Some of the lower-quality Internet firms had already experienced heavy selling, such as eToys (falling from a peak of $70 to $20), iVillage (from $130 to $20), and Value America (from $75 to $5), but on the whole, Nasdaq valuations remained lofty (including Yahoo!, which enjoyed a price-to-earnings ratio of 2,174).

Cash-rich Internet start-ups had already made arrangements to have a big media splash by way of television ads during the Super Bowl. Because of the strong demand for ads, the producers of Super Bowl XXXIV demanded $2 million for each 30 seconds of commercial play, a new record. No fewer than 17 different Internet companies bought ads, including such now-forgotten firms as computer.com, epidemic.com, onmoney.com, lifeminders.com, kforce.com, and ourbeginning.com.

The E*Trade advertisement, one of the 17, made no apologies for the obvious insanity that was happening. The entire 30 seconds featured nothing more than two men in a garage and a monkey clapping (off-tempo) to some music. The ad had nothing to do with any particular features or benefits the E*Trade might be able to offer prospective clients. It simply was two men and a monkey, none of whom had been blessed with any rhythmic sensibilities. The tag line read, "We just wasted two million bucks," which would probably have been an appropriate tag line for each of the dot-com ads being broadcast that day.

The IPO calendar was still crowded with new offerings, with 10 IPOs slated for just a single day, February 11, 2000. One of these IPOs was (it should go without saying) money-losing pets.com, a firm that apparently lacked an appreciation for what the cost burden of shipping 40-pound bags of dog food around the country might be to their finances. Pets.com garnered a meager $6 million in revenue for 1999, and from that, it managed to lose $62 million.

The reception of the stock that day was a subtle sign that unlimited interest in Web stocks may have been waning: the stock was priced at $11 per share, and although it rose to $14 that day, it fell back down to a closing price of $11. Coming just two months after a nearly 700 percent gain from VA Linux, a 0 percent change on its first outing was a chilly reception for pets.com. Within a couple of days, it closed at $7.50, in spite of the Nasdaq's continuing higher.

Within days of the ultimate top for the Nasdaq, one event in the stock market was especially stunning which, given the circumstances of late 1999 and early 2000, was a very high bar to jump. The stock in question was a spin-off from an existing public company, 3Com. 3Com owned the Palm handheld device technology, and the popularity of the product compelled the firm to spin it off as its own organization. 3Com arranged to sell 5 percent of the firm, retaining 95 percent ownership of Palm.

On March 2, 2000, symbol PALM went public. The investment bankers originally targeted a price of $12, but demand was so strong that, on offering day, the bankers more than tripled the price to $38 before taking the firm public. Trading opened at $60 and zoomed higher from there, closing just as $95 per share. This gave Palm Computing a value of $54.3 billion.

What is remarkable about this is that Palm was now worth *twice* as much as 3Com, but 3Com still owned 95 percent of Palm. This suggested that 3Com, an established, profitable organization, had a value of *negative* $22 billion.

On Friday, March 13, 2000, the Nasdaq peaked at 5,132.52 and closed at 5,048.62. It would, even more than a decade later, represent the highest valuation in Nasdaq history. The average price-to-earnings ratio was over 100 (as opposed to the more typical 14 of normal stock markets), and some of the biggest companies in the world were technology giants Lucent, Nortel, and Sun Microsystems.

The end-of-day commentary on the CNN Money site remarked, in a surprisingly blase fashion:

> The Nasdaq composite eked out its 16th record of the year Friday, rising for the third time in three sessions, as money chased proven technology leaders such as Dell Computer, Microsoft and Qualcomm. But the Dow Jones industrial average fell, unable to build on two days of gains, as investors dumped drug makers Merck and Johnson & Johnson, and financials J.P. Morgan and Citigroup, all seen as sensitive to higher interest rates. The divergence between the blue chips and technology is symbolic: The Nasdaq finished above the key 5,000 mark, while the Dow ended below 10,000.

The article immediately went on to state: "Analysts see the trend continuing." But, in fact, the top was in. The Nasdaq, which had moved from 3,000 to 5,000 in only four months—an annualized rate of growth of 200 percent—was about to begin one of the most brutal bear markets in financial history.

The beginning of the twenty-first century was a wonderful time for Prophet. We were creating terrific products for traders; we were garnering recognition with awards; and our ability to hire talented people greatly improved with the bursting of the Internet bubble.

The costs associated with running our business, from office rent to personnel, plunged dramatically, while at the same time, our revenue continued to inch higher each month with more subscribers and more licensees of our charting products.

In short, Prophet bucked the trend of the Internet collapse by thriving in the midst of chaos and business failures. The competitors who had been given tens of millions of dollars in funding had gone belly-up, and the quality of our products was winning people over. Our customers also liked that they were working with a small business that was motivated, engaged, and excited about its products.

Because we were in the business of financial information, it became increasingly important for us to ensure system uptime around the clock. All-night programming and equipment setup sessions started to become the norm. There were over twenty folks at Prophet in 2002, and at the time most of us were young enough—and childless enough—to continue to pour ourselves completely into the business.

Since our products now involved real-time data and streaming charts, the pressure on all of us to deliver something that was reliable was far greater than when were just an end-of-day data business, but Prophet was blessed with some amazing talent.

What surprises me most about the people at Prophet is, to put it bluntly, that they stayed in the first place. I have a lot of great memories, but a big part of that is because I founded Prophet and was there during much leaner, less happy times. But the fact is that these people could have gone elsewhere and done better for themselves. Prophet's salaries weren't very high; no one ever believed we would be bought for a princely sum, making the employees rich; except for a regular supply of drinks and snacks in our kitchen, there really wasn't any special privilege or luxury to working at the place.

But I think what bound people together—what made them stay— was that they truly enjoyed working with each other, and each of

(Continued)

them could see a direct and positive contribution they were making to the firm as a whole. We were large enough to get attention, but small enough that everyone could really feel they made a difference.

The one person that everyone recognized as our product leader was, of course, Alex Dobrovolskiy. Alex created just about all the Web-facing products that Prophet had. His principal creation was JavaCharts, which was a full-blown charting applet that put Prophet on the map.

This one creation absolutely made the company because it gave us something that brokerages were actually interested in licensing. So over 20 different firms licensed the product, and it gave us a steady, hearty stream of recurring revenue.

As JavaCharts usage grew from thousands to millions to tens of millions of hits every month, the pressure was always on to improve both the product and its underlying infrastructure. But, as with any software product, JavaCharts was starting to show its age, and Alex wanted to created something completely new to replace it.

In 2002, he embarked on a new project called *Kandinsky* (which ultimately would become the ProphetCharts product that is used around the world today). Even though JavaCharts was a really good product, we knew that Alex's experience with it would provide him a foundation to create something that was better. So his long days at the office continued—and his life was all the more complete now that his wife and son had joined him (equipped, as he now was, with a Green Card) in the United States.

At 8:16 P.M. on November 8, 2002, Alex was—as was often the case—the last one at the office. He wrote himself an e-mail of sites he wanted to check first thing on Monday morning. The subject line, in typical Alex fashion, was humorously meaningless. He even signed the e-mail, even though he was sending it to himself. I imagine at this point he shut down his computer, locked the door, and started to walk across the street to get into his car.

The next morning, I was sitting in the Chinese restaurant Fu Lam Mum in Mountain View with my family, and my cell phone rang. It was Alex's wife, Eugenia, whose English was more limited than her husband's.

"Hello. I'm sorry to bother you."

"It's no bother. Is something wrong?"

"Alex was hit by a car. I thought you should know. He's at Stanford Hospital."

She wasn't crying; she wasn't hysterical; and she seemed to feel genuinely bad about calling me on a Saturday morning. Needless to say, we all left immediately for the hospital, not knowing what had happened or how bad it was.

We met Eugenia at the hospital, and she remained very composed—stoic, even. My wife asked to see Alex, whom she adored, even in his horribly damaged condition. I couldn't bear to go in there; he wasn't conscious, and he was being kept alive by machines.

According to the police, a hit-and-run driver mowed Alex down as he was crossing Alma. He was thrown at least 40 feet. He was as good as dead at that point, and once they turned the machines off, at Eugenia's request, he was gone.

This brilliant man was dead—the man who had made everything we succeeded at in our company possible—and whose wife and child had joined him in a new land. He was killed by someone with probably half his IQ and one-fiftieth of his morals. Somewhere out there is the person who ran him over and didn't have the courage to face the consequences of his actions.

As we told our employees that Monday morning, privately, one by one, the reactions were understandable—shock, grief, and a fear of what was going to happen. After all, we were each, to a degree, riding on Alex's coattails. His was the brain behind our creations.

I was particularly moved by the outpouring of support we received from the community. Both strangers and friends wired money into his memorial fund in order to support his survivors. And, of course, people were outraged that the wrongdoer got away with it. But Prophet would continue, and the technology Alex created and the company he helped construct would be his legacy.

◼ Burning Up

There is an old saying in the world of trading that no one rings a bell at the top of the market, and mass media, instead of providing valid turning points, often acts as a contrary indicator. It isn't often that a mass media publication serves up a notice that a market has reached a particular extreme. On March 20, 2000, *Barron's* did something unusual by doing precisely that.

The cover story was called "Burning Up," and it stated "... *during the next 12 months, scores of highflying Internet upstarts will have used up all their cash.*" The article was not conjecture or guesswork; instead, it systematically examined, company by company, all the public Internet firms, their cash, and the "burn rate" of how quickly they were going through that cash.

Barron's pointed out that the 371 Internet companies profiled represented about $1.3 trillion in value, about a tenth of the entire stock market, and that within 12 months at least 50 of the firms profiled would have no cash left. These numbers were collectively a kind estimate, considering the low-caliber firms crowding the public markets, but the article from the normally bullish *Barron's* sent shock waves through the market. *Barron's* is published on Saturday, but when the market opened on Monday, the Nasdaq fell 188 points, or about 4 percent.

A week later, on March 28, even the almost-always-bullish Abby Joseph Cohen announced that it was time to lighten up on stocks slightly, changing her model portfolio from 70 percent invested in common stocks to 65 percent. A suggested allocation of 0 percent would have prevented subsequent losses for her followers, but for someone as bullish as Cohen to suggest even a slight diminishment in equity ownership was another signal that perhaps the bull run was at an end. In what must be one of the great euphemisms of financial market history, Cohen described the market in March 2000 as "no longer undervalued" (see Figure 23.7).

The companies most prone to suffering early on were those that had been formed relatively recently. Old-timers such as Yahoo! may have still have been overpriced, but they had been around long enough and had a large enough user base to weather the storm ahead. In contrast was the likes of Boo.com, which had been founded in 1998 and had launched its website only four months earlier, in November 1999.

Boo had been flooded with $185 million in investor capital based on the premise that it would create a successful website to sell expensive fashion clothes. Its employees were well paid and had such perks as generous benefits, stock options, and fresh fruit delivered to the office daily. As with many

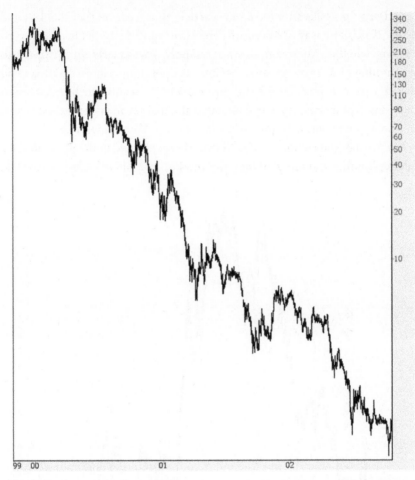

340
290
250
210
180
150
130
110
90
70
60
50
40
30
20
10

99 00   01   02

FIGURE 23.7   Akamai, one of the later companies to have a public offering, experienced a steady drop in its stock price for years after it sold its shares to the public.

well-funded start-ups in the late 1990s, the company was in a position to *act* like a successful, profitable firm without the bother of actually having to *be* one.

Once the website was at long last up and running, it wasn't particularly good and, ironically, it didn't even work on Macintosh computers (which was the platform of choice for a more fashionable demographic, ostensibly Boo's target market). In their first few months as a going concern, Boo was able to cobble together a little over $1 million in sales, but there was no more investor funding forthcoming to cover the unending losses. On May 17, the company closed its doors and filed for bankruptcy.

A couple of weeks after the *Barron's* article appeared, another shock would hit the Nasdaq by way of Microsoft. The U.S. Supreme Court had been considering whether Microsoft was a monopoly, particularly with respect to its bundling of its browser software into its operating system. Netscape had played a part in pushing for the government to scrutinize Microsoft and its business practices, since it dominated the market for operating systems, microcomputer business software, and—now—Web browsers.

On April 3, the ruling was issued that Microsoft was, in the government's legal opinion, a monopoly. Once the market was open again, on April 4,

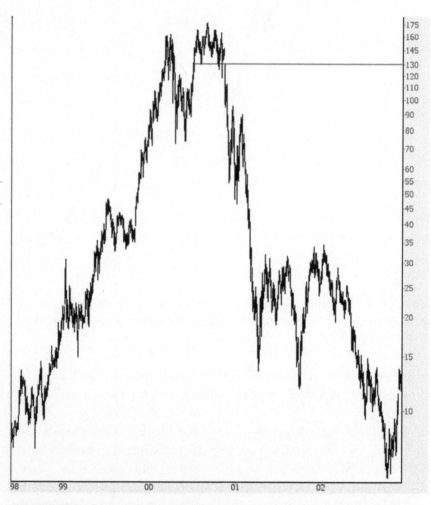

FIGURE 23.8 Many stocks, such as Broad.com, saw their stock prices go "full circle," ascending dramatically in the late 1990s and losing the entirety of those gains in the first couple of years of the new century.

the NASDAQ went into convulsions, plunging from 4,382 to 3,649, and then back up to 4,223. It was the most volatile date in the entire history of the Nasdaq market. Once the trading week was over, the Nasdaq was down a third of its value from just the prior month, and the Internet composite had collapsed by 50 percent. In just the week of April 3, over $2 trillion in market value had been wiped clean (see Figure 23.8).

It is a truism in equity markets that stocks fall much more quickly than they rise, and the swiftness of the Nasdaq's drop held true to that fact. As startling as a one-third drop in value a single month was, some individual equities had even more spectacular drubbings. From March 10 2000 to April 14, the losses suffered by a few Internet firms were:

- Akamai down 78.1 percent

- Ariba down 79.6 percent

- Commerce One down 74.4 percent

- Internet Capital Group down 72.2 percent

- TheGlobe.com down 62.5 percent

Unlike the brief, relatively mild drops in 1997 and 1998, this one seemed serious and, perhaps, much longer lasting. *Barron's* had come very closing to calling the top, and another 30 months of bear market were in front of a public that for nearly a decade had grown accustomed to prices that did almost nothing but go up every day.

■ Startup.com—The Movie

At almost the exact peak of the Internet bubble, a documentary was made about a dot-com start-up that superbly captured the *zeitgeist* of the time. The filmmakers didn't know it when they began filming, but the formation of the company at the center of the movie—GovWorks.com—was at the very height of the fundraising and investment mania having anything to do with the commerical Internet. Late in 1998, Kaleil Tuzman and Tom Herman, two friends who had met in high school, decided to start a company together.

The company was originally called Public Data Systems, but after some meditation (literally), Kaleil decided on the name GovWorks.com. The site's purpose would be to provide citizens an electronic means of interacting with government, such as applying for fishing licenses, paying parking tickets, or communicating with elected officials.

The company was formed in New York City's "Silicon Alley," and Kaleil left a lucrative job at Goldman Sachs to join the eight-person outfit that his friend Tom had already assembled. Kaleil's first focus, and a task which occupies much of the documentary, is fund-raising. The start-up is not greeted instantly with open checkbooks; on the contrary, the elite firm Kleiner Perkins turns GovWorks down for a variety of reasons, not the least of which is that they are based on the East Coast, far away from the Silicon Valley nexus.

Because so many of the dot-coms that were created left no artifacts except for a large figure representing how much money investors lost, the movie *Startup.com* provides a unique insight into the rise and fall of a high-tech company. The ascent and crash is at a vastly accelerated pace, particularly because the firm was assembled at what would, in retrospect, be recognized as the end of that particular business era known as the dot-com bubble.

GovWorks finally did raise its first funding—$17 million—and began focusing on its business plan. The extraordinary fact, of course, is that they were able to raise so much without a well-defined plan in the first place. But, given the start-up climate at the time, even without a website, revenue, or profits, the founders already anticipate their virtually assured wealth. One of the company's employees tells Kaleil on camera, "We're gonna go IPO in six months, and you're gonna be a billionaire" (see Figure 23.9).

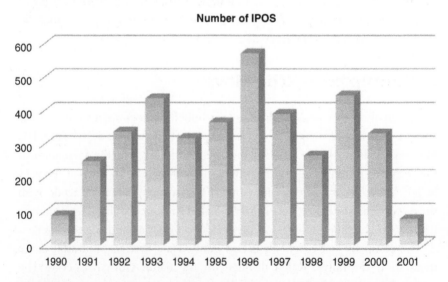

FIGURE 23.9 The number of IPOs actually peaked in 1996, before the ultimate top in the market. By 2001, very few companies made the choice to go public.

With almost any new Web business, the majority of cash is spent on personnel, and GovWorks' rapid hiring begins to burn through the substantial funds the firm was able to raise. In October 1999 the firm had 70 employees, growing to 120 in January 2000. There are two problems with commencing rapid hiring in a market like the one at the end of the twentieth century.

First, the vastly increased demand for a relatively fixed supply of talent means that the talent is going to be expensive, and the really *good* talent will, in all likelihood, already be employed elsewhere. Second, hiring dozens of employees every month (particularly by a firm whose management is inexperienced with hiring) will invariably lead to a less-than-optimal group of employees. It is difficult to make that many optimal decisions in such a short span of time.

Although GovWorks had only just launched its site and was, at best, years away from profitability, Kaleil was invited to the White House and was personally introduced by President Clinton to a gathering of business executives to discuss his new firm. The massive publicity GovWorks received on top of having an audience with the president of the United States was the peak for the company, as the reality of operating a business began to sink in.

As the film portrays it, the business quickly runs into a variety of real-life, day-to-day problems that many new companies face. The website is buggy; governments are slow to sign up as paying clients; the GovWorks office is burglarized; and the strains of dealing with business troubles are straining the working relationship of the two founders.

On May 28, 2000, Tom Herman found an envelope on his computer keyboard at work. Inside it was a signed letter from his friend and founding partner notifying him that he had been terminated effective immediately. As Tom discusses the situation with his parents, he mentions, "I'd rather see GovWorks fail than risk personal relationships."

The company quickly shrank from that point, down to 60 employees in November of 2000, and by January, what's left of the firm is sold off to First Data Corporation at a substantial loss to all the investors. The founders, far from being billionaires, received absolutely nothing for their shares, and Kaleil had, in fact, *personally* guaranteed over a million dollars of loans the firm had received. The Chapter 11 bankruptcy filing from March 2001 indicated assets of $8 million and liabilities of $40 million from the $70 million that was raised in all. GovWorks, like many of its peers, was at an end.

■ Horror and Terror

While the Super Bowl in early 2000 had been crowded with Internet ads, Super Bowl XXXV had a mere three dot-com advertisements, not even one-fifth of the prior year's. That spring, in one of the last hurrahs of dot-com excess, a start-up firm called iWon.com had a television special on which it gave away $10 million to a lucky contestant.

The quantity and size of dot-com burnouts increased as the Nasdaq passed the first anniversary of its peak. On March 7, 2001, eToys went out of business, having burned through $274 million in investor capital. eToys had once been richly valued, peaking at $10 billion, but after declaring bankruptcy, the only thing left for it to sell was its toy inventory at a steep discount.

With competition such as Amazon.com extending its reach into all manner of product lines, it is easy to see why a niche online retailer like eToys would have no reason to be in business. To do so would be little different than someone setting up a shop specializing in just soap and shampoo next door to a Wal-Mart.

One year after the Nasdaq's peak, the index stood at 2052.78, representing a loss of $3.5 trillion in shareholder wealth. One of the best-known Internet firms in the world, Yahoo!, was selling at a mere one-tenth its peak price. The broad Internet Composite itself was down 84.2 percent in just one year's time.

Another high-flier, theglobe.com, had withered away to $0.16 per share, and the Nasdaq exchange delisted the stock and relegated it to the "pink sheets," which is the domain of thinly traded companies, some of them teetering on the brink of bankruptcy. On August 3, theglobe.com shuttered its website altogether. The company has, in the many years since then, operating largely as a shell corporation. A recent annual report cites assets of about $6,000 and liabilities of about $3.2 million.

Not long thereafter, the largest recipient of Internet start-up capital, WebVan, closed its doors as well. Having spent $1.2 billion, WebVan found there wasn't a real need for online grocery shopping. The founder, Louis Borders, miscalculated the appeal of being able to shop for groceries on the Web (and perhaps had underestimated how much people actually enjoy shopping for groceries in person). Borders saw his earlier success, the Borders bookstore, also go bankrupt a decade later, on February 16, 2011.

The bear market ground away at the "old company" stocks starting in January 2000 and the "new company" stocks commencing in March 2000, chipping away at values month after month. As uneasy as the country was about both the economy and the stock market, a much bigger shock took place without any warning on September 11, 2001.

The terrorist attacks on the mainland United States wiped away once and for all the notions from 1999 about the United States being a capitalist utopia, living in a geographic bubble, spared the hardships of the outside world and able to travel an unending path of prosperity. The nation's mood, in less than two years, had gone from ceaselessly sunny to desperately dark (see Figure 23.10).

FIGURE 23.10 The Nasdaq Composite took many years to reach its peak over 5,000. A couple of years later, almost all the gains from the 1990s were eliminated.

Any hopes that smaller or more obscure Internet firms could continue to survive were quickly dispatched; some of the corporate carnage included:

- GeoCities, bought by Yahoo! for $3.57 billion in January 1999 and shuttered on October 26, 2009.

- Norris Communications, which changed its named to e.Digital (EDIG) in January 1999, catapulting its stock from 6 cents up to $24.50 by January 24, 2000, but henceforth plummeting back to just pennies per share.

- FreeInternet.com, the fifth largest Internet service provider in the United States, which canceled its IPO and filed for bankruptcy in October 2000. In 1999 it lost $19 million on less than $1 million in revenues;

- Startups.com, "the ultimate dot-com start-up," whose site, as of this writing, is nothing more than a solicitation for anyone who wants to buy the domain name startups.com.

- Broadcast.com, which was bought by Yahoo! in 1998 for $5.9 billion but was later shuttered (Mark Cuban, the cofounder of Broadcast, retained his billionaire status by shrewdly betting *against* Yahoo! near the stock's price peak).

- The Learning Company, bought by Mattel in 1999 for $3.5 billion and sold for $27.3 million in 2000, a loss of well over 99 percent.

- InfoSpace, which, on a split-adjusted basis, peaked at $1,305 per share only to drop to $22 in by April 2001.

A little more than a year after the terrorist attacks, on October 9, 2002, the Nasdaq finally hit bottom at 1,114.11, nearly an 80 percent loss from its peak in the spring of 2000. Millions of retail investors felt burned by the losses, and a meaningful portion of them would never invest in individual stocks again. In the years ahead, the indexes would recover, but even a dozen years later, the Nasdaq was still nowhere near its high, in spite of broader indexes like the Dow Jones 30 and the S&P 500 beating their old records (see Figure 23.11).

■ Picking Up the Pieces

In spite of the losses incurred during the bursting of the Nasdaq bubble, many Internet companies would survive, and some of them would go on to become the most valuable companies in the world. The rise and fall of the

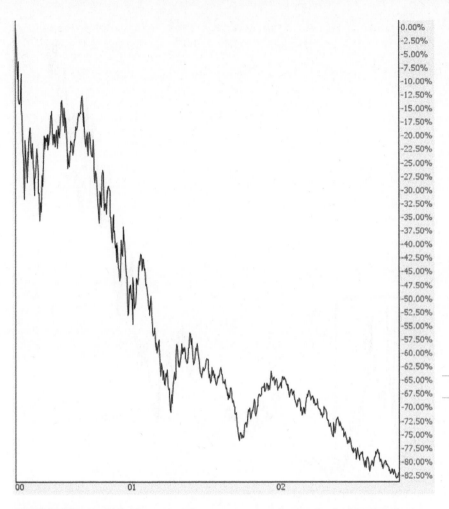

0.00%
-2.50%
-5.00%
-7.50%
-10.00%
-12.50%
-15.00%
-17.50%
-20.00%
-22.50%
-25.00%
-27.50%
-30.00%
-32.50%
-35.00%
-37.50%
-40.00%
-42.50%
-45.00%
-47.50%
-50.00%
-52.50%
-55.00%
-57.50%
-60.00%
-62.50%
-65.00%
-67.50%
-70.00%
-72.50%
-75.00%
-77.50%
-80.00%
-82.50%

00   01   02

FIGURE 23.11 This illustrates the percentage change in the Nasdaq from its peak. Soon after the 9/11 attacks, it seemed that perhaps the market had final reached a climactic bottom, but the real bottom wouldn't come for about another year.

Internet had plenty of victims, but it also yielded the likes of Google, eBay, Amazon, and other giants that were never in any danger of going out of business (see Figure 23.12).

The path from October 2002 to better times would be a long one, however, and plenty of companies would not survive the journey. By October 2003, it was widely agreed that AOL–Time Warner was the worst corporate merger in history. The business combination had become such an

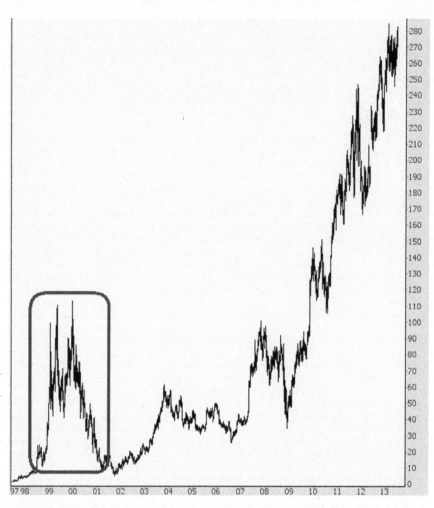

FIGURE 23.12 Amazon's stock price, in spite of losing almost all its 1990s gains, actually went on to much higher prices following the Internet mania. Even those who bought Amazon at the price peak late in 1999 would still have enjoyed exceptional profits, as long as they stayed with the stock through the substantial downturn in price.

embarrassment that Time Warner dropped AOL from its name completely. The firm also wrote off $99 billion in goodwill from its balance sheets, the largest accounting write-down ever recorded.

Warren Buffett's maxim, mentioned earlier in this chapter, "Only when the tide goes out do you discover who's been swimming naked," rang true during the bear market of 2001 and 2002. Corporate scandals become regular news items, with such titans as WorldCom, Enron, and Adelphia being exposed for massive frauds and accounting malfeasance.

Just as *Time* magazine pegged the top of the market with its Jeff Bezos "Man of the Year" cover story in December of 1999, it unwittingly signaled the bottom of the market by naming as its "Person of the Year" in December 2002 "The Whistleblowers." On the cover were three women, arms crossed, staring at the camera: Cynthia Cooper of WorldCom, Coleen Bowley of the FBI, and Sherron Watkins of Enron. The celebration of corporate whistle-blowers signaled an important psychology inflection point in American atti-tudes toward business.

The realm of investment banking and stock analysts did not go unscathed either. Banks were ordered to disgorge hundreds of millions of dollars in profits, and sweeping new rules from Congress (most notably the The Sar-banes-Oxley Act of 2002) made going public a far less alluring prospect. The expense and paperwork involved in being public would render IPOs far less attractive for many years to come.

Individual analysts, too, were made to account for their glowing recom-mendations made during the bubble (while simultaneously denigrating in private the very stocks they were touting in public). Henry Blodget, for example, agreed to a fine of $4 million and was banned from the securities industry for the rest of his life. Mary Meeker managed to emerge without being charged with any wrongdoing.

One analyst who was not so lucky was Jack Grubman, who in 1999 was the highest-paid analyst on Wall Street (earning $25 million per year) and a widely followed telecommunications industry expert. One particular rec-ommendation that came back to haunt him was an upgrade of AT&T from "neutral" to "buy" in 1999. He later admitted that he did so for one surpris-ing reason: to assure that his twin daughters would get into a coveted pre-school program in Manhattan.

Living History

The Silicon Valley was a very different place after the Internet bubble finally burst. Traffic jams abated; stock market obsession disappeared; even the quality of employees in "normal" jobs like waiting tables improved noticeably, because people realized that not everyone was entitled to get rich simply by virtue of being in the (650) area code.

(Continued)

Ironically, the situation with my own high-tech start-up improved drastically once the bubble was over. These advantages took several forms:

- *Talent reappeared.* During the bubble, anyone skilled with computers would be given a generous salary by any of the well-funded start-ups, or already-rich tech giants, thus creating an absolute dearth of talent for very small businesses like mine. At the height of the bubble, the only people left were really quite poor at their jobs, and even they expected to be well paid. Once a normal economy returned, it was much easier to find talented workers that were eager for a reasonable, if not exorbitant, salary.

- *Personnel costs dropped.* From consultants to full-time employees, expectations about compensation requirements dropped substantially. I distinctly remember one individual who was a network consultant. In 1999, he demanded $100 per hour, and in spite of us paying his rate, he left us for Cisco not long thereafter. Early in 2002, he sheepishly came back to the office and asked for us to hire him again. I asked him how much he wanted. He responded: "$20 per hour. $15 per hour. Anything. I've got to eat!"

- *Much cheaper office space.* The "office" we were renting was a ramshackle old house that was never intended as an office space. In any other part of the country, the house would probably have rented from $1,000 per month, if that. During the bubble, we were paying $17,500— plus utilities—every month. Once we had other office options, the rent plunged, and I was able to renegotiate the fee multiple times until it was less than one-third what we were paying before. Shortly thereafter, we were able to move to a much larger, more professional-looking space at a small fraction of the cost we had been paying for the old house.

Prophet's small size worked to its advantage, and there were still enough online investors that wanted a quality website to keep us growing. We almost sold the business in the summer of 2004, but the deal fell through at the last minute. That autumn, I found several other parties interested in Prophet, and on January 26, 2005, we sold the business for $8 million to a firm called Investools.

It was, in the context of the Silicon Valley, a microscopic event, but for me, it was the biggest day of my life. Thirteen years of hard work had finally paid off, and I had achieved what I had sought all my life: to create, grow, and sell a successful, profitable technology company. I would continue working there for a number of years afterward, free from the strains of worrying about revenue, making payroll, or dealing with administrative matters. It was a wonderful end to what had been a surprisingly long journey.

■ The Bubble's Legacy

As dramatic as the bursting of the dot-com bubble was, on the whole, the changes it brought were positive. Millions of investors, from venture capital giants to the smallest retail customer, lost trillions during the 2000–2002 bear market, but once all the dust had cleared, several lasting changes had taken place:

- *Giants came and stayed.* Many successful corporations serving millions of customers and employing tens of thousands of people each emerged from the tumult of the 1990s. Some of these names include eBay, Amazon, and Google, and over the long haul, investments in all these companies have paid off very well for everyone, irrespective of when they bought. Many other smaller firms have thrived as well, such as Priceline and Salesforce.com.

- *Start-up expectations changed.* Power shifted in favor of the entrepreneurs, and start-ups found themselves able to demand better terms from investors, even after the financial carnage the VC world suffered at the beginning of the 2000s. This would be particularly important to the wave of "Web 2.0" companies that were put together around the 2004–2006 period.

- *IPOs became much less attractive.* Although not necessarily a good change, depending on one's point of view, there is no doubt that the post-scandal regulation, particularly in the form of Sarbanes-Oxley, made the option of going public far less attractive to small companies. Firms like theglobe .com would almost certainly not seek to go public in this new environment, and instead would seek a lucrative buyout, particularly from a large firm like Google or Yahoo.

- *The fame and appeal of the Valley increased.* Even though the Silicon Valley was hardly a secret in 1995, its reputation and fame increased markedly thanks to the Internet mania. Although dozens of places around the world tried to copy the success of the Santa Clara region, none of them really succeeded, and the San Francisco Bay Area remains the world's hub for high-tech start-ups.

- *The groundwork was laid for future technology.* Plenty of "overbuilding" took place during the bubble, but eventually all that infrastructure did get used, and it paved the way for another wave of successful firms such as Facebook, LinkedIn, Yelp, Open Table, and Groupon. Some of the ideas of the late 1990s were actually quite good, but in many cases, the world wasn't quite ready for them. Once computing power, communications infrastructure, and browser technology caught up, some really outstanding concepts from the bubble which had failed at first were able to be resurrected and thrive.

The Internet bubble was an extraordinary event, and its scope and reach were probably unprecedented. There will no doubt be instances of such manias around technology in the future, and one thing is almost guaranteed: that it will be "different this time."

CHAPTER 24

The Great Recession

A fter the dot-com crash and the subsequent bear market, the United States faced the prospect of a deep, lengthy recession. Through a series of aggressive rate cuts, Alan Greenspan, the chairman of the Federal Reserve, replaced one bubble—Internet stocks—with another: real estate. By dramatically relaxing lending standards and interest rates, the U.S. government put inflated an enormous credit bubble that fueled consumer spending, real estate values, and the global economy, only to see it collapse into the worst financial crisis since the 1930s.

415

■ The American Dream

The seeds for the recession that spanned December 2007 through June 2009 were sown 80 years earlier, during the Great Depression. The FDR administration recognized that the housing industry was of paramount importance. The special place residential construction has in America is due to the fact that its own health benefits so many other aspects of the American economy: timber, professional trades, consumer appliances, and all the other materials and services that are required to build and furnish a home.

In 1938, the Federal National Mortgage Association (FNMA, often referred to as "Fannie Mae") was created as part of FDR's New Deal. Its purpose was to purchase mortgages from banks, bundle those mortgages into securities, and sell those securities into the secondary public markets. The value in doing so was that banks would continue to have a rich reserve of cash to lend instead of having it tied up in a slow but steady cash flow than spanned 30 years of repayment.

Fannie Mae was a government-sponsored entity (GSE); that is, it was created and supported by the federal government, but it was an independent (and, as of 1968, publicly traded) corporation. A companion GSE was formed in 1970 called the Federal Home Loan Mortgage Corporation ("Freddie Mac") which was created to purchase mortgages on the secondary market, package (or "securitize") them, and sell these packages as mortgage-backed securities.

Thus, the government played an important role in taking the tens of millions of relatively tiny mortgages spread through the nation and building a liquid, active market based upon them. The objective was to make the market for mortgages as liquid as possible, in turn making the mortgages required for home purchases as affordable as possible.

The federal government of the United States has a long history of providing incentives for home purchases and ownership. One of the most prevalent is the tax treatment of mortgages. For many Americans, the deductibility of mortgage interest is one of the most valuable tax-saving aspects of their annual tax return.

The U.S. government forsakes tens of billions of dollars year after year with this benefit, and in 1986, the government made it even more valuable since it eliminated tax deductions for interest paid on credit cards. This encouraged people to borrow against their homes for their cash requirements, as opposed to borrowing from credit cards, for which the tax benefits had been eliminated.

In 1992, the government used Fannie Mae and Freddie Mac in another assertion of policy, by requiring them to dedicate a percentage of their mortgage purchases to affordable housing. The logic was that the government should focus its efforts on helping secure mortgages for Americans who were least able to attain them. The government authorized the Department of Housing and Urban Development (HUD) to dictate the percentage of mortgage purchases related to affordable housing.

When the directive was issued in 1992, the percentage was set at 30 percent, but it increased in future years. In 1995, HUD increased the percentage to 40 percent, rising to 42 percent the next year, 50 percent in 2000, and 52 percent in 2005. By 2008, a full 58 percent of Fannie Mae and Freddie Mac purchases were tied to affordable housing, and the two organizations eventually held $5 trillion of low-income and minority loan commitments.

As *the New York Times* reported on September 30, 1999:

> Fannie Mae, the nation's biggest underwriter of home mortgages, has been under increasing pressure from the Clinton Administration to expand mortgage loans among low and moderate income people and felt pressure from stock holders to maintain its phenomenal growth in profits. In addition, banks, thrift institutions and mortgage companies have been pressing Fannie Mae to help them make more loans to so-called subprime borrowers

Besides the deductibility of mortgage interest, there was another benefit added to the tax code for homeowners: tax-free capital gains. This benefit was initially introduced in July 1978 during the Carter administration, allowing for a tax-free capital gain of up to $100,000 from the sale of a home by those 55 years or older. This exemption was increased to $125,000 in 1981 and then raised much more substantially to $250,000 (for a single person) and $500,000 (for a married couple) in 1997.

Thus, the government had created a way for a couple of enjoy as much as $500,000 in profits from the sale of their home clear of any taxation. This spurred on interest in real estate investing, including, for wealthier Americans, investments in vacation homes.

If there was any trend in the late twentieth and early twenty-first centuries that encouraged Americans to invest in real estate, the most persistent and prevalent one was plunging interest rates. In 1982, interest rates exceeded 18 percent for the most creditworthy customers.

Over the next three decades, rates would move generally downward. After the dot-com crash, the Federal Reserve became especially aggressive about dropping rates, reducing its own interest rate to 1 percent. With every quarter-point drop in interest rates, mortgage payments become affordable for a larger pool of Americans.

However, in spite of its reputation as a wonderful investment, the "American dream" of a single-family home is actually a rather moribund instrument for capital growth. Over the long haul, residential real estate in the United States has barely kept pace with inflation. During most of the 1990s, when the "hot money" was in Internet stocks, the value of U.S. homes barely budged. From the beginning of 1990 to the beginning of 1997, home prices moved up only 8.3 percent, and that figure does not even take into account inflation over the seven-year period.

After 1997, however, the pace of appreciation increased markedly. There were many forces behind this, such as the tax incentives cited above, but perhaps the most important was the tremendous growth in "easy money" that would be flooding the United States real estate market over the next decade.

■ A Yield-Seeking Ocean of Money

In spite of the dip in the economy in 2001–2002, the world—particularly the oil-producing world—was still very rich, and it needed a place to put its wealth. The rapidly shrinking interest rates meant that the $70 trillion in fixed income investments was generating an increasingly meager rate of return on its capital. The money was intended for safe, not speculative, purposes, and its stewards were on a constant quest to find investments that were simultaneously high in safety and relatively high in yield.

The solution was found in the always-resourceful financial engineering of United States investment banks. To understand the solution, a comprehension of its elements is important, specifically, subprime lending, credit default swaps (CDSs), and collateralized debt obligations (CDOs).

The subprime lending market, as the name implies, is targeted at individuals with relatively low-quality credit ratings. Because the risk for the lender is higher, the interest rates attached to these loans have traditionally been higher than those in the "prime" lending market. A person with excellent credit might be paying 6 percent on his mortgage, whereas someone else with lower credit might pay 10 percent on the same-sized mortgage.

The latter is the kind of market that Fannie Mae and Freddie Mac were directed to serve in increasing large proportions. By the very nature of poor credit risks, it becomes more difficult to find those in the subprime category who meet qualification standards, so the standards have to be lowered if loans are to be approved. So through the late 1990s and early 2000s, both the private market and the GSEs supporting the mortgage market found themselves on an increasingly slippery slope of lowering their requirements for loan approvals.

Before this liberalization of standards began, the subprime market was relatively small. In 1994, subprime mortgages accounted for about $35 billion of the new originations, which was about 5 percent of the overall market. It increased to 9 percent in 1996, 13 percent in 1999, and 20 percent in

2006. Thus, in a dozen years, new subprime markets grew from $35 billion to $600 billion in newly issued home mortgages.

As standards relaxed, new lending products were created to make it easier for lower-income families to afford the payments. Interest-only mortgages were one popular choice (accounting for nearly 50 percent of all new mortgages in San Diego in 2004), in which monthly payments didn't pay down a single penny of the mortgage's principal.

Another style of loan was the "stated income loan" in which the borrower could provide whatever financial information they wanted without having to provide any proof. The colloquial term for these was *liar loans,* since it is a virtual certainty that, in many cases, stated incomes were significantly higher than reality.

The liberal loans came in a variety of styles, each denoted by a four-letter acronym. The SIVA loan was Stated Income, Verified Assets, in which the borrower could declare whatever income they wanted but only prove that had a job, and they had to show proof of cash in a bank account.

The NIVA stood for No Income, Verified Assets, in which proof of a bank account was also required, but proof of a job was not. The most liberal of all was the NINA loan, which stood for No Income, No Assets, in which case no proof of any stated facts was required. The borrower could claim whatever income and assets they were willing to write on the application.

Perhaps the most extraordinary example of new loan product was the "interest-only negative-amortizing adjustable-rate subprime mortgage." With this product, a borrower not only was assessed for just the interest on the monthly payment, but he could choose not to make a payment at all and simply let the interest due for that month be added to the amount of the loan (hence "negative amortization"). Therefore, not only was the loan not being brought down, but the loan could actually increase in size as the interest payments went unpaid (see Figure 24.1).

If that were the extent of the financial innovation, it would seem unhelpful for the trillions of dollars seeking a safe, high-yielding home. The subprime market took care of half the problem—"high yield"—but it certainly was not safe. The kinds of debtors that would undertake high-interest, easily-approved loans were not good credit risks, and the likelihood of default was far higher than a borrower with superb credit.

This is where additional financial products become relevant. First, there is the credit default swap (CDS), which is in essence a financial insurance policy. There are three principal entities relevant to a CDS: a buyer, a seller,

U.S. Subprime Lending Expanded Significantly 2004–2006

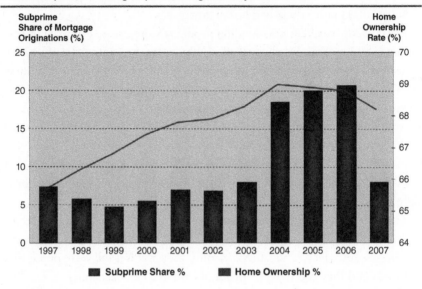

FIGURE 24.1 The quantity and value of subprime loans soared from 2004 through 2006.

Sources: U.S. Census Bureau; Harvard University-State of the Nation's Housing Report 2008

and a debt (otherwise known as a "reference bond"). The buyer agrees to pay the seller regular payments over a period of time. If the bond does not default during that time, the seller keeps all the payments and the transaction is complete.

However, if at any time during the course of the agreement the bond defaults, the seller of the CDS is required to pay the buyer the value of the default, and the seller takes possession of the bond.

For example, a CDS might be created requiring a buyer to pay $200,000 every year for 10 years to a seller, with the reference bond being a loan of $20 million. (The buyer and seller may or may not have anything to do with the reference bond). If, five years into the CDS, the bond defaults, even though the buyer has paid out $1 million already, he is entitled to receive $20 million from the seller (and will also not be required to make any more payments).

The asymmetric nature of CDSs makes them highly attractive for high-end speculators, since risking $1 million for a potential payout of $20 million (as with the preceding example) could be seen as an attractive gamble. The growth of the CDS market, which was only created in 1994, was explosive. By the end of 2007, the nominal amount of CDS contracts outstanding was $62.2 trillion, which is larger than the entire global economy.

There is another financial instrument known as a collateralized debt obligation (CDO), which is a collection of individual bonds or other assets that is allocated to buyers in a series of slices known as tranches. To cite a simple example, 1,000 mortgages might be bought in the open market and bundled into a CDO. Those 1,000 mortgages have different levels of quality, depending upon the credit risk of each, and they are organized within the CDO into tranches.

In turn, those tranches are sold off to buyers, with the lowest-risk tranches yielding the lowest interest and being sold to more conservative buyers. The highest-risk tranches within the CDO would offer correspondingly higher yields, but the buyers run the risk of not being paid in full, or at all, if their tranche of the CDO defaults.

■ Unreliable Ratings

The key to bridging the gap between all the cash seeking a safe, high-yielding instrument and the CDOs made up of subprime mortgages was found in the ratings system. Ratings agencies, such as Moody's, S&P, and Fitch, made a business of giving ratings to financial products. The stated purpose of these agencies was to offer an objective, unbiased, and independent analysis of a financial product and give it a grade—its rating—as a way of declaring the risk associated with the product.

A high-risk product might warrant a BBB rating, meaning the market would demand a higher interest rate to compensate for the increased risk, whereas a Treasury Bond from the U.S. government, widely recognized as the most risk-free investment, would receive an AAA rating. It would be extremely safe, but it would also pay the lowest interest.

The "bundles" of subprime mortgages that were being gathered up and packaged into saleable CDOs should have been given the low ratings that their credit risk warranted. After all, these were mortgages whose payment depended on the promises of relatively low-income individuals with impaired credit histories.

However, the rating industry is arranged in such a way that the parties paying the fees to have the ratings done are the same organizations creating the financial products in the first place. It would be similar to having all the largest commercial meat producers in the country paying for the

Department of Agriculture's ratings for meat quality. Naturally, if the entity whose products you are judging is the same entity that is responsible for your revenue, some conflicts of interest are bound to occur.

Thus, even though the hundreds of billions of dollars of subprime mortgage CDOs being created by the investment banks warranted relatively low ratings (after all, the mortgages were "*sub*-prime"), the overwhelming majority of them were blessed with a AAA rating, the highest possible. To return to the meat producer analog, it would be equivalent to partly spoiled, low-grade cuts of meat being packaged and priced as it they were filet mignon.

The difference, of course, is that a person in a grocery store buying meat would not, in spite of the filet mignon label affixed to the package, purchase the product when they saw what was inside, whereas a purchaser of a CDO has to trust the grade given to it by a globally recognized ratings agency. The sheer volume of the CDOs created between 2004 and 2007 was an astonishing $1.4 trillion, and most of these CDOs satisfied the two requirements of the yield-seeking fixed-income stewards: safety and above-market returns.

CDOs were not widely known or widely issued until the 2000s, but they soon gained popularity based on their ability to act as a tool for securitizing mortgages in a highly profitable fashion. In the first quarter of 2004, about $20 billion CDOs were issued by investment banks, but this figure rose steadily to over $180 billion by the first quarter of 2007, just three years later.

When the CDOs were first becoming popular, most of them consisted of high-quality debt instruments. As the real estate boom began to take hold, and subprime loans became more common, the percentage of subprime mortgage debt grew to over one-third of all CDOs outstanding by 2007. The remarkable thing is that, in spite of the overall plunge in the quality of the underlying assets, the AAA ratings did not change.

The ratings agencies enjoyed surging revenue growth from 2004 to 2007 from the business of rating these products, since they could not only charge substantial fees to rate them, but also because the sheer volume of CDOs being generated (each of which required a rating) was ascending. Moody's Structured Finance Division, which specialized in rating instruments such as CDOs, was responsible for 44 percent of Moody's corporate revenue in 2006.

Insurance giant AIG had a division dedicated to specialized financial derivatives called AIG Financial Products (AIGFP). It sold credit default swaps based on the subprime CDOs, and the fee they were charging, about twelve-hundredths of a single percentage point against the value of the debt, did not reflect the risk of the CDO.

The low pricing of the CDS simply reflected the AAA rating given to the CDO, but doing so was similar to giving a teenager driver with multiple traffic violations the same insurance rate as a 40-year old driver with a spotless record. The risk pricing did not reflect the reality.

■ Bubble Denial

Whereas real estate had been a relatively moribund investment for most of the 1990s, home prices from 1997 to 2006 began to accelerate, increasing by 124 percent. One measure of housing affordability is the ratio of household income to the average price for a home. In the 1980s and 1990s, this ratio was about 3 (in other words, the average price of a home equaled three years of household income), but this figure increased to 4.6 by 2006. Under normal circumstances, such an increase would have put home ownership out of reach of millions who might have been able to afford it earlier.

In 2003, Alan Greenspan had lowered interest rates to a mere 1 percent, which was the lowest level in 45 years. Very low interest rates were a major driving factor in the real estate boom, since they compelled investors to not only seek out better-yielding investments (since fixed income paid so poorly) and they made monthly payments lower.

Demand for housing was also greater, since lower lending standards meant that a much larger population of potential buyers were in a position to make bids on properties for sale. A much larger pool of capital was at work, and that capital was accessible to a larger percentage of the population than ever before.

In one example of liberal lending standards, a buyer in Southern California, a migrant worker who picked strawberries for a living and made $17,000 a year doing so, was able to secure a loan for a $754,000 house.

In America, the typical split between owners and renters was two-thirds and one-third. The 66 percent ownership rate in America crept higher, thanks largely in part to the government's push (aided by the burgeoning market for mortgage derivatives by investment banks) to make buying a home more affordable for a larger portion of the population. In 2004, home ownership reached a high of 69.2 percent in the United States, a national record.

The housing mania was strongest in what were colloquially known as the "sand states" of California, Arizona, Nevada, and Florida. The word *flipping* entered the popular vernacular, which was a term used to describe the process of buying a house in need of some repairs and improvement, quickly renovating the home, and then selling it for a substantial profit. Magazines and books touted how everyday Americans could take part in, and profit from, the boom in residential real estate flipping.

Some of these titles included *Are You Missing the Real Estate Boom?* and *Why the Real Estate Boom Will Not Bust—And How You Can Profit from It*. The June 13, 2005, cover of *Time* magazine captured the popular zeitgeist by featuring a painting of a man embracing his house under the headline "Home Sweet Home," with the subtitle "Why we're going gaga over real estate." A student of financial history might have taken the cover as a cue that the top was close at hand, particularly given *Time*'s prominence in popular culture.

Even for those who had no interest in being part of the boom, millions of existing homeowners refinanced their mortgages to lower rates. Mortgage brokers had never had so much business before.

In addition to an active mortgage refinancing market, another aspect of popular financial activity was equity lines of credit. Because interest paid on home equity was deductible (whereas credit card debt was not), homes became a favored source of borrowing. With an equity line of credit, homeowners could borrow tens or hundreds of thousands of dollars for cars, boats, consumer electronics, or even second homes. In 2005 alone, U.S. homeowners borrowed three-quarters of a trillion dollars against the value of their homes, and these expenses helped fuel a healthy economy based mostly on consumer spending.

The comforting and oft-cited fact of this era was that, ever since the Great Depression, housing prices had not fallen in the United States even one single year. Nowhere else could one point—not bonds, not equities—to any investment choice that featured so stable a performance. Thus, even in the midst of rapidly-ascending prices, investment banks, home builders, and home buyers could all take solace in the fact that United States real estate had a multi-decade run of consistent growth, and all indications were that this steady appreciation would persist.

An important aspect of this appreciation, however, was how modest it was, and in contrast how abnormal the gains from 1997 to 2005 were. Although home prices had been steadily increasing, the increase was on average less than 1 percent per year. Adjusted for inflation, home prices increased a mere 0.4 percent per year from 1890 to 2004.

The double-digit annual growth seen in some metropolitan areas of the United States was far out of line with historical norms, and the modest historical ascent in prices up to that point was no guarantee that at some point home prices would not revert to the mean.

Popular news outlets offered few such warnings. In a June 21, 2005 *Bloomberg Businessweek* article, the chief economist of Freddie Mac, Frank Nothaft, stated, "I don't foresee any national decline in home price values. Freddie Mac's analysis of single-family houses over the past half-century hasn't shown a single year when the national average housing price has gone down."

October 27 of the same year, the *Washington Post* published an article titled "Bernanke: There's No Housing Bubble to Go Bust." The article cited the 25 percent increase in home prices over the past two years, but stated Bernanke's assurance that the increases "largely reflect strong economic fundamentals" and that "a moderate cooling in the housing market, should one occur, would not be inconsistent with the economy continuing to grow at or near its potential next year." Alan Greenspan was also quoted in the article, asserting that he saw no bubble in home prices in the United States, in spite of some "froth" in local markets.

Even after housing prices peaked and were clearly on the decline, Bernanke offered assurances that there was no cause for alarm. In his testimony before Congress on March 28, 2007, Chairman Bernanke stated:

> The principal source of the slowdown in economic growth that began last spring has been the substantial correction in the housing market. ... So far this year, sales of existing homes have held up, as have other indicators of demand such as mortgage applications for home purchase. ... In addition, a large increase in early defaults on recently originated subprime variable-rate mortgages casts serious doubt on the adequacy of the underwriting standards for these products, especially those originated over the past year or so ... *however, the impact on the broader economy and financial markets of the problems in the subprime market seems likely to be contained.* In particular, mortgages to prime borrowers and fixed-rate mortgages to all classes of borrowers continue to perform well, with low rates of delinquency.

The National Association of Realtors sought to tamp down concerns of a bubble as well, distributing "Anti-Bubble Reports" in August 2005, which stated "... there is virtually no risk of a national housing price bubble based on the fundamental demand for housing and predictable economic factors." A few months later, President George Bush offered his own opinion on housing bubble concerns, stating, "If houses get too expensive, people will stop buying them."

The assumption was that all the players involved were behaving in an economically rational sense, and that because transactions were taking place at certain prices, those transactions must therefore be sensibly priced, since buyers and sellers had reached an agreement.

In the midst of all these assurances, there were some experts who tried to warn others of what was going on. The chief economist of the International Monetary Fund, Raghuram Rajan, spoke at the 2005 gathering at Jackson Hole, Wyoming, sponsored every year by the Federal Reserve Bank of Kansas City. He stated that the deregulation that had taken place in finance, and the focus on short-term profits in spite of all the risks being taken, could lead to catastrophe. The speech got a chilly reception, with Larry Summers, the president of Harvard at the time, calling the speech "largely misguided."

■ Financial Fissures

With the Internet bust and 9/11 terrorist attacks years behind, and the economy performing so well, the Federal Reserve began pushing up interest rates from the historically low 1 percent level. They did this in small steps, but they did so 17 consecutive times, lifting the Fed rate from 1 percent to 5.25 percent from 2004 to 2006. High rates meant higher monthly payments for mortgage holders across the nation, the vast majority of whom had adjustable rates. The situation was worse yet for those with subprime loans, since their low "teaser" rates would, upon expiration, be replaced by exorbitantly higher interest payments.

The data revealed that higher rates were starting to have a negative impact. The S&P/Case-Shiller Index recorded its first year-over-year decline in nationwide prices in the first quarter of 2007, which hadn't happened for the past 16 years.

Delinquencies and foreclosures began to rise, and the situation became acute by March 2007 when over 25 subprime lenders either went bankrupt or reported severe financial distress. While most of these lenders were small, the sheer number of business failures in this one sector was strongly indicative of a systemic problem.

Any doubts about the situation's severity were set aside the next month when, on April 2, 2007, New Century Financial, already the target of investigations by the U.S. Justice Department and the largest subprime lender in the country, declared bankruptcy with liabilities in excess of $100 million.

Although the stock market kept rising, other signs of trouble began to emerge. In July 2007, two hedge funds run by Bear Stearns collapsed. Their names were the Bear Stearns High-Grade Structured Credit Fund and the Bear Stearns High-Grade Structured Credit Enhanced Leveraged Fund. Investors in each fund would soon discover there was not much "high-grade" about either of them.

Some of the assets within the funds were derivatives linked to subprime mortgages, and the investment bank notified investors that they would get virtually nothing back due to "unprecedented declines." This surely came as a shock to at least some of the investors, since the ratings given to the failure securities were AAA, which theoretically should have been absolutely safe from such a wipeout.

The declining values of the subprime market and its derived financial products spread from funds to the investment banks themselves. In October 2007, Merrill Lynch posted its third quarter earnings report. Along with the regular quarterly information on revenues and profits, management also issued a shocking admission: a $7.9 billion loss on CDOs. The financial products that the banks had been creating were starting to severely backfire on the originating banks.

In August 2007, American Home Mortgage filed for bankruptcy, and the gigantic Countrywide Financial was pushed to the brink of bankruptcy itself before securing $11 billion in loans from a consortium of banks. Before the month is over, another large subprime lender, Ameriquest, also shuttered its doors.

CEOs of the largest investment banks began to flee the damage. Stanley O'Neal resigned from Merrill Lynch in October 2007, and the next month, Citigroup's Chairman and CEO left his post due to the "significant impact" his firm's fourth quarter earnings were going to suffer due to the plunge in CDO values. Bear Stearns added to the bad news when it reported a $1.2 billion loss from mortgage-related securities in November 2007, generating the first loss for the company in its entire 83-year history.

Although the Federal Reserve began to cut interest rates, slashing them from 6.25 percent to 4.75 percent in a matter of months, the upward trend in home prices, the mortgage market, and economic sentiment had all broken and were gathering downside momentum. In October 2007, the

Case-Shiller housing index printed its tenth consecutive decline in prices. By the end of the year, foreclosures were up 75 percent from 2006, and the number of homes in the foreclosure process had doubled from the year before.

■ Fiscal Free-Fall

The year 2008 would be the fiercest stage of the financial crisis and mortgage meltdown, with trillions of dollars of wealth in the United States alone wiped out. As 2008 began, there had already been some damage to the stock market, but 2007 overall still produced gains for most indexes, with the Dow enjoying about a 750 point profit in spite of its slump from the October 11, 2007, peak of 14,101.

The Dow continued its skid in January, but in February and March, markets began to stabilize, as the investing public began to assume that the worst of the problems with subprime mortgages were behind it and that a recovery from the damage was already beginning.

Attention turned to Bear Stearns which, nine months after its hedge fund failures, seemed to be the only financial institution at serious risk. On March 14, 2008, a $25 billion loan was arranged by the Federal Reserve Bank of New York to give the investment bank a month to stabilize its financial operations and shore up public confidence in the bank's liquidity. However, the Fed withdrew this loan and instead directed a more substantial loan—$30 billion—to JPMorgan, coupled with an agreement that JPMorgan would buy rival Bear Stearns for a mere $2 per share (see Figure 24.2).

The announcement of a $2 per share price for Bear was astonishing to Wall Street. The same stock had traded hands for $172 per share in 2007, and even a few weeks prior to the loan arrangement and following its hedge fund debacle, Bear Stearns still enjoyed a share price of $93. The shareholders were outraged at the agreement and filed suit, so the Fed and JPMorgan increased the agreed-upon price to $10 per share.

Even though it was quintuple the original amount, it still represented a 94 percent drop from the stock's peak the prior year and was a humbling end to a once-proud financial giant that was nearly nine decades old.

The stock market, however, greeted the news enthusiastically, as the low point for the year had been reached on January 22, and the Dow had been making tentative steps higher from month to month. By mid-May, the stock market reflected the attitude that Bear's absorption by a larger, healthier

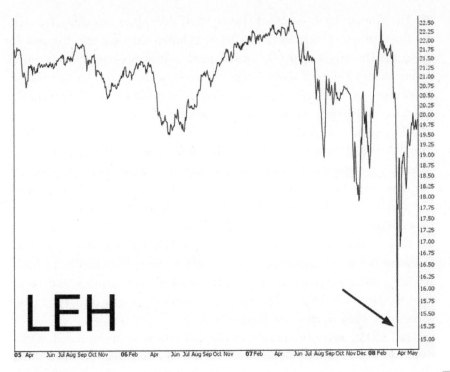

22.50
22.25
22.00
21.75
21.50
21.25
21.00
20.75
20.50
20.25
20.00
19.75
19.50
19.25
19.00
18.75
18.50
18.25
18.00
17.75
17.50
17.25
17.00
16.75
16.50
16.25
16.00
15.75
15.50
15.25
15.00

LEH

05 Apr   Jun Jul Aug Sep Oct Nov   06 Feb   Apr   Jun Jul Aug Sep Oct Nov   07 Feb   Apr   Jun Jul Aug Sep Oct Nov Dec 08 Feb   Apr May

FIGURE 24.2   The fire-sale price assigned to Bear Stearns sent shock waves in the investment banking world, briefly sending companies in the same industry tumbling in March 2008, such as Lehman Brothers.

bank had cleansed Wall Street of its subprime problem, and the equity market could return to its focus on growth and earnings instead of mortgage derivatives.

However, the Dow Jones weakened as spring turned to summer, and by June 16, 2008, the market was breaking to new lows for the year. The festering problems of the multitrillion-dollar derivatives market were still a fiscal drag on the banks, and housing prices were continuing to weaken and foreclosures continued to rise. The market meandered throughout the summer, but the real chaos would ensue in September.

Lehman Brothers would be the new epicenter of financial concern. The bank was viewed as the weakest large investment bank on Wall Street, now that Bear Stearns was gone. However, the Korean Development Bank was reported to be interested in buying Lehman, which helped shore up not only the price of its stock but also general confidence that a wider financial crisis would be averted.

The Korean bank reported that it faced difficulties attracting partners to the deal, so on September 9, 2008, Lehman's stock price dropped 45 percent. The investing public sensed another Bear Stearns collapse was at hand, and the Dow fell about 300 points in sympathy with Lehman's plunge. Confidence in the bank continued to erode as it fell another 7 percent the next day and 40 percent more on September 11.

During the weekend of September 13–14, a meeting was hosted by New York Fed chief Timothy Geithner (who later would be President Obama's Treasury secretary). The purpose of the meeting was to discuss what should be done with Lehman Brothers. It was decided that, unlike Bear Stearns, no purchase of Lehman would be arranged, nor would any loan package be assembled.

Hours before the U.S. markets opened on Monday, September 15, 2008, Lehman Brothers announced that it would be filing for Chapter 11 bankruptcy, ending 158 years in business. The stock plunged another 90 percent, and the Dow sold off by over 500 points, marking one of the largest point drops in trading history (see Figure 24.3).

The CDS market began to seize up, because as an unregulated market with no reporting requirements, no one knew who had positions, what those positions were, and what cumulative risk exposures were. The bankruptcy of Lehman caused $400 billion of CDS-based payouts to become due (although this was greatly diminished by offsetting positions), and the overall notional value of all CDS contracts outstanding was nearly $70 trillion. Warren Buffett's famed quotation that derivatives were a "weapon of mass financial destruction" seemed to be unfolding in real time.

AIG was singularly vulnerable to CDS risk, since it had insured $441 billion in securities that had been given an AAA rating which were now understood to be anything but AAA-grade. The day after the Lehman bankruptcy announcement, AIG faced a liquidity crisis that threatened its own existence. The U.S. federal government swiftly put together an $85 billion credit package for the firm, the largest government bailout in the nation's history, in a desperate attempt to shore up a crisis of confidence that was overwhelming Wall Street (see Figure 24.4).

The panic became so great that massive withdrawals began taking place in money market funds, with $144.5 billion in withdrawals during a single week, a 20-fold increase from the week preceding. At one point, the market "broke the buck," meaning that custodians of money market funds were paying out slightly less than the full dollar value of the account.

FIGURE 24.3 The drop Lehman suffered in March 2008, marked here with an arrow, is barely a blip compared to the gigantic collapse that lay ahead for it in September 2008.

Governments in both the United States and Europe attempted more dramatic measures to reverse the slide of the markets. On September 18, regulators in the United Kingdom announced an outright ban on short-selling of financial stocks. America's own Securities and Exchange Commission (SEC) followed suit, forbidding short-selling on 799 specifically named corporations in the financial sector (see Figure 24.5).

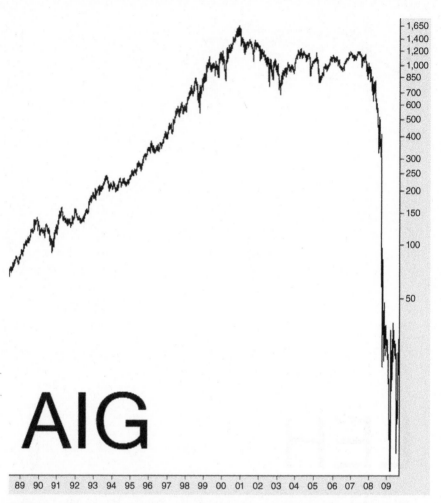

FIGURE 24.4 For decades a steady performer, AIG suddenly went into a free-fall, falling to prices even lower than the bear market of 1974. Forty years of gains were erased in four months.

■ Bailout

Treasury Secretary Henry Paulson and Fed Chairman Ben Bernanke met on September 18 with congressional leaders to propose a $700 billion rescue package called TARP, which stood for Troubled Asset Relief Program. Its purpose was to buy the toxic securities from financial institutions, infusing the financial sector with much-needed liquidity and stability. Bernanke emphasized to the congressional delegation the crucial nature of the TARP bill, speculating that "if we don't do this, we may not have an economy on Monday."

BAC

FIGURE 24.5   Normally staid stocks such as Bank of America were collapsing during the financial crisis, compelling government regulators to forbid anyone selling the stock short, which they felt was exacerbating the decline.

The market rallied on the news, with the Dow leaping about 1,000 points from its low of September 18 to its high of September 19. Some stocks briefly soared to lifetime highs, as it seemed the federal government was, by way of its short-selling ban and the nearly trillion-dollar cash pledge, forbidding the market from going any lower.

Paulson's printed proposal on TARP was brief, and Congress took his blueprint for the program and constructed a substantial bill around it to submit for a vote. The bill was expected to pass on September 29, but as the tallies updated on the screen, it was a much closer split between Yay and Nay votes than most anticipated. When the gavel finally came down at 2:10 P.M., TARP had lost, and the markets began plunging again. The Dow lost 777.68 points, the largest one-day point drop in its history.

The selloff in stocks continued as uncertainty remained about what, if anything, the government would do about the crisis that would pass congressional muster. From October 1 through October 9, the S&P 500 lost 251 points, wiping out nearly 22 percent of its already-depleted value. Every day investors saw their 401(k) accounts shrink, as trillions of dollars were lost on the collective equity holdings of both citizens and businesses. European and U.S. central banks put trillions of dollars into the financial system as they continued to wait for legislative action.

The TARP bill was passed when it was submitted to Congress again, and President George W. Bush signed it into law on October 3, 2008. Ironically, the Dow fell again on this day, as it would continue to do until March 6, 2009, when it would finally bottom at 6,469.95, a calamitous 55 percent drop from its peak of 14,198.10 just two Octobers prior (see Figure 24.6).

The TARP program authorized the U.S. Treasury to purchase up to $700 billion of mortgage-based derivatives or any other assets whose purchase was deemed to be constructive to promoting stabilization in the financial sector. The government's hope was that by getting the "toxic" assets off the bank books, and by infusing the banks with capital, financial firms would be willing to make loans to shore up the damaged economy as opposed to hoarding their capital. Some of the cash outlays included:

- $205 billion to buy shares in banks.

- $21.9 billion to buy mortgage-related securities.

- $40 billion to buy shares in Citigroup and Bank of America.

FIGURE 24.6 As with the Dow Industrials, the Nasdaq 100 dropped severely during the financial crisis, but the drop was dwarfed by the much larger drop it had already suffered between 2000 and 2002.

- $79.7 billion in loans to U.S. auto manufacturers.

- $67.8 billion to buy preferred shares in AIG.

The bad financial news continued to come in. Case-Shiller reported the largest price drop for home prices in history, and foreclosures continued to climb. About 3.1 million foreclosures were executed in 2008, and another 4 million would be filed in 2009, with a similar number in 2010 (see Figure 24.7).

By the end of 2008, the devastation on the economic sector was extraordinary: a third of the top 30 mortgage lenders were gone; all 5 of the largest investment banks had either gone bankrupt, been acquired, or converted to commercial institutions; and about half of peak equity values had been wiped out. Joblessness was on the ascent, too, as the unemployment rate pushed into the double digits for the first time in a quarter-century (see Figure 24.8).

Homeowners, who had been assured that there had never been a year-over-year decline in average property values, had suffered a nearly one-quarter loss in the value of their properties from the peak two years prior.

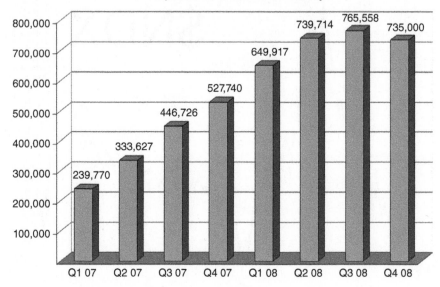

Properties with Foreclosure Activity

FIGURE 24.7 New foreclosures continued to accumulate each quarter, reaching a peak in the third quarter of 2008.

Newer homeowners found themselves "underwater"—that is, they owed more on their homes than the home itself was worth. As early as March 2008, over 10 percent of all homeowners had negative equity, and by September 2010, a full 23 percent of U.S. homes had a value lower than the mortgage outstanding on the property.

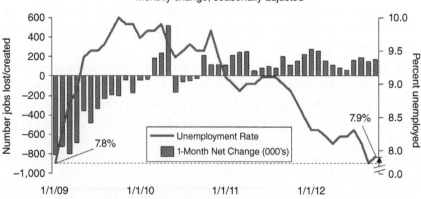

United States Employment Statistics Jan 2009 – Oct 2012
Monthly change, seasonally adjusted

FIGURE 24.8 Unemployment reached a double-digit peak in early 2009 then beginning a slow descent in the years following.

Unlike some other countries, such as Spain, residential mortgages in the United States are nonrecourse, which means that a person can simply abandon the property (and the mortgage) with no other consequence than a negative mark on their credit rating. Thus, millions of newer homeowners simply turned in their keys and left the banks with billions of dollars of losses. The diminishment in prices for homes slightly exceeded the loss in value from the Great Depression, the last time in American history that any drop in price at all had taken place.

■ A Nation on the Mend

Barack Obama won a decisive victory in the U.S. presidential election in November 2008, but the stock market would continue to weaken for his first couple of months in office. However, just as FDR's entrance into the White House in 1933 caused a sea change in economic confidence, so, too, did Obama's.

During the first couple of years of Obama's first term, he would mention countless times how his administration had "inherited the worst financial crisis since the Great Depression" to make clear that not only was he not responsible for the ongoing economic woes, but that his administration would need time to repair the damage.

The damage, of course, was not confined to the United States. Fifty million people worldwide were said to have lost their jobs to the crisis, and unemployment rates in Europe were almost all in the double digits, with unemployment rates for young people exceeding 50 percent in some countries.

Due to a series of economic stimulus packages, particularly trillions of dollars of "quantitative easing" executed by the Federal Reserve, asset values began to climb again. The total net worth of U.S. households had plunged from $67 trillion in 2007 to $52 trillion in 2009, but by late 2012, the lost value in assets had been fully recovered, mostly by an increase in both equity and real estate values (see Figure 24.9).

The cost for this recovery was substantial, however, with the U.S. national debt growing from $9 trillion in 2007 to $17 trillion in 2013. More important, the percentage of national debt in relation to the gross domestic product soared to levels never seen, with the exception of a brief period during World War II. Before the financial crisis struck in 2008, total debt was 66 percent of GDP, but by the end of 2012, the percentage crossed into the triple digits with no sign of abating (see Figure 24.10).

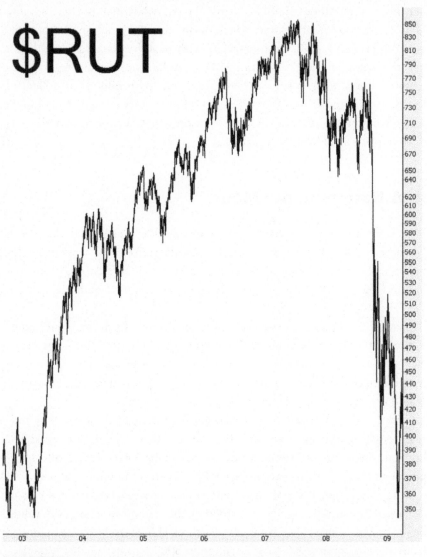

FIGURE 24.9   The drop in the Russell 2000 index in 2008 and 2009 was dramatic, but it would go on to reach new lifetime highs by 2013.

The public sought someone to blame, as they always do at the end of any crisis. The federal government assembled a working group for this purpose, and at the beginning of 2011, the U.S. Financial Crisis Inquiry Commission issued its report, which stated in part:

> … the crisis was avoidable and was caused by: *Widespread failures in financial regulation,* including the Federal Reserve's failure to stem

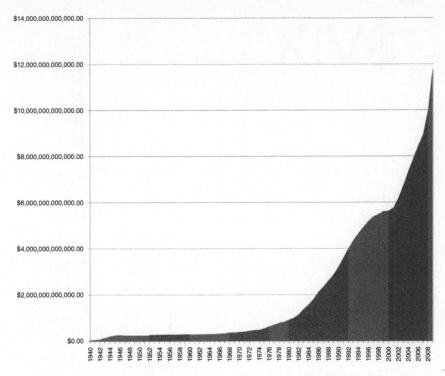

FIGURE 24.10   The U.S. federal debt exploded during the financial crisis.

the tide of toxic mortgages; *Dramatic breakdowns in corporate governance* including too many financial firms acting recklessly and taking on too much risk; *An explosive mix of excessive borrowing and risk by households and Wall Street* that put the financial system on a collision course with crisis; Key policy makers ill prepared for the crisis, lacking a full understanding of the financial system they oversaw; and *systemic breaches in accountability and ethics* at all levels.

If a person in early 2007 had entered hibernation and emerged five years later, they would have witnessed very little evident change. None of the hundreds of investment bank personnel who might have been charged with criminal wrongdoing were prosecuted, the largest investment banks had simply grown larger, and interest rates were still historically low. Almost all the financial losses suffered had been recovered, thanks to the government's persistent, multiyear intervention.

The only real changes that had taken place were (1) a sensational rise in the amount of debt that had been undertaken by U.S. taxpayers to bail out,

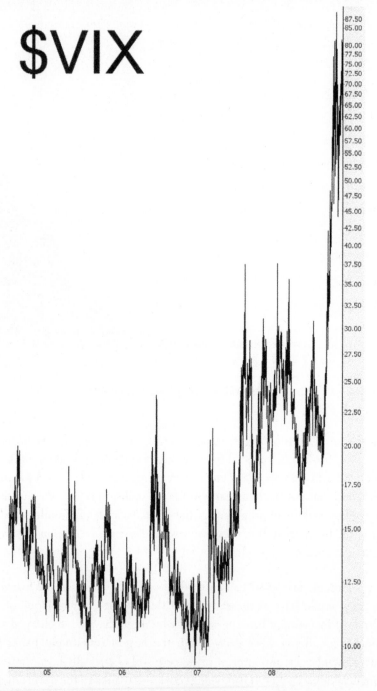

FIGURE 24.11 During the autumn of 2008, the VIX, colloquially known as the "fear index," spiked from the single digits to nearly 90, a level never before seen in the history of the indicator. As normalcy returned during the Obama administration, the VIX would drift back down to the subteen levels.

to the tune of many trillions of dollars, the economy from the financial crisis and (2) a return to the mean for home prices. The subprime market had been all but eliminated, and the individuals in the economic sector that had been renters prior to 1997 had returned to renting.

The unknown outcome from the entire crisis as of this writing is what will become of the staggering and persistent deficits that the U.S. government is generating. The cure for the ills of the financial crisis may, in the end, require another cure of its own (see Figure 24.11).

CHAPTER 25

History in the Making

Having surveyed so much of history over the span of five centuries, can any conclusions be drawn? Can any generalities be divined from these historical lessons that can help inform future decisions? Although answering either of those questions to a certainty would be impossible, there are some broad themes that wind their way through the 24 chapters that precede these closing remarks.

■ The Ties That Bind

Although the great variety of nations, cultures, and events prevent any single theme from binding together all of these episodes, there are certainly some common themes that can be used to gather some of them together into similar groupings:

■ *How obvious things seem in hindsight.* As the old saying goes, hindsight is 20/20, and upon reading tales of the savings-and-loan (S&L) fiasco and the Internet bubble, one can be forgiven by puzzling over how the public and its leadership could have been so foolhardy. After all, allowing parties to buy S&Ls with federally insured money and in turn permit them to invest in anything they pleased seems like lunacy today, but that's what took place not so very long ago. Likewise, any price chart of equity markets using any fundamental metric would have illustrated how completely insane anyone would have needed to be in order to buy Internet stocks in the beginning of 2000, but tens of millions did so anyway. The same could be said for tulip bulbs, South Sea shares, or Japanese real estate. Only after the bubble has deflated can people sit back in their chairs, rub their chins, and wonder how on earth such a thing could have happened and pledge to never behave in such a way ever again.

■ *The analogs that exist with separate events.* It is easy to see how parallels can be drawn between one situation and another from these chapters, even if the circumstances are separated by centuries. For example, the mania around tulip bulbs and the one surrounding Internet stocks has been cited many times before, even while it was happening, because of the similarities in price ascension, public fervor, and novelty. There will undoubtedly be more "tulips" in the decades ahead, although whether they revolve around nanotechnology, space exploration, biotechnology, or some other breakthrough we cannot currently conceive, only time can tell.

■ *How one event can provoke another unrelated one.* Perhaps the most fascinating aspect of all these episodes is how some of them can create a chain reaction to lead to another, even if it seems too far away or unrelated to be germane. For example, the Asian currency crisis had been addressed by early 1998, and Russian finances were completely detached from anything having to do with Asian currency. However, in the summer of 1998, one of the principal reasons for investors' fleeing Russian assets was the recently painful memory of events in Asia. The two economies were for all practical purposes unlinked, but had there not been an Asian crisis and the angst surrounding it, it is likely the Russian crisis would have been far less severe. Similar cause-and-effect relationships could be described with the Mississippi Scheme and the South Sea bubble, or the energy crisis and the mania around precious metals. The episodes may be detached, but the memory and mentality of the investing public binds them together.

■ *The moral hazard of asymmetric bets.* When bets are "tilted"—that is, when a party has the opportunity to either make a lot of money or lose practically nothing, then caution and good sense will make a swift exit. This was evident with the subprime derivatives that led to the Great Recession as well as the FSLIC-insured deposits of the S&L fiasco. If a party isn't presented with a reasonable balance of risk and reward, then there is no reason to believe that economically rational decisions will be made.

■ What Makes an Event a Historical Force?

What we call "history," of course, happens constantly around us, in every country, every day of the year. What separates the commonplace from the tiny fraction of a percent that actually goes down into history books is whether or not a given occurrence yields either a lasting impact or provokes an important inflection point in the course of human events.

The episodes chronicled in this book were in some cases about positive occurrences and at other times about negative circumstances. It was not necessarily plain to see at the time these were taking place whether the outcome would be good or bad. What are some of the general circumstances surrounding a situation can suggest the nature of its outcome?

The occasions that led to positive outcomes tended to have these properties:

- *A long base of inactivity*: there is no better time for prosperity to arrive than when it's been absent for a long time. Long bouts of economies doing little more than marking time are often the time when the seeds are being planted for future growth. The massive bull market of the 1980s and 1990s in America came on the heels of a profoundly moribund 1970s, and the Asian miracle took place in a series of mostly third-world nations that were far behind the industrial global giants. Growth and prosperity are usually healthiest when emerging from valleys instead of mountain peaks.

- *A supportive and constructive political/legislative environment.* It is crucial that an economy can depend on a relatively honest and reliable political and legal structure in order to survive in the long term. Whereas the Russian economy of the 1990s had every opportunity to thrive in an overall booming global atmosphere, it was held back largely by corruption, cronyism, and calcified internal dependencies. In contrast, nations such as Singapore blossomed into astonishing capitalist success stories, since the rule of law yielded a business environment in which other parties could be relied upon to keep their word or else face consequences for failing to do so.

- *The early capture of a major shift.* In the various periods of asset appreciation described in earlier chapters, the biggest profits were made by those who caught trends earlier before they became saturated with public attention. In spite of their eventual fall, the markets for gold in the 1970s, Russian stocks in 1997, Internet stocks in the late 1990s, and Japanese assets in the 1980s were all fabulous investments. In each case, a sea change had taken place in the circumstances surrounding the asset. Only when overwhelming attention was being paid to these gains, long after early adopters had made their winnings, did the fortunes reverse for each of them.

However, situations that led to worsening circumstances tended to have these characteristics:

- *Proximal troubles.* Trouble tends to beget trouble, and in circumstances in which problems are taking place that are geographically or temporally proximal, the risk of a negative contagion is increased. The Great Depression, the Latin American debt crisis, and the Asian currency collapse are just a few examples of how trouble can spread swiftly, and its potential speed is only accelerating as technology promulgates and communication become instantaneous.

- *Saturation of participation.*: The more prominent any idea, trend, or opportunity is known, the more likely it is that a top is at hand. The well-known "cover curse" is a good example of this, since the mass media often unwittingly lets it be known when any popular concept has become so saturated that there usually aren't any new buyers left. The converse is true as well, as famously illustrated by the *Business Week* cover story on "The Death of Equities," which was published before one of the greatest multidecade increases of equity prices ever seen before.

- *Dependence on external parties.* When a nation or an enterprise is dependent upon the munificence or mercy of an external party, the risk of failure is higher. In these pages, the third party has taken the form of the IMF, the Federal Reserve, the Bank of Japan, and the Iranian Revolutionary Council. The more external parties are involved, the more dangerous an impasse becomes, particularly if the interests of the disparate parties are not necessarily aligned.

■ The Road Ahead

At the beginning of this book, I wrote:

My hope is that, having read these accounts, the reader can gain perspective—specifically, perspective of how consistent human behavior has been over the centuries, and how in spite of extraordinarily techno-

logical, political, and legal changes, the templates that govern humanity's relationship with both opportunity and fear are surprisingly steady.

There will undoubtedly be new "chapters" in your own lifetime of
globally important events that move both markets and sentiment. In the
end, I hope the reader can be better armed to comprehend the world's
complexities and changes by way of the knowledge and insights this
book endeavors to provide.

Now that we find ourselves at the end of our survey of financial history, I
wanted to echo the same sentiments I had expressed at the beginning. Being
a part of history, and an active knowledge observer of it, makes life more
interesting, both as a citizen and as an investor. I truly hope the journey I've
put together in these pages will be of aid to your thinking and your understanding in the years to come.

Tim Knight is a money manager and founder of www.SlopeofHope.com, a popular trading blog started in 2005 that is one of the most active forums for discussion among traders on the Internet. Previously, he was founder of Prophet Financial Systems, a web-based service that was bought by Ameritrade and was consistently rated the number one website for technical analysis by both *Barron's* and *Forbes*. Prior to starting Prophet, Knight was vice president of technology products for Montgomery Securities and worked at Apple in Strategic Planning. Knight has traded for over 25 years, primarily using technical analysis and price charts as the basis for his decisions, and he owns and operates a short-bias hedge fund from his home town of Palo Alto, California.

NOTE: Page references in *italics* refer to photos, illustrations, and figures.

A

O